INTERESTS IN SECURITIES

INTERESTS IN SECURITIES

A Proprietary Law Analysis of the International Securities Markets

Dr Joanna Benjamin

OXFORD

UNIVERSITY PRESS

This book has been printed digitally and produced in a standard specification
in order to ensure its continuing availability

OXFORD
UNIVERSITY PRESS

Great Clarendon Street, Oxford OX2 6DP

Oxford University Press is a department of the University of Oxford.
It furthers the University's objective of excellence in research, scholarship,
and education by publishing worldwide in

Oxford New York

Auckland   Cape Town Dar es Salaam Hong Kong Karachi
Kuala Lumpur Madrid Melbourne Mexico City Nairobi
New Delhi Shanghai Taipei Toronto
With offices in
Argentina Austria Brazil Chile Czech Republic France Greece
Guatemala Hungary Italy Japan South Korea Poland Portugal
Singapore Switzerland Thailand Turkey Ukraine Vietnam

Oxford is a registered trade mark of Oxford University Press
in the UK and in certain other countries

Published in the United States
by Oxford University Press Inc., New York

ISBN 978-0-19-826992-2

Printed and bound by CPI Antony Rowe, Chippenham and Eastbourne

To Robert Reiner

CONTENTS—SUMMARY

IV REPACKAGED PRODUCTS

V CONCLUSIONS

CONTENTS

III INFRASTRUCTURE PRODUCTS AND SERVICES

IV REPACKAGED PRODUCTS

V CONCLUSIONS

PREFACE

This book considers the proprietary aspects of the international securities markets. It argues that the computerisation of custody and settlement[1] arrangements in these markets has fundamentally altered the legal nature of the assets which are held by investors and collateral takers. It is hoped that this analysis will assist in managing legal risk in cross border investment and collateral arrangements.

Today most investors and collateral takers hold their assets indirectly, through one or more depositaries, custodians or other intermediaries. Such intermediaries generally have large numbers of clients, and they hold the interests of their clients in any particular type of securities together in a commingled pool, so that the interest of each client is unallocated. The interests of the intermediaries' respective clients in these commingled pools are recorded in electronic accounts maintained by the intermediary. A client may be separated from the issuer of the underlying securities by a chain of intermediaries spanning a number of jurisdictions. (In certain repackaging arrangements (discussed in Chapter 12) 10 or even 15 such intermediaries would not be unusual.)

This book argues that such intermediation significantly affects the legal nature of the asset. It will distinguish between securities, which are held directly (so that the investor is in a direct relationship with the issuer), and interests in securities, which are held through one or more intermediaries on an unallocated basis. The book shows that the status of interests in securities under domestic law and private international law differs from the status of securities in a number of important respects.

In the light of this analysis, the book considers a range of domestic and cross border financial techniques and products involving interests in securities, with special reference to the collateralisation of financial exposures and the impact of insolvency. In many cases, market participants mistakenly assume that such arrangements relate to securities (rather than interests in securities). This is a source of legal risk.

In order to keep the size of the book within reasonable limits, some important legal aspects of securities business remain outside its scope, including the regulation, taxation and accounting treatment of the securities markets, and the provisions of company law relating to corporate securities. Derivatives are also outside the scope of this book, except to the extent that interests in cash securities (ie non-

---

[1] Settlement means delivery, as discussed in Chapters 1 and 9.

derivative securities) are used to collateralise derivatives exposures. The disclosure of interests in shares is not addressed.

The material in this book is intended to be up to date as at June 2000. At the time of writing, the international securities markets are in a state of rapid transformation, and thus the subject matter of this book is a moving target. Some of the detailed references, such as those to market standard documentation and the procedures of settlement systems, may soon become out of date. However, it is hoped that the underlying legal analysis will remain pertinent over the longer term, and will assist market participants, service providers and their regulators in managing legal risk.

This analysis in this book accords with the general approach informing articles 8 and 9 of the US Uniform Commercial Code. Professor Sir Roy Goode has proposed that (English and possibly UK) commercial law should be codified. In the author's view, the position of London as a financial centre would be strengthened by the codification of the area of law to which this book is devoted. Prior to such codification, however, this book seeks to clarify the existing principles of English domestic and private international law, and suggests that in general they produce an appropriate result.

A number of distinguished authors have contributed to this area of legal analysis. In particular, the author wishes to acknowledge the work of the following: (on the US position) Professor James Rogers, Professor Jean Schroeder, and Steven Schwarcz; (on the English position) Professor Sir Roy Goode; and (on the international position) Randall Guynn and Richard Potok. In relation to the custody of securities, see the welcome publication of *Custody of Investments* (Oxford University Press, 2000) by Timi Austen Peters, who is practising in Lagos, Nigeria, and also the author's *The Law of Global Custody* (Butterworths, 1996, 2nd edn forthcoming 2001).

This book is not intended to offer a general overview of the legal issues within its scope, and it is not intended to give legal advice. Legal advice should always be sought in relation to particular financial market transactions and arrangements.

Note on terminology

The third person feminine has been used in preference to the third person masculine (so that, for example, 'the investor' is referred to as 'she'). However, the third person neuter has been used to refer to institutions (so that, for example, collateral takers and participants in settlement systems are referred to as 'it'). As indicated above, this book distinguishes between securities and interests in securities. However, where it is appropriate to refer to both types of asset together, they are referred to collectively as '(interests in) securities'. For ease of reference, the markets in both type of asset are referred to as 'the securities markets', collateral comprising both types of asset is referred to as 'securities collateral' and settlement of both types of asset is referred to as 'securities settlement'.

ACKNOWLEDGEMENTS

My greatest debts are to the members of my family. In particular I wish to thank Robert Reiner (for finding space within his own publishing timetable to offer unflagging support) and Lesley Benjamin (for contributing to the ideas that lie behind Chapter 13, and also for reviewing several chapters and giving me the tactful benefit of her considerable writing skills).

Also, I am grateful to Nina Farhi for her wise comments towards the end of the project.

At a practical level, I am indebted to the following practitioner and academic colleagues who reviewed particular chapters and/or offered general comments: Ed Bradley, Partner, Clifford Chance (Chapter 1); Professor David Hayton, King's College London (Chapter 2); Professor Ian Fletcher, The Centre for Commercial Law Studies, Queen Mary and Westfield College (Chapter 7); Mark Kirby, Head of Legal Affairs, CRESTCo (Chapter 9); Tim Herrington, Partner, Clifford Chance and Madeleine Yates, Senior Associate, Clifford Chance (Chapter 11); Andrew Coates, Partner, Clifford Chance (Chapter 12), and Simon James, Partner, Clifford Chance, Dermot Turing, Partner, Clifford Chance, A Cohen, Partner, Clifford Chance, Peter Taylor, Partner, Clifford Chance, Charmaine Joshua and Matt Huggett of Clifford Chance (generally).

My thanks go to the staff of Oxford University Press, and particularly Chris Rycroft and Becky Allen, for their helpful professionalism. I am also grateful to Nauraj Gabisi for research assistance on general law issues, to Andrew Nicola for financial markets references and generally to the information officers at Clifford Chance for their patient help. Debbie Hulme, my secretary at Clifford Chance, provided invaluable help in the delivery of the manuscript.

The origin of this book is a postgraduate course on Interests in Securities which I used to teach at King's College London, and currently teach at The Centre for Commercial Law Studies, Queen Mary and Westfield College. My final thanks, therefore, go to my students, whose comments helped to refine the detail of this book, and whose enthusiasm is a continuing pleasure.

ABBREVIATIONS

ACD   authorised corporate director
ADR   American depositary receipt
AIM   Alternative Investment Market
APACS   Association for Payment Clearing Services
AUTIF   Association of Unit Trusts and Investment Funds
CBO   collateralised bond obligation
CCP   central counterparty
CDO   collateralised debt obligation
CGO   Central Gilts Office
CHAPS   Clearing House Automated Payment System
CIS   collective investment scheme
CLO   collateralised loan obligation
CMO   Central Moneymarkets Office
CRR   counterparty risk requirement
DBV   delivery by value
DCC   Depository and Clearing Centre
DMO   Debt Management Office of HM Treasury
DR   depositary receipt
DTC   Depositors Trust Company
DVP   delivery versus payment
EASDAQ   European Association of Securities Dealers Automated Quotation
            System
ECN   Electronic Communication Network
ECSDA   European Central Securities Depositories Association
EDR   European depositary receipt
ETT   electronic transfer of title
EURIBOR   Euro Interbank Offered Rate
FIX   Financial Information eXchange
FSA   Financial Services Authority
GDR   Global depositary receipt
GEMM   Gilt edged Market Maker
GMSLA   Global Master Securities Lending Agreement
GSTPA   Global Straight Through Processing Association
IOI   indication of interest
IOSCO   International Organization of Securities Commissions

IPE	International Petroleum Exchange
IPMA	International Primary Markets Association
ISDA	International Swaps and Derivatives Association
ISITCI	Industry Standardisation for Institutional Trade Communications Committee
ISLA	International Securities Lenders Association
ISMA	International Securities Market Association
LCH	London Clearing House
LIBOR	London Interbank Offered Rate
LIFFE	London International Financial Futures and Options Exchange
LME	London Metal Exchange
MMI	money market instrument
MTN	medium term note
NIF	note issuance facility
OEIC	open-ended investment company
OTC	over the counter
PPS	Protected Payments System
PVP	payment versus payment
QIB	qualified institutional buyer
RUF	revolving underwriting facilities
SBLI	Stock Borrowing and Lending Intermediaries
SEATS	Stock Exchange Alternative Trading Service
SEAQ	Stock Exchange Automated Quotation System
SETS	Stock Exchange Electronic Trading Service
SPV	special purpose vehicle
STP	straight through processing
TARGET	Trans-European Automated Real-Time Gross Settlement Express Transfer System
TRS	Trade Registration System
UCP	Uniform Customs and Practices for Documentary Credits of the International Chamber of Commerce

GLOSSARY

The allocation question	The question whether it is possible to create a valid trust over an unallocated part of a pool of assets, as described in chapter 2.
Assets	Things which can be the subject of property rights.
Bearer securities	Securities issued in the form of paper instruments, the transfer of which is effected by delivery of possession of the instrument, as described in chapter 2.
Clearing	A process to manage credit exposures arising after trading and before settlement, by interposing a clearing house between the original parties to a trade, as described in chapter 8.
Collateral assets	Assets delivered for the purposes of collateralisation.
Collateral, Collateralisation	A technique for addressing credit risk by supporting a personal obligation with a right of recourse against identified assets, as described in chapter 4.
Collateral giver	The person delivering collateral assets.
Collateral taker	The person receiving collateral assets.
Collateralised Bond Obligation, CBO	A type of repackaged asset described in chapter 12.
Convertibles	Bonds which can be converted, at the election of the bondholder, into another form of security such as equities.
Credit risk	The risk that a debt or other personal obligation will not be performed because of the insolvency of the debtor or other obligor.
Dematerialisation	An arrangement permitting electronic settlement involving the issue of securities in paperless form, as described in chapter 1.
Depositary receipts	A form of repackaged asset, described in chapter 11.
Electronic settlement	The delivery of (interests in) securities by debiting and crediting electronic accounts maintained by a settlement system, as described in chapters 1 and 9.
Equities	Ordinary shares in a company.
Equity of redemption	The right of a collateral giver, which arises under a security interest, to the redelivery of the collateral assets upon the discharge of the collateralised obligation.
Equivalent redelivery	Arrangements whereby a custodian or collateral taker redelivers assets equivalent to, but not identical with, the assets that were originally delivered to it, as described in chapter 6.

Eurosecurities	(Interests in) securities issued outside their domestic market into more than one jurisdiction.
Fungible	Interchangeable within a class, as described in chapter 2.
Fungible asset	An asset in respect of which the customary redelivery obligation is equivalent and not in specie, as described in chapter 2.
Fiduciary	A relationship of special trust as described in chapter 2.
Gearing	Borrowing.
Global custody	A service involving the safekeeping, administration and settlement of international portfolios of securities, as described in chapter 10.
Hedge fund	A type of unregulated managed fund offering a high return to participants by a range of mathematically complex investment techniques, as described in chapter 10.
Immobilisation	A arrangement permitting electronic settlement involving placing securities in traditional paper form with a depositary that is linked to a settlement system, as described in chapter 1.
Insolvency displacement	The rules of insolvency law permitting an insolvency official to challenge transactions entered into by the insolvent, as described in chapter 4.
In special redelivery	Arrangements whereby a custodian or collateral taker redelivers the identical assets that were originally delivered to it.
Interests in securities	The assets of a client for whom an intermediary holds (interests in) securities on an unallocated basis, commingled with the interests in securities of other clients.
(Interests in) securities	Securities or interests in securities.
Insolvency set off	The ability of set off mutual debits and credits with an insolvent counterparty, as described in chapter 6.
Intangible	Having no physical existence.
Issuer	The company, government agency or other person creating securities.
Lex situs	The law of the place where an asset is located, as described in chapter 7.
Long position	Holding an asset.
Managed fund	An arrangement whereby the assets of different investors are pooled and invested on a collective basis by a professional manager as described in chapter 11.
Margin	The excess in the value of collateral assets over the value of the collateralised exposure, as described in chapter 6.
Margining	Marking to market.
Marking to market	A technique for preserving the agreed margin throughout the life of a collateral transactions, as described in chapter 6.
Mortgage	The delivery of title to an asset by way of security, as described in chapter 5.

Outright collateral transfer	A type of collateral arrangement whereby the collateral giver transfers to the collateral taker the whole of its property rights in the collateral assets, subject to personal rights of equivalent redelivery, as described in chapter 6.
Pari passu principle	The general principle of insolvency law that all unsecured creditors should be treated equally, as described in chapter 4.
Perfection	The process of rendering a security interest enforceable against third parties, usually by formalities involving publicity such as notarisation or registration, as described in chapter 4.
Personal right	A legal right (such as a debt) which is enforceable only against a person, and not against any particular asset, as described in chapter 13.
Pledge	The delivery of possession of a tangible asset by way of security, as described in chapter 5.
Primary markets	New issues of securities to their original holders.
Prime brokerage	A complex package of financing, custodial, brokerage and other services, as described in chapter 10.
Property right	A legal right (such as ownership or a security interest) which is enforceable against assets, as described in chapter 13.
Registered securities	Securities the transfer of which is effected by entering the name of the transferor in place of the name of the transferee in a register maintained by or on behalf of the issuer.
Rehypothecation	The delivery to a third party of assets which have been received under a security interest, as described in chapter 5.
Repackaging	The creation of new types of (interests in) securities on the legal and economic basis of existing (interests in) securities or other financial assets, as described in chapters 1, 11 and 12.
Repo or repurchase Agreement	A type of transaction traditionally used to raise short term cash using (interests in) securities as collateral, as described in chapter 6.
Secondary markets	The transfer of securities from holder to holder.
Securities	A type of transferable financial asset, of which equities and debt securities are examples, as described in chapter 1.
Securities lending	A type of transaction traditionally used to fill temporary short positions in securities, as described in chapter 6.
Security interest	A limited property right in assets that is delivered for the purposes of collateralisation, as described in chapter 5.

Settlement	The delivery of (interests in) securities, usually against cash, to fulfil contractual obligations such as those arising on trading.
Settlement system	An electronic system permitting settlement.
Short position	Being obliged to deliver an asset which one does not currently hold.
Special purpose vehicle	A company, trust or partnership established for the purpose of a particular transaction or series of transactions, as described in chapter 12.
Straight through processing	The automation of the processing of transactions, as described in chapter 10.
Tangible	Physical.
Trading	Buying and selling (interests in) securities.
Treasuries	Medium- to long-term debt securities issues by government agencies.
Trust	A relationship between one or more persons known as trustee and one or more persons known as beneficiary in respect of trust assets, whereby the trustee holds the trust assets for the benefit of the beneficiary, as described in chapter 2.

TABLES OF CASES

TABLES OF LEGISLATION

UK STATUTORY INSTRUMENTS

NATIONAL LEGISLATION FROM OTHER JURISDICTIONS

EC/EU LEGISLATION

INTERNATIONAL TREATIES AND CONVENTIONS

Part I

OVERVIEW

1

INTRODUCTION TO SECURITIES, INTERESTS IN SECURITIES, THE SECURITIES MARKETS AND SETTLEMENT*

Knowledge of these things would be much easier learnt in the City than in the courts.[1]

A. The Distinction Between Securities and Interests in Securities

1.01 The central idea in this book is that interests in securities are legally distinct from securities.

---

* The author is grateful to Ed Bradley, Partner, Clifford Chance, for kindly reviewing this chapter. The opinions expressed in it and any errors are her own.
[1] Blackstone, quoted in C H S Fifoot, 'The Development of the Law of Negotiable Instruments and the Law of Trusts' (1938) *Journal of the Institute of Bankers*, lix, 433–456.

(1) Securities

1.02 Securities are a type of transferable financial asset. The meaning of the term 'securities' has varied over time.[2] Originally the term was used to denote security interests (such as mortgages and charges) supporting the payment of a debt or other obligation.[3] In the early modern period, companies and government agencies began to raise capital from the public by issuing transferable debt obligations; the repayment of these debt obligations was secured on the assets of the issuer.[4] By a process of elision, these secured debt obligations came to be known as 'securities'.[5] Since late medieval times, commercial companies have raised funds by issuing participations or shares. In the Victorian era the transferability of these shares under the general principles of company law was put beyond doubt.[6] As shares became more readily transferable, their functional likeness to debt securities became clearer, and both forms of investment became known as 'securities'. More recently, the term 'securities' has been extended to include units in investment funds and other forms of readily transferable investment.[7]

1.03 One form of security is a debt security. This is akin to an IOU, and constitutes the acknowledgement by the issuer of the security that it owes money to the security holder. The holder is entitled to interest and the repayment of the principal sum at the times specified under the terms of the security. Another form of security is an equity security or ordinary share. The holder of an equity security is a shareholder or participant in the company that issues it, as discussed later in this chapter.

---

[2] 'The word [securities] is not a term of art, but only a word of description. It is a commercial word which will vary with the history of commerce': *Re Rayner* [1904] 1 Ch 176, per Vaughan Williams LJ at 185.

[3] See *British Oil Mills Co v Inland Revenue Commrs* [1903] 1 KB 689, per Stirling LJ at 697, 698. See also *Singer v Williams* [1921] AC 41, per Viscount Cave at 49: 'My Lords, the normal meaning of the word "securities" is not open to doubt. The word denotes a debt or claim the payment of which is in some way secured'. Security interests are discussed in Chapter 5.

[4] Such secured corporate debt obligations are called debentures.

[5] See *Re Smithers* [1939] Ch 1015 per Crossman J at 1017–1020.

[6] See the discussion in Chapter 3.

[7] ' "Securities" means shares, stock, debentures, debenture stock, loan stock, bonds, units of a collective investment scheme within the meaning of the Financial Services Act 1986, and other securities of any description': Stock Transfer Act 1963, s 4, as amended. See also the Income and Corporation Taxes Act 1988, s 710(2). The connotation of a security interest has now been lost: 'finally, we do not consider there is any requirement for a security to confer a proprietary interest in the fund or assets to which it relates': letter, Dilwyn Griffiths, HM Treasury, to Iain Saville, CRESTCo, 19 July 2000.

See also *Re Douglas' Will Trusts, Lloyds Bank v Nelson* [1959] WLR 744 per Vaisey J at 749: 'I am prepared to make a declaration that "securities" includes any stocks or shares or bonds by way of investment'. See the discussion of the meaning of the term in *Re Rayner* [1904] 1 Ch 176 per Romer LJ at 189, per Stirling LJ at 191.

(2) Interests in Securities

'Interests in securities' are the assets of a client for whom an intermediary holds **1.04** securities (or interests in securities) on an unallocated basis, commingled with the interests in securities of other clients.

The distinction between securities and interests in securities is often overlooked **1.05** in practice. It will be argued that this is a source of legal risk. In this book, the distinction will be drawn. Where a comment relates to both types of asset, they will be referred to together as '(interests in) securities'.

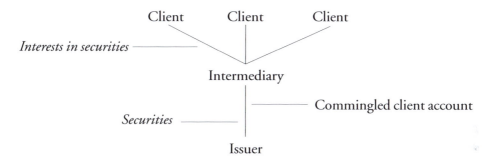

Figure 1.1: Securities and interests in securities

B. The Uses of (Interests in) Securities

The uses that are made of (interests in) securities have changed over time, both for **1.06** the issuer and for the holder.

(1) For the Issuer

Traditionally, issuers have used securities as a means of raising new capital.[8] **1.07** Another use has developed in recent decades, as securities have been issued in order to repackage existing financial assets, including existing (interests in) securities, as discussed below.[9]

---

[8] Indeed, the purpose of capital raising has sometimes been taken to be a defining characterisic of securities.

[9] Some instruments such as bills of exchange and promissory notes have traditionally been issued together with letters of credit in order to finance trade (ie to purchase goods and services). However, the use of such instruments in trade finance is declining, as they are replaced by deferred payment undertaking under the UCP (the Uniform Customs and Practices for Documentary Credits of the International Chamber of Commerce). A detailed discussion of trade finance is beyond the scope of this book.

New capital

1.08   Commercial enterprises need capital in order to run their businesses. If their own retained profits are not sufficient, external sources of finance are required. Equally, government agencies need to raise capital if taxation and other income are insufficient to meet public expenditure, so that there is a budget deficit.[10] Bank loans may be relatively expensive and short term, and therefore not an attractive source of finance.[11] An alternative is to raise capital through the issue of securities. In this case, capital is provided by the investors who purchase the securities.

Repackaging

1.09   In more recent decades, securities have developed a different function. They are issued, not to raise new capital, but to repackage existing assets. This can serve a range of different purposes. For example in a traditional securitisation, a financial institution may wish to remove assets from its balance sheet in order to achieve regulatory capital efficiencies[12] or to accelerate its receipt of cash flow from the original assets. Alternatively, an intermediary may wish to make a profit by acquiring financial assets and repackaging them in a way which makes them more attractive to investors, in a CBO issue, depositary receipt programme or a managed fund. The financial assets underlying these arrangements may themselves be (interests in) securities. These structures are discussed in Chapters 11 and 12.

Identity of issuers

1.10   Typical issuers of securities are commercial companies, government agencies, local authorities and international and supranational organisations (such as the World Bank). Debt securities issued by government agencies are referred to as sovereign debt.[13] Sovereign debt generally carries a lower interest rate than corporate debt (ie debt securities issued by commercial companies), because of the perceived lower risk of default by the issuer. In the case of repackaged securities, the issuer is generally a company[14] established for the purpose of the repackaging, and is referred to as a special purpose vehicle, or SPV.

---

[10]   Governments may require financing either because of budget deficits, or because the timing of expenditure and receipts does not coincide, for example because taxation is received at annual or biannual intervals only, while expenditure is constant.

[11]   Another relative disadvantage of bank loans as a source of financing is that the bank may seek a measure of control over the business of the borrower, by imposing (and monitoring) financial covenants.

[12]   See Chapter 12 for an explanation of these arrangements.

[13]   As discussed below, medium or long sovereign debt securities are called 'treasuries'.

[14]   Or, in some cases, a trust or limited partnership.

(2) For the Holder

An individual or institution may hold (interests in) securities for investment pur- **1.11** poses, or alternatively as collateral.

Investment

The traditional economic function of the purchase of (interests in) securities is **1.12** investment, with a view to receiving income and/or achieving capital growth. Debt securities generally offer a higher rate of interest than bank deposits, and equities may offer the prospect of capital growth (although their income stream is uncertain).[15]

Collateral

The last decade has seen an enormous growth in the use of (interests in) securities **1.13** as collateral, as discussed further in Chapter 4. Where A is owed a debt or other obligation by B, A may require B to deliver property rights in (interests in) securities (called collateral) to A. These property rights enable A to satisfy its claims in the event that B becomes insolvent.

Collateral arrangements are divided into two broad categories, namely security **1.14** interests (discussed in Chapter 5) and outright collateral transfers (discussed in Chapter 6). Collateral takers are not investors, and (generally speaking) are not entitled to the benefit of income[16] from or capital growth in the (interests) in securities that serve as collateral.

Identity of holders

Investors may be retail, ie members of the public investing other than by way of **1.15** business. However the greatest part by value of securities investment is wholesale, ie by financial institutions acting on their own account, or on behalf of clients. Important institutional investors include investment banks, insurance companies, pension funds and other managed funds.[17]

---

[15] As discussed below, there is no automatic right to income. Equity investment may also offer control of the business of the issuer.

[16] With equitable security interests, the collateral giver retains legal title and therefore the right to receive income. With legal security interests, it is customary for the collateral taker to pass any income it receives back to the collateral giver. In the case of outright transfers, income is paid to the collateral taker as the legal owner, but the collateral contract provides for a sum equal to this income to be paid by the collateral taker to the collateral giver.

[17] 'Institutional shareholders accounted for 52.3% of UK ordinary shares at 31 December 1998, with a combined value of £787 billion. Of this, the largest components were insurance companies and pension funds (each with £326 billion)': *CREST Newsletter*, April 2000, Issue No 73, p 18.

1.16 It is relatively unusual for individuals to take securities collateral. However, all types of financial institutions act as collateral takers. Commercial banks, investment banks and government agencies are very significant collateral takers.[18] See Chapters 4 to 8 for a detailed discussion of collateral.

C. The Securities Markets

1.17 The following is an extremely brief overview of the securities markets. A number of excellent books are available which provide more detailed discussion.[19]

(1) The Primary and Secondary Markets

1.18 The securities markets are divided into the primary markets and the secondary markets. The primary markets are also known as the capital markets. The primary markets comprise issues of new securities to their first holders.

1.19 Issuers usually retain investment banks to assist them in finding buyers for the issue of securities. The investment bank agrees to seek to sell the (interests in) securities to investors (or broker dealers who will in turn sell the (interests in) securities to their clients) and, in many cases, to buy the (interests in) securities itself if sufficient investors are not found. This arrangement is known as underwriting. The risk of underwriting is usually spread between a group of sub-underwriters (in UK domestic transactions) and between a group or syndicate of managers (in international transactions).[20] (Managers are investment banks acting in international issues of securities who agree with the issuer to market the securities; managers assume underwriting liabilities for a shorter period of time than underwriters of domestic issues).[21] In recent years the business of managing or underwriting issues of securities has been concentrated in the hands of a small number

---

[18] As indicated below in the discussion of treasuries, governments provide liquidity to national financial systems through money market operations, in which they advance money to selected institutions against securities collateral, usually under repurchase agreements (repos), but sometimes under security interests. See Chapter 6 for a discussion of repos.

[19] In particular, see P Wood, *Comparative Financial Law* (London: Sweet & Maxwell, 1995); R Tennekoon, *The Law and Regulation of International Finance* (London: Butterworths, 1991); S Valdez, *An Introduction to the Global Financial Markets* (2nd edn, London: Macmillan, 1997). For a student guide that is equally useful to practitioners, see D Adams, *Banking and Capital Markets*, ILPC Resource Book (Jordans, 1999), chs 17 and 18.

[20] The underwriting obligation to the issuer is undertaken in the Subscription Agreement; the Agreement Among Managers serves to regulate the relationship between (and the liabilities of) the syndicate members in respect of the underwriting obligation. See R Tennekoon, *The Law and Regulation of International Finance* (London: Butterworths, 1991), ch 10, for a fuller discussion. Standard forms of agreement are provided in the *Handbook* of IPMA, the trade association for the primary securities markets (discussed below).

[21] Managers do not assume underwriting commitments at the beginning of the selling period, but only do so at a later stage and for a shorter period of time, after investors have given indications of interest in the issue.

of investment banks.[22] The International Primary Markets Association (IPMA) is the trade association of banks and other investment institutions who are active in the primary markets.[23]

Transferability is an essential characteristic of securities.[24] In the secondary markets, existing (interests in) securities move from holder to holder. The International Securities Market Association (ISMA) is the trade association for the banks and other investment institutions that are active in the secondary markets.[25] **1.20**

(2) Public Offers, Private Placements, Auctions of Sovereign Debt

In the primary markets, (interests in) securities may be offered to the public in a public offer. Alternatively, they may be offered privately to a limited number of persons in a private placement. Often a combination of the two is used. The distinction between public and private offers is important from the point of view of securities regulation and company law. However, it is less important to the proprietary analysis with which this book is concerned. **1.21**

Sovereign debt is generally sold by auction to a specialised class of dealers. **1.22**

(3) Domestic and International Issues

In international issues, (interests in) securities are targeted at investors in a number of different jurisdictions. In domestic issues, (interests in) securities are targeted at investors in the jurisdiction of the issuer. (Interests in) securities are often denominated in the currency which is legal tender in the jurisdiction into which they are primarily targeted. **1.23**

(4) Programmes

In a securities programme, multiple issues of securities are made from time to time on the basis of a single set of underlying documents. Short supplements are prepared for each issue, setting out the particular details of the issue, and bringing **1.24**

---

[22] 'The growing concentration of market share in the hands of the top banks has coincided with an explosion in the global capital markets during the 1990s, from total volume of less than $1,500bn at the start of the decade to almost $4,000bn last year . . . The top 10 are Goldman Sachs, Morgan Stanley Dean Witter, Merrill Lynch, Salomon Smith Barney, Credit Suisse First Boston, Warburg Dillon Read, Deutsche Bank, J.P. Morgan, Chase Manhattan and Lehman Brothers': 'Consolidation in Investment Banking Sector, Japan Retreats from Market', *Financial Times*, 1 March 1999.

[23] The IPMA *Handbook* contains a series of recommendations relating to many aspects of the issue of securities, including disclosures, the execution of underwriting agreements and fees.

[24] Indeed, the repackaging of relatively illiquid assets into readily transferable assets is known as 'securitisation', as discussed in Chapter 12.

[25] ISMA sets out rules and recommendations relating to many aspects of the secondary markets in international debt securities, including dealing, reporting and settlement. See the ISMA website at www.isma.org

information disclosed in the original selling document up to date.[26] This arrangement is designed to save costs and provide the convenience of standardisation.

1.25 A medium term note (MTN) programme is used as a facility to enable an issuer to raise capital from a group of investment banks. It is agreed that the issuer may issue and the investment banks may purchase and/or find purchasers for the notes which the issuer will issue from time to time on pre-agreed terms.

(5) Listing and OTC Dealing

1.26 A stock exchange is an organised and officially recognised market on which (interests in) securities are bought and sold. A stock exchange also performs a regulatory role. Its listing rules[27] may restrict the types of issuer whose securities can be listed and impose disclosure requirements, while its trading rules may regulate the behaviour of exchange members with a view to achieving a fair, transparent and orderly market, and avoiding market abuse. Issuers may seek listings for their (interests in) securities in order to attract investors, by ensuring that there is a liquid[28] and regulated market in which investors will be able to buy and sell (interests in) securities at a fair price. Indeed, some investors such as regulated funds are subject to investment restrictions that may prevent them from purchasing (interests in) securities which are not listed on particular exchanges.

1.27 However, large volumes of (interests in) securities are bought and sold otherwise than on stock exchanges. This is called dealing 'over the counter', or OTC. OTC dealing involves buyers and sellers dealing with each other by telephone or electronically on the basis of prices that are displayed electronically, usually by commercial information vendors such as Reuters and Bloombergs.

1.28 The somewhat misleading term 'eurosecurities' means (broadly) (interests in) securities that are issued outside their domestic market into more than one jurisdiction.[29] The prefix 'euro' does not necessarily denote Europe or the EU, and is used for historic reasons: the original eurobond issues in the early 1960s were tar-

---

[26] These are usually called 'pricing supplements' and set out matters such as maturity, interest rate and issue price of the issued securities.

[27] Note that in the United Kingdom, listing authority was transferred from the London Stock Exchange to the Financial Services Authority on 1 May 2000.

[28] A liquid market is one in which assets can be bought and sold without delay.

[29] See the definition of 'Euro-securities' in the Prospectus Directive (89/298/EEC): "Euro-securities" shall mean transferable securities which:
  —are to be underwritten and distributed by a syndicate at least two of the members of which have their registered offices in different States, and
  —are offered on a significant scale in one or more States other than that of the issuer's registered office, and
  —may be subscribed for or initially acquired only through a credit institution or other financial institution.'
In some cases, the term is taken to mean securities denominated in a currency other than that which is legal tender in the jurisdictions into which it is marketed.

geted at 'eurodollars' held in Europe. 'Eurodollars' means US dollar deposit held with banks outside the USA.[30] Transactions in (interests in) securities take place OTC. Nevertheless, eurosecurities are generally listed on the Luxembourg Stock Exchange or admitted to listing in London. The reasons for listing eurobonds include regulatory and tax considerations, as well as the investment restrictions indicated above.[31]

Traditionally, stock exchanges have attracted very large volumes of business and **1.29** have therefore been important sources of liquidity in the securities markets. However, the explosive growth in informal electronic trading systems in recent years has challenged the traditional business of stock exchanges.[32]

(6) Debt Securities and Equities

Securities are traditionally divided into debt securities and equities. Each type of **1.30** security has pros and cons for issuers and holders alike.[33]

Debt securities

Any type of issuer (whether or not it is a company) may issue debt securities. The **1.31** holder of a debt security is owed a debt by the issuer and is entitled (on the due dates) to the payment of principal and interest, together with other personal rights under the terms of issue of the securities, such as the right to receive certain information. Debt securities are generally issued for a fixed term and redeemable by the issuer at the end of that term.[34]

---

[30] A large fund of eurodollars built up in the 1960s and 1970s through a desire of depositors to avoid US regulatory and tax restrictions.

[31] See Tennekoon (n 19 above), 318, for a fuller discussion.

[32] See the discussion in Financial Services Authority, *Market Infrastructure* (Consultation Document, January 2000).

Examples of new or proposed ECNs are Jiway (in relation to equity business including retail business); E-Crossnet (in relation to the wholesale equity business of fund managers) and BrokerTech (in relation to (interests in) bonds and bond derivatives).

[33] For issuers, pre-emption rights in favour of existing shareholders may present an obstacle for the issue of new equity securities in some circumstances. Existing shareholders may not favour the issue of new equities, which will dilute the rights (to vote, receive dividends etc) attaching to their shares. The issue of debt at a relatively fixed cost may enable the company to enhance profits for existing shareholders. This technique is called 'gearing' or 'leverage'.

For the investor, debt securities generally carry a higher rate of interest, and their market value is generally less volatile than equities. They may therefore be more suitable for the cautious or short term investor. Equities generally carry a lower rate of income, but may offer the prospect of capital appreciation. They may be more suitable for long term or speculative investment, and investors looking for a mix of interest and capital return.

[34] This is called 'bullet' redemption. An alternative is for eurobonds to be redeemable over a period of years. Each year, the proportion of eurobonds to be redeemed is selected by drawing lots.

1.32 Debt securities generally carry an automatic right to income. The rate of income may either be fixed[35] or floating.[36] An alternative is deep discounted debt (or zero coupon bonds), which is issued at, for example, 80 per cent of the price at which it is redeemed. No interest is paid, and the discounted issue price reflects the interest foregone by the holder.[37] The issuer usually pays income to investors through banks appointed by the issuer to act as paying agents.[38] As the issuer's creditor, the holder of debt securities is entitled to be repaid in advance of shareholders in the event of the issuer's insolvency.

1.33 Debt securities may be secured or unsecured. Where the debt securities are secured, investors will be paid in priority to ordinary creditors.[39] UK domestic debt securities are often secured, whereas international debt securities are generally unsecured (with the exception of repackaged securities: see Chapter 12). Secured debt securities are called debentures. Debentures are usually issued by companies. The obligations of the issuer to pay holders are secured either on the whole undertaking of the issuer, or on specific assets. Because of this security, the interest rate is usually lower than for unsecured debt securities.

1.34 As indicated above, secured debt securities rank ahead of unsecured debt securities. Other possible rankings for securities are as follows. Subordinated debt securities rank behind both secured and unsecured debt securities, and holders of subordinated debt securities are repaid only after all the claims of general creditors have been met. Unsecured debt securities which are not subordinated are referred to as senior debt securities. Convertible bonds (see below) are often subordinated. Subordinated debt securities are sometimes called junior debt securities.

1.35 In many cases, trustees are appointed to protect the interests of the holders of debt securities. Where a trustee is appointed, the issuer enters into certain covenants in favour of the trustee in a trust deed. The trustee holds these covenants for the benefit of holders of the debt securities. The issuer covenants to pay principal and interest to the trustee as well as to provide financial and other information. The payment covenants run in parallel to the promise to pay the holder which is writ-

---

[35] ie a fixed annual percentage of the value of the debt. The market value of fixed interest rate debt securities is affected more by interest rates than by the performance of the issuer, which does not generally affect the value of the debt, unless the credit worthiness of the issuer is affected.

[36] ie an annual percentage of the value of the debt calculated by reference to a floating rate of interest, eg 2 per cent above a reference rate such as LIBOR or EURIBOR. LIBOR is the London Interbank Offered Rate: this is the average lending rate offered for deposits by the major banks in the London interbank money market. EURIBOR is a floating rate calculated by the European Banking Federation.

[37] This is sometimes referred to as 'intrinsic interest'.

[38] Where (interests in) debt securities are held through an international settlement system, the paying agent generally pays the money on to the settlement system, which in turn credits the accounts of participants.

[39] See Chapter 4 for a discussion of priorities in relation to security interests.

ten on the face of the instruments constituting the securities.[40] In order to ensure that holders are not paid twice, the rights of enforcement of the holders are limited, and in the normal course only the trustee is permitted to enforce the obligations of the issuer.

It is the duty of trustees to monitor the performance by the issuer of its obligations **1.36** to holders. An important reason for appointing a trustee is to ensure that the enforcement of holders' rights is orderly and also appropriate, guarding against the possibility that a holder might declare an event of default by the issuer following a trivial or technical breach of the issuer's obligations.[41]

Trustees are generally appointed in UK domestic debt issues, but are becoming **1.37** less common in international issues.[42] Where no trustee is appointed, the issuer will appoint a fiscal agent. As discussed below, trustees owe fiduciary duties to beneficiaries, but a fiscal agent does not owe fiduciary duties towards holders and has a more limited role than a trustee, akin to that of a principal paying agent.

The debt markets

This section will briefly consider three different markets in debt securities, namely **1.38** the markets in treasury bonds, in money market instruments and in international debt securities respectively.

Treasury bonds

Medium or long term debt securities issued by sovereign governments or their **1.39** agencies are known as treasury bonds or 'treasuries'. As with all sovereign debt securities, treasuries carry a lower rate of interest than corporate bonds.[43] In addition to serving as a source of finance for governments, treasuries are used to manage the money supply in the money market operations of central banks. Money is

---

[40] This discussion assumes that the bearer security is in the form of a traditional paper instrument. See the discussion of computerisation below.

[41] This is commonly known as 'the mad bondholder problem'. 'If there was no trustee vested with the discretion to be flexible on the occurrence of a technical default it would be open to one "mad bondholder" to accelerate his bond and precipitate a series of accelerations and activate cross-default clauses giving rise to the possibility of a liquidation of the issuer. The absence of a trustee who is in control of acceleration on default would also prevent a commercial compromise which would be advantageous to all creditors and which could stave off a liquidation': Tennekoon (n 19 above) 212, 213.

[42] However, in convertible bonds (see below), trustees are invariably appointed, and have a more substantive role than in relation to non-convertible securities, with responsibility for supervising the conversion agent and making sure that investors get a fair conversion rate.

[43] Anecdotally, UK gilts recently provided an exception to this rule. 'By issuing gilts at long maturities and mostly at fixed rates of interest, the UK government has locked the British taxpayer into a higher cost of funding . . . Other European countries, notably Italy and Belgium, had concentrated their funding at short maturities and at a floating rate of interest. This had enabled them to benefit from the sharp reduction in interest rates over the past few years . . .': 'Bond Policy Costs UK £3bn a year', *Financial Times*, 13 October 1999.

injected into the economy by the central banks advancing money to financial institutions against the provision of government bonds, usually under repurchase programmes.[44] US treasury bonds are very widely used to collateralise exposures between commercial participants in the international financial markets.

1.40　UK treasuries are known as gilt-edged securities or 'gilts'. They bear a fixed rate of interest. Gilts are denominated in sterling. The Debt Management Office of HM Treasury ('the DMO') has taken over responsibility for the issue of gilts from the Bank of England. Gilts are issued on regular dates to specialist dealers called 'gilt edged market makers' or GEMMs.[45]

1.41　The London Stock Exchange provides a secondary market for gilts, which it regulates on a day to day basis.[46] Trades in gilts are settled through CREST,[47] as discussed in Chapter 9.

1.42　The UK gilts market was significantly liberalised over the course of the 1990s along the lines of the US treasuries market.[48] Changes have included the introduction of a gilt strips market[49] and an open gilt repo market.[50]

Money market instruments

1.43　Money market instruments are short term[51] debt instruments, such as certificates of deposit, commercial paper and certain bills of exchange. They are highly liquid and are sometimes referred to as 'near cash'.

1.44　Secondary market dealings in money market instruments are largely limited to banks and other financial institutions dealing either with each other and/or with their institutional clients on a wholesale basis (ie for large values). In the United Kingdom, a light regulatory regime applies to such dealings. Money market instruments are settled through the Central Moneymarkets Office (CMO). As discussed in Chapter 9, it is proposed that the CMO will be merged with CREST, which settles UK equities.

---

[44] Repos involve outright transfers of collateral, and in some jurisdictions where outright collateral transfers are not recognised, securities collateral is taken in money market operations under security interests. See Chapters 5 and 6 for further discussion.

[45] This status is awarded by the DMO. GEMMs must be members of the London Stock Exchange, and are subject to its rules.

[46] The DMO is involved with the issue and admittance of gilts, and does not become involved in the day to day regulation of dealing practice.

[47] Prior to the merger of the Central Gilts Office with CREST in July 2000, gilts were settled through the Central Gilts Office. See Chapter 9.

[48] This was in order to reduce the cost to the government of issuing and administering gilts, or the cost of finance.

[49] In which the right to interest is separated from the right to principal, and trades separately from it.

[50] Until 1996, gilt repos were restricted to GEMMs.

[51] Of up to one year's duration.

The international debt markets: eurobonds and euronotes

As indicated above, the somewhat misleading term 'eurosecurities' means (broadly) securities issued internationally outside their domestic market. Eurosecurities include eurobonds and euronotes. **1.45**

A bond is a debt security bearing a fixed rate of interest[52] and having a medium to long term maturity (ie over one year). A *euro*bond is a bond which is issued internationally outside the domestic market of the issuer.[53] Eurobonds are characteristically underwritten,[54] and not secured,[55] and interest is paid gross. **1.46**

Notes are short term debt securities. *Euro*notes are short term debt securities issued outside the domestic market of that currency. A euronote may take the form of euro-commercial paper or ECP (short term borrowings by a company)[56] or euro-certificates of deposit (short term borrowings by a bank). **1.47**

London is the centre of the eurosecurities markets. There was a huge rise in the eurosecurities market in London in the early 1980s. Settlement of trades in eurosecurities is currently effected through two European computerised systems called Euroclear (in Belgium) and Clearstream (formerly Cedelbank in Luxembourg).[57] **1.48**

Equities

Whereas companies and non-companies alike can issue debt securities, equities can only be issued by companies. An equity is an ordinary[58] share in a **1.49**

---

[52] Where a floating rate of interest is payable, the security is generally called a floating rate note, or FRN.

[53] 'The international securities traded subject to ISMA's rules . . . are frequently denominated in a currency other than that of the country of the issuer and are intended to be traded internationally as well as domestically, and syndicated on that basis . . . The international financing of state and private projects has existed since the 19th century. The international securities market in its current form, however, dates from the early 1960s (arguably, the first Eurobond was issued on July 16, 1963: a US$ 15m loan for Autostrada)': ISMA *Handbook* (January 1998) 9.

[54] See the discussion of underwriting in the section on the primary markets above.

[55] See the discussion of secured and unsecured securities in the section on debt securities above.

[56] ECP programmes are short term (usually 45–60 days) and have no trustee. ECP usually does not pay interest but is issued at a discount.

ECP has come to replace revolving underwriting facilities (RUFs) and note issuance facilities (NIFs).

[57] See the discussion of settlement below, and the detailed discussion in Chapter 9.

[58] 'The rights attached to ordinary shares ("equities") may be stated quite shortly. Except insofar as the memorandum, articles or terms of issue provide otherwise, an ordinary shareholder is entitled to receive dividends when declared (subject to any priority as to dividend enjoyed by preference shareholders), to have his appropriate proportion of the company's assets after payment of creditors paid or transferred to him on a winding up (subject again to any priority enjoyed by preference shareholders) and to exercise one vote for each share that he holds at the general meetings of the company. [See Companies Act 1985, s 370(6)]': Byles and Sykes, *Gore-Browne on Companies* (44th edn, Jordans, 1986), Supplement 27, para 14.3.

company.[59] The holder of an equity is a shareholder, owning a share, or fractional part of the issuer. This means that the equity investor shares in all the assets, as well as all the liabilities of the issuing company,[60] participating in both the risks and the rewards of its business.[61] If the issuer prospers, the market value of the share (or the price for which it can be sold in the secondary market) will increase to reflect the increase in the value of the company's business.

1.50 In the case of a limited liability company, the exposure of shareholders to the liabilities of the company is limited by the face value of their shares. If the shares are fully paid, the shareholder may lose her investment, but (in normal circumstances) will face no further liability. If the shares are partly paid, the shareholder may face a call for the unpaid portion of the face value of her shares. In the case of unlimited companies, the exposure of shareholders for the liabilities of the company are unlimited. However, partly paid shares, and shares of unlimited companies are not normally found in the secondary markets.

1.51 An ordinary share does not carry an automatic right to income. However, if the company is profitable, available income is usually distributed to shareholders in the form of dividends. Thus the income generated by a share is variable, depending on the performance of the company.

1.52 The issue of shares is generally subject to pre-emption restrictions.[62] UK companies are subject to rules on maintenance of capital,[63] which place restrictions on the ability of companies to redeem their own shares. In very broad terms, therefore, investors' capital investment is only returnable *by the issuing company* in its liquidation, and an investor wishing to liquidate her investment must find a purchaser for her shares.[64]

---

[59] It is an ordinary share as distinct from a share having special preferred or postponed rights, such as a preference share: see below.

[60] 'The word "share" does not denote rights only—it denotes obligations also': *National Bank of Wales, Taylor, Phillips and Rickards' Case* [1897] 1 Ch 298, per Lindley LJ at 305.

[61] Whereas the investor in debt securities is concerned generally only with the payment of interest and principal, the equity investor is concerned with all aspects of the business of the issuer.

[62] In most European jurisdictions, including the United Kingdom, new shares, which are issued for cash, must be offered first to existing shareholders, unless existing shareholders renounce their rights of pre-emption. New issues, which raise further equity subject to the pre-emption rights of existing shareholders, are called 'rights issues'. This is subject to disapplication of pre-emption rights under the articles of the company or by special resolution. See the Companies Act 1985, ss 89–95.

[63] Gore-Browne discusses '. . . the principle of maintenance of capital, whereby a company with a share capital is bound to obtain a proper consideration for the shares which it issues and to refrain from handing back any or all of the fund so acquired to its members except by a lawful distribution of dividend or statutory reduction approved by the court. This is a principle of general law, though in most respects the general law has been superseded by statute, especially Part V of the Companies Act 1985': *Gore-Browne* (n 58 above) para 13.1.

[64] See Part V of the Companies Act 1985. A special regime applies to open-ended investment companies (OEICs), which are able readily to redeem their shares at net asset value. See Chapter 11.

Upon liquidation, a shareholder is not entitled to have her investment repaid **1.53**
unless and until all creditors are repaid first.[65]

Hybrid securities

A type of securities known as hybrid securities combines some of the characteris- **1.54**
tics of debt securities with some of the characteristics of equities. Examples of
hybrid securities are preference shares, convertibles and equity warrants.

Preference shares (or prefs) form an intermediate class of security between equities **1.55**
(or ordinary shares) and debt. They are called preference shares because they carry
the right in the liquidation of the issuer to receive interest and/or a return of
capital in priority to ordinary shareholders. Rather than a variable dividend, prefs
usually carry a fixed interest rate. In the case of cumulative preference shares, any
dividend which cannot be paid in one year remains owing by the company and is
carried forward to the following year for payment.[66] Usually prefs carry no voting
rights.

Convertibles are bonds which can be converted, at the election of the bondholder, **1.56**
into another sort of security such as equities.

Equity warrants are contractual entitlements to purchase shares on pre- **1.57**
determined terms. They are often issued together with bonds or existing equities,
but are detachable from them and separately tradable.

The equity markets

The London equity markets have traditionally been dominated by the London **1.58**
Stock Exchange, which provides a market for UK equities and certain overseas
equities.[67] On 1 May 2000 the UK Listing Authority transferred from the London
Stock Exchange to the Financial Services Authority. Full listing is available for certain UK companies.[68] Smaller and less well-established companies may be listed

---

[65] See the Insolvency Act 1986, s 107.

[66] If preference shares carry additional rights to participate in the profits of the company, they are
called 'participating preference shares'. With non-cumulative preference shares, the dividend is only
payable out of available profits each year.

[67] Other securities traded on the London Stock Exchange include gilts, bonds, depositary
receipts, covered warrants and traditional short-dated options on UK equities.

[68] Normally, a three-year track record is required. However, with effect from January 2000,
chapter 25 of the Listing Rules, controversially 'sets out a concessionary route for listing innovative
high growth companies without a three year record . . . The company must demonstrate its ability
to attract funds from sophisticated investors, have a market capitalisation at the time of listing of at
least £50 million and, unless the Exchange agrees otherwise, undertake a marketing of at least £20
million at the time of listing': 'Note to Subscribers to the Listing Rules, Amendment No 14'.

Securities included in the FTSE 100 index are traded on the Stock Exchange Electronic Trading
Service (SETS). This is an order-driven system. Buyers and sellers specify the prices at which they
are willing to trade, and the system automatically implements trades between matching orders.
A potential problem with order-driven systems is illiquidity when matching orders do not

and admitted to trading on the Alternative Investment Market ('AIM').[69] International equities are also listed and admitted to trading on the London Stock Exchange.[70] Most London Stock Exchange trades in UK securities are settled through an electronic system called CREST (see Chapter 9).

1.59 Two important trends are affecting the international equity markets. First, the traditional markets are being consolidated, particularly within Europe and between Europe and New York. With the introduction of the euro, large financial institutions are leading the demand for a single pan-European trading platform,[71] with links to New York. New initiatives involving the traditional exchanges are announced on a regular basis.[72] An important example is the alliance of the Paris, Amsterdam and Brussels bourses which is (at the time of writing) also understood to be exploring links with Nasdaq.[73]

1.60 Secondly, the traditional exchanges are facing a challenge from more recently established alternative trading systems.

---

spontaneously arise. Since SETS was introduced in 1997 it has experienced illiquidity and also price abnormalities.

Other fully listed securities for which two member firms are willing to act as market makers may trade on The Stock Exchange Automated Quotation System (SEAQ). This is a quote-driven system. Market makers are a special class of broker dealer (or stock exchange member), which enjoy special privileges in exchange for assuming an obligation to quote continuous two-way (ie buy and sell) prices for the securities in respect of which they are market makers. Market makers' prices are displayed on screen by SEAQ, and broker dealers conclude trades on the basis of those prices by telephone. Market makers deal with other market makers through Inter-Dealer Brokers. In exchange for the obligation to quote continuous prices, the usual trade disclosure rules are relaxed in favour of market makers. Other privileges are exemption from stamp duty and the ability to quote prices on SEAQ. The use of market makers is designed to ensure liquidity. However, quote-driven dealing has been criticised for lack of transparency due to the relaxed reporting obligations of market makers.

[69] AIM securities trade on The Stock Exchange Alternative Trading Service (SEATS). In addition, fully listed securities that are unable to attract two market makers also trade on SEATS. Broker dealers may choose between using the using a quote-driven system or an order-driven system.

[70] Non-UK equities are traded on The Stock Exchange Automated Quotation System International (SEAQ International).

[71] The EU has indicated its commitment to facilitating the wholesale financial markets within Europe. 'The prospect of a single currency is spurring a market-driven modernisation of EU wholesale markets. However, the single currency will not of itself deliver an optimally functioning wholesale market. A coherent programme of action to smooth out remaining legislative, administrative and fiscal barriers to cross-border floatations and investment-related activities can deliver significant economic dividends': Commission Communication, *Financial Services: Building a Framework for Action* 2.

[72] On May 2000 the London Stock Exchange announced a proposed merger between itself and Deutsche Börse. However, following a hostile takeover bid from the OM group in August 2000, the proposals for the Deutsche Börse merger have now been withdrawn, and the London Stock Exchange has no immediate plans for a merger or alliance with another exchange.

[73] This alliance is known as Euronext.

EASDAQ[74] is a Brussels-based exchange for equities in European high-growth or **1.61** 'venture capital' companies, particular technology companies. It was established with the aim of creating a pan-European market, using the 'passport' freedoms under the Investment Services and Prospectus Directives.[75] However, significant volumes of business have not yet been achieved. EASDAQ trades are settled through the Swiss settlement system, SIS SegaIntersettle.

In 1995, Tradepoint launched an alternative order-driven electronic market for **1.62** leading UK equities. Transactions concluded on Tradepoint are settled through the London Clearing House. Tradepoint was acquired by a consortium led by Instinet, a US-based agency brokerage firm offering electronic order routing services. In a bid to offer consolidated pan-European equity trading, clearing and settlement, Tradepoint announced plans for an enhanced system, to be launched towards the end of 2000, whereby its international trades are cleared and settled through London Clearing House and Euroclear.

A further significant challenge to the business of the traditional exchanges comes **1.63** from Jiway, a new electronic equity market formed in a joint venture between Morgan Stanley and the OM Group. Trading, clearing and settlement will be available for a range of European and US equities, with settlement taking place through links to local depositaries.

Much wholesale business in international equities is concluded OTC between **1.64** brokers and fund managers. This business is currently concluded largely by telephone and fax, but there are moves to introduce a higher degree of automation, led in London by the Global Straight Through Processing Association, or GSTPA. (See the discussion of straight through processing in Chapter 10.)

D. Introduction to Settlement

Settlement is the plumbing of the securities markets. Understanding the structure **1.65** of the securities settlement industry is the key to understanding the legal nature of interests in securities.

---

[74] European Association of Securities Dealers Automated Quotation System.
[75] Under the Investment Services Directive, firms who are authorised in their home Member State may carry on investment business in other Member States without additional authorisations. This freedom is known as the 'general passport'. A broadly similar general passport is available for banks under the Second Banking Co-ordination Directive (Second Council Directive of 15 December 1989 on the coordination of laws, regulations and administrative provisions relating to the taking up and pursuit of the business of credit institutions (89/646/EEC)).

1.66   In the past, settlement was relatively neglected by lawyers. However it now attracts significant legal attention, as regulators and practitioners endeavour to manage risk through settlement efficiencies. Settlement is a major industry, and this industry is in a process of rapid and continuous transformation.

(1) What is Settlement?

1.67   Securities settlement is the process whereby (interests in) securities are delivered, usually against payment, to fulfil contractual obligations, such as those arising under securities trades.[76]

1.68   In the past, securities settlement involved the physical movement of paper instruments, or certificates and transfer forms. Payment was usually made by cheque. Paper-based settlement was labour intensive.[77] It was also risky, as paper instruments, certificates and transfer forms were relatively easy to lose, steal and forge. Above all, it was slow. As the volume of business in the securities markets increased, settlement could not keep up. In the 1970s, the US markets experienced what has become known as 'the paper crunch', as settlement delays threatened to disrupt the operation of the securities markets. In the United Kingdom, the weakness of paper-based settlement was exposed by a programme of privatisation of nationalised industries in the 1980s, and the Big Bang[78] of 1986 led to an explosion in the volume of trades, and settlement delays became significant. In the crash of 1987, many investors sought to limit their losses by selling their securities, but found that the failure of timely settlement left them exposed.

(2) Electronic Settlement

1.69   In 1989, a New York-based think tank for the international financial markets called the Group of Thirty ('G30')[79] published a major report entitled *Clearance and Settlement Systems in the World's Securities Markets* (known as 'the G30 Report'). This report made nine recommendations with a view to achieving more efficient settlement.[80] The G30 Report put the need for electronic settlement beyond doubt.

---

[76] Alternatively, the relevant contractual obligation may arise under a margin call; see Chapter 10.

[77] In the era of paper-based settlement, securities houses employed huge numbers of settlement clerks, known collectively as 'the back office'.

[78] The Big Bang is the colloquial name for reforms that were made to the rules of the London Stock Exchange, which fundamentally altered the structure of the London equity market.

[79] See the G30 website at www.group30.org

[80] These recommendations related to: trade comparisons; trade confirmations/affirmations; central securities depositaries; trade netting; delivery versus payment or DVP; payments; rolling settlement and shorter settlement intervals; securities lending; and securities numbering systems. See Chapter 7 for a fuller discussion

With electronic settlement, (interests in) securities are delivered through elec-   **1.70**
tronic settlement systems. Electronic settlement takes place between participants
in such systems.[81] The interests of participants are recorded by credit entries in
securities accounts maintained in their names by the operator of the system. The
operator also maintains participant cash accounts. When participant A (a seller)
and participant B (a buyer) agree that (interests in) securities will be delivered
against payment from A to B, they instruct the settlement system to debit the
securities account of A and credit that of B. At the same time they instruct the system to debit the cash account of B and credit the cash account of A.[82] This
arrangement offers quick and efficient settlement by removing the need for paperwork. It also permits the synchronisation of the delivery of (interests in) securities
with the payment of a corresponding cash sum;[83] such synchronisation is called
delivery versus payment or DVP.[84]

For many years the G30 Report provided the model for standards in the settle-   **1.71**
ment industry. As new electronic technologies are developed, the settlement
industry is able to meet and even exceed the G30 standards.[85] More than a decade
after the report was published, commercial pressure for increased settlement efficiencies is more intense than ever. Indeed, the recent development of electronic
securities trading has brought about settlement pressures akin to the paper crunch
of the 1970s and 1980s, rendering the need for further efficiencies urgent.[86]
Recent developments in securities settlement are discussed in Chapter 9.

(3) The Legal Significance of Settling a Trade

Settlement involves the delivery of (interests in) securities to perform contractual   **1.72**
delivery obligations. Settlement usually also involves the corresponding payment
of the purchase price.

---

[81] If a non-participant wishes to settle its interests in securities electronically, it must do so
through a participant acting as its custodian.

[82] Of course, cash accounts are not debited and credited in a free delivery, ie a delivery of (interests in) securities without a corresponding cash payment. Free deliveries are widely used in marking
to market; see Chapter 6.

[83] This cash sum would be the purchase price in the case of purchases, and the loaned cash in the
case of collateral deliveries.

[84] See the discussion of DVP in Chapter 9.

[85] See Morgan Guaranty Report, *Cross-Border Clearance, Settlement and Custody: Beyond the G30
Recommendations* (1993).

[86] The urgency of achieving rapid settlement is in part due to the growth of electronic trading
in securities. 'At the present time, internal and industry-wide systems are straining to manage
the rapidly growing volumes resulting from an explosion of self-directed investment for defined
contribution plans, growth in cross-border activity and the advent of electronic communication
networks (ECNs) and electronic trading. This strain will intensify with the planned expansion
of trading hours': SIA, *Institutional Transaction Processing Committee: White Paper, version 1.5*
(1 December 1999) 2.

1.73 The legal significance of settlement is most clear when one considers the legal position of the purchaser. After the trade and before settlement, her rights are contractual and therefore personal.[87] Because they are merely personal, her rights are at risk in the event of the insolvency of the vendor.[88] After settlement, the purchaser owns (interests in) securities and her rights are proprietary. In normal circumstances,[89] these property rights will not be affected by the insolvency of the vendor. Settlement is the delivery of (interests in) securities to complete trades; it involves upgrading personal rights into property rights and thus protects market participants from the risk of the default of their counterparties.[90]

1.74 Settlement is described as a 'back office' function, in order to distinguish it from trading activity ('front office' activity) and post-trade, pre-settlement processing (which take place in 'the middle office').[91]

(4) The Contrast Between Trading and Clearing

1.75 It is important to distinguish settlement both from trading and from clearing.

Trading

1.76 Trading involves entering into contracts of sale and purchase.[92] Trading does not include settlement (ie payment and delivery).

Clearing

1.77 Settlement is different from clearing, although the two terms are often confused in practice. Clearing has long been used in the derivatives markets, but more recently has been extended to the non-derivative (ie the cash) securities markets. Where clearing takes place, it follows trading and precedes settlement.[93] As already indicated, settlement involves delivery (and usually payment) in fulfilment of contractual obligations, which are assumed on trading or otherwise.[94] Clearing involves modifying those contractual obligations so as to facilitate settle-

---

[87] A contractual right is a form of personal right. The purchaser has a personal right, arising under the contract of sale, to require the vendor to perform the bargain.

[88] See Chapter 4 for a discussion of the impact of insolvency on personal rights. A further discussion of the distinction between personal and property rights follows in Chapter 13.

[89] See the discussion of insolvency displacement in Chapter 3.

[90] The position for the vendor is similar. Before settlement she is merely owed the purchase price; this debt is at risk in the purchaser's insolvency.

[91] Middle office activity involves the processing of trades after they have been concluded but before they have been settled. It involves steps such as confirmation, matching, the allocation of agency trades to clients and regulatory reporting.

[92] Trading may take place on an organised exchange or OTC, as discussed above.

[93] However, it is not usually intended to be included in the term 'the middle office'.

[94] A delivery or payment obligation might also arise under a collateral arrangement.

ment, usually by netting and novation.[95] Clearing is usually performed by a well capitalised entity called a clearing house. It is discussed in more detail in Chapters 8 and 9.

(5) Distinctions Between Settlement Systems

A number of distinctions may be made between different kinds of settlement sys- **1.78**
tem. The following distinctions are particularly important in the legal analysis of interests in securities.

Immobilisation and dematerialisation

There are two broad models for electronic settlement, namely immobilisation and **1.79**
dematerialisation. The G30 Report recommends immobilisation as an interim stage towards the ultimate goal of dematerialisation.[96]

Immobilisation

Immobilisation entails the use of securities in paper form and the use of deposi- **1.80**
taries, which are linked to a settlement system. Securities (either constituted by paper instruments or represented by paper certificates) are immobilised[97] in the sense that they are held by the depositary at all times.[98]

The depositary does not own the securities beneficially. It may hold the securities **1.81**
directly for participants in the settlement system to whose accounts interests in the relevant securities are credited.[99] Alternatively the depositary may hold the securities for the operator of the settlement system, which in turn holds its interests in the securities for participants.[100] The interests of participants may arise under bailment,[101] or trust,[102] or under a special statutory arrangement.[103]

An example of a national immobilisation system is the Central Moneymarkets **1.82**
Office or CMO in London, which is discussed in Chapter 9. Euroclear[104] and Clearstream Banking, Luxembourg ('Clearstream')[105] are two important

---

[95] Very broadly, netting is the off-setting of mutual obligations. Novation is the replacement of an old contract with one or more new contracts in like terms to the original contract but with different parties.

[96] See G30 Report, discussion of recommendation 3.

[97] They are immobilised on a continuing basis (ie before, during and after settlement).

[98] The depositary retains possession of bearer securities, and its (or its nominee's) name is entered in the register of registered securities.

[99] This is the case in the Central Moneymarkets Office, the UK settlement system for money market instruments, which is proposed to be merged with CREST: see Chapter 9.

[100] This is the case with Euroclear and Clearstream, discussed below.

[101] As in the case of the CMO.

[102] As in the case of the Hong Kong Clearing and Settlement System (HKCSS).

[103] As in the case of Euroclear and Clearstream.

[104] See the Euroclear website at www.euroclear.com

[105] See the Clearstream website at www.clearstream.net

examples of international immobilisation systems. The legal and operational structures of these two systems are similar in many respects.

1.83   Euroclear is based in Brussels and operated by the Brussels branch of Morgan Guaranty Trust Company of New York.[106] Clearstream Banking, Luxembourg is the entity formerly known as Cedelbank (renamed in 2000 following the merger of the business of Luxembourg-established Cedel International with the German Deutsche Börse Clearing). Euroclear and Clearstream originally settled eurobonds, but now a wide range of international securities are settled through them including many types of sovereign debt and equity securities.

1.84   In relation to eurobonds and equity securities, the normal arrangement in each system is for the underlying securities to be held by a depositary acting for both Euroclear and Clearstream (and therefore called a 'common depositary').[107] In the case of bearer securities, it is usual for the paper in the hands of the depositary to consist not of individual bonds in definitive form ('definitives'), but rather one single instrument (called a global bond or 'global') which represents the entire issue of definitives.[108]

1.85   In turn, Euroclear and Clearstream hold their interest in the securities for their respective participants in accordance with the credit entries made to the participants' Euroclear or Clearstream securities accounts. This arrangement arises in accordance with each system's General Terms and Conditions and local statute. The relevant statute is (in the case of Euroclear) the Belgian Royal Decree No 62 of 10 November 1967 (as amended),[109] and (in the case of Clearstream) the Luxembourg Grand-Ducal Decree of February 1971 (as amended). These statutes provide in effect that in the insolvency of the operator of the settlement

[106] Morgan Guaranty operates the Euroclear system under contract with the Euroclear Clearance System Société Coopérative, which in turn is owned by some 1,500 Euroclear participants.

[107] In order to ensure that international securities are attractive to investors, issuers usually arrange for them to be eligible for settlement in both Euroclear and Clearstream.

The depositary acknowledges that it holds the securities for Euroclear and Clearstream in the relevant proportions, which it will record from time to time. The proportion held for Clearstream will increase for example, if a Euroclear participant sells interests to a Clearstream participant. Such settlements are recorded across a special software link called 'the Bridge'.

Euroclear and Clearstream obtain opinions from local lawyers practising in the jurisdictions where the common depositaries are based confirming that in the event of the depositaries' insolvency the securities will not be available to its general creditors.

[108] Originally, temporary globals were used for a 40-day period, after which definitives were issued. This practice was driven by US regulatory and tax concerns. However, increasingly permanent globals are used and definitives are never issued except on the default of the issuer or the clearing system.

[109] 'First, Articles 10 to 13 of the Royal Decree, as interpreted by leading Belgian scholars and practising lawyers, defines the interest of an investor or secured creditor in securities held through accounts with C.I.K. or its affiliates as a package of personal rights and co-property rights in favour of the collectivity of persons credited with interests in securities of the same type': Guynn and Tahyar, *Modernising Securities Ownership, Transfer and Pledging Laws* (London: IBA, 1996).

system, interests in securities will not be available to the general creditors of the operator.[110]

Whereas the holder of *securities* has a claim against the issuer of those securities, **1.86** the interest of a participant in an immobilisation system is in the normal course not enforceable against the issuer, but only enforceable against the operator of the system.[111]

Each of Euroclear and Clearstream has links with many national settlement systems. These cross-border links are discussed in Chapter 9. **1.87**

Dematerialisation

While immobilisation entails immobilising paper instruments or certificates, **1.88** dematerialisation involves dispensing with them altogether. Dematerialised (interests in) securities are issued 'straight onto the screen' of the settlement system and only exist in the form of electronic records.

Dematerialisation generally requires statutory support. This is because the rules **1.89** of traditional company law and property law generally require the use of paper instruments, certificates and transfers; these requirements must be disapplied by statute.[112]

The legal impact of dematerialisation differs in relation to bearer and registered **1.90** securities respectively. It will be shown in Chapter 2 that registered securities are intangible assets, comprising bundles of claims. (The physical certificate issued in respect of a registered security merely evidences, and does not constitute, the security.) Therefore, the elimination of paper certificates and transfer forms in relation to registered securities is merely a procedural matter, and does not fundamentally alter the legal nature of the security, which is intangible in both dematerialised and non-dematerialised form.

With bearer securities, however, the impact of dematerialisation is greater. It will **1.91** be shown in Chapter 2 that a traditional bearer security is a tangible asset, because the paper instrument is treated as constituting (and not merely evidencing) the claim on the issuer. With dematerialisation, physical instruments are replaced by electronic records, so that tangible assets are replaced by intangibles.

---

[110] '[T]he package of rights includes a right of *revendication*, exercisable in the event of the insolvency of the intermediary. That right entitles the holder to the return of a specific quantity of securities or interests in securities, which right is superior to the claims of the intermediary's general creditors. This right has been characterised by leading Belgian scholars and lawyers as reflecting a co-proprietary right to a notional portion of the pool of securities of the same type held by the intermediary on behalf of the collectivity of its interest holders': Guynn and Tahyar (n 109 above).

[111] As discussed below, it is customary to provide participants with direct rights in the event of issuer default under a deed poll.

[112] In the United Kingdom, the statutory basis for dematerialisation in CREST is the Uncertificated Securities Regulations 1995, SI 1995/3272, as discussed in Chapter 9.

1.92 This is important for a number of reasons. First, commercial techniques traditionally used in the bearer securities markets (including negotiation, bailment and pledge)[113] rely on the possession of a tangible asset, and are not possible in a dematerialised environment.[114] Secondly, whereas the tangible assets have physical locations, intangibles do not. This is significant in the conflict of laws.[115]

Direct and indirect

1.93 A further important distinction is that between settlement systems in which participants hold the underlying securities[116] directly, and those in which the interest of the participants in the underlying securities is indirect. It was indicated above that immobilisation necessarily involves the use of a depositary. A depositary holds the underlying securities, and stands in the chain of ownership between participants and issuers.

1.94 With dematerialisation, the system may be either indirect or direct. Depositaries may optionally be used in dematerialised settlement systems, holding title to the underlying securities on behalf of the system or its participants (but not holding physical instruments or certificates, for none exist). Alternatively, a dematerialised system may involve no depositary, and may act as mere conduits for communications between participants and the issuers of securities, thus permitting participants to hold title to the underlying securities directly.

Direct

1.95 In a direct system, participants hold the underlying securities directly. The settlement system does not stand in the chain of ownership, but merely serves as a conduit for communications of participants to issuers. CREST in the United Kingdom is an example of a direct system.[117]

Indirect

1.96 In contrast, where a depositary is used, the depositary stands in the chain of ownership between participant and issuer, so that the interest of the participant in the underlying securities is indirect. Euroclear and Clearstream hold certain securities[118] on a dematerialised basis, and do so indirectly.

1.97 Under the customary[119] terms of issue of securities, the issuer does not recognise the rights of any participant in an indirect settlement system in respect of the secu-

---

[113] These terms are discussed in Chapter 2.

[114] See Chapter 2 for a discussion of these issues.

[115] See Chapter 7. As discussed in that chapter, the conflict of laws, or private international law, are the rules that govern the legal aspects of cross-border situations.

[116] The term 'underlying securities' is used to denote the securities in which the participant has direct or indirect property rights, and from which any interests in securities derive.

[117] See Chapter 9.

[118] Many types of treasury securities are so held.

[119] More recently, some issues of securities have permitted such direct rights to arise.

rities (in the absence of default or the removal of definitive securities from the settlement system).[120]

Settlement systems generally restrict direct participation to a small number of **1.98** institutions, imposing financial and sometimes nationality criteria.[121] The number of investors and collateral takers greatly exceeds the number of participants in settlement systems. Those who wish to hold interests in securities, but are not participants in the relevant settlement systems, must hold such interests indirectly, through participants who act as their custodians. Thus, the custodian stands in the chain of ownership between investors and issuers, just as the depositary stands between the issuer and participants in indirect settlement systems. (This pattern of intermediation is repeated in the cash and derivatives markets, with participation in large value settlement systems being restricted to large institutions, and with smaller institutions participating indirectly.)[122] Thus, even where the settlement system chosen by the issuer gives participants a direct interest, the interest of most investors in the securities remains indirect, because of the use of custodians.

Another source of intermediation is the formation of links between local settle- **1.99** ment systems. Such links usually involve one system (A) acting as depositary for another system (B), so that A stands in the chain of ownership between participants in B and issuers.[123]

Thus, a consequence of the widespread use of intermediaries in settlement is that **1.100** the assets of investors and collateral takers are indirect, in the sense that these assets do not confer direct rights of action against the issuers of the underlying securities.

Allocated and unallocated

A further key distinction between different settlement systems is whether the **1.101** interests of participants are allocated or unallocated.[124]

---

[120] Moreover the records of the depositary indicate that it holds the securities for the operator of the settlement system, and not for their participants. Although some issues now provide for direct rights of enforcement by participants in the event of default, there is usually no clear method by which participants can mount a claim against the issuer. Thus, the participant does not have a direct entitlement to the immobilised securities, recoverable against either the depositary or the issuer, but rather an indirect entitlement. (In practice, payment is made by paying agents crediting the account of the settlement system, which in turn credits the account of the participant.)

[121] Interestingly, CREST imposes no financial criteria, but rather requires participants to have settlement banks. In practice, settlement banks are only willing to act for clients with adequate financial resources.

[122] For example, in the United Kingdom participation in the CHAPS wholesale sterling settlement system is narrowly restricted, as is clearing membership of the London Clearing House, as discussed in Chapter 8.

[123] For more detail, see the discussion in Chapter 9.

[124] A fuller discussion is given in Chapter 2. The same distinction arises in custody, as discussed in Chapter 10.

Allocated

1.102 In allocated arrangements, particular (interests in) securities are allocated to particular participants. Allocated arrangements are becoming less and less common, as greater settlement efficiencies are possible with unallocated arrangements.[125]

Unallocated

1.103 With unallocated arrangements, there is no link between particular participants and particular (interests in) securities. The interests of all participants holding the relevant (interests in) securities are held together by the settlement system in a commingled pool. The settlement system records how many (interests in) securities are held for each participant, but not which ones. Unallocated settlement renders a settlement system more flexible, and any error or delay relating to the settlement of one trade is less likely to affect the settlement of other trades.

1.104 With unallocated arrangements, the participants' rights do not attach to particular (interests in) securities, but rather relate to a pool of (interests in) securities, as do the rights of all other participants to whose accounts the relevant (interests in) securities are credited. They are therefore co-proprietary rights.[126] In many jurisdictions, special legislation is needed to permit such co-proprietary rights to arise.[127] Because participants would not enjoy such property rights but for such local legislation, such rights arise under the law under which the settlement system operates, and not under the law under which the underlying securities were issued, as discussed further in Chapter 7.

E. Interests in Securities

1.05 For these reasons, the interests of the participant in unallocated settlement and custody arrangements are not the same assets as the underlying securities. To take the example of the asset of a participant in Euroclear (which is located in Belgium) in respect of Italian bonds, the interest of the participant is indirect and unallocated. It arises under Belgian law on the basis of a Belgian account entry. It does not attach to particular underlying bonds. For these reasons it is intangible. In contrast, the depositary acting for Euroclear directly holds the underlying bonds. This holding is allocated (attaches to particular bonds) and arises under Italian law on the basis of possession. Because it attaches to the physical paper held by the

---

[125] An example of an allocated system is the CMO and the Depository and Clearing Centre owned and operated by Bank One NA (DCC).

[126] See, however, the discussion of *C A Pacific* [2000] BCLC 494 in Chapter 2.

[127] Examples are the Belgian Royal Decree No 62 of November 1967 in the case of Euroclear, the Luxembourg Grand-Ducal Decree of 17 February 1971 in the case of Clearstream, and (some would argue) reg 25 of the Uncertificated Securities Regulations 1995 in the case of CREST.

depositary, the asset of the depositary is tangible. It follows that the asset of the participant is different from the asset of the depositary. The economic value of the former derives from the latter, but the two are legally distinct.[128]

Interests in securities are often heavily intermediated, with a series of custodians, **1.106** depositaries and other intermediaries standing in the chain of ownership between the investor and the underlying issuer. The investor may be further removed from the underlying issuer where its asset has been repackaged under securitisation, depositary receipt or investment fund arrangements, as discussed in Chapters 11 and 12. Normally, each link in such a chain shares the characteristics of unallocated settlement, in that the interest of the client is indirect, unallocated and intangible.

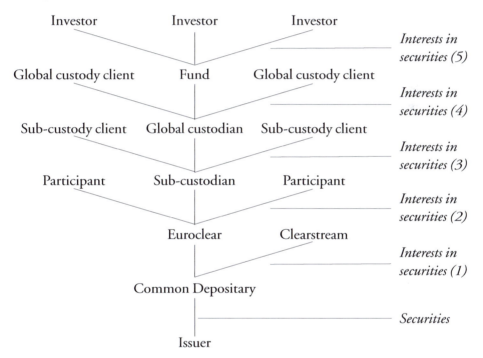

Figure 1.2: Chain of interests in securities

---

[128] It may be helpful to equate the use of unallocated depositary arrangements with a form of repackaging. Settlement in the international equity markets has long been more fragmented than international bond settlement. As discussed in Chapter 11, the traditional technique for overcoming this fragmentation has been the use of depositary receipts (DRs). For example, at the time of writing, Indian share settlement can take several weeks. To enable investors to acquire an interest in Indian shares, without suffering the delay of Indian settlement, a depositary bank might take legal title to a pool of Indian shares. It would issue US or English law DRs in respect of these shares, and agree to hold the shares on trust for holders of the DRs. The DRs may be settled conveniently through the DTC, and/or Euroclear and Clearstream. The DR programme is unallocated in that the DR holders have co-proprietary rights in the pool of shares held by the depositary. Although the

1.107   Although the underlying securities and the interest of the investor are legally distinct, they are the same in economic terms[129] (on the basis that the investor's asset is not at risk in the event of the insolvency of any intermediary). In economic terms the holder of interests in securities has all the risks and rewards of ownership of the underlying securities. This accords with the balance sheet[130] and regulatory capital[131] treatment of interests in securities.

1.108   Such intermediation suggests the image of a series of Russian dolls, one inside the other, with the smallest doll containing a jewel. Each doll is different from every other doll, although the value of all the dolls derives alike from the jewel. The jewel equates by analogy to the underlying securities, and each doll to a different interest in securities.

1.109   This legal analysis informs the drafting of the revised article 8 of the US Uniform Commercial Code.[132] Legislation in Belgium[133] and Luxembourg[134] takes the same approach, which accords with article 9(2) of the Settlement Finality Directive[135] in relation to conflict of laws issues. While further legislative clarification in the Unied Kingdom would be welcome, the author would argue that the treatment of securities and interests in securities as separate assets is correct under the existing principles of English law.

DR represents an interest in the underlying Indian shares, it is a different asset, and is governed by a different system of law.

DRs are less widely used in the bond markets, because of the availability of the international settlement systems, Euroclear and Clearstream. The author would argue that the legal impact of the use of unallocated depositary arrangements in DRs and in settlement is the same.

[129]   Of course, the investor faces the risk of the fraud and negligence of the intermediaries; this should not be significant if they are regulated institutions.

[130]   The investor shows securities, and not interests in securities, on its balance sheet.

[131]   The regulatory capital weighting of interests in securities follows the credit rating of the issuer of the underlying securities, and not that of the intermediary.

[132]   It informs the concept of 'securities entitlements'; see s 8-102(a)(17) and (generally) Part 5 of article 8.

[133]   The Royal Decree No 62 of November 1967.

[134]   The Grand-Ducal Decree of 17 February 1971.

[135]   Directive 98/26/EC. See Chapter 7.

2

THE LEGAL NATURE OF SECURITIES
AND INTERESTS IN SECURITIES*

So continuous is legal history that the lawyers do not see that there has been a new departure until this has for some time past been an accomplished fact.[1]

This chapter will consider in turn the legal nature of securities and that of interests in securities. The difference between the two illustrates the legal impact of intermediation in the securities markets.   **2.01**

A. The Legal Nature of Securities

The legal nature of securities will be considered first.   **2.02**

(1) Key Distinctions

Securities are traditionally categorised by two sets of distinctions, the first being **2.03** that between debt and equity securities, and the second being that between bearer and registered securities. The first distinction, which was considered in Chapter 1, concerns the nature of the rights of the holder in relation to the issuer. In contrast, the distinction between registered and bearer securities, which is considered

---

* The author is grateful to Professor David Hayton of King's College London for kindly reviewing this chapter. The opinions expressed in it and any errors are her own.
[1] F Maitland, *The Forms of Action at Common Law* (Cambridge University Press, 1997, first published 1909) 43.

below, concerns the manner in which the legal rights of the holder are formally acquired, recorded and transferred.[2]

(2) Bearer and Registered Securities

2.04 This section will consider the differences between bearer and registered securities.

Bearer securities

2.05 Bearer securities are issued in the form of a paper instrument; on the face of the instrument is written the promise of the issuer to pay the bearer (or holder) of the instrument. By a legal fiction, the instrument is deemed to constitute the debt of the issuer and/or other rights comprised in the security, and not merely to represent them. The person who for the time being has possession[3] of the instrument (its holder)[4] is the legal owner of the bearer security. Bearer securities are transferred by delivering the instrument from person to person.[5]

2.06 Regulatory and fiscal authorities sometimes regard bearer securities in a negative light, as they may be used to facilitate the evasion of regulatory restrictions and tax. In the United Kingdom, the issue of bearer securities was heavily restricted during the era of exchange control, and today bearer securities remain less common than registered securities.[6] The sale of bearer securities to US persons is generally prohibited. However, eurobonds are traditionally issued in bearer form, as discussed in Chapter 1.

Registered securities

2.07 Although certificates bearing the name of the holder are issued in relation to registered securities,[7] such certificates merely *represent* the registered securities. Certificates do not *constitute* the securities, and a person does not automatically

---

[2] This discussion concerns technical ownership, or legal title. Where legal title to a security is with one person, it is possible for other persons to enjoy beneficial or equitable interests in the same security at the same time, under a trust. This is discussed further below.

[3] Possession is the physical control of a tangible asset, as discussed below.

[4] '"Holder" means the payee or indorsee of a bill or note who is in possession of it, or the bearer thereof': Bills of Exchange Act 1882, s 2.

[5] Delivery is the transfer of possession. See the discussion of possession below. In some cases, transfer is by endorsement, or signing the back of the instrument, and delivery.

[6] 'Bearer securities are much less common than they were before the Second World War. The Exchange Control Act 1947 provided that no person in the United Kingdom might issue any bearer certificate or coupon without the permission of the Treasury [s 10]. The position was alleviated to some extent by the Finance Act 1963, which provided that the registered holder of British Government stock was entitled to exchange it for bearer bonds subject to certain conditions [s 711]. That provision was introduced for the benefit of foreign investors. Finally, all United Kingdom exchange controls were removed in 1979. In spite of the removal of exchange controls, bearer securities are comparatively rare at the present day': J Milnes Holden, *The Law and Practice of Banking* (8th edn, London: Pitman, 1994) vol 2, 190.

[7] Except in the case of dematerialised securities; see the discussion of CREST in Chapter 9.

acquire legal ownership of the security by having possession of the certificate.[8] The issuer[9] maintains a register[10] in which details of the holders of the securities are entered and updated as appropriate. A transfer of registered securities is effected by amending the register, so that the securities stand in the name of the transferee, rather than in that of the transferor.[11]

Examples of registered and bearer securities

In the United Kingdom, equities are always in registered form.[12] UK debt securities **2.08**
may be issued in either bearer or registered form.[13] UK domestic issues of debt are usually registered and international debt issues are characteristically in bearer form.

(3) Tangible and Intangible Securities

A tangible thing is something that one can touch. Personal assets[14] are divided into **2.09**
tangible personal assets (called 'choses in possession' or 'chattels') and intangible personal assets (called 'choses in action' or 'claims').[15] The term 'chose' is old legal

---

[8] The term 'certificate' is used to denote a document representing registered securities, and the term 'instrument' is used to denote a document constituting bearer securities. Legal title is determined by registration. However, the holder of a certificate may acquire an equitable security interest in the securities: see Chapter 5.

[9] The issuer usually appoints a registrar to maintain the register on its behalf. In the UK settlement system, CREST, it is proposed that CRESTCo will maintain the register (or part of the register) on behalf of issuers, under proposals for electronic transfer of title; see Chapter 9.

[10] Traditionally registers were maintained in the form of books or ledgers. More recently, registers are generally computerised.

[11] Registration is required to transfer legal title: *Société Generale de Paris v Walker* (1895) 11 App Cas 20. An equitable interest in shares may be delivered by a trust or charge, without reregistration; see below, and Chapter 5.

In order to achieve registration, the transferee must (in the case of registered securities in traditional form) submit to the registrar the certificate of the transferor together with a transfer form made out in the transferee's favour, and executed by the transferor. In due course the registrar replaces the name of the transferor with of the transferee in the register, cancels the transferor's certificate and issues a new certificate in favour of the transferee. For the procedure in relation to dematerialised registered securities, see the discussion of CREST in Chapter 9.

[12] However, share warrants may be issued in bearer form: see the Companies Act 1985, s 188. Also, shares of open-ended investment companies (discussed in Chapter 11) may be in bearer form.

[13] There is a relatively small volume of corporate registered debt in issue. An enormous volume of international corporate debt in bearer form is in issue.

[14] Assets are divided into real assets (including most interests in land) and personal assets. 'The objects of dominion of property are *things*, contradistinguished from *persons*: and things are by the law of England distributed into two kinds; things *real*, and things *personal*'. Blackstone, *Commentaries on the Laws of England* (facsimile of 1st edn: Chicago, University of Chicago Press, 1979) vol 2, 16. See also Megarry, *The Law of Real Property* (7th edn, London: Sweet & Maxwell, 1993) 13, 14.

[15] 'Having thus considered the several divisions of property in *possession*, which subsists there only, where a man hath both the right and also the occupation of the thing; we will proceed next to take a short view of the nature of property in *action*, or such where a man hath not the occupation, but merely a bare right to occupy the thing in question; the possession whereof may however be recovered by a suit or action at law: from whence the thing so recoverable is called a thing or *chose*, *in action*': Blackstone (n 14 above) vol 2, 396, 397. 'According to my view, all personal things are either in possession or in action. The law knows no *tertium quid* between the two': *Colonial Bank v*

French for 'thing'. An example of a chose in possession is a ship. An example of a chose in action is a debt. The terms 'chose in possession' and 'chose in action' derive from the method of enforcing rights in relation to those assets. Because a chose in possession is a physical asset, the owner can assert her rights in it simply by seizing the asset (ie by taking possession), without recourse to the courts. However a claim can be enforced only by suing the obligor (ie the person against whom the claim arises), in a court action, and hence the term 'chose in action'.

2.10 The general rule is that securities are intangible and therefore constitute choses in action. For example, a registered share comprises a bundle of intangible rights[16] including the right of the shareholder to share in all the assets of a company, subject to all the liabilities of the company.[17] As indicated above, tangible share certificates may be issued, but they only represent the share and do not constitute it.

2.11 There is an important exception to the rule that securities are intangible. Bearer securities in their traditional form (ie in the absence of computerisation) comprise pieces of paper, which read on their face, 'I promise to pay the bearer . . .'. As discussed above, the paper instrument is treated by a legal fiction as *constituting* the debt. This means that bearer securities are tangible, and therefore constitute choses in possession.[18]

(4) Divided and Undivided Securities

2.12 A second distinction is that between divided and undivided securities. With some types of securities, each individual security constitutes a separate asset, which is legally distinct from each other security in the same issue. These will be called 'divided securities'.

2.13 With other types of securities, the entire issue makes up one single asset, with each of the securities being a fractional part of this undivided whole. These will be called 'undivided securities'.[19]

Whinney (1885) 30 Ch D at 285 per Fry LJ, dissenting judgment upheld in House of Lords (1886) All ER Rep 468.

[16] The original term for a share in a company was an 'action'. See F Maitland, 'Trust and Corporation' in *Selected Essays* (Cambridge University Press, 1936) 208.

[17] 'A share is the interest of a shareholder in the company, measured by a sum of money for the purpose of liability in the first place and of interest in the second, but also consisting of a series of mutual covenants entered into by all the shareholders inter se in accordance with s 16 of the Companies Act 1862 [now s 14 of the Companies Act 1985]. The contract contained in the articles of association is one of the original incidents of the share. A share is not a sum of money settled in the way suggested, but is an interest measured by a sum of money, and made up of various rights contained in the contract, including the right to a sum of money of a more or less amount': per Farwell J in *Borland's Trustee v Steel Brothers & Co Ltd* [1901] 1 Ch 279 at 288.

[18] *Hornblower v Proud* (1819) 106 ER 389. Further references are given in the discussion of negotiation in Chapter 3.

[19] Note the definition of the term 'Undivided interest' in the US Statement of Financial Accounting Standards No 125: 'Partial legal or beneficial ownership of an asset as a tenant in common with others . . .'.

Shares in the secondary markets are always undivided.[20] The issuer owes only one **2.14** set of obligations to shareholders under its memorandum and articles of association and company law. A share[21] represents an undivided fractional part of the issuing company.[22] To say that X owns 1,000 shares, is simply a way of measuring X's entitlement. It does not mean that X owns 1,000 different assets. The traditional name of the company, the 'joint stock company' emphasises the joint, or undivided nature of the investor's share in the capital. Registered debt securities also have this undivided nature.[23]

In contrast, in the case of bearer securities in their traditional (or pre-electronic) **2.15** form, each instrument reads on its face 'I promise to pay the bearer . . .'. Each such instrument constitutes the separate covenant of the issuer and is a separate debt. Therefore traditional bearer securities are divided.

Chapter 1 indicated that where bearer securities are immobilised, it is not cus- **2.16** tomary for the issuer to issue individual definitive instruments, but rather to issue a single global instrument in respect of the entire issue. There is only one covenant to pay on the face of the global instrument. In other words, the use of global securities renders immobilised securities undivided.

More generally, the term 'interests in securities' has been defined as the assets of **2.17** the client for whom an intermediary holds (interests in) securities on an commingled basis together with the interests in securities of other clients. Interests in securities are, by definition, undivided.

---

[20] This comment relates to shares of the same class, which rank pari passu and are fully paid up. This will always be the case with listed shares. Shares in the secondary market are in practice unnumbered. Numbering is optional for shares, which are fully paid and rank pari passu: Companies Act 1985, s 182(2).

Even numbered shares are legally undivided, as the number is for administrative convenience only, and does not render one share a different asset from another share: see *Ind's Case* (1872) 7 Ch App 485.

[21] The same word, 'share' is used more generally to mean a participation or undivided entitlement to any asset. This is not a pun, but two uses of the same word.

[22] The ancestor of the modern company is the joint stock company of the early modern period. Registered securities were developed as a means of permitting interests in joint stock to be transferable: *In re Bahia and San Francisco Railway Co* (1865) per Blackburn J at 595, 596. 'The term "stock" is used in a general way as co-extensive with the whole property, but is more frequently applied to what may be termed the trading or floating capital': R R Formoy, *The Historical Foundations of Modern Company Law* (London: Sweet & Maxwell, 1923) 6. This accords with the balance sheet treatment of registered securities, with, in general, no allocation between the two sides of the balance sheet. It also reflects the historic links between companies and partnerships, because partnership property is held by partners under a joint tenancy (modified, in the case of company assets, by the exclusion of the right of survivorship).

[23] Most domestic registered debt takes the form of stock. With stock, the issuer makes only one set of covenants to pay principal, interest etc. These covenants are made to trustees, who hold them for the benefit of stockholders. The issuer does not make a series of different sets of covenants direct to stockholders. Thus the whole issue of stock constitutes one debt of the issuer, of which different stockholders hold undivided fractions.

(5) Fungible and Non-Fungible Securities

2.18 The terms 'divided' and 'undivided' relate to the proprietary nature of a security or an interest in securities, ie whether it constitutes a separate asset or an undivided part of an asset. In contrast, the terms 'fungible' and 'non-fungible' relate to the way in which (interests in) securities are held. The word 'fungible' denotes the redelivery obligation that is customary in respect of an asset. If an asset is fungible, this means that when such an asset is lent, or placed with a custodian, it is customary for the borrower or custodian to be obliged at the end of the loan or custody arrangement to return assets equivalent to the original asset, rather than the identical asset. In other words, the redelivery of fungibles is equivalent and not *in specie* (ie identical).[24]

2.19 Undivided (interests in) securities are always fungible by logical necessity. If one security or interest in securities is undivided (and therefore indistinguishable) from another, a lender cannot complain that a borrower has failed to redeliver the original asset.[25]

2.20 Divided securities may or may not be fungible, depending on market practice. The clear trend is towards fungible arrangements.[26]

B. The Legal Nature of Interests in Securities

2.21 The previous part of this chapter considered the legal nature of securities. In contrast, this part will consider the legal nature of interests in securities.[27]

(1) Intangible Assets

2.22 As indicated above, securities may be tangible (in the case of bearer securities) or intangible (in the case of registered securities). In contrast, interests in securities are always intangible. The only evidence of them comprises electronic records (ie the positive balances in the client securities accounts maintained by the relevant intermediary).

---

[24] See the discussion of the loan of fungibles (*mutuum*) and of non-fungibles (*commodatum*) in Justinian's *Institutes* J.III.14.

[25] As will be seen in Chapter 10, it is market practice somewhat inaccurately to refer to non-fungible custody arrangements in relation to registered securities. By this it is meant that the custodian records the interests of a particular client in a separate account.

[26] For example, money market instruments (MMIs) held in the CMO prior to its merger with CREST, are held on a non-fungible basis. Each instrument is issued with a distinctive serial number and they are held in the CMO on a segregated basis, so those particular instruments were allocated to particular participants. In contrast, when the CMO is merged with CREST, MMIs will be settled on a fungible basis. See Chapter 9 for a further discussion.

[27] Interests in securities were defined in Chapter 1 as the assets of a client for whom an intermediary holds (interests in) securities on an unallocated basis, commingled with the interests in securities of other clients.

Interests in securities confer property rights in relation to the underlying securities, and in some cases these underlying securities comprise tangible bearer instruments. However, this does not mean that interests in securities are themselves tangible. To conclude that it does is to confuse rights of property with the assets to which they relate. Western lawyers have been warned against such confusion for some 1,500 years.[28] Interests in securities are unallocated, and therefore do not attach to any tangible asset. **2.23**

Commentators have emphasised the importance of intangible assets in the contemporary economy. This is often attributed to the decline in manufacturing and the rise of service industries. The rise of interests in securities is another factor contributing to the development of the 'weightless economy'.[29] **2.24**

An important legal consequence of the intangible nature of interests in securities is that they are incapable of possession at common law.[30] Broadly speaking, possession is the physical control of a tangible asset, coupled with the intention to possess.[31] English law recognises actual (physical) possession,[32] legal possession ('the state of being a possessor in the eye of the law')[33] and constructive possession (or the right to possession).[34] Possession of goods may be delivered symbolically as well as actually.[35] However, both constructive possession and legal possession derive from actual possession,[36] and therefore can only relate to choses in possession. Choses in action cannot be possessed. **2.25**

---

[28] See for example Justinian, *Institutes* II.2.2; *Bracton on the Laws and Customs of England* (S Thorne (trans), Cambridge, Massachusetts: Harvard University Press, 1968) vol 2, 48; Blackstone (n 14 above) vol 2, 20, 21; Hohfeld, *Fundamental Legal Conceptions* (New Haven: Yale University Press, 1919); Jeanne Schroeder, 'Death and Transfiguration: the Myth that the U.C.C. Killed "Property"' (1996) 6a Temple Law Review (No 4) 1281.

[29] The phrase was coined by Professor Danny Quah.

[30] Reference is made to possession 'at common law' in order to distinguish it from the concept of an equitable interest 'in possession', which can relate to intangibles. Hereafter, reference to possession will mean possession at common law.

[31] One does not possess items slipped into one's pocket without one's knowledge. See *Lockyer v Gibb* [1966] 2 All ER 653, per Lord Parker CJ at 655. In Roman law, from which the common law of possession in part derives, 'the facts needed to acquire possession were physical control, "corpus possessionis" and an awareness of the situation, "animus" . . . ': R M Dias, *Jurisprudence* (5th edn, London: Butterworths, 1985) 274.

[32] 'Physical control, detention, or *de facto* possession. This, as an actual relation between a person and a thing, is matter of fact': Pollock and Wright, *An Essay on Possession in the Common Law* (Oxford: Clarendon Press, 1888) 26.

[33] 'Possession in the legal sense may exist without physical possession': ibid 26. See also *R v Martin* [1948] OR 963 at 966, per Laidlaw JA.

[34] Thus, a principal has constructive possession of assets held for her by an agent.
'Right to possess, when separated from possession, is often called "constructive possession"': Pollock and Wright (n 32 above) 27.

[35] 'Handing over a key is a symbolic act, which at common law carried with it possession of that to which the key is the means of access': *Holt v Dawson* [1939] 3 All ER 635, per Scott LJ at 637.

[36] While there is no clear answer to the question, 'Is Possession a matter of fact or a right?' (Pollock and Wright (n 32 above) 16), the final basis of possession is always fact rather than law because 'the existence of the *de facto* relation of control or apparent dominion [is] required as the foundation of the alleged right' (ibid 10).

2.26   A number of legal concepts that have traditionally been widely used in the securities markets are based on possession. As intangible interests in securities replace tangible bearer instruments, the use of these possession-based concepts in the securities markets needs to be reassessed.

2.27   Pledge is the delivery of possession by way of security.[37] Traditionally, the delivery of bearer instruments by way of pledge has been widely used in the securities markets to collateralise financial exposures. (The delivery of certificates to registered securities has also been widely used in collateral arrangements. However, because registered securities are not tangible assets, the legal effect of such delivery is generally characterised not as pledge, but rather equitable mortgage, as discussed in Chapter 5).[38]

2.28   A pledge cannot take effect in relation to intangible assets such as interests in securities. A purported pledge over intangible assets may be recharacterised as a floating charge in some circumstances, which in turn may be void for want of registration. This risk is discussed in Chapter 4.[39]

2.29   Negotiability has been an important concept in the traditional bearer securities markets. Traditional forms of bearer securities are treated as negotiable instruments. Negotiable status has a number of advantages, including (most importantly) security of transfer, as discussed in Chapter 3. The 'holder in due course' of a negotiable instrument (very broadly, the good faith purchaser) takes the instrument free from prior claims, and can get good title from a thief.

2.30   The law relating to negotiable instruments presumes the existence of a physical instrument. An intangible asset such as an interest in securities cannot be a negotiable instrument, as discussed in Chapter 3. The question whether the absence of negotiable status reduces security of transfer in the securities markets is also considered in Chapter 3.

2.31   The custody of securities has long predated the development of electronic settlement systems, and the custodian of bearer securities has traditionally been categorised as bailee.[40] The essence of bailment is the delivery of possession without the delivery of title.[41] Thus the bailee acquires possession of the bailed assets, while

---

[37] See Chapter 5 for a fuller discussion.

[38] As also discussed in Chapter 5, such arrangements can be construed as delivering a pledge of the certificates, although not of the underlying registered securities.

[39] This risk was particularly relevant when certificates of deposit were dematerialised in the Central Moneymarkets Office in 1994.

[40] See *Re Hallett's Estates* [1874–80] All ER Rep 793, per Jessell MR at 708; *Kahler v Midland Bank* [1950] AC 24, HL.

[41] See *Palmer on Bailment* (2nd edn, London: Sweet & Maxwell, 1991) 2. See the famous definition of the forms of bailment per Holt CJ in *Coggs v Bernard* (1703) 2 Ld Raym 909, 916–917).

the bailor retains title to them.[42] Other examples of bailment are the storage of goods in warehouses and the placing of jewellery in safety deposit boxes.

However, because bailment is based on possession, it can only relate to tangible **2.32** assets. Interests in securities cannot be the subject of bailment, because they are intangible.[43] The rise of interests in securities therefore requires the traditional custodial relationship to be reappraised, as discussed below.[44]

(2) Indirect Interests

Interests in securities confer on their holders rights of property in relation to the **2.33** underlying securities.[45] However, they only do so indirectly, as against the intermediary in whose account the interests in securities are recorded. As discussed in Chapter 1, the holder of an interest in securities does not have a direct claim against the issuer of the underlying securities.[46] She has an economic interest in the underlying securities, but this must normally be enforced through the intermediary or intermediaries that stand between her and the issuer in the chain of ownership.

Chapter 13 will consider the difference between personal and property rights. It **2.34** will argue that intangible assets (such as interests in securities) are only subject to property rights *as against* intermediaries. Thus, where debt securities are held for an investor by a custodian, the rights of the investor *as against the custodian* are proprietary, in the sense that they will not be at risk in the insolvency of the custodian. However, as against the issuer, any rights in relation to the debt securities are personal, because of course the rights of investors are at risk in the insolvency of the issuer. See Chapter 13 for a further discussion.

Intermediary credit risk; bailment and trust

Whenever a client entrusts her assets to an intermediary, she is concerned to **2.35** ensure that her assets will not be treated as part of the intermediary's own estate, but that they will be treated as a separate fund (ie separate from the intermediary's own assets). This is because she wishes to ensure that creditors of the intermediary

---

[42] Although in the normal course, delivery of a bearer instrument passes title, the effect of delivery can be varied by the intention of the parties. Thus, delivery for the purposes of safekeeping creates a bailment (and delivery by way of security creates a pledge). The bailee acquires a limited legal interest, which enables it to pass good title to a purchaser.

[43] Equally registered securities cannot be bailed, because they are also intangible.

[44] See also the discussion of custody in Chapter 10.

[45] To be exact they confer indirect rights on the underlying *(interests in)* securities. However, for the sake of simplicity, it will be assumed in this discussion that the asset held by the intermediary in whose accounts the interests in securities are recorded, are securities, so that only one intermediary is involved.

[46] As indicated in Chapter 1, this is the usual position. A participant in a settlement system may be given conditional rights against the issuer under deed poll, which arise in the event of default. For the meaning of the term 'deed poll', see Blackstone (n 14 above) vol 2, 296.

will not have recourse to her assets, whether the intermediary is solvent[47] or insolvent.[48] If the intermediary holds client assets as a separate fund, the client is protected from the intermediary's credit risk.

2.36 Under English law, the traditional legal arrangement whereby bearer securities are held by an intermediary for a client as a separate fund, is bailment. On the basis that interests in securities are intangible assets, this author has argued[49] that an alternative legal characterisation of the arrangement is necessary. The author has argued also that the only alternative under English law, which will enable the assets of the client to be treated as a separate fund, is a trust.[50]

2.37 A trust is a legal relationship between one or more trustee and one or more beneficiary in respect of assets (known as trust assets), whereby the trustee holds the trust assets for the benefit of (ie on trust for) the beneficiary or beneficiaries.[51] The trustee has legal (ie technical) title to (ie ownership of) the trust assets, and the beneficiary has equitable (ie beneficial or economic) ownership.

2.38 In the normal course, as far as third parties are concerned, the trustee as legal owner is the true owner of the securities. Thus, the issuer of the securities will properly pay the income to the trustee and will accept its voting instructions. The issuer does not have to deal with the beneficial owner.[52] However, the trustee is required to pass on these benefits of ownership to the beneficiary under the terms of the trust. Also, a good faith purchaser of the securities can acquire good title from the trustee as legal owner.

2.39 The general rule is that third parties can deal with the trustee as if it were full legal and beneficial owner. However, as between the trustee and the beneficiary, the trustee is obliged to hold the benefit of the trust assets for the beneficiary. This means that it must account to the client for the income and proceeds of sale, and

---

[47] ie, if a creditor obtains judgment against the intermediary in respect of a debt, it will not be able to enforce that judgment against the client's assets.

[48] ie, if the intermediary becomes insolvent, the client's assets will not be treated as part of the intermediary's estate and therefore available to meet the claims of its creditors.

[49] See *The Law of Global Custody* (London: Butterworths, 1996) ch 4.

[50] The traditional uses of trusts in the financial markets are discussed in C Duffet, 'Using Trusts in International Finance and Commercial Transactions' (1992) 1 JITCP 23–31. The above analysis suggests a much wider use for trusts, as characterising the custodial relationship between all securities intermediaries and their clients.

Where an agent holds client property on a segregated basis, it will do so as trustee: *Burdick v Garrick* (1870) 5 Ch App 233 per Giffard LJ at 243. See *Bowstead and Reynolds on Agency* (16th edn, London: Sweet & Maxwell, 1996) para 51, 253–255 and *Halsbury's Laws*, vol 1(2), para 98, 68.

[51] 'A trust is an equitable obligation, binding a person (who is called a trustee) to deal with property over which he has control (which is called the trust property), for the benefit of persons (who are called the beneficiaries or cestuis que trust), of whom he may himself be one, and any of whom may enforce the obligation': D J Hayton, *Underhill and Hayton, Law Relating to Trusts and Trustees* (15th edn, London: Butterworths, 1995) 3.

[52] See the Companies Act 1985, s 360.

can only exercise voting and other rights and otherwise deal with the securities in accordance with the client's instructions.

The three certainties

A trust of land must be evidenced in writing[53] but a trust of personal property **2.40** requires no formalities.[54] However, three matters must be certain or ascertainable in order for a valid trust to arise.[55] These are certainty of intention, certainty of beneficiary and certainty of subject matter. Together, they are known as 'the three certainties'.

In order to show certainty of intention, it is not necessary that the term 'trust' **2.41** should be used in any client documentation.[56] Persons are deemed to intend the legal consequences of their actions.[57] If the parties clearly intend that the client's intangible assets should form a separate fund in the hands of the intermediary, certainty of intention to create a trust will be present because a trust is the only way to give legal effect to that intention.[58]

Certainty of beneficiary is rarely a problem in the securities markets. The require- **2.42** ment is that the beneficial owner or owners should be known or ascertainable,[59] and an intermediary will as a matter of course record the identities of its clients.[60]

The general rule is that to achieve certainty of subject matter, it is necessary to **2.43** establish which assets in the hands of the trustee are held on trust for the beneficiary. Interests in securities have been defined as the assets of a client for whom an intermediary holds (interests in) securities on an unallocated basis, commingled

---

[53] Law of Property Act 1925, s 53(1)(b).

[54] *Paul v Constance* [1977] 1 All ER 195.

[55] *Knight v Knight* (1840) Beav 148, 9 LJ Ch 354.

[56] See *In re Kayford Ltd (in liquidation)* [1975] 1 WLR 279. No formal wording is required: *Tito v Waddell (No 2)* [1977] Ch 106.

[57] *Swiss Bank v Lloyds* [1979] 1 Ch 548 at 569.

[58] Indeed, this would be treated as an express trust and not an implied trust because it gives effect to the express intention of the parties.

[59] Broadly, in the case of a fixed trust, it must be possible to draw up a complete list of beneficiaries at any time (*Re Gulbenkian's Settlement Trusts* [1970] AC 508), and in the case of a discretionary trust, it must be possible to say with certainty whether any individual is or is not a beneficiary (*McPhail v Doulton* [1971] AC 424). The requirement does not apply in the case of a trust for charitable purposes. Of course, a custody trust will fall into the first category.

[60] Although in some cases they may identify them by code name, for example where a custodian has been instructed by a fund manager to hold assets for the managed funds for whom the manager acts as agent.

The requirement for certainty of beneficiary will also be satisfied in the case of a trust in favour of a changing class of beneficiaries, so long as, at any one time, the individual beneficiaries can be ascertained at any time. Indeed, in legal history the desire to hold property for a changing class of persons has been a major factor in the commercial development of the trust, informing the law of companies, partnerships and other unincorporated associations. Many trusts in the securities markets are in favour of changing classes of beneficiary where securities are commingled in the hands of intermediaries acting for clients or investors from time to time.

with the interests in securities of other clients. The question therefore arises whether the requirement for certainty of subject matter can be established, in the absence of allocation to the client of particular assets in the hands of the intermediary. This question has generated much discussion in the London legal community, and is considered at length below.

Fiduciary duty[61]

2.44   The trust is a useful concept in the securities markets, as it enables intermediaries to hold clients' interests in securities without exposing them to the credit risk of the intermediary. However, if the ring-fencing of client assets is the benefit of trust status for intermediaries, fiduciary status is its burden.

2.45   'A fiduciary is someone who has undertaken to act for or on behalf of another in a particular matter in circumstances which give rise to a relationship of trust and confidence.'[62] Thus the term 'fiduciary' characterises certain relationships. '[I]t is possible to divide fiduciaries into two categories, status-based fiduciaries and fact-based fiduciaries.'[63]

2.46   Status-based fiduciaries 'include people who, by virtue of their involvement in certain relationships are considered, without further inquiry, to be fiduciaries. Such relationships include those between trustee-beneficiary, solicitor-client, agent-principal, director-company and partner-partner'.[64] 'Often these relationships are described as ones in which a party reposes trust and confidence in the other'.[65] Trusteeship 'is the most intense form of fiduciary relationship'.[66] While bailees may also be fiduciaries,[67] the characterisation of an intermediary as a trustee increases the implied level of implied fiduciary duty.[68]

---

[61]   Fiduciary duty is a difficult area of law. 'This area of law is highly complex, poorly delimited, and in a state of flux': Law Commission Consultation Paper (May 1992) 26, 27. It has been suggested that 'the fiduciary relationship is a concept in search of a principle': Sir Anthony Mason, 'Themes and Prospects' in P D Finn (ed), *Essays in Equity* (1985), quoted at 54, 55. See also *Bristol and West Building Society v Mothew* [1998] Ch 1, per Millett LJ at 16: 'this branch of the law has become bedevilled by unthinking resort to verbal formulae'.

[62]   *Bristol and West Building Society v Mothew*, per Millett LJ at 18.

[63]   Law Commission Consultation Paper, *Fiduciary Duties and Regulatory Rules* (May 1992) 27.

[64]   ibid 28. See also P D Finn, 'The Fiduciary Principle' in T G Youdan (ed), *Equity, Fiduciaries and Trusts* (Toronto: Carswell, 1989) 33: 'We have little difficulty in accepting the fiduciary characterisation of relationships such as trustee and beneficiary, partners, principal and agent, and director and company. Such is the law's perception of the legal relationship itself that it characterises, as a matter of course, the purpose of the relationship and the role and reason of one party in it as being to promote the interest of the other, or the joint interest, and not his own'.

[65]   Finn (n 64 above) 33.

[66]   *Fiduciary Duties and Regulatory Rules* (n 63 above) 84.

[67]   See *Re Andrabell Ltd (in liquidation), Airborne Accessories Ltd* [1984] 3 All ER 407, per Peter Gibson J at 413, 414. Whether or not a bailee is a fiduciary depends on all the circumstances and the terms of the bailment; it would be prudent to assume that a global custodian holding and administering client securities as bailee is a fiduciary. See *Reading v Attorney General* [1949] 2 KB 232 and *In re Brooke Bond & Co Ltd, Trust Deed* [1962] 1 Ch 357.

In relation to fact-based fiduciary relationships, '[h]ere the courts have not limited **2.47** fiduciary relationships to those presumed as a matter of law. They can arise *ad hoc* because in the actual circumstances of a relationship the requisite ascendancy or trust has in fact been obtained, or given, or confidential information has in fact been acquired'.[69]

The law of equity implies certain duties in fiduciary relationships,[70] so that the **2.48** fiduciary is required to put the client's interests above her own interests.[71] She owes duties of confidentiality and of undivided loyalty to the client. She must avoid any conflict of interest[72] and she must not profit at the client's expense.[73]

The typical broker or bank that acts as intermediary in the securities markets acts **2.49** for reasons other than altruism. With the deregulation of the financial markets and the rise of multi-function financial institutions, conflicts of interest routinely arise. Client data is a commercially exploited asset. The need to avoid conflict

---

[68] However, provided appropriate limitation clauses are in place, the contractually modified level of duty is the same; see the discussion of limitation clauses below.

[69] Finn (n 64 above) 43. See also *Fiduciary Duties and Regulatory Rules* (n 63 above) 27–28.
'In order to establish a fact-based fiduciary relationship, what must be shown, in the writer's view, is that the actual circumstances of a relationship are such that one party is entitled to expect that the other will act in his interests in and for the purposes of the relationship. Ascendancy, influence, vulnerability, trust, confidence or dependence doubtless will be of importance in making this out, but they will be important only to the extent that they evidence a relationship suggesting that entitlement': Finn (n 64 above) 46.

[70] 'fiduciary law's concern is to impose standards of acceptable conduct on one party to a relationship for the benefit of the other where the one has a responsibility for the preservation of the other's interests': Finn (n 64 above) 2.

[71] 'The "fiduciary" standard for its part enjoins one party to act in the interests of the other—to act selflessly and with undivided loyalty': Finn (n 64 above) 4.

[72] See *Prince Jefri Bolkiah v KPMG* [1999] 1 BCLC 1, in which it was held that an ad hoc Chinese wall was not effective in addressing a conflict of interest.

[73] 'The exact scope of the fiduciary's obligations and the consequences of breach vary according to the particular circumstances but the duties may conveniently be summarised in the following basic rules: (i) *the 'no conflict' rule* A fiduciary must not place himself in a position where his own interest conflicts with that of his customer, the beneficiary. There must be a 'real sensible possibility of conflict'; (ii) *the 'no profit' rule* A fiduciary must not profit from his position at the expense of his customer, the beneficiary; (iii) *the undivided loyalty rule* A fiduciary owes undivided loyalty to his customer, the beneficiary, not to place himself in a position where his duty towards one customer conflicts with a duty that he owes to another customer. A consequence of this duty is that a fiduciary must make available to a customer all the information that is relevant to the customer's affairs; (iv) *the duty of confidentiality* A fiduciary must only use information obtained in confidence from his customer, the beneficiary, for the benefit of the customer and must not use it for his own advantage, or for the benefit of any other person': Law Commission Report, *Fiduciary Duties and Regulatory Rules* (Cm 3049, December 1995).
See also Millett LJ in *Bristol and West Building Society v Mothew* [1998] Ch 1 at 18: 'The distinguishing obligation of a fiduciary is the obligation of loyalty. The principal is entitled to the single-minded loyalty of his fiduciary. This core liability has several facets. A fiduciary must act in good faith: he must not make a profit out of this trust; he must not place himself in a position where his duty and his interest may conflict; he may not act for his own benefit or the benefit of a third person without the informed consent of his principal. This is not intended to be an exhaustive list, but it is sufficient to indicate the nature of fiduciary obligations'.

between implied fiduciary duty and commercial practice has much judicial comment,[74] and has been considered at length by the Law Commission.[75]

2.50　An important part of the legal effort that goes into documenting intermediary arrangements is expended with a view to managing implied fiduciary duty. In general implied fiduciary duties can be reduced to commercially acceptable levels by contract. The key cases are *Kelly v Cooper*[76] and *Clark Boyce v Mouat*.[77] Intermediaries rely on wording in their terms of business under headings such as 'Confidentiality' and 'Conflicts of interest etc'. These are relieving provisions, intended to disapply implied fiduciary duty.[78] They are read together with duty defining clauses (which specify the level of care which the intermediary is contractually obliged to take in performing services under the agreement) and limitation of liability clauses (which limit the liability of the intermediary in the event of breach of duty). The effectiveness of such clauses is discussed in *Midland Bank Trustee (Jersey) Ltd*,[79] in which it is indicated that a limitation of liability to liability for gross negligence[80] may be enforceable (unless this is prohibited by statute).

---

[74] In a number of judgments it is stressed that implied fiduciary duty should not distort a contractual commercial relationship. See for example *Kelly v Cooper* [1992] 3 WLR 936, per Lord Browne-Wilkinson at 942; *Clark Boyce v Mouat* [1994] 1 AC 428, per Lord Jauncey of Tullichettle at 437; *Target Holdings Ltd v Redferns*[1995] 3 WLR 352, per Lord Browne-Wilkinson at 362.

[75] Law Commission Consultation Paper, *Fiduciary Duties and Regulatory Rules* (May 1992) and Law Commission Report (December 1995). This friction provided one of the original motives for the introduction of regulation to the UK financial services industry: see J Black, *Rules and Regulators* (Oxford: Clarendon Press, 1997) 53, 54.

[76] [1993] AC 205. See also *Hospital Products International Ptr Ltd v US Surgical Corp* (1984) 156 CLR 41, per Mason J at 97, quoted by Lord Browne-Wilkinson in *Kelly* at 215: 'That contractual and fiduciary relationships may co-exist between the same parties has never been doubted. Indeed, the existence of a basic contractual relationship has in many situations provided a foundation for the erection of a fiduciary relationship. In these situations, it is the contractual foundation which is all important because it is the contract that regulates the basic rights and liabilities of the parties. The fiduciary relationship, if it is to exist at all, must accommodate itself to the terms of the contract so that it is consistent with, and conforms to them. The fiduciary relationship cannot be superimposed upon the contract in such a way as to alter the operation which the contract was intended to have according to its true construction'.
Following *Kelly*, the Law Commission comments as follows: '[The judgment in *Kelly*] confirmed that where a fiduciary relationship arises out of a contract, a clearly worded duty defining or exclusion clause will circumscribe the extent of the fiduciary duties owed to the other party': *Law Commission Report* (December 1995) 4. See pp 85, 86 and 24 for a discussion of conditions for this principle to apply, and circumstances in which it will not.

[77] [1994] 1 AC 428. 'A fiduciary duty . . . cannot be prayed in aid to enlarge the scope of contractual duties' per Lord Jauncey at 437. See also *Target Holdings Ltd v Redferns* [1995] 3 WLR 352, per Lord Browne-Wilkinson at 362.

[78] It is important to note that, even with the benefit of such clauses, the intermediary remains a fiduciary, albeit one whose implied duties have been modified. Such clauses are construed contra proferentem, or strictly against the intermediary seeking to rely on them: *Photo Production Ltd v Securicor Ltd* [1980] AC 827 and *Midland Bank Trust Company (Jersey) Limited v Federated Pension Services* (1995) JLR 352 at 391. See also *Underhill and Hayton* (n 51 above) 559.

[79] *Midland Bank Trust Company (Jersey) Limited v Federated Pension Services* [1995] JLR 352, per Le Quesne JA at 391.

[80] See that judgment for a discussion of the meaning of gross negligence.

As a matter of good commercial practice it is customary to accept liability for ordinary negligence.[81] In some circumstances, statutory restrictions apply to limitation clauses.[82]

The fiduciary status of intermediaries holding interests in securities for their **2.51** clients has two important commercial consequences. First, for the intermediary, it renders undocumented business particularly risky, because of the high levels of duty that are implied in the absence of contractual modification. Secondly, for persons buying interests in securities from an intermediary, or accepting interests in securities as collateral from an intermediary, it is crucial to address the risk that the intermediary has acted in breach of its fiduciary duty of undivided loyalty or its equitable duties of care.[83] If it has, the purchaser or collateral taker may face liability under a tracing action or an action for constructive trusteeship.[84]

Tracing and constructive trusteeship

Breach of fiduciary duty may give rise to special types of legal action. In particu- **2.52** lar, when an intermediary holds interests in securities for clients as fiduciary, and where it delivers such interests to a third party, it is important for the third party to satisfy itself that the transaction does not involve a breach of the intermediary's duties to its clients. If there has been a breach of fiduciary duty, then, (very broadly) if the third party knew or ought to have known of the breach of duty, it may be sued by the clients under a tracing action or as constructive trustee.

---

[81] ie negligence which is not gross negligence. Custodians who are regulated in the conduct of their investment business in the UK are required to accept liability for their own negligence. The Law Commission in its 1995 Report, *Fiduciary Duties and Regulatory Rules*, discusses the requirements for effective limitation clauses and other provisions that serve contractually to modify fiduciary duty.

[82] Under the Unfair Contract Terms Act 1977, s 3, exclusion clauses contained in standard terms of business are subject to a reasonableness test. The Unfair Terms in Consumer Contracts Regulations 1999, SI 1999/2083 apply (broadly) to terms which have not been individually negotiated, in contracts between business and consumers; they impose requirements of fairness and (broadly) plain English. The provisions of the Trustee Bill 2000 restrict the ability of a trustee to permit its delegate contractually to modify its implied fiduciary duties in some circumstances. See clauses 14(2) and 14(3) (broadly, trustees appointing an agent must not authorise it to restrict its liability or permit conflicts of interest 'unless it is reasonably necessary for them to do so').

Because London standard custody documentation does restrict the custodian's liability and permit conflicts, it is likely that a custodian will reject trustees' requests to remove such restrictions so that such restrictions will be reasonably necessary to obtain the services of the reputable custodian in question. Similar provisions are included in relation to custodians appointed by trustees in clauses 20(2) and 20(3).

[83] *Bristol and West Building Society v Mothew* [1998] Ch 1, per Millett LJ at 16. Millett LJ distinguishes between breach of fiduciary duty and breach of the equitable duty of care at 17.

[84] Although 'not every breach of duty by a fiduciary is a breach of fiduciary duty': *Bristol and West Building Society v Mothew*, per Millett LJ at 16.

Proprietary liabiliy via the tracing process

2.53 Tracing is a process[85] which becomes available to beneficiaries when their assets have been disposed of by a trustee or other fiduciary in breach of its duty. It enables the beneficiaries to identify the assets which are subject to their claims in the hands of third parties (either in their original form or in the form of substitute assets).[86] The beneficiaries can then claim either ownership of all or a proportionate part of such assets or, if the assets have depreciated, a charge over such assets as security for their claim.

2.54 Depending on the circumstances, a tracing claim may be brought either under the rules of common law, or the rules of equity.[87] Tracing in equity can follow assets through a pool in which they are mixed with other assets, but the general rule is that tracing at law cannot.[88] The fact that many interests in securities comprise

---

[85] 'Tracing properly so-called, however, is neither a claim nor a remedy but a process . . . It is the process by which the plaintiff traces what has happened to his property, identifies the persons who have handled or received it, and justifies his claim that the money which they handled or received (and, if necessary, which they still retain) can properly be regarded as representing his property; he has to do this because his claim is based on the retention by him of a beneficial interest in the property which the defendant handled or received': *Boscawen and others v Bajwa and another* [1996] 1 WLR 328, per Millett LJ at 334. See also *Foskett v McKeown* [1997] 3 All ER 392, CA.

[86] For example, where the trust assets have been sold and their proceeds of sale reinvested in new assets, the beneficiaries can trace against the new assets. 'Of course, "tracing" or "following" property into its product involves a decision by the owner of the original property to assert his title to the produce in place of his original property': *Lipkin Gorman v Karpnale* [1991] 2 AC 548, per Lord Goff at 573.

In *The Law of Tracing* (Oxford: Clarendon Press, 1997), Lionel Smith distinguishes between following original assets in the hands of third parties, and tracing substitute assets in the hands of third parties, and claiming such assets: see ch 1 section II.

Where the traceable trust fund has been mixed with other assets (for example where the proceeds of sale of the original trust assets form part of the purchase price of a new holding of securities), the plaintiff may claim an equitable charge on the amalgam, or a proportionate share of it: *Re Tilly* [1967] 2 All ER 303, per Ungoed-Thomas J at 310. The former option would be more valuable to the plaintiff where the new holding has dropped in value; the latter option would be more valuable where it has appreciated.

[87] In the past, the decisions of different courts generated different bodies of law. The common law courts generated the rules of common law, and the Chancellor's courts generated the rules of equity. (Equally, the mercantile courts developed the rules of the law merchant.) Following a process of consolidation of the different courts (and therefore of the different bodies of law) culminating in the Judicature Acts of 1873 and 1887, English case law is now a unified whole. However, different bodies of rules remain, so that the rules of common law (which govern legal title to assets) differ from the rules of equity (which govern equitable interests in assets).

Because the asset of a trust beneficiary is equitable, she must bring any tracing action for it in equity. Where the legal owner of an asset is wrongfully deprived of the asset, she may be able to bring a tracing action at law. See *Trustees of the Property of F C Jones & Sons v Jones* [1996] 3 WLR 703.

[88] 'at common law, property in money, like other fungibles, is lost when it is mixed with other money': *Lipkin Gorman*, per Lord Goff at 572. See also *Re Diplock* [1948] Ch 465 at 520.

Detailed rules have been developed in case law to identify traceable trust assets when they have been mixed with the assets of the trustee (see in particular *Re Hallett's Estate* (1880) 13 Ch D 695, *Re Oatway* [1903] 2 Ch 356, *Roscoe v Winder* [1915] 1 Ch 62) and the assets of other beneficiaries or

foreign assets (located in jurisdictions that do not recognise trusts) is not necessarily a bar to tracing, as it is possible as a matter of English law to trace through foreign jurisdictions into trust jurisdictions in some circumstances.[89]

Where it is proposed to purchase interests in securities or to accept them as collateral, it should be established whether the interests in securities belong beneficially to the vendor or collateral giver. If they do not or may not, it is important to establish that, in the event that the proposed transaction involves the vendor or collateral giver in breach of fiduciary duty to its clients, the purchaser or collateral taker would be able to defend any tracing action brought by the clients.   **2.55**

A number of defences are available to a tracing action.[90] For the purchaser or collateral taker in the securities markets, the most important defence is likely to be that it received the assets as 'equity's darling', ie a bona fide purchaser[91] of the legal estate for value without notice of the breach of trust.[92] A purchaser for value includes a mortgagee[93] and chargee.[94] Notice for this purpose includes actual notice, imputed and constructive notice.[95]   **2.56**

Generally speaking, a person has actual notice of matters within her knowledge,[96] and of matters contained in documents of which she has possession. A person has   **2.57**

---

innocent third parties (see in particular *Clayton's Case* (1816) 1 Mer 572, *Re Diplock* [1948] Ch 465 and *Barlow Clowes International v Vaughan* [1992] 4 All ER 22).

[89] See *El Ajou v Dollar Land Holdings plc* [1993] 3 All ER 717, per Millett J at 736, 737.

[90] The right to trace is lost if the trust assets are dissipated, because a precondition of tracing is the existence of a continuing trust fund: *Re Diplock* [1948] Ch 465 at 566, but a person dissipating trust assets known to be such or suspect of being such can be personally liable as a constructive trustee.

More recently, the defence of change of position has been accepted in relation to restitutionary claims: *Lipkin Gorman v Karpnale Ltd* [1991] 2 AC 548, per Lord Goff at 580: 'At present I do not wish to state the principle any less broadly than this: that the defence is available to a person whose position has so changed that it would be inequitable in all the circumstances to require him to make restitution, or alternatively to make restitution in full. I wish to stress however that the mere fact that the defendant has spent the money, in whole or in part, does not of itself render it inequitable that he should be called upon to repay, because the expenditure might in any event have been incurred by him in the ordinary course of things . . . It is, of course, plain that the defence is not open to one who has changed his position in bad faith . . .'. Although this case concerned a claim for restitution at common law and not a tracing claim in equity, the judgment may be interpreted to mean that the change of position defence should be extended to cases of equitable tracing; per Lord Goff at 581: 'while recognising the different functions of property at law and in equity, there may also in due course develop a more consistent approach to tracing claims, in which common defences are recognised as available to such claims, whether advanced at law or in equity'.

[91] Equity will not assist a volunteer, ie a person who has not given value.

[92] Mere notice of the existence of the trust (as opposed to breach of trust) does not make the defence unavailable. Generally for this defence, see *Pilcher v Rawlins* (1872) 7 Ch App 259.

[93] See the Law of Property Act 1925, s 205(1)(xxi): 'In this Act "purchaser" means a purchaser in good faith for valuable consideration and includes a . . . mortgagee'.

See also *Kingsworth Finance Co v Tizard* [1986] 1 WLR 783.

[94] See the Companies Act 1985, s 396(4): 'In this Chapter, "charge" includes mortgage'.

[95] See generally *Underhill and Hayton* (n 51 above) 919–925.

[96] See *Underhill and Hayton* (n 51 above) 922.

actual notice of matters to which she deliberately turns a blind eye.[97] Many participants in the securities markets are companies, and the rules whereby notice of matters of which a member of staff has notice is attributed to the company, are relevant to the management of fraud risk. 'In *El Ajou v Dollar Land Holdings plc*[98] the Court of Appeal emphasised that an individual's knowledge can be attributed to a company either if the individual was its directing mind and will in relation to the act or omission in point or was its agent in the relevant transaction'.[99] It is therefore necessary for companies receiving interests in securities under purchase or collateral arrangements to have procedures whereby staff actively engaged in the transaction communicate any concerns immediately to a responsible officer.

2.58 A principal generally has imputed notice of matters of which her agent has actual or constructive notice, provided the information was received by the agent in the same transaction for which she acts for the principal.[100]

2.59 A person has constructive notice of matters that she ought reasonably to have known. The doctrine of constructive notice originated in conveyancing (ie the procedure for land transfer), where it is customary to investigate title, by searches and enquires.[101] A purchaser of land has constructive notice of matters she would have discovered had she investigated title in the usual way. In the securities markets, it is not customary to investigate title. A purchaser or collateral taker is allowed to assume that everything is in order, unless there are circumstances that should arouse suspicion in an honest and reasonable person. If there are, and she fails to make reasonable enquiries, she will have constructive notice of matters which such enquiries would have revealed.[102] In practice, purchasers and collateral

---

[97] 'The test is actual knowledge or suspicion and deliberate abstention from inquiry lest the truth be discovered': *Macmillan v Bishopsgate (No 3)* [1995] 3 All ER 747, per Millett J at 756. At 769 the judgment discusses 'actual notice (including "wilful blindness" or "contrived ignorance", where the purchaser deliberately abstains from an inquiry in order to avoid learning the truth)'.

[98] [1994] 2 All ER 685.

[99] *Underhill and Hayton* (n 51 above) 925.

'Since a company is an artificial person, the knowledge of those who manage and control it must be treated as the knowledge of the company . . . This is nothing to do with the law of agency. Those who "constitute the directing mind and will of the company are the company for this purpose . . . Their minds are its mind; their intention its intention; their knowledge its knowledge. Where the company is a one-man company, or all the directors possess the relevant knowledge, there is ordinarily no difficulty. Where the directors are merely nominees with no executive authority, or where only one of several directors has the necessary knowledge, different considerations come into play" ': per Millett J in *El Ajou v Dollar Land Holdings plc* [1993] 3 All ER 740. See also *Fiduciary Duties and Regulatory Rules* (n 75 above) 14–18.

[100] See the discussion in *Underhill and Hayton* (n 51 above) 923. This is an argument for effective dialogue between solicitors and clients.

[101] See the Law of Property Act 1925, s 199(1).

[102] *Macmillan v Bishopsgate (No 3)* [1995] 3 All ER 747, per Millett J at 769: 'The doctrine of constructive notice has developed in relation to land, where there is a recognised procedure for investigating the title of the transferor. There is no room for the doctrine of notice in the strict conveyancing sense in a situation in which it is not the custom and practice to investigate the transferor's

takers require vendors and collateral givers to represent and warrant that they are the beneficial owner of the interests in securities, or alternatively that they are duly authorised by the beneficial owners. In addition, when accepting securities from an intermediary, it is important that compliance procedures are in place so that any suspicious circumstances, of which a senior or responsible member of staff has notice, are investigated.

An element of the defence of 'equity's darling' is that the defendant should acquire **2.60** a legal interest in the assets. This represents a particular challenge in the computerised securities markets. As discussed in more detail below, the interest of a beneficiary under a trust is equitable and not legal. On the basis that interests in securities are trust interests, the defence of equity's darling is therefore not generally available to their purchaser or collateral taker. However, as indicated above other defences may be available, depending on the circumstances.[103]

Personal liability via the interposition of notional or constructive trusteeship

With a successful tracing action, the defendant is only obliged to hand back the **2.61** disputed assets if she still has them (in their original form, or in the form of identifiable substitute assets into which they have been economically converted). In other words, dissipation is a defence to a tracing action.[104] However, in a personal action arising from constructive trusteeship, the defendant must restore the value of the trust assets whether or not she still has them, if necessary by digging into her own pocket.[105] This personal action can be more financially onerous for the defendant than a proprietary tracing action. Unlike the proprietary action, the personal action carries the implication of bad faith; the basis of the potentially

---

title. But in the wider sense it is not so limited . . . It is true that many distinguished judges in the past have warned against the extension of the equitable doctrine of constructive notice to commercial transactions (see *Manchester Trust v Furness* [1895] 2 QB 539 at 545–546 per Lindley LJ) but they were obviously referring to the doctrine in its strict conveyancing sense with its many refinements and its insistence on a proper investigation of title in every case'. Per Millett J at 783: 'Account officers are not detectives. Unless and until they are alerted to the possibility of wrongdoing, they proceed, and are entitled to proceed, on the assumption that they are dealing with honest men. In order to establish constructive notice it is necessary to prove that the facts known to the defendant made it imperative for him to seek an explanation, because in the absence of an explanation it was obvious that the transaction was probably improper'. The judgment goes on to consider previous cases in which it is stated that commercial dealings are undertaken on the basis of trust and not distrust.

[103] See *Underhill and Hayton* (n 51 above) 916, 932.

[104] 'The equitable remedies presuppose the continued existence of the money either as a separate fund or as part of a mixed fund or as latent in property acquired by means of such a fund. If . . . such continued existence is not established, equity is as helpless as the common law itself. If the fund, mixed or unmixed, is spent upon a dinner, equity, which dealt only in specific relief and not in damages, could do nothing': *Re Diplock* [1948] Ch 465, at 521. See *Underhill and Hayton* (n 51 above) 296, 297.

[105] This is on the basis that constructive trusteeship gives rise both to a proprietary claim against the traceable assets (if any) in the hands of the defendant and also to a personal claim against the defendant.

severe penalties associated with constructive trusteeship is the proposition that the conscience of the defendant is affected.[106] A tracing action has no such implication of bad faith.[107]

2.62   There are two forms of constructive trusteeship, namely 'knowing receipt' (better regarded nowadays as 'dishonest dealing') and dishonest assistance.

2.63   Where a person receives trust property in breach of the trustee's duty and for her own benefit,[108] then once she had knowledge of the breach of trust but goes on to deal with the property inconsistently with the terms of the trust[109] she is liable to account as constructive trustee on the basis of knowing receipt.[110] The relevant time is the time of the receipt (or later while she retains the assets). Knowledge for this purpose can be actual knowledge, shutting one's eyes to the obvious or wilfully or recklessly failing to make reasonable enquiries where impropriety is suspected.[111] Dishonesty or want of probity is needed for the purposes of liability for dishonest dealing or knowing receipt, and in order to establish constructive notice for the purposes of a tracing action.[112]

2.64   Personal liability via constructive trusteeship on the basis of dishonest assistance can arise even when the defendant did not receive trust assets, if she dishonestly assisted in the breach of trust.[113] This may be relevant, for example, for fund man-

---

[106] See for example *In re Montagu's Settlement* [1987] 1 Ch 264, per Megarry VC at 285: 'the basic question is whether the conscience of the [defendant] is sufficiently affected to justify the imposition of such a trust'. See also Lord Browne-Wilkinson in *Westdeutsche v Islington Borough Council* [1996] AC 669, 705, 707, 709.

'A constructive trust of property is a trust imposed by equity in respect of property on proof of a variety of special circumstances . . . where equity considers it unconscionable for the owner of a particular property to hold it purely for his own benefit': Underhill and Hayton (n 51 above) 42.

[107] In contrast, one can be the defendant in a successful tracing action without any wrongdoing, merely because one had the misfortune to deal with a fraudster in circumstances where no defence was available. For example, the defence of equity's darling is not available to one acquiring an equitable as opposed to legal interest.

[108] ie not merely on behalf of another; see *Cigma Life Insurance NS v Westpac Securities* [1996] 1 NZLR 80.

[109] ie does not return the trust property to be held on trust for the beneficiaries.

[110] 'The plaintiff must show, first, a disposal of his assets in breach of fiduciary duty; secondly, the beneficial receipt by the defendant of assets which are traceable as representing the assets of the plaintiff; and, thirdly, knowledge on the part of the defendant that the assets he received are traceable to a breach of fiduciary duty': *El Ajou v Dollar Land Holdings plc and another* [1994] 2 All ER 685, per Hoffman LJ at 700.

[111] See *Re Montagu's Settlement Trusts* [1987] 1 Ch 264 per Megarry VC at 285.

A 'recipient is not expected to be unduly suspicious and is not held liable unless he went ahead without further inquiry in circumstances in which an honest and reasonable man would have realised that the money was probably being misapplied': *El Ajou v Dollar Land Holdings plc* [1993] 3 All ER 717 at 739.

[112] See for example *Macmillan Inc v Bishopsgate Investment Trust* [1995] 1 WLR 978, at 1000, 1014.

[113] See *Agip (Africa) Ltd v Jackson* [1990] 1 Ch 265, per Millett J at 293: 'The true distinction is between honesty and dishonesty'.

agers arranging for the purchase of securities for the account of a fund from an intermediary acting in breach of trust.[114] Such a constructive trustee has accessory liability to make good the loss. *Royal Brunei Airlines v Tan*[115] established that the test of dishonestly for this purpose has both an objective element (would an honest person regard it as honest to behave as the defendant did) and a subjective element (was the defendant dishonest, taking account of the defendant's knowledge, experience, intelligence and reasons).[116] The broad meaning of dishonesty is conscious impropriety.[117]

In order to manage the risk of personal liability via constructive trusteeship, firms **2.65** which receive securities in purchase or collateral transactions should establish whether they are or might be dealing with intermediaries. If so, it is important to establish that there are no circumstances that suggest that their counterparties are acting in breach of duty to their clients. The level of due diligence that would serve to defend a tracing action would a fortiori defend an action for constructive trusteeship.

Priorities

It was indicated above that trust assets are treated as a separate fund in the hands **2.66** of the trustee, and are not available to the trustee's creditors.[118] The basis for this is the proposition that, in equity, trust assets do not belong to the trustee, but rather belong to the beneficiaries. Because the interest of the beneficiary is recognised in equity (but not at common law), it is known as an equitable interest.

A legal interest is an interest that is recognised by the common law. Where a per- **2.67** son holds securities directly from the issuer, her interest is legal. Also, when a person holds securities through an intermediary acting as bailee, her interest is also

---

[114] Note that there is no requirement for the intermediary which is a fiduciary, as opposed to the defendant manager, to act dishonestly: see *Royal Brunei v Tan* (n 115 below) per Nicholls LJ at 109.

[115] [1995] 3 WLR 64.

[116] ibid per Lord Nicholls at 389: 'in the context of the accessory liability principle acting dishonestly, or with lack of probity, which is synonymous, means simply not acting as an honest person would in the circumstances. This is an objective standard. At first sight this may seem surprising. Honesty has a connotation of subjectivity, as distinct from the objectivity of negligence. Honesty, indeed, does have a strong subjective element in that it is a description of a type of conduct assessed in the light of what a person actually knew at the time as distinct from what a reasonable person would have known or appreciated . . . Thus for the most part dishonesty is to be equated with conscious impropriety. However, these subjective characteristics of honesty do not mean that individuals are free to set their own standards of honesty in particular circumstances. The standard of what constitutes honest conduct is not subjective. Honesty is not an optional scale, with higher or lower values according to the moral standards of each individual. If a person knowingly appropriates another's property, he will not escape a finding of dishonesty simply because he sees nothing wrong in such behaviour'.

[117] *Royal Brunei Airlines v Tan* [1995] 2 AC 378 at 389.

[118] See *Underhill and Hayton* (n 51 above) 6.

legal, because (as discussed above) bailment involves the transfer of possession, but not title, to the bailee.

2.68 Thus, the change in the status of intermediaries in the securities markets from bailee to trustee has the effect of changing the nature of the interest of the client from legal to equitable. This may represent a disadvantage that results from the rules of priority. These rules apply where there has been fraud or successive dealings in assets, so that competing claims arise in relation to the same assets.

2.69 The rules of priority are complex, and are discussed elsewhere in this book.[119] However, the general rule is that equitable interests have weaker priority than subsequent legal interests taken without notice of them (so that a client's equitable interest may be defeated if an intermediary wrongfully transfers legal title to a good faith purchaser). Also, the general rule is that subsequent equitable interests have weaker priority than prior equitable interests, so that the purchaser or collateral taker cannot eliminate the risk of adverse claims, even where it gave value and acted in good faith.[120] See Chapter 4 for a fuller discussion.

Common law and civil law

2.70 Trusts are not recognised in all jurisdictions. Very broadly speaking, trusts are recognised in the domestic law of common law jurisdictions,[121] but not under the domestic[122] law of civil law jurisdictions.[123] Although the civil law concept of bailment may be sufficiently wide to relate to intangible assets, it may not be possible under the general principles of civil law for the client to assert property rights in unallocated assets in the hands of the custodian. Thus, alternative techniques are used in civil law jurisdictions to ring fence the interests in securities of clients in the hands of intermediaries. National intermediated settlement systems are given

---

[119] See Chapter 4.

[120] 'The absence of notice of the earlier interest by the party who acquired the later interest is irrelevant, even if he gave value. He cannot gain priority as a bona fide purchaser of the legal estate without notice if he has not acquired the legal estate': *Macmillan v Bishopsgate (No 3)* [1995] 3 All ER 747, per Millett J at 768.

[121] These are jurisdictions with a system of law which is influenced by English common law. Common law jurisdictions include Ireland, New York, Australia, New Zealand, Hong Kong and India.

[122] Certain civil law jurisdictions recognise trusts under their rules of private international law under the Hague Convention of the Law Applicable to Trusts and their Recognition.

[123] These are jurisdictions whose law is codified and based on Roman law principles. Civil law jurisdictions include countries in continental Europe, the former Soviet Union and South America. Philip Wood has pointed out that the basis of the civil law objection to the trust is the policy against 'false wealth'. If the legal owner appears to own the asset, it would be unfair to creditors of the legal owner, if those assets were placed beyond the reach of creditors under hidden trusts. See P R Wood, *Principles of International Insolvency* (London: Sweet & Maxwell, 1995) 36.

special statutory regimes,[124] whose jurisprudential effect is similar to the common law trust.[125]

Of course, many intermediaries to whose accounts interests in securities are credited do not operate under English law. As an important example, the rights of participants in Euroclear are governed by Belgian law.[126] As a civil law jurisdiction, Belgian law does not recognise trusts. However, this does not prevent the English courts as characterising the relationship between the operator of Euroclear and participants as akin to a trust for the purposes of English law, by analogy.[127]   **2.71**

(3) Unallocated Interests

It was seen above that interests in securities are intangible assets, and that they confer indirect rights of property in relation to the underlying securities. A third feature of interests in securities, which is related to the first two, is that the rights of property which they confer are unallocated, in the sense that the client's rights do not attach to particular assets in the hands of the intermediary.   **2.72**

Global client holdings

Where an intermediary has holdings in the same type of asset both for clients and for itself beneficially, it is normal practice for it to segregate the two types of holdings.[128] Where the assets in question are bearer security in the intermediary's possession, this may be achieved by the physical segregation of instruments.[129] Where   **2.73**

---

[124] It is understood that in civil law jurisdictions intangibles can like tangibles be deposited with bailee-custodians. But where the custodian holds intangibles on an unallocated basis, the client cannot bring a proprietary revindication action because that requires identifying specific assets. Hence the need for statutory provision to permit a proprietary claim in respect of an appropriate undivided fraction of the pool held by the custodian.

[125] Examples are (in Belgium) Royal Decree No 62 of 1967; (in Luxembourg) Grand-Ducal Decree of February 1971.

In civil law jurisdictions, private custodial arrangements, which do not have the benefit of any special statutory regime, may rely on the law of agency; this has the operational disadvantage that the (interests in) securities must be held in the name of the client.

[126] This is because such rights arise under Belgian legislation (Royal Decree No 62 of 1967) and the Belgian law Terms and Conditions for Participants in Euroclear.

[127] See Millett J in *Macmillan v Bishopsgate (No 3)* [1995] 3 All ER at 769, 770: 'Legal estates and equitable interests are, of course, concepts of English law which may not have their counterparts in the jurisprudence of other legal systems. Where, therefore, a question arises whether a transaction in England and governed by English law created a legal estate or an equitable interest in foreign property such as shares in a foreign corporation, then recourse must be had to the foreign law in order to ascertain, not how the interest resulting from the transaction would be characterised by that law, but what rights are conferred by that law on the owner of the interest. Once the nature of the interest is known, its characterisation as legal or equitable must be determined in accordance with English law'.

[128] Such segregation is required by trust law, and by regulation of many jurisdictions.

[129] Alternatively, because each traditional bearer instrument has a distinctive serial number, individual client designation can be achieved by keeping a record that allocates particular instruments by serial number to particular clients. It has the same legal effect as physical separation because it makes it possible to attribute particular securities to particular clients.

the assets are registered securities which are registered in the intermediary's name (or that of its nominee), such segregation can be achieved by separate entries in the register of the issuer.[130] Where the assets are interests in securities recorded in the accounts of another intermediary ('the second intermediary'), segregation is achieved by having the second intermediary open separate house and client accounts in the name of the first intermediary.

2.74 However, as indicated in Chapter 1, it is not customary for intermediaries to hold the assets of each client separately from the assets of each other client. Intermediaries find such individual client segregation operationally inconvenient, and settlement systems may charge significant additional costs for opening individual client accounts. Indeed, Euroclear does not offer such a service. In other words, the most common arrangement is for intermediaries to pool the like assets of different clients. Thus, in the case of bearer securities, there will be one physical holding of client securities, and in the case of registered securities, one entry for clients generally. In the case of interests in securities, there will be one global or omnibus client account in the books of the second intermediary.[131]

2.75 In considering the legal effect of a global client holding, it is assumed that the clients consent to the pooling of their assets.[132] Earlier in this chapter a distinction was made between divided securities (such as traditional bearer bonds) and undivided securities (such as registered securities). The legal effect of a global client holding in cases where the underlying assets held by the intermediary are divided, and where they are undivided, will be considered in turn.

Divided underlying assets

2.76 This section will consider the position when *divided* assets such as traditional bearer securities belonging to different clients are commingled in the hands of an intermediary. The Roman term for mixtures of assets comprising units which retain their unitary nature in the mixture, is '*mixtio*' or '*commixtio*'.[133] The effect in Roman[134] and in English law[135] of consensual *commixtio* is that the original

---

[130] The name of the intermediary would appear twice in the register, and one entry would be designated 'client account', or otherwise distinguished. Strictly speaking, this practice is in breach of the Companies Act 1985, s 360, which says that no note of any trusts will be entered on the register. However, it is common practice.

[131] In practice, there may be more than two accounts because of the different tax treatment of different clients.

[132] This will usually be the case, where the intermediary deals on standard terms which provide for such commingling. The legal effect of non-consensual mixing may be different.

[133] See 'Mixtures' by Peter Birks, in Palmer and McKendrick (eds), *Interests in Goods* (2nd edn, London: LLP, 1998) 227, which gives a very clear discussion of Roman and English law in this area.

[134] Justinian, *Institutes* 2.1.28, quoted by Birks (n 133 above) 233.

[135] See *Buckley v Gross* (1863) 3 B & S 566, 122 ER 213; *Spence v Union Marine Insurance Co Ltd* (1868) LR 3 CP 427; *Indian Oil Corn Ltd v Grindstone Shipping SA, The Ypatianna* [1987] 3 All ER 893, and other cases considered in *The Law of Global Custody* (n 49 above) ch 5.

owners cease to own individual units of the assets, and instead become owners in common of the commingled mass.[136]

Undivided underlying assets

The analysis may be slightly different where the asset held by the intermediary is undivided.　**2.77**

Suppose two clients transfer shares out of their respective names and into the name of the intermediary, to be registered together in the intermediary's name without individual designation. The Roman term for the mixing together of assets which belong to different persons and which are not divided into distinct units, is *confusio*.[137] Again, in Roman[138] and English law,[139] the effect of *consensual confusio* is co-ownership.　**2.78**

However, the position is different where the underlying asset is a permanent global security. This is because such interests are not only unallocated in the hands of the intermediary, but also incapable of allocation, since the underlying asset is undivided and indivisible. Such interests are necessarily unallocated from the time global security is originally issued; at no time do clients hold allocated interests. Therefore this is not a case of mixing, which occurs when pre-existing and allocated interests are subsequently commingled. This situation gives rise to a legal question, which will be called 'the allocation question', and which is discussed below.　**2.79**

The allocation question

The allocation question is as follows: can a trust arise in favour of a client whose interests in securities are held by the intermediary together with those of other clients on a commingled basis, or does such a purported trust fail for want of certainty of subject matter?[140] There has been an active debate in the London legal community in recent years concerning the allocation question.　**2.80**

---

[136] Generally, see Birks (n 133 above) 233. See also Blackstone (n 14 above) vol 2, 181: 'Tenants in *common* are such as hold by several and distinct titles, by unity of possession; because none knoweth his own severally, and therefore they all occupy promiscuously'.

[137] 'Confusio is the latin word for the mixing of goods belonging to two different owners, so that they cannot be separated': per Staughton J in *Indian Oil Corp Ltd v Greenstone Shipping SA, The Ypatianna* [1987] 3 All ER 893 at 894.

[138] Justinian, *Institutes* 2.1.27, quoted by Birks (n 133 above) at 233.

[139] *Coleman v Harvey* (1989) 1 NZLR 723, per Cooke P; Judge Paul Baker QC in *Re Stapylton Fletcher* [1994] 1 WLR 1181, 1199. Where the mixing is accidental, the result is the same: see for example *Buckley v Gross* (1863) 3 B & S 566, per Blackburn J at 574, 575; *Spence v Union Marine Insurance Co Ltd* (1868) LR 3 CP 427, per Bovill CJ at 437; *The Ypatianna* per Staughton J at 907, 908.

[140] The debate was triggered by the case of *Re London Wine (Shippers) Ltd* [1986] PCC 121. In this judgment, Oliver J, relying on older authority (and in particular *Re Waite* [1927] 1 Ch 606), held that clients could not establish a trust in their favour over assets (wine) for which they had paid

2.81 The rules relating to mixing discussed above do not answer the allocation question, because they apply in cases where the individual ownership of different assets predates the mixing of those assets. In the allocation question, the timing is reversed because the commingled mass predates purported property rights in it.[141]

2.82 Two broad approaches have been taken by commentators to the allocation question. The first approach (which the author considers prudent) is that the requirement for certainty of subject matter will not be satisfied if it is sought to establish individual trusts concerning a specific number of (interests in) securities in favour of each client of the intermediary. However, the requirement will be satisfied if a single trust is established over the global client holding. All clients of the intermediary to whose accounts in the books of the intermediary interests in the relevant (interests in) securities are credited will be beneficiaries under this single trust. Thus, all such clients together beneficially co-own the pool of assets in the intermediary's hands; they own fractional shares of the pool. There is no uncertainty of subject matter, because the trust property comprises the entire client holding.[142]

2.83 There is some basis for the view that, where client assets are segregated from the intermediary's house assets, co-ownership rights arise by operation of law.[143] However, prudent institutions have expressly provided for such co-ownership in their client documentation.[144]

2.84 An attraction of this approach is that the legal results of consensual mixing and the allocation question coincide; co-ownership rights arise in either case. This is desir-

---

and which they had agreed to leave in the hands of a custodian, because such assets had not been separately identified in the hands of the custodian.

The same issue arises at law as well as in equity. In relation to the sale of goods, the old rule that property does not pass prior to ascertainment was modified by the Sale of Goods (Amendment) Act 1995, which (very broadly) provides that title to goods in ex bulk sales passes on payment of the purchase price.

[141] The author sought to make this distinction in *The Law of Global Custody* (n 49 above) 45: 'English case law makes a clear distinction between two situations. The first is where there is a purported transfer of an unidentified part of a fungible bulk without appropriation. The second is where property belonging to several persons is commingled into a fungible bulk without segregation'. Peter Birks makes the distinction more elegantly in 'Mixtures' (n 133 above) 228, using Roman terms.

[142] Of course, this approach will only be effective where a pool of assets (such as a commingled client account) exists: see *Re Goldcorp Exchange Ltd (in receivership)* [1995] 1 AC 74.

[143] See *Re Stapylton Fletcher Ltd (in administrative receivership), Re Ellis Son & Vidler Ltd (in administrative receivership)* [1995] 1 All ER 192, per Judge Paul Baker QC at 210: 'If a number of cases or bottles of identical wine are held, not mingled with the trading stock, in store for a group of customers, those cases or bottles will be ascertained . . . even though they are not immediately appropriated to each individual customer. Property will pass by common intention . . . They will take as tenants in common'.

[144] *Stapylton Fletcher* (n 143 above) related only to legal interests arising in the sale of goods; *Re London Wine (Shippers) Ltd* [1986] PCC 121 considered the position both at law and in equity, and indicated (per Oliver J at 137), that very clear wording would be required in order for an equity in common to arise. (On the other hand, in *London Wine* client assets were not separated from house assets as they were in *Stapylton Fletcher*, and as they are required to be in the custody of securities.)

able in the interests of legal certainty, because (in an active custody account) it will be impracticable to establish whether any interest of any client is a case of mixing[145] or the allocation question.[146]

The co-ownership approach raises what Professor Birks has called the problem of unilateral partition. If client assets are co-owned, does each client require the consent of the other clients to dispose of her interest?[147] In relation to goods, a statutory solution is provided in the new sections 20A and 20B of the Sale of Goods Act 1979.[148] Of course, intangibles such as interests in securities are not goods, and they fall outside the scope of these provisions. However, Professor Birks suggests that 'the day may not be far off when a solution on those lines' will be judicially developed to provide a general solution to the problem of unilateral partition.[149] The author shares his faith in the common sense of our judges. **2.85**

A second approach to the allocation question follows the judgment in *Hunter v Moss*.[150] In this case, the allocation question was considered in relation to a pool of shares. It was held that the need for certainty of subject matter does not apply in relation to shares, because they are intangible.[151] Detailed reasoning to support this proposition was not supplied in the judgment. *Hunter v Moss* was reluctantly followed in *Re Harvard Securities Ltd*[152] and (less reluctantly) in the Hong Kong case of *CA Pacific*.[153] **2.86**

---

[145] eg where the client held (interests in) securities in its own name prior to transferring them into the name of the custodian.

[146] eg where the client purchased the (interests in) securities from a third party, who transferred them directly into the name of the custodian.

[147] 'If one owner in common takes his quantity from the co-owned mass, every molecule that he takes remains co-owned save so far as the other co-owner or co-owners consent to the transfer of their interests to him': Birks (n 133 above) 229.

[148] These provisions were introduced by the Sale of Goods (Amendment) Act 1995, which provides (in s 20A) for implied co-ownership and (in s 20B) for unilateral partition.

[149] This 'will eliminate from the law a good deal of unnecessary complexity': Birks (n 133 above) 230.

[150] [1993] 1 WLR 934; [1994] 1 WLR 452.

[151] 'The defendant did not identify any particular 50 shares for the plaintiff because to do so was unnecessary and irrelevant. All 950 of his shares carried identical rights . . . Any suggested uncertainty as to subject matter appears to me to be theoretical and conceptual rather than real and practical': *Hunter v Moss* [1993] 1 WLR 934, 946.

[152] *Harvard Securities (in liquidation), Holland v Newbury and another* [1997] 2 BCLC 369. In this case a securities broker became insolvent while holding client shares on a commingled basis. The allocation question arose both under English law (in relation to certain shares) and under Australian law (in relation to others). It was held that the requirement for certainty of subject matter does not apply to intangibles under English law but does under Australian law, which is very strange, as both are common law jurisdictions: 'Under English law, in the light of the decision of the court of Appeal in *Hunter*, by which I am bound, the US shares and the Australian shares sold to former clients after 14 July 1986, are held beneficially for Harvard's former clients . . . In relation to Australian shares acquired before 14 July 1986, former clients have no such beneficial interest': per Neuberger J at 388.

[153] *Re CA Pacific Finance Ltd (in Liquidation) and another* [2000] BCLC 494. The latter case considered the nature of the assets of clients of brokers whose interests in securities were held on an unallocated basis in the Hong Kong settlement system, HKCSS. It was held that the clients' assets

2.87   *Hunter v Moss* has attracted serious criticism on a number of grounds.[154] First, it erroneously assumed that because a testator could leave 50 of her 950 shares to X and 50 to Y, it followed that a settlor could in her lifetime declare a trust of 50 of her 950 shares and retain her own interest in 900. Moreover, there is no basis in the law of trusts to treat trusts of intangibles differently from trusts of tangible assets.[155] In any case there is clear authority that the requirement for certainty of subject matter does apply to trusts of cash.[156]

2.88   In the author's view, it is currently unsafe to rely on the suggestion in *Hunter v Moss* that property rights can arise under a trust without attaching to any particular asset, as this is inconsistent with a large body of case law.[157] Therefore it would be prudent to prefer the co-ownership approach, and seek to reconcile *Hunter v Moss* with it.[158] Further arguments in support of the co-ownership approach are as follows. In a wide range of repackaging arrangements, the interests of investors arise under express co-ownership provisions, as discussed in Chapter 11. The legal analysis of the securities markets is tremendously simplified if the legal nature of interests in securities arising under such repackagings, and those arising under custodial and settlement arrangements, are understood to be the same.

---

were proprietary and did not merely comprise personal rights against the brokers. However, it was further held that these property rights were individual rights, not in the nature of co-ownership rights. See also the discussion of *Hunter v Moss* in T Austen-Peters, *The Custody of Investments* (Oxford University Press, 2000), paragraphs 3.36–3.38.

[154]   See in particular D J Hayton, 'Uncertainty of Subject-Matter of Trusts' (1994) 110 LQR 335.

[155]   'In view of the weak reasoning in *Hunter v Moss* and of the ringing endorsement of *Re London Wine Co (Shippers) Ltd* by the Privy Council in *Re Goldcorp Exchange Ltd* . . . it is respectfully submitted that *Hunter v Moss* should not be followed: there is no sound reasoning for distinguishing trusts of goods from trusts of intangibles': *Underhill and Hayton* (n 51 above) 65.

[156]   *Mac-Jordan Construction Ltd v Brookmount Erostin Ltd (in receivership)* [1992] BCLC 350. For a discussion of this and subsequent case law, see A J M Blacker, 'Retention Monies in UK Building Contracts' in Palmer and McKendrick (eds), *Interests in Goods* (2nd edn, 1998).

[157]   In relation to the law of trusts, see in particular the rejection of *Space Investments Ltd v Canadian Imperial Bank of Commerce Trust Co (Bahamas) Ltd* [1986] 3 All ER 75 in *Re Goldcorp Exchange Ltd (in receivership)* [1995] 1 AC 74.

[158]   It might be sought to argue that the true basis of the judgment was not the intangible nature of shares, but rather their indivisible nature, as follows. A holding of registered securities such as shares is not only undivided; it is also indivisible because the entire issue of registered securities comprises one asset, in which shareholders participate as co-owners. In contrast, cash may be segregated by placing it in a separate bank account, for each bank account in credit represents a separate debt of the bank. However, shares cannot be so segregated, because one share is not a separate asset from another share, but rather (as its name suggests) an undivided share in the undertaking of the company: see *Ind's Case* (1872) 7 Ch App 485. Because multiple shareholdings can only take effect by way of co-ownership, co-ownership may be safely assumed to arise by operation of law. Therefore an interest in registered securities automatically takes effect as a co-ownership right. No further allocation is either necessary or possible.

This argument suggests that the true ratio of *Hunter v Moss* is akin to that in *Stapylton Fletcher*, ie not that the requirement for allocation is not applicable, but that it is automatically satisfied by co-ownership of the whole. It does, however, involve rejecting the approach of *CA Pacific* (n 153 above).

Further, Western law has always treated a share in a pool of undivided assets as different from an individual asset owned outright.[159] The effect of mixing to create such a pool is a form of substitution; the contributors to the pool cease to own the original assets outright, and in their place acquire co-ownership rights in the pool. This provides support for argument that interests in securities are located with the account of the intermediary in which they are recorded, and not with the underlying securities. As discussed in Chapter 7, this approach is commercially helpful. In contrast, the view that clients have outright interests in the underlying assets would not support this approach.

However, the law of equity may continue to develop following *Hunter v Moss*, so as to provide a conceptual basis for relieving property rights in intangibles from the requirement to attach to particular assets. Chapter 13 seeks to indicate such a basis, in the Roman law reification of obligations. It is not suggested that this represents the current state of English law. However, such a development would be welcome in view of the economic importance of interests in securities.

(4) Bearer or Registered?

As discussed above, the assets of the holder of traditional bearer securities are tangible, and her interests are allocated and based on possession. In contrast, the assets of the holder of traditional registered securities are intangible, and her interests are unallocated and based on an entry in the register. It has been argued above that the assets of the holder of interests in securities are intangible, and that her interests are unallocated and based on entries in the account maintained by the intermediary in her favour. On this basis, interests in securities may be properly characterised as a form of registered securities, even where the underlying securities are in bearer form. (The significance of this in the conflict of laws will be discussed in Chapter 7.)

2.89

2.90

2.91

---

[159] See Justinian's *Institutes* 2.1.27–28, and the discussion of it by Birks in 'Mixtures' (n 133 above) 233: 'The underlying rationale of the distinction [between granular and fluid mixtures] was as follows. In the case of fluids and molten metals (*confusio*) it was the interpenetration of the contributions arising from the loss of the physical integrity of the constituent units which accounted for the change in their proprietary status'.

PART II

DELIVERIES

3

TRANSFERS

... for no *chose* in action could be assigned or granted over, because it was thought to be a great encouragement to litigiousness, if a man were allowed to make over to a stranger his right of going to law.*

A. Introduction

A key component of market capitalism is the secondary securities market, in **3.01** which (interests in) securities are bought and sold. As discussed in Chapter 1, transferability is a defining characteristic of securities. English law has developed a number of techniques for the transfer of securities, which will be considered in this chapter.

'Transfer' is not a technical legal term. It describes the economic result of a trans- **3.02** action whereby a transferee acquires the asset that was previously held by the transferor.[1] This economic result can be achieved by a variety of legal means of which novation, assignment and negotiation are particularly relevant to the securities markets.[2] Each of these will be considered in turn.

---

* Blackstone's *Commentaries on the Laws of England* (facsimilie of the 1st edn, 1765–1769, University of Chicago Press, 1979) vol 2, 442.

[1] To be exact, in the case of novation, the transferee does not acquire the same asset, but rather a new asset in like form.

[2] Sub-participations and declarations of trust are also widely used in the context of securitisations (which are discussed in Chapter 11). See 'Securitisation and Asset Transfers' in FSA, *Guide to*

3.03　It is important for transfers to be convenient (so that transfers can take place rapidly with the minimum of formality). It is also important for transfers to be secure (so that the good faith purchaser of (interests in) securities is confident that she will be able to retain the purchased assets free from adverse claims). Techniques of transfer, formalities of transfer and security of transfer will be considered in turn.

B.　Techniques of Transfer

3.04　The following techniques of transfer are relevant to a legal analysis of the secondary markets in (interests in) securities.

(1)　Novation

3.05　Transfer by novation[3] is a technique for transferring contractual claims. It is best explained by example. Suppose there is a contract between A and B. B wishes to transfer her interest under the contract to C. This can be achieved by novation if A, B and C agree together that a new contract between A and C shall replace the old contract between A and B. To be accurate, novation is not a form of transfer, because C's asset arises under a new contract, and is therefore not the same as B's asset, which is extinguished by the contract.[4] However, it has the same economic effect as a transfer, because the old and new contracts are on like terms.

3.06　It was seen in Chapter 2 that registered securities are transferred by registration. Registration involves substituting the name of the transferee for that of the transferor in the register of the issuer. Thus, the transfer of registered securities involves the participation of the issuer.[5] Registration may therefore be characterised as a form of novation, by equating the issuer with A in the above example. By its actions in registering the transfer, the issuer implicitly agrees with the transferor and the transferee that the latter should stand in the place of the former.[6] The regimes for the transfer of registered equities and gilts has been given a statutory

---

Banking Supervisory Policy section 5.1.2. Sub-participations are also widely used in the secondary markets in bank loans. They do not so much transfer existing assets as create new ones; however, as long as the parties are solvent, the effect of a sub-participation may be the same as that of a transfer. The author is grateful to Simon James, partner, Clifford Chance, for this point.

　　[3] Novation means making anew. As well as being used as a technique of transfer, novation is also used as a technique of netting. The author is grateful to Richard Firth of Barclays Bank for this observation.

　　[4] 'It should, however, be noted that the effect of a novation is not to assign or transfer a right or liability, but rather to extinguish the original contract and replace it by another': *Chitty on Contracts* (28th edn, London: Sweet & Maxwell, 1999), para 20-086, 1067.

　　[5] In practice, the ability of the issuer to decline to register a transfer may be limited; if it is not, the ability to transfer is much reduced.

　　[6] See the discussion of the effect of registering a transfer of units in a unit trust in Kam Fan Sin, *The Legal Nature of the Unit Trust* (Oxford: Clarendon Press, 1997) 319.

basis under the Companies Act 1985 and the Stock Transfer Act 1963 respectively.[7] Nevertheless, it is argued that the original common law for basis transfers of registered securities is novation.[8]

Historically, the novation of contracts was long recognised by English common law.[9] However, in some circumstances the necessary involvement of the obligor in novation presents a disadvantage. An alternative technique of transfer, which does not involve the participation of the obligor, is assignment. **3.07**

(2) Assignment

If A owes a debt to B, B may[10] unilaterally (ie without involving A) transfer the debt to C by way of assignment. In contrast to novation, it is the same debt in the hands of both A and B. **3.08**

The old common law rule

A rule of medieval common law prohibited the assignment of choses in action. This rule was based on an aspect of medieval social policy, namely the policy against maintenance. Maintenance is trafficking in claims, which was feared as a social abuse that might undermine the operation of justice in medieval England.[11] The approach of the medieval courts was that a claim was personal as between the obligor and the obligee, and the law should therefore not contemplate its transfer without the active involvement of the obligor.[12] This ancient rule continued to have general effect (subject to specific statutory exemptions in favour of certain type of chose in action)[13] until a general regime for the legal assignment of choses in action was created in the nineteenth century (see below). **3.09**

Equitable assignment

Long before legal assignment became possible through statute (see below), the Courts of Chancery offered support to the early capitalists by permitting assignment in equity.[14] However, the position of the equitable assignee is weaker **3.10**

---

[7] The statutory regime for dematerialised securities is made under the Companies Act 1989. See Chapter 9 for more details.

[8] Of course, novation involves one tri-partite contract, and it might be argued that transfer by registration involves three bi-partite contracts.

[9] A procedural restriction on actions for novation was overcome by the development of the action of assumpsit in the early modern period. See W S Holdsworth, *A History of English Law* (Methuen & Co) vol VIII, 85–88.

[10] It is assumed that the contract under which the debt arises does not prohibit assignment.

[11] See Holdsworth (n 9 above) vol III, 394 et seq, vol V, 201 et seq and vol VIII, 397 et seq. For the current position, see also *Chitty on Contracts* (n 4 above) 859 et seq.

[12] See Holdsworth (n 9 above) vol VII, 525, 526, 532 et seq.

[13] eg the Policies of Assurance Act 1867 permits the assignment of insurance policies.

[14] See Holdsworth (n 9 above) vol V, 299.

than that of a legal assignee, as discussed in the section on advantages of legal over equitable assignment below.

3.11 An equitable assignment can only take effect in equity. Thus, whether the interest of the assignor is legal or equitable, all the assignee can take is an equitable interest.

3.12 An equitable assignment requires fewer formalities than a legal assignment. Indeed, in many cases purported legal assignments that cannot take effect at law because they do not comply with some statutory requirement for legal assignment (see below), take effect in equity.[15]

3.13 However, even an equitable assignment requires writing. This is because of section 53(1)(c) of the Law of Property Act 1925, which requires dispositions of equitable interests to be in writing.[16]

Statutory legal assignment

3.14 The Victorians made further concessions to the demands of market capitalism, by permitting statutory legal assignment. In 1873 there was enacted the predecessor of section 136 of the Law of Property Act 1925.[17] This creates an exception to the common law restriction, by permitting the legal assignment of choses in action provided certain formalities and restrictions are observed.[18] These are, broadly,

---

[14] See Holdsworth (n 9 above) vol V, 299.

[15] eg an assignment of a debt without notice to the debtor and assignment of part of a debt take effect in equity.

[16] Section 53(1)(c) provides 'a disposition of an equitable interest or trust subsisting at the time of the disposition, must be in writing signed by the person disposing of the same, or by his agent hereunto lawfully authorised in writing or by will'. This requirement does not apply to constructive or resulting trusts (s 53(2)). Section 53(1)(c) replaces the Statute of Frauds 1677, s 9 (repealed), which provided as follows: 'all grants and assignments of any trust or confidence shall likewise be in writing, signed by the party granting or assigning the same, or by such last will or devise, or else shall likewise be utterly void and of none effect'.

A purported equitable assignment that does not comply with the section will not be effective to confer property rights and will take effect in contract only. This means that the rights of the purported assignee will be personal only and will bind only the purported assignor, and not third parties. This leaves the assignee vulnerable to the double-dealing and insolvency of the purported assignor. However, as discussed below, a number of arguments are available to avoid the restrictions in this section.

[17] Supreme Court of Judicature Act 1873, s 25(6) (repealed).

[18] Law of Property Act 1925, s 136, provides as follows: '(1) Any absolute assignment by writing under the hand of the assignor (not purporting to be by way of charge only) of any debt or other legal thing in action, of which express notice in writing has been given to the debtor, trustee or other person from whom the assignor would have been entitled to claim such debt or thing in action, is effectual in law (subject to equities having priority over the right of the assignee) to pass and transfer from the date of such notice—
(a) the legal right to such a debt or thing in action;
(b) all legal and other remedies for the same; and
(c) the power to give a good discharge for the same without the concurrence of the assignor'.

that the assignment is absolute, that the assignment is in writing, and that written notice of the assignment is given to the obligor. The requirement that the assignment is absolute means that it must dispose of the entirety of the interest of the assignor.[19]

There are two requirements for writing: first, a written assignment or instrument **3.15** of transfer and secondly a written notice to the debtor or other obligor. Of course, there does not necessarily need to be two pieces of paper, as one writing can serve both functions. In many transfers of financial assets it is not considered feasible to comply with the requirement for written notice to the debtor because of the formality and disclosure involved.[20] However, where written notice to the debtor is given, this provides an additional advantage under the rule in *Dearle v Hall.*[21] This rule relates to priorities, or the rules for the ranking of competing claims to the same asset. It will be discussed in detail in Chapter 4.

Advantages of legal over equitable assignment

Both legal and equitable assignments require writing. The advantages of legal over **3.16** equitable assignments are as follows. First, equitable interests are relatively weak in priority, and so may be vulnerable to adverse claims, as discussed in detail below. Secondly, an equitable assignee cannot in general sue the issuer in its own name but must join the assignor in any action against the issuer.[22] Thirdly, if the assignor owes money to the issuer, the issuer may in some circumstances[23] set this off against its payment obligation under the assigned claim.

Limitations of assignment

In general even legal assignment is not an ideal technique of transfer in the sec- **3.17** ondary securities markets, for a number of reasons.

Benefit and burden

The general rule is that an assignment can transfer the benefit, but not the burden, **3.18** of a contract.[24] This is based on the principle that a creditor should be able to choose her debtor and should not be deprived of the ability to sue B, when B unilaterally assigns to C. Securities in the secondary market are generally fully paid, so no debt obligations are imposed on holders. However, other restrictions may be

---

[19] The assignment of part of a debt cannot pass legal title but does operate in equity to transfer the part assigned and constitutes the assignee a creditor in equity of the original debtor: *Re Steel Wing Co* [1921] 1 Ch 349, per Lawrence J at 355.

[20] See the discussion of CBOs and securitisation in Chapter 12.

[21] (1828) 3 Russ 1; [1824–34] All ER Rep 28.

[22] See *Chitty on Contracts* (n 4 above) paras 20-037–20-040.

[23] Legal set off requires a judgment; equitable set off requires a connection between the two debts.

[24] See *Chitty on Contracts* (n 4 above) paras 20-075–20-078.

imposed, such as limitations of liability and other waivers, or representations and warranties of residence or other issues of regulatory status.

Subject to the equities

3.19 A further disadvantage of assignments is the general rule that assignments are subject to the equities.[25] This rule might be illustrated as follows. B has a debt against A for £10, and she assigns this debt to C. B owed money to A under another debt for £6 which is connected with the assigned debt. In this case, A can set off the debt of £6 against its obligation to pay C £10 (reducing this to £4), provided the debt of £6 accrued before A had notice of the assignment.[26] This is clearly unsatisfactory for C.

3.20 For the above reasons, assignment is generally not a satisfactory basis for secondary market activity.[27] A more attractive alternative is negotiation.

(3) Negotiation

3.21 It was seen that legal assignment did not generally become available to the securities markets until the Victorian era, and that the formalities involved in novation meant that that technique could not meet the needs of the mercantile community for conveniently transferable debt securities.[28] Therefore an alternative form of transfer was developed for certain instruments in the medieval period onwards[29] by the law merchant. This is known as negotiation, which is a modified form of assignment. A negotiable instrument is transferable by delivery or, in some cases, endorsement and delivery.[30] Delivery means the transfer of possession (ie handing over the paper).[31] Endorsement means signing the back of the instrument.[32]

---

[25] See *Business Computers Ltd v Anglo African Ltd* [1977] 1 WLR 578.

[26] *Chitty on Contracts* (n 4 above) 1059–1060.

[27] In contrast, assignment is widely used in the secondary markets in bank debt, and in securitisation structures. Arguably, these markets show a higher tolerance for adverse claims that the securities markets, where the use of electronic settlement systems creates a particular intolerance for systemic risk.

[28] Strictly speaking, bills of exchange and promissory notes do not constitute debts, but rather promises to pay. However, for ease of reference, the term 'debt security' will continue to be used.

[29] See Blackstone, *Commentaries*, vol 4, 434 and Holdsworth (n 9 above) 113 et seq. Arguably, bills of exchange were in use in the Mediterranean area in ancient times. The use of bills and other financial techniques continued in the Middle East after the fall of the Western Roman Empire. They were rediscovered by the West at the time of the crusades. See W A Bewes, *The Romance of the Law Merchant* (London: Sweet & Maxwell, 1923).

[30] 'Endorsement can be spelled with either an "e" or "i". While the Bills of Exchange Act 1882 uses 'indorsement', this paper uses the more common spelling of "endorsement"': *The Future of Money Market Instruments* (Bank of England, November 1999) 17. Interestingly, in relation to the dematerialisation of money market instruments, discussed in Chapter 9, it is proposed to drop 'endorsement'. See *The Future of Money Market Instruments* 18 and *The Future of Money Market Instruments, Next Steps* (Bank of England, March 2000) 7, 15. There must also be the intention to transfer title by the delivery, so that delivering a bearer instrument to a custodian for safekeeping does not make the custodian the owner of the instrument, but rather its bailee.

[31] Delivery is defined in the Bills of Exchange Act 1882, s 2, as: 'transfer of possession, actual or constructive, from one person to another'.

[32] For the requirements of valid endorsement, see the Bills of Exchange Act 1882, s 32.

The original meaning of the term 'negotiable' was transferable. This was because, **3.22** historically, negotiable instruments were not subject to the common law restrictions on assignment discussed above. However, as these restrictions were relaxed in the Victorian era, the term 'negotiable' came to have a new connotation, relating to security of transfer.[33]

Not all instruments are negotiable instruments. An instrument can acquire nego- **3.23** tiable status either by statute or by commercial custom. The original forms of negotiable instruments were bills of exchange and promissory notes. The Bills of Exchange Act 1882 codified the law relating to bills of exchange, promissory notes and cheques.[34] Other forms of debt security have subsequently been added to the list by commercial custom, in accordance with the law merchant.[35] Most forms of non-computerised bearer debt securities are negotiable instruments.

As indicated in Chapter 2, the concept of negotiability is based on a legal fiction. **3.24** The law merchant asserted that a negotiable instrument was not an intangible debt, but rather a physical piece of paper. In other words, the debt in respect of which the paper was issued was treated as being locked up in the paper.[36] Therefore, when the paper moves from hand to hand in the secondary markets the debt moves with it. By simply handing over the instrument, one transfers the debt.

Another consequence of this fiction is that negotiable instruments are treated as **3.25** choses in possession.[37] This means that negotiable instruments can be bailed and pledged. Further, in conflict of laws, the situs of a negotiable instrument is the physical location of the paper, as discussed in Chapter 7.

The first great advantage of negotiable status is the availability of negotiation as a **3.26** convenient technique of transfer. The second great advantage of negotiable status is security of transfer. Very broadly, the good faith purchaser of a negotiable instrument (known as the holder in due course) takes it free of adverse claims, and can acquire a better title than the transferor had. This will be discussed in more

---

[33] See J S Ewart, 'Negotiability and Estoppel' (1900) 15 LQR 135, 140, 141: 'The truth is that "negotiable" has an original and an acquired signification. Originally, it meant transferable; but afterwards it was used to indicate the effects of transfer, namely, that the transferee (1) took free from equities, and (2) could sue in his own name'.

[34] The law relating to cheques was further modified by the Cheques Act 1957 (as amended by the Cheques Act 1992).

[35] These include bearer bonds, whether foreign or domestic, corporate or government (see *Edelstein v Schuler* [1902] All ER Rep 884) and certificates of deposit (see *Libyan Arab Foreign Bank v Bankers Trust Co* [1988] 1 Lloyds Rep 259).

[36] This might be described as a form of metonymy.

[37] Negotiable instruments are treated as a form of chattel. See *R v Sadi and Morris* (1787) 168 ER 336 (bank-notes); *Hornblower v Proud* (1819) 106 ER 389 (bills of exchange); *Cumming v Baily* (1830) 130 ER 1320, 1323 (bills of exchange) *Edwards v Cooper* (1847) 116 ER 386, 388 (bills of exchange). See also the general discussion, F Ryder et al (eds), *Byles on Bills of Exchange* (26th edn, London: Sweet & Maxwell, 1988) 5.

detail below. For participants in the secondary market, negotiability is a real advantage. However, negotiable status is not available to registered securities, or (it will be argued below) to any form of interest in securities.[38]

(4) Transfers of Interests in Securities

3.27 It was argued in Chapter 2 that interests in securities are akin to registered securities, because the account of the intermediary in which they are recorded is comparable to a register. It was argued above that registered securities are transferred by novation. On this basis, transfers of interests in securities by debits and credits to the account of the intermediary also involve novation. This view is supported by the case of *R v Preddy*.[39]

Preddy and novation

3.28 *R v Preddy* is a criminal law case relating to mortgage fraud. It concerned the legal effect of the payment of money by book entry, ie by debiting the account of the payor and crediting the account of the payee. The decision in the case applies by analogy to deliveries of interests in securities by book entry.

3.29 In *Preddy*, the appellants had obtained mortgage advances from building societies and others on the basis of misrepresentations. The advances were made by debiting the account of the lender and crediting the account of the appellants or their solicitors. The appellants were convicted under section 15(1) of the Theft Act 1968.[40] The House of Lords quashed the conviction, on the basis that the actions of the appellants did not involve obtaining property *belonging to another*. Payment from one deposit account to another involves the reduction or extinction of one chose in action, and the increase or creation of another. The fraudulent payee's chose in action against its bank (represented by the credit balance on its account) did not represent property belonging to another, as it was never owned by the payor.

3.30 This is consistent with novation, which involves the extinction of the claim of the transferor and the creation of a new claim in favour of the transferee.

Neither negotiation nor assignment

3.31 Interests in securities are evidenced by account entries, and their transfer is effected by book entry. *Preddy* shows that, following a book entry transfer, the asset of the transferee is different from the asset of the transferor. This is consistent

---

[38] The term 'interests in securities' has been defined in Chapter 1 (broadly) as the interest of a client for whom an intermediary holds (interests in) securities on a commingled basis.

[39] [1996] AC 815.

[40] 'A person who by any deception obtains *property belonging to another* [emphasis added], with the intention of permanently depriving the other of it, shall on conviction on indictment be liable to imprisonment for a term not exceeding ten years.'

with novation, but inconsistent with assignment. This tends to support the view that transfers of interests in securities involve novation.[41]

The disadvantages of assignment were discussed above. Although widely used in certain financial markets,[42] assignment provides less security of transfer than novation.[43] Therefore the conclusion that the secondary markets in interests in securities do not involve assignment will be generally welcome. However, a less welcome conclusion, which is developed below, is that these markets do not involve negotiation. The shift from negotiation to novation, which (it will be argued) is the consequence of the computerisation of the bearer bond markets, may serve to reduce security of transfer, as discussed below.   **3.32**

The argument that transfers of interests in securities take effect by novation further supports the view that they are a form of registered security.   **3.33**

Net settlement

It is customary for financial institutions dealing in the secondary markets to settle their securities transactions on a net basis. Thus, for example, where investment bank A is obliged to deliver 2,000,000 ABC shares to investment bank B under transaction 1, and where B is obliged to A deliver 1,000,000 ABC shares to A on the same day under transaction 2, the delivery obligations of both banks under both transactions will be discharged on a net basis by A delivering 1,000,000 ABC shares to B.   **3.34**

Netting increases efficiency and reduces risk in settlement. However, it has the interesting legal consequence of severing the link between particular trades and particular deliveries.[44] Deliveries of securities cannot be allocated to the particular contractual obligations which they serve to discharge. The familiar jurisprudential model of personal rights (which arise on contract) evolving into property rights (upon allocation or delivery) may therefore be misleading.   **3.35**

C. Formalities of Transfer: the Requirement for Paper

As indicated in Chapter 1, interests in securities are intangible assets, which are transferred by debiting and crediting of securities accounts maintained by intermediaries. In these respects they differ from securities, the transfer of which has traditionally involved paper. Thus bearer securities are transferred by the delivery   **3.36**

---

[41] See the discussion in J E Penner, *The Idea of Property in Law* (Oxford: Clarendon Press, 1997) 147 and Kam Fan Sin, *The Legal Nature of the Unit Trust* (Oxford: Clarendon Press, 1997) 288.
[42] In particular, in the secondary market for bank loans and in securitisations: see Chapter 12.
[43] This is because assignment is subject to the equities, as discussed above.
[44] To the author's knowledge, this point was first raised by Professor Jim Rogers.

of a physical instrument, and registered securities have traditionally been delivered by the use of stock transfer forms.[45] This section will consider the legal aspects of the paperless transfer of interests in securities.

3.37 As indicated above, section 136 of the Law of Property Act 1925 requires legal assignments of choses in action to be in writing, and section 53(1)(c) of that Act requires dispositions of equitable interests to be in writing.

3.38 The author would argue that section 136 does not apply to transfers of interests in securities, because these take effect by novation and not by assignment.[46]

3.39 However, section 53(1)(c) relates to *dispositions* of equitable interests. As discussed in Chapter 2, interests in securities generally comprise equitable interests as a matter of English law. The term 'disposition' in this context has been widely interpreted in case law, and is clearly not limited to assignments.[47] It would be prudent to assume that a novation is a disposition.[48]

3.40 Various arguments are available to the effect that the section does not apply to transfers of interests in securities.[49] It might be argued that the transferee is protected under a trust.[50] Alternatively, it might be argued that transfers of interests in securities take effect, not as dispositions, but by a form of succession.[51]

---

[45] The transfer of registered securities is permitted by the Stock Transfer Act 1963 provided a written transfer form is used. The provisions of this Act apply (inter alia) to company shares, gilts and units in authorised unit trust schemes; see s 1(4). In the case of dematerialised securities, the requirement for written transfers is removed by the Uncertificated Securities Regulations 1995, SI 1995/3272 (made under the Companies Act 1989, s 207).

[46] For this reason, the disapplication of the Law of Property Act 1925, s 136 in the Uncertificated Securities Regulations 1995 may have been cautious rather than necessary.

[47] The meaning of the term is considered at length in *Grey v IRC* [1959] 3 All ER 603. In this case, a trustee was orally directed to cease holding shares for the settlor, and instead to hold them for the settlor's grandchildren. It was argued that the direction was not a 'disposition' for the purposes of s 53(1)(c), and that that term was limited to grants and assignments, but that argument failed. 'If the word "disposition" is given its natural meaning, it cannot, I think, be denied that a direction given by Mr Hunter whereby the beneficial interest in the shares theretofore vested in him became vested in another or others is a disposition' (per Viscount Simonds at 506).

[48] A counter-argument would be that novation extinguishes the original asset, and therefore is not a disposal. The author is grateful for Simon James of Clifford Chance for this point.

[49] These points were developed by the author in her position paper for the Trust Law Committee, *Equitable Problems in the Securities Markets* (1998).

[50] Under the rule in *Chinn v Collins* [1981] AC 533, HL, a vendor holds the purchased assets for the purchaser prior to delivery of those assets, when the purchase price is paid. (This rule is discussed in Chapter 9.) Thus, even if a contract of sale is prevented from delivering interests in securities by s 53(1)(c), the same result is achieved by trust.

[51] The co-ownership rights of a client holding interests in securities arise under pooled arrangements, under which the intermediary holds, for example, all the ICI shares in its commingled custody account rateably for all clients to whose accounts it has credited ICI shares. A client's interest in the pool arises by virtue of its joining the class of clients to whose accounts IC shares are credited. The position is akin to changes in the membership of unincorporated associations. Although new members become entitled to equitable interests in association property, writing has never been required for changes in association membership (see, eg *Carne v Long* (1860) 2 De GF & J; 45 ER

However, a legislative disapplication of section 53(1)(c) would be welcome, in order to put the matter beyond doubt. It is hoped that this will be done under section 8 of the Electronic Communications Act 2000. **3.41**

D. Security of Transfer

A transfer is secure if the transferee, being a good faith purchaser, is able to retain the transferred asset free from adverse claims. Adverse claims may come from three sources. These are: the transferor's liquidator (insolvency displacement); the issuer of the security (issuer's claims); and third parties (third party claims). Each of these will be considered in turn. **3.42**

(1) Insolvency Displacement

If the transferor of securities is affected by insolvency at the time of transfer or shortly thereafter, the transfer may be challenged under the provisions of insolvency law. The general policy behind such provisions is a desire to protect the interests of general creditors. **3.43**

Dispositions made after commencement of insolvency proceedings are generally void.[52] After the commencement of insolvency proceedings, a number of days may pass before they become public. Further, under 'zero hour rules', the timing of the commencement may be moved back to the beginning of the 24 hour day. This means that at any particular time, the transferee has no way of knowing if the transferor will subsequently be treated as having been insolvent at that time. It follows that the transferor cannot know whether any transfer to it may be avoided as a post-insolvency disposition.[53] **3.44**

The periods leading up to insolvency are colloquially known as the 'hardening periods'. Transactions entered into during a statutory hardening period may be set aside under displacement provisions designed to protect general creditors. **3.45**

Examples are the setting aside of transactions which are entered into at an undervalue[54] and the invalidation of transactions which are deemed to constitute preferences in favour of certain creditors.[55] **3.46**

---

550 and *Neville Estates Ltd v Madden* [1961] 2 All ER 769). Property rights are acquired by an individual assuming a certain status that automatically confers a property interest.

[52] In the United Kingdom, see the Insolvency Act 1986, s 127.

[53] The court can ratify transfers in these circumstances, and often will if they were made for value.

[54] ie broadly, the company either received no consideration or insufficient consideration in return for the value which it provided: Insolvency Act 1986, s 238. The hardening period for this section is six months, or two years if (broadly) the transferor and transferee are connected: s 240.

[55] ie broadly, the company was influenced when entering into the transaction by a desire to improve the position of the collateral taker in its insolvency: s 239. As with s 238, the hardening

3.47 As a general rule, transferees of interests in securities may ensure that the transfers will not be challenged as transactions at an undervalue or preferences if the assets are transferred pursuant to bargains entered into at market value and in good faith at arm's length commercial terms.[56] However, it is harder to ensure that a transfer will not be avoided under section 127 of the Insolvency Act 1986.

3.48 The risk of insolvency displacement is particularly problematic in settlement systems, where one delivery often is interdependent on another, and the disruption of delivery may introduce systemic risk, as discussed in Chapter 9. For this reason, special statutory regimes have been introduced to protect settlement systems from the rules of insolvency displacement.[57]

(2) Issuer's Claims

3.49 The transferee of securities may face adverse claims from the issuer of the securities. This is best illustrated by example. If A is the issuer of securities and B is a holder, and if B owes money to A, A may wish to offset the debt of B against its obligation to pay B under the securities.[58] If B then transfers its securities to C, C will be concerned to ensure that A is not able to offset the debt of B against its obligation to pay C under the securities. It will be assumed for the purposes of this discussion that the securities are fully paid.

3.50 In the case of traditional bearer debt securities, negotiable status protects transferees from issuer's claims.[59] More generally the doctrine of estoppel is taken to protect the transferees of both bearer and registered securities. This operates as follows. In the case of bearer securities, the issuer's promise to pay the bearer appears on the face of the instrument. This promise estops the issuer from claiming that it is not obliged to pay the bearer because of debts owed to it by a predecessor in title.[60] With registered securities, entry of the name of the transferee in

---

period for s 239 is six months, or two years if (broadly) the transferor and transferee are connected: s 240. Also, floating charges are invalidated in certain circumstances, where they are given in respect of a pre-existing debt; see s 245.

[56] Where the transfer is by way of a security interest, it should be in relation to new debt, ie not securing existing unsecured debt, because of the provisions avoiding certain floating charges.

[57] Where interests in securities are delivered within settlement systems, the Settlement Finality Directive (98/26/EC) is designed to provide protection in certain circumstances from such insolvency displacement. In the United Kingdom, anti-displacement measures are also provided for key markets and settlement systems under Part VII of the Companies Act 1989. Both of these pieces of legislation are discussed in Chapter 9.

[58] Issuer's claims are unlikely to be a problem in practice. Even as between A and B, it is unlikely that A would have a defence to B's claim, unless the claims were connected. A would have a counterclaim, not a set off, which would not prevent B from obtaining summary judgment (although if A also obtained summary judgment at the same time, there might be a legal set off), though B would face an argument for stay of execution. The author is grateful to Simon James of Clifford Chance for this point.

[59] See for example *Re Agra and Masterman's Bank* (1867) LR 2 Ch at 397.

[60] See the discussion in Ewart (n 33 above).

the register and the issue of a certificate is generally taken to estop the issuer from setting up equities against the holder. Thus issuer's claims do not present a problem in practice for transferees.

(3) Third Party Claims

Third party claims present more of a problem in practice. Third party claims may **3.51** arise where the transferred assets belong beneficially to the clients of the transferor, but the transferor transferred the assets without her clients' authority. The clients as beneficial owners may seek to claim the transferred assets in the hands of the transferee.[61]

Security of title and security of transfer

Some might argue that the fundamental principles of English commercial law are **3.52** clear and readily understood. However, they regularly conflict with each other. The principle of security of transfer provides that a transfer of assets to a good faith purchaser should not be reversed. The principle of security of title provides that fraud should not be effective to deprive a person of her assets. The question of third party claims brings these two principles into direct collision.

A central function of commercial law is to deal with the competing claims that **3.53** arise as a consequence of fraud and insolvency. Of course, fraud and insolvency often go together.[62] The following factual scenario recurs in case law. A entrusts her securities to B, retaining property rights in them. B fraudulently sells A's securities to C or delivers them to C as collateral. C acquires the securities for value and in good faith, without notice of B's breach of duty. A discovers the fraud, and sues C for the return of the securities. By this time B has absconded or become insolvent. The court therefore hears a dispute between A[63] and C.[64]

There is no easy way to resolve this perennial dispute between the defrauded true **3.54** owner and the bona fide purchaser. Assuming both A and C have acted in good faith and without negligence, each is innocent, but one has to lose, and so the law has to select a victim. The doctrine of security of title favours A, and the doctrine

---

[61] Third party adverse claims (which are based on breach of pre-existing fiduciary duty) should be distinguished from questions of priority which arise where there has been double dealing (for example where the same asset is subject to two competing security interests). The rules of priority are discussed in Chapter 5. The rules for dealing with third party claims are similar but slightly different. For example, the rule in *Dearle v Hall* forms part of the rules of priority, but does not apply to adverse claims (perhaps because of the policy considerations associated with breach of fiduciary). See the discussion of Millett J in the first instance decision of *Macmillan v Bishopsgate (No 3)* [1995] Ch 747, at 756, 757.

[62] Fraud often only comes to light on the insolvency of the fraudster, and may arise in an attempt to stave off insolvency.

[63] Who says to C, 'Those are my securities and I want them back'.

[64] Who says, 'I didn't know they were yours and I gave good money for them'.

of security of transfer favours B. The different branches of English law deal with this problem in different ways.

Common law

3.55 The rule of common law is *nemo dat quod non habet*, or no-one can give that which she does not have. C cannot win, because the assets were not B's to give. The common law evolved certain limited exceptions to this rule, including the rule in favour of market overt, now abolished.[65] Clearly, this approach favours security of title over security of transfer, and is unhelpful in a market economy.

3.56 The common law rule applies unless either the rule of the law merchant or the rule of equity, discussed below, displaces it.[66]

Law merchant

3.57 A fundamentally different approach is taken by the law merchant. Unsurprisingly, this approach reflects market values, and favours security of transfer over security of title. It was seen above that a negotiable instrument is transferable without formalities by delivery (or in some cases by endorsement and delivery). The second great advantage of negotiable status is that honest acquisition confers good title.[67] The holder in due course of a negotiable instrument can (unknowingly) acquire good title from a thief.[68] A holder in due course is defined in the Bills of Exchange Act 1882[69] and includes a pledgee as well as a purchaser.[70] While a holder in due course is under no general duty to investigate title,[71] she has a duty to investigate any sus-

---

[65] Sale of Goods Act 1979, s 22(1) provided 'Where goods are sold in market overt, according to the usage of the market, the buyer acquires a good title to the goods, provided he buys them in good faith and without notice of any defect or want of title on the part of the seller'. The ancient rule applied to sales from shops in the City of London and, outside the City of London, to sales from any open, public and legally constituted market, including fairs. It did not apply to Scotland or in Wales, or to ships, or to goods belonging to the Crown. The rule was highly technical in its application and replete with artificiality. It was abolished by the Sale of Goods (Amendment) Act 1994, which came into force on 3 January 1995, and applies to any contract for the sale of goods made after that date. See *Benjamin's Sale of Goods* (5th edn, London: Sweet & Maxwell, 1997).

[66] In practice, the common law rule will apply, where A (and not B) had legal title prior to the fraud, and where the disputed assets are not negotiable instruments. This would be the case, for example, where A was a sponsored member of CREST, and B was her sponsor; see Chapter 9.

[67] The second advantage is more often emphasised today, as the first advantage (ease of transfer) has become less significant with the creation of a statutory regime for the assignment of choses in action.

[68] See the Bills of Exchange Act 1882, s 38. However, even the holder in due course may be affected by a forgery.

[69] 'A holder in due course is a holder who has taken a bill, complete and regular on the face of it, under the following conditions; namely, (a) that he became the holder of it before it was overdue, and without notice that it had been previously dishonoured, if such was the fact: (b) that he took the bill in good faith and for value, and that at the time the bill was negotiated to him he had no notice of any defect in the title of the person who negotiated it': s 29(1).

[70] *London Joint Stock Bank v Simmons* [1892] AC 201.

[71] See *London Joint Stock Bank Ltd v Simmons* [1892] AC 201.

picious circumstances.[72] This now accords with the rule in equity, as discussed below. The holder in due course must have given value, but value is presumed.[73]

Thus, where the disputed assets comprise negotiable instruments, the rule of the law merchant will displace the common law rule. **3.58**

Equity

If the common law favours security of title and the law merchant security of trans- **3.59** fer, the rules of equity represent a compromise between these two extremes. The rules of equity whereby a defrauded beneficial owner may claim trust assets in the hands of a third party were discussed in Chapter 2. As discussed in that chapter, a number of defences to such claims are available, the most important of which is that in favour of equity's darling. Equity's darling is a bona fide purchaser of the legal estate for value, without notice.

The rules of equity apply where the plaintiff is suing in equity, ie if, prior to the **3.60** fraud, her interest in the disputed assets was beneficial and not legal.

(4) Interests in Securities and Security of Transfer

This section will consider how the rules discussed above apply to transfers of inter- **3.61** ests in securities. To recap, the common law rule will apply to a dispute about security of transfer, unless it is displaced by either the rule of the law merchant or that of equity. The common law rule will be displaced by the rule of the law merchant if the disputed asset is a negotiable instrument. It will be displaced by the rule of equity if the plaintiff is suing in equity; the plaintiff will sue in equity if the asset of which she has been deprived is an equitable interest. This will be the case where the fraudulent transferor was a custodian who held her assets under a custody trust.

Loss of negotiability

Negotiation involves the transfer of possession of an instrument. As discussed in **3.62** Chapter 2, possession involves the physical control of a tangible asset. As intangibles, interests in securities cannot be possessed and therefore cannot be negotiated. Furthermore, the traditional understanding of the term 'instrument' is of a formal paper document.[74] Moreover the law relating to negotiable instruments

---

[72] *Jones v Gordon* (1877) 2 App Cas 616.

[73] Bills of Exchange Act 1882, s 27(2).

[74] The Bills of Exchange Act 1882 defines both bills of exchange (in s 3(1)) and promissory notes (in s 83(1)) as being 'in writing', and provides that ' "writing" includes print' (in s 2). *Byles on Bills of Exchange* (26th edn, London: Sweet & Maxwell, 1997) provides (at 2988) that 'Bills of exchange, and promissory notes are usually, but it would seem not necessarily, written on paper. It is conceivable that they might be written on parchment, linen, cloth, leather or any other convenient substitute for paper, not being a metallic substance'. The Interpretation Act 1978 provides (in s 5 and Sch 1) that statutory references to 'writing' are presumed to include printing, lithography and photography. Unsurprisingly, because the traditional understanding of the term 'instrument' pre-dates the electronic era, this traditional understanding does not extend to electronic records.

presumes that a negotiable instrument will take the form of a physical document, which can be delivered, signed on its face and endorsed.[75]

3.63 On this basis, an interest in securities cannot be a negotiable instrument,[76] and the rule in favour of holders in due course cannot apply to purchasers of interests in securities.[77] Therefore the common law rule will apply, unless it is displaced by the rules of equity.

Loss of the defence of equity's darling

3.64 As indicated able, the rules of equity apply where the defrauded true owner sues in equity. On the basis that intermediary custodians hold their clients' assets as trustee, such clients will sue in equity when they are defrauded. It was seen above that the most important defence to an action in equity (that of equity's darling) involves the acquisition of a legal interest. Interests in securities are by definition the interest of a client holding assets through an intermediary. Where English law governs the relationship with the intermediary, that relationship is likely to constitute a trust. On this basis, interests in securities are equitable and not legal. Thus if the assets acquired by transferee are interests in securities, the defence of equity's darling will not be available.

Conclusions

3.65 The author has argued that, under the general law, the transition from securities to interests in securities has reduced security of transfer in the secondary markets. While the correct balance between security of transfer and security of title is a question of policy, there may be a case for statutory provision to reverse some of the losses to security of transfer that have been brought about by the computerisation of the securities markets.

---

[75] See the many references to delivery, signing and endorsement in the Bills of Exchange Act 1882.

[76] This approach is taken in *The Future of Money Market Instruments* (Bank of England, November 1999), in Appendix II. That excellent discussion was drafted by Guy Morton of Freshfields. For further detail supporting this argument, see Benjamin, *The Law of Global Custody* (London: Butterworths, 1996) ch 3.

In *Banking Services: Law and Practice Report by the Review Committee* (Cm 622, 1989) (the Jack Report), statutory provision conferring negotiable status on (broadly) interests in securities was called for: '[A] new Act should contain provisions giving to transactions taking place in a screen based or book entry depositary (or dematerialised) system operated by an Approved Depositary and satisfying certain basic statutory requirements the same status as equivalent transactions in negotiable instruments generally' (para 8(9), 74). However, a different approach was taken in relation to money market instruments in CREST, as discussed in Chapter 9. More generally, consultation among bankers and practitioners conducted by the author and Hugh Pigott of the Centre for Law Reform on behalf of the Law Commission in 1999 and 2000 indicated that there was little appetite in London for a new Bills of Exchange Act.

[77] Because traditional bearer securities are negotiable instruments, this represents a significant legal consequence of the computerisation of the securities markets.

4

SECURITIES COLLATERAL

It is far better to be possessor than to be plaintiff*

This chapter will provide an introduction to the use of (interests in) securities as **4.01** collateral.

A. Overview

The purpose of collateral is to protect the collateral taker against the risk that its **4.02** counterparty (the collateral provider)[1] will become insolvent.

Most financial assets consist of personal obligations such as debts. A personal **4.03** obligation is generally enforceable only by suing the obligor. When an obligor becomes insolvent, debts and other personal obligations are generally unenforceable against it. The obligee must prove its claim as an unsecured creditor in the liquidation of the obligor, will experience delay in payment and (depending on

---

 * *Justinian's Institutes* (Birks and McLeod (trans), London: Duckworth, 1987) 143, J4.15.4.
 [1] While it is possible for the person whose obligation is being secured, and the collateral provider, to be two different people, this is not common.

the outcome of the liquidation) may receive only a fraction of the sum owed, or even nothing at all. The risk for the obligee that its claims will be affected in this way by the insolvency of the obligor is called credit risk.

4.04 Collateralisation is the technique for addressing credit risk by supporting a personal obligation (which may be defeated by insolvency) with a right of recourse against identified assets (which should not).[2]

4.05 The normal practice is for the collateral taker to require that the value of the collateral assets exceed the value of the collateralised exposure by a margin.[3] Increasingly, financial institutions seek to manage their collateral arrangements in respect of all transaction types on a centralised basis, in order to make the most efficient use of available collateral assets, and also better to manage risk.[4]

(1) Importance of Collateral

4.06 Collateral is becoming increasingly important in the international financial markets. As indicated above, the use of collateral reduces credit risk. Collateral therefore enables financial institutions to undertake more business, and in particular more business with counterparties whose credit risk is poor,[5] than would be possible on an uncollateralised basis within the terms of the institution's credit policy. Collateral also has an important function in reducing the burden of regulatory capital. In order to address liquidity and credit risks, regulated entities such as banks and brokers are required by their regulators to maintain minimum levels of capital. These regulatory capital requirements are calculated by reference to the risks assumed by the entity from time to time. One element of the calculation of regulatory capital is known as counterparty risk requirement (CRR). CRR is calculated by reference to a regulated firm's credit exposures to counterparties. CRR is very significantly reduced if credit exposures are collateralised. Collateralisation therefore means that a regulated firm is able to undertake more business with its available capital, and therefore generate more profits.

---

[2] *The New Oxford Dictionary of English* (Oxford: Clarendon Press, 1998) shows the derivation of the term from medieval Latin '*collateralis*' ('*col*' ('together with') and '*lateralis*' ('side')).

[3] 'In practice, it is necessary to strike a balance between protection against large, rapid valuation changes and the commercial realities that limit the amount of collateral that counterparties are willing or able to post': *ISDA 1999 Collateral Review* (ISDA, 1999) 29.

[4] 'Over time, most collateral practitioners have centralized collateral management for an array of products. This is done mainly for reasons of operational efficiency, but is also a key factor in risk management control. It minimizes the possibility, in volatile markets, of swap collateral (for example) being returned to a counterparty while a different part of the institution waits for repo collateral to be delivered. Indeed, an important lesson from the market crises of 1998 was that a centralized collateral management area can become a key provider of information and risk to business managers, and can act as a vital point of control around payments to distressed counterparties': *ISDA 1999 Collateral Review* 11.

[5] ie counterparties for whom the risk becoming insolvent is significant.

(2) (Interests in) Securities as Collateral

In the international financial markets, the most sought-after form of collateral **4.07** asset is cash (and in particular US dollars). After that, (interests in) securities (and in particular US treasuries) comprise the most acceptable form of collateral. (Interests in) securities are highly liquid,[6] and are easily valued. They are used to collateralise vast financial exposures under bank loan, custody, settlement, swaps, repo and securities lending arrangements. In addition to these private commercial arrangements, central banks use securities collateral in their money market operations, as indicated in Chapter 1.

A number of factors have increased the demand for securities collateral in recent **4.08** years. These include a new concern to manage credit exposures following the market turbulence of 1998, and the need to achieve new regulatory capital efficiencies in an increasingly competitive market. The result of this increased demand is that high quality securities collateral has become a relatively scarce commodity. Collateral takers are not always able to insist on (interests in) US treasuries, other forms of collateral are becoming more widely accepted, including (interests in) treasuries issued from any OECD state, corporate debt securities and even equities.[7] Demand often exceeds supply,[8] and the markets are increasingly intolerant of delays in the securities' delivery.

(3) Settlement Systems

In practice, the vast majority by value of securities collateral is held and delivered **4.09** through national and international settlement systems. Therefore the practicalities of creating, perfecting and enforcing collateral arrangements should be considered in the light of the operation of such systems. A discussion of international and UK settlement is given in Chapter 9.

(4) Legal Risk and Reform

In recent years, significant attention has been focused on the legal issues involved **4.10** in taking cross border securities collateral.[9] By 'cross border securities collateral' is meant collateral which consists of interests in securities which are issued from a jurisdiction or jurisdictions other than that of the collateral taker. A number of settlement systems, investment banks and other market participants have

---

[6] In contrast to interests in land, for example, interests in securities can be readily sold in the secondary markets and thus converted into cash.

[7] Generally, equities are less acceptable because of their price volatility.

[8] For example, after the market disturbance in the second half of 1998, the market experienced a 'flight to quality' as major sums were invested in treasuries. Anecdotally, liquidity in treasuries dried up almost entirely.

[9] This is in part due to adverse market conditions in the late 1990s: 'extreme market stresses experienced in late 1997 through 1998 focused attention on credit risk, and, therefore, on collateral': *ISDA 1999 Collateral Review* (n 3 above) 13.

undertaken extensive legal studies of cross border securities collateral arrangements. Where legal risks have been identified, there has been a call for law reform. Both a Report of the Giovannini Group[10] and a recent ISDA project[11] have identified areas where reform is needed within Europe, and a new European Directive on the cross border use of collateral is proposed.[12]

B. Two Categories

4.11   Collateral arrangements are divided into two broad legal categories. These are security interests[13] and outright collateral transfers. The difference between them is best illustrated by example. If B wishes to borrow money from A, and A requires B to provide collateral for this debt, the collateral arrangement may be structured either as a security interest or alternatively as an outright collateral transfer.

(1) Security Interests

4.12   In the case of a security interest, A will acquire a limited interest (its security interest) in the collateral assets. Upon B's default, A will be able to enforce its security interest by selling the assets and applying the proceeds of sale to discharge the

---

[10] Report of the Giovannini Group, *EU Repo Markets: Opportunities for Change* (Brussels, October 1999). 'Action is also needed in the form of legislative reforms. As a first step, a full and detailed survey of current legislation and market rules on "netting" in each Member State should be undertaken. Reforms would enable repo activity to be undertaken across the EU on the basis of sound and effective credit risk management practices': at 6.

[11] In 1999, the ISDA Collateral Law Reform Committee conducted a cross border survey in a large number of European jurisdictions to identify legal challenges to cross border securities collateral within Europe. See the ISDA website at www.isda.org.

[12] In its Financial Markets Action Plan of May 1999 (Commission Communication of 11 May 1999, *Financial Services: Implementing the Framework for Financial Markets: Action Plan* (COM (1999) 232)) the European Commission stated that 'Work on the implementation of the Settlement and Finality Directive shows the importance of common rules for collateral pledged to payment and securities settlement systems. Priority should be given to further progress in the field of collateral beyond this field. The mutual acceptance and enforceability of cross-border collateral is indispensable for the stability of the EU financial system and for a cost-effective and integrated securities settlement structure. At present, these conditions are not fulfilled: there is a higher risk of invalidation of cross-border collateral arrangements and uncertainty as regards enforceability should the collateral provider become insolvent. If such difficulties are not resolved, cross-border securities transactions will be subject to higher costs and risks' (at 8). The document sets out an action plan for financial services, in which a directive on the cross border use of collateral is identified as a 'priority 1 action' and therefore as 'crucial to the realization of the full benefits of the euro and to ensuring the competitiveness of the Union's financial services sector'. The objective of the proposed directive is 'Legal certainty as regards validity and enforceability of collateral provided to back cross-border securities transactions'. An optimal timeframe is indicated in which consultations begin in autumn 1999, a proposal is made at the end of 2000 and adopted in 2003.

[13] Security interests should not be confused with interests in securities. Security interests are a class of collateral arrangement comprising mortgages, charges, pledges and liens. Interests in securities has been defined as the asset of a client for whom an intermediary holds (interests in) securities on an unallocated basis, together with the interests in securities of other clients; see Chapter 1.

secured debt.[14] Because A has a security interest in the collateral assets, the liquidator of B is not able to make those assets available to general creditors. In other words, the security interest enables A as secured creditor to take the collateral assets out of the liquidation of B.[15] However, until such default and enforcement, A is not free to dispose of the assets, and B retains the right to have them redelivered to it upon repayment of the debt. This right of B is called 'the equity of redemption'.

(2) *Outright Collateral Transfers*

In contrast, under an outright collateral transfer, the collateral assets belong **4.13** entirely to A from the moment of delivery, so that A is free to sell them or deal with them as it wishes, whether or not B has defaulted. When B repays the loan, A is obliged to deliver to B assets which are *equivalent* to the assets originally delivered to A. For example, if B originally delivered 50 XYZ shares to A, A is required to deliver 50 XYZ shares to B, although not necessarily the same ones that were originally delivered to it. If B defaults, A's protection lies in insolvency set off. The collateral agreement will provide that upon the default of either party, the obligation of A to deliver equivalent collateral to B, will be set off against the obligation of B to repay A (or otherwise to discharge the collateralised obligation). It is important for A to ensure that the insolvency regime affecting B permits such set off, as discussed in more detail in Chapter 6. The liquidator of B is not permitted to claim the collateral assets for the general creditors of B, because B has no interest in them.

(3) *The Alternatives*

As indicated above, with a security interest, the collateral taker acquires an inter- **4.14** est in the collateral assets, which is less than outright ownership. The collateral taker holds the collateral assets subject to a residual interest of the collateral giver, which is the right to the return of the same assets upon discharge of the secured obligation, or the equity of redemption. In contrast, with outright collateral transfers, the assets are delivered outright, and the collateral giver retains no residual interest in them. (Its right to receive equivalent collateral is contractual only, and does not amount to an interest in the collateral.)

Outright collateral transfers have a long history in English law.[16] In spite of this, **4.15** greater use has traditionally been made of security interests to collateralise

---

[14] And meet the reasonable costs of enforcement. An alternative method of enforcing a security interest, other than exercising a power of sale, is foreclosure. Here, the collateral taker appropriates the collateral asset. However, this is not customary in relation to securities collateral.

[15] 'Creditors who are fully secured are largely unaffected by the liquidation process. They can remove their security from the pool and realize it to satisfy what is due to them, accounting to the liquidator for any surplus': R M Goode, *Principles of Corporate Insolvency Law* (2nd edn, London: Sweet & Maxwell, 1997) 167.

[16] See the many nineteenth century cases discussed in Chapter 7 in the context of recharacterisation risk.

exposures in the financial markets. More recently, however, attention has focused on certain disadvantages that are associated with security interests. As discussed below, the collateral taker under a security interest cannot deal freely with the collateral assets. Moreover, certain security interests must be registered under Companies Act registration requirements, and under the rules of conflict of laws, a security interest requires to be perfected under the law of the jurisdiction where the charged assets are located, or lex situs. The last requirement in particular has been a perceived source of legal uncertainty in relation to interests in securities held in cross border settlement systems. This is because opinion has differed as to the true situs of such assets.[17] Also, certain security interests (such as floating charges) may require judicial action for enforcement. For these reasons, the last ten years or so have seen a major shift from security interests to outright collateral transfers in international finance.

4.16 More recently, however, it has become evident that certain disadvantages are also potentially associated with outright collateral transfers. First, such transfers rely on insolvency set off, which is not available in some jurisdictions. Also, in some cases, the risk may arise that an outright collateral transfer may be recharacterised by the courts as a security interest; this is known as recharacterisation risk.[18] A further discussion of the pros and cons of outright collateral transfers is given in Chapter 6.

4.17 This chapter gives a brief overview of these two collateral structures. A detailed discussion of security interests will follow in Chapter 5, and of outright collateral transfers in Chapter 6.

C. Steps in Taking Collateral

4.18 A number of steps are involved in taking collateral. These fall into two broad categories. The first category comprises the steps necessary to form a valid, binding and enforceable collateral agreement. The second category comprises the steps necessary for the collateral taker to acquire and, if necessary, successfully enforce, a property interest in the collateral assets. It is customary for the collateral taker to obtain the opinion of independent local counsel covering many of the steps indicated below. A discussion of these steps under the conflict of laws is given in Chapter 7.

---

[17] Within Europe, such uncertainty is addressed in some circumstances by the implementation of the Settlement Finality Directive (98/26/EC). See Chapter 7 for a full discussion.

[18] See Chapter 6 for a full discussion.

(1) Formation of Collateral Contract

As a precondition of acquiring any interest *in the collateral assets*, the collateral **4.19** taker must establish that it has acquired appropriate rights *against the collateral giver* under the collateral contract. This involves a number of steps as follows.

Material validity

It must be established that the collateral agreement is materially (or essentially) **4.20** valid. This means that there is nothing in its essential nature that would invalidate it, such as being contrary to public policy, or want of consideration. English law requires the giving of consideration (or value) by both parties in order for agreements to be enforceable as contracts. However, if the collateral agreement is executed as a deed, it does not need to be enforceable as a contract.

Formal validity

It must also be established that the collateral agreement is formally valid, ie that it **4.21** complies with any applicable formal requirements, such as being in writing, signed or notarised. In general, English law imposes few formal requirements, although certain types of agreement are currently required to be in writing.[19] However, it is hoped that many of these requirements will be disapplied in the near future under section 8 of the Electronic Communications Act 2000.

Power

In most cases the collateral giver will not be an individual acting on her own **4.22** account, but rather a local authority, an insurance company, a pension fund acting through its trustee or some other type of institution. The power of such an institution to act is limited by its constitution and/or by applicable law. It is therefore important to establish that the collateral giver has power (or vires) to enter into the collateral agreement. The consequences of the collateral giver acting beyond its powers (or ultra vires) varies from case to case. In the case of a statutory corporation such as a local authority, an ultra vires contract is void.[20] In the case of an ordinary English limited company, broadly speaking, third parties dealing in good faith with the directors of a company are able to enforce an ultra vires contract.[21] Where a trustee contracts in breach of trust, the counterparty may be able

---

[19] See, for example, the Statute of Frauds Act 1677, s 4 (guarantees), the Law of Property Act 1925, s 136 (legal assignments of choses in action) and the Law of Property Act 1925, s 53(1)(c) (dispositions of equitable interests).

[20] See *Hazell v Hammersmith and Fulham Council* [1992] 2 AC 1.

[21] Under the Companies Act 1985, s 35.

to enforce the contract against the trustee personally, but its interest may not be enforceable against the trust assets.[22]

Authority

4.23 A company is not a natural person and can only act through its members of staff.[23] Where the collateral giver is a company, it must be established that the individual executing the agreement on behalf of the company has authority to bind it. This is in addition to establishing that the company has power to enter into the contract.

Authorisations

4.24 It must be established that the collateral giver has obtained and complied with the terms of any regulatory authorisations which are necessary to enter into the collateral agreement and perform its obligations under it. Also, it must be established that the collateral arrangements are within the scope of any local law restrictions affecting the business of the collateral giver.

Due execution

4.25 The collateral giver must establish that the collateral taker has taken all necessary steps to enter into, execute and deliver the collateral agreement.

(2) Interest in the Collateral Assets

4.26 The second stage is for the collateral taker to ensure that it acquires an interest in the collateral assets which it is able, if necessary, successfully to enforce. This also involves a number of different steps.

Attachment[24]

4.27 The process whereby the collateral taker acquires an interest in the collateral assets is generally called attachment. No particular formalities are required for attachment under English law, provided the collateralised obligation is a current obligation and the collateral assets are present (ie not future) assets and identified. As indicated above, English law recognises floating charges (which do not attach to particular assets), but many jurisdictions do not.

---

[22] In general, a trustee has a right of reimbursement out of the trust fund for all expenses properly incurred: see D J Hayton, *Underhill and Hayton, Law Relating to Trusts and Trustees* (15th edn, London: Butterworths, 1995) 787, 788. In the insolvency of the trustee, third party creditors generally have a right of subrogation to this indemnity. However, this right of subrogation is generally only available where the indemnity would have been available, and does not generally arise in respect of expenses incurred in breach of trust.

[23] See *Gower's Principles of Modern Company Law* (6th edn, London: Sweet & Maxwell, 1997) 178.

[24] Professor Sir Roy Goode identified this as a separate step under English law.

Perfection[25]

In order for the interest of the collateral taker to be enforceable against third par- **4.28** ties, it is generally necessary to perfect it. The requirements for perfecting a security interest differ from jurisdiction to jurisdiction. Perfection generally involves some act of publicity, whereby notice of the interest of the collateral taker is given to the world at large. In legal theory, because a security interest binds third parties, it should not arise in circumstances where it is not apparent to third parties.[26]

Under English law, few formalities are required for perfection. Any physical **4.29** bearer instrument should be taken into possession.[27] If the collateral taker is imprudent enough to leave the instruments in the hands of the collateral giver, it should ensure that they are clearly segregated from the collateral giver's own unencumbered assets. Where interests in securities are held through an intermediary, the intermediary should be notified of the security interest.[28]

Other jurisdictions impose more formal requirements, involving notarisation, the **4.30** service of notice, registrations and/or special wording in the collateral agreement. Where security interests are taken over interests in securities held through a settlement system, the rules of that system and/or local law may require special account entries to be made.[29]

Registration

Many jurisdictions impose registration requirements in relation to security inter- **4.31** ests. The English law registration requirements under section 395 of the Companies Act 1985 are discussed in Chapter 5.

Strictly, registration is not a perfection requirement, but a special statutory **4.32** requirement. The consequences of failure to register are slightly different to those of failure to perfect,[30] and the conflict of laws aspects of the two steps differ.[31]

---

[25] The meaning of the word 'perfection' in this technical sense is narrower than its general meaning; it means making enforceable against third parties, and not making perfect. Students are sometimes disappointed to learn that a perfected security interest may still be defective from the point of view of the collateral taker, for example because it is weaker in priority than another competing perfected security interest.

[26] See P Wood, *Comparative Law of Security and Guarantees* (London: Sweet & Maxwell, 1995) 4, 5.

[27] Possession for this purpose may be actual or constructive; see Chapter 2.

[28] Such notification also fixes the priority of the security interest, under the rule in *Dearle v Hall*; see n 36 below.

[29] eg it may be a requirement that the collateral is credited to the general account or collateral account of the collateral taker. Some systems permit the collateral to be credited to the collateral account of the collateral giver, although this may involve enforcement problems. See the discussion of escrow balances in CREST in Chapter 9.

[30] Unlike failure to perfect, failure to register renders the secured debt immediately due and payable.

[31] As discussed in Chapter 7, perfection is determined by lex situs, whereas registration is determined by the location of the collateral giver.

Priorities

4.33 Priorities are relevant where the same collateral assets are subject to more than one perfected interest, for example where the collateral giver has granted successive security interests (double dealing). Where there are such competing perfected security interests, the rules of priority determine the order in which the different security interests will be satisfied out of the collateral assets. (If the assets are insufficient to meet all the interests in full, the order of priority is crucial.) Naturally, the collateral taker wishes to establish that, in the event of competing interests, its interest will have the highest priority.

4.34 The English rules of priorities are complex and the following is a rough guide. The general rule is that interests rank in the order of creation, so that the first in time prevails. This is subject as follows. Any equitable interest[32] is overridden by a subsequent legal interest acquired in good faith without notice of that prior equitable interest.[33] A floating charge is in general[34] overridden by a subsequent fixed charge.[35] However, a floating charge may have priority if it prohibited the creation of subsequent fixed charges and the fixed chargee had actual notice of this.

4.35 Where the collateral consists of intangible assets, the above general rules are modified by the rule in *Dearle v Hall*.[36] This provides that where there are successive assignments (or, by extension, other dealings in) a debt (or, by extension, other choses in action) priority is determined by the order in which notice is given to the debtor (or, by extension, other obligor). Where security interests are given over interests in securities, the rule in *Dearle v Hall* is interpreted in practice to require notice to be given to the intermediary in whose account the interest of the collateral giver is recorded.[37]

---

[32] A charge over personal property is always equitable; see Chapter 5.

[33] 'In English law the order of priority between two competing interests in the same property depends primarily on whether they are legal or merely equitable interests. Where both interests are equitable—or both legal, for that matter—the basic rule is that the two interests rank in the order of their creation. In the case of equitable interests the order of priority may be reversed in special circumstances, but "where the equities are equal, the first in time prevails" . . . Where, however, the first is equitable and the second is legal the position is different. A bona fide purchase for value who obtains the legal estate at the time of his purchase without notice, actual or constructive, of a prior equitable right is entitled to priority in equity as well as at law: see *Pilcher v Rawlins* (1972) LR 7 Ch App 259": *Macmillan v Bishopsgate (No 3)* [1995] 3 All ER 747, per Millett J at 768.

[34] As discussed in Chapter 5, the subsequent fixed charge will not take priority if it had notice of a negative pledge in the prior floating charge at the time the fixed charge was created.

[35] See Chapter 5 for a discussion of fixed and floating charges.

[36] (1828) 3 Russ 1; [1824–34] All ER Rep 28.

[37] This is assuming that the collateral assets remains in an account maintained by such intermediary. If the assets are delivered out of the hands of the intermediary, to the collateral taker or its custodian, no such notice would be required.

Beneficial ownership

Many collateral givers are institutions that offer a custody service to clients. It is **4.36** important for the collateral taker to ascertain whether the collateral giver beneficially owns the collateral assets. However, it is normal in some contexts for intermediaries to deliver their clients' assets as collateral for their own exposures, for example in prime brokerage[38] and on exchange derivatives collateral[39] arrangements. If the collateral giver does not beneficially own the collateral assets, it is crucial it has the authority of the beneficial owners to enter into the collateral agreement. This issue is normally addressed by requiring the collateral giver to provide a standard representation and warranty in the collateral agreement.[40]

Of course, the collateral taker cannot exclude the risk that the collateral giver will **4.37** wrongly use its client's assets as collateral for its own exposures, without authority from its clients, in breach of representation and warranty. It is therefore important for the collateral taker to establish that, in the event that it faces an adverse claim from defrauded clients for the return of the collateral assets, it would be able successfully to defend it.

As discussed in Chapter 3, in defending such an adverse claim, it is crucial for the **4.38** collateral taker to show that it did not have notice (actual, imputed or constructive) of the breach of duty to clients by the collateral giver. In order to show that it did not have constructive notice, it is important to investigate any suspicious circumstances when the collateral is taken or thereafter as long as the collateral is retained. See Chapter 3 for a fuller discussion.

Enforcement

If and when a collateral giver defaults, it is important for the collateral taker to be **4.39** able to enforce its interest in the collateral securities immediately. Any delay in enforcement may expose the collateral taker to market risk; if the value of the collateral falls after default, the collateral giver may be unlikely to comply with margin calls.[41] In a turbulent market, enforcement delay may expose the collateral taker to significant losses. The ideal position for the collateral taker is to be able to enforce its interest immediately or by selling the collateral at the best market price on simple notice to the collateral giver. Care should be taken to establish that applicable law and/or the rules of the settlement system in which the collateral is held do not impose any delays or formalities, such as giving a period of notice to

---

[38] See Chapter 10.
[39] See Chapter 8.
[40] ie that it either is, or is authorised by, the beneficial owner of the collateral assets to enter into the arrangements.
[41] See Chapter 6 for a discussion of margin.

the collateral giver, a court order or a public auction. The conflict of laws aspects of enforcement are considered in Chapter 7.

4.40 Under English law, where collateral is taken under a security interest, the collateral taker is required to make demand for payment before enforcement, and to obtain the best price reasonably obtainable when exercising a power of sale. Other restrictions on statutory powers of enforcement under the Law of Property Act 1925 are usually disapplied in the collateral agreement.[42] Where the security interest is given by an English company, enforcement may be frozen if the company goes into administration, under section 11(3)(c) of the Insolvency Act 1986.

4.41 As a practical matter, the collateral taker is obviously in a better position when the collateral has been delivered to its general or collateral account (so that it can immediately enforce its interest). If the collateral has remained in the general or collateral account of the collateral giver, it must arrange for the collateral to be delivered into its account or to its order in order to enforce. Where the collateral is not delivered to the collateral taker, it is customary for the collateral taker to obtain a power of attorney from the collateral giver enabling it to procure the delivery to it of the collateral in the event of default. In the United Kingdom, problems have been associated with acting under such powers of attorney in relation to collateral held through CREST, as discussed in Chapter 9.

4.42 Where collateral is delivered under an outright collateral transfer, it is not necessary for the collateral taker to exercise a power of sale, because it is already the outright owner of the collateral. Its recourse in the event of the default of the collateral giver is to exercise a right of set off, as discussed in Chapter 6. Any contractual or operational restriction on its ability to apply set off may raise recharacterisation risk, as discussed in Chapter 6.

Remittance

4.43 It is also important to ensure that the proceeds of enforcement can be remitted to the collateral taker, and are not subject to exchange control.

Displacement

4.44 Even after enforcement, a collateral taker may face a challenge to its interest in the collateral. One possible risk is that of an action from defrauded beneficiaries, in circumstances where the collateral consisted of client assets delivered by the collateral giver in breach of its duties to clients, as discussed briefly above, and in greater detail in Chapter 3.

4.45 A further risk is insolvency displacement. Both security interests and outright collateral transfers protect the collateral taker by conferring an interest in the col-

---

[42] Restrictions are imposed by the Law of Property Act 1925, s 103.

lateral assets. This interest in turn provides the collateral taker with recourse in the insolvency of the collateral giver, which would not be available to unsecured creditors under the general principles of insolvency law. In this way, collateral cuts across the normal operation of these principles and for this reason, there are circumstances in which insolvency law may invalidate collateral arrangements. These circumstances are referred to in this discussion as 'insolvency displacement'.

4.46 Insolvency displacement reflects a principle informing insolvency law known as the 'pari passu principle'. The context of the pari passu principle is the ranking of creditors in insolvency.

4.47 The assets of an insolvent company may be insufficient to meet all the claims of its creditors.[43] Because not all creditors' claims will be met, it is important to identify the winners and losers. This is done by insolvency ranking, or determining the order in which such claims are to be met. The position of a creditor in that order, or its priority in insolvency, may determine whether it gets paid in full, in part or not at all.

4.48 The general rule is that the costs and expenses of the liquidation are met first.[44] After that, preferential debts[45] are paid, and thereafter the claims of other creditors are met and lastly, if there is anything else, members (ie shareholders) of the insolvent company have their capital returned to them.

4.49 The general rule is the all non-preferential creditors should rank equally. This means that they are all paid rateably in proportion to their admitted claims, so that the same proportion of each creditor's claims is met. This equal treatment of creditors is known as the pari passu principle, and generally reflects a deep policy commitment in insolvency law.[46]

4.50 There are a number of exceptions to the pari passu principle. One exception is made where a creditor has a valid security interest. Another exception is made where insolvency set off is available.[47] (As indicated above, outright collateral transfers rely on insolvency set off.) However, in order to protect the pari passu principle, these exceptions are narrowly defined. Moreover, collateral arrangements are required to

---

[43] They may be sufficient where the company became insolvent because of liquidity and not credit problems.

[44] See the Insolvency Act 1986, s 175(2)(a). If this were not so, it might be hard to get anyone to agree to act as liquidator.

[45] Preferential debts include monies owed to the Inland Revenue, to Customs and Excise, Social Security contributions, contributions to occupational pension schemes and employees' remuneration. See the Insolvency Act 1986, ss 175, 386, Sch 6.

[46] 'The most fundamental principle of insolvency law is that of pari passu distribution, all creditors participating in the common pool in proportion to the size of their admitted claims': Goode, (n 15 above) 141.

[47] As discussed below, insolvency set off is not available in all jurisdictions.

clear a number of additional legal hurdles if they are to be effective in rescuing collateral takers from the ranks of unsecured creditors. As will be seen below, in the case of security interests two such hurdles are statutory registration requirements, and perfection under lex situs. A third class of hurdle comprises the rules of insolvency displacement.

4.51 Clients and students are sometimes surprised at the number of legal tests that collateral arrangements are required to pass in order to be effective, and the readiness of the courts to reduce the collateral taker to the status of unsecured creditor. This may be explained by the deep influence of the pari passu principle.

4.52 The duty of the liquidator is to maximize the assets that are available to general creditors. In order to assist her (and in order also to enforce the pari passu principle), a number of provisions of insolvency law exist which may serve to undermine collateral arrangements. These insolvency displacement provisions differ from jurisdiction to jurisdiction. The provisions under UK insolvency law were briefly indicated in Chapter 3.

4.53 As discussed in more detail in Chapters 5 and 6, market standard documentation provides for the original collateral to be withdrawn and other assets substituted from time to time. Also, where the value of the collateral or the collateralised exposure varies over the life of the transaction, 'marking to market' provisions in market standard documentation provides for surplus collateral to be released, or new collateral delivered, so as to restore the original ratio between the value of the collateral and the collateralised exposure.

4.54 When collateral arrangements are entered into, it is customary for the collateral taker to obtain a legal opinion which addresses the impact of the collateral giver's insolvency on the collateral arrangements. It is important, however, to consider the impact of insolvency not just on the original collateral delivery, but also on subsequent deliveries of assets between the parties under substitution and marking to market provisions. In particular it is important to establish that these deliveries are not subject to challenge under insolvency displacement rules. Any such challenge would clearly undermine the effective management of credit risk.

4.55 Under English law, the position is generally favourable. In relation to the invalidation of preferences under section 239 of the Insolvency Act 1986, it is not clear how any desire to prefer[48] could be shown in the case of margining; excess collateral is released by the collateral taker in order to discharge a pre-existing contractual obligation. Although the collateral taker has no contractual obligation to consent to substitution, it is not clear how this could amount to a preference.[49] For the purposes of the invalidation of transactions at an undervalue under section

---

[48] See Insolvency Act 1986, s 239(5).
[49] See ibid s 239(4).

238, it is necessary to show that the company received either no consideration under a transaction, or significantly less consideration than it gave.[50] Clearly, where collateral securities are substituted the provision of new collateral amounts to adequate consideration for the withdrawal of old collateral having equal value. In relation to marking to market deliveries it should be arguable that adequate consideration is given by the extension of credit under the arrangements as a whole; the release of margin does not amount to a separate transaction. Thus it should be possible under English law to achieve a broad measure of comfort that the above heads of challenge should not be problematic in relation to substitution and margin deliveries. However, a greater problem is posed by the avoidance of post-petition dispositions under section 127 of the Insolvency Act 1986, and rule 4.90(3) of the Insolvency Rules 1986 (which may take deliveries of margin outside the scope of insolvency set off).[51]

ISDA 1999 Collateral Review, referred to above, identified a number of problems **4.56** in relation to substitution, margining and insolvency displacement in certain European jurisdictions.

D. Collateral and Electronic Settlement

Chapter 7 considers the lex situs rule in the context of interests in securities, and **4.57** argues that the use of cross border electronic settlement systems has important implications for the rules of conflict of laws applicable to perfecting security interests. This section will briefly consider a number of other respects in which the use of electronic settlement systems affects the legal analysis of securities collateral.

(1) Computerisation and the Unavailability of Pledge

As briefly indicated in Chapter 2, the use of pledging language in security docu- **4.58** mentation raises special concerns in the context of electronic settlement. In a pre-electronic environment, security interests over securities often took the form of pledges. As discussed in Chapter 5, pledges are attractive to the collateral taker, because they are not registrable and also because they take effect at law and therefore have priority over prior equitable security interests of which the pledgee has no notice at the time the pledge is taken. Pledge is based on common law possession and can therefore only relate to tangible assets such as negotiable instruments.[52] If

---

[50] See ibid s 238(4).

[51] '(3) Sums due from the company to another party shall not be included in the account taken under paragraph (2) if that other party had notice at the time they became due that a meeting of creditors had been summoned under section 98 or (as the case may be) a petition for the winding up of the company was pending.'

[52] While shares, being intangible, cannot be pledged, share certificates can: see for example *Colonial Bank v Cady and Williams* (1890) 11 App Cas 426.

security documentation is not amended to reflect the impact of computerisation, there is a danger that a purported pledge over intangible assets will be recharacterised as a charge. This would have the following possible disadvantages. A charge over personal property can only take effect in equity and therefore may be postponed to a subsequent legal security interest. As well as this priority disadvantage, if the collateral giver retains control over the collateral assets, the security interest may be treated as a floating charge which in turn may be avoided for non-registration.[53]

(2) Intermediation and Multiple Security Interests

4.59 Much securities collateral consists of interests in securities which are held through a number of intermediaries. For example, collateral may consist of interests in eurobonds, where the underlying bonds are held through a local depositary, on behalf of an international settlement system, on behalf of a sub-custodian, on behalf of a global custodian, on behalf of the collateral taker. It is important to note that each of these intermediaries is likely to have a security interest over the assets they hold, with which the interest of the collateral taker will have to compete.

4.60 Such competing security interests may arise under the terms of the contracts pursuant to which custodial and settlement services are provided, or even by operation of law. Even if the collateral taker is able to argue that these competing security interests are not perfected, it faces the practical problem that its competitors may have de facto control of the disputed assets. The prudent collateral taker will therefore engage in due diligence to substantiate the warranty of no prior encumbrance routinely given by the collateral giver.

(3) Commingled Client Accounts and Cross Subsidisation

4.61 The discussion of global custody in Chapter 10 considers the risk for custody clients that a shortfall may arise in the insolvency of the custodian. In this case, the total (interests in) securities credited to the accounts of clients in the books of the custodian would exceed the assets held by the custodian on behalf of clients. The risk of such shortfall may arise when a commingled custody client uses its asset to collateralise its exposures to a third party. This is best illustrated by example. Suppose three clients of a custodian, A, B and C, each have interests in 100 ICI shares credited to their accounts in the books of the custodian. The custodian holds 300 ICI shares in a commingled client account in CREST, and has a entry in its name of 300 on the register of ICI.[54] A grants a charge to X over the balance of its account. Later A buys 50 ICI shares from Y, with settlement to the custodian's account (raising the balance of the custodian's account to 350, and of its

---

[53] See Chapter 5 for a discussion of the other disadvantages of a floating charge.
[54] See the discussion of CREST in Chapter 9.

account in the books of the custodian to 150) and subsequently sells 50 shares (restoring the two balances to 300 and 100 respectively). A defaults and X enforces the charge. In accordance with its terms, the custodian delivers 100 ICI shares to X, reducing A's balance to 0 and its own balance to 200. Thereafter CREST informs the custodian that the transfer from Y has been avoided by the liquidator of Y as a transaction at an undervalue. CREST reverses the associated credit of 50 to the custodian's account, reducing the custodian's balance to 150. There is a shortfall in the assets held by the custodian for its clients, and in effect the assets of B and/or C have been used to collateralise the debts of A.

In these circumstance, it may be possible for the custodian to bring an action on behalf of B and C to recover the assets from X, but the outcome of such litigation would be uncertain. As long as the possibility of bad deliveries (due to fraud, error or insolvency) are not excluded from settlement systems, this 'cross-subsidisation' risk will always be inherent in the grant of security interests by commingled custody clients. **4.62**

(4) Collateralisation of Settlement Exposures and Netting

As discussed in Chapter 9, an important development is the introduction of clearing arrangements to the settlement of (interests in) securities, whereby a central counterparty is introduced between buyer and seller during the settlement interval, in order to address the risk of default by either party. As explained in Chapter 8, central counterparties offering a clearing service require the delivery of cash and (interests in) securities to collateralise their exposures. In relation to any particular transaction, as the market value of (interests in) securities changes between trade and settlement, the size of the credit exposure of the central counterparty to either party also changes. Where such exposure is reduced, a collateral surplus may arise; conversely, where it increases, a collateral shortfall may arise. **4.63**

In order to make the most efficient use of their available assets, market participants wish to ensure that collateral is called on a net basis, so that a collateral shortfall on one transaction is met by a collateral excess on another. While such netting between transactions settled within a single settlement system may be straightforward, netting between systems may present a challenge on which the international securities markets may work for years to come. **4.64**

5

SECURITY INTERESTS

When movables are deposited as gage and the creditor is given seisin for a fixed term, he is bound to keep the gage safely and may not use it or deal with it in any way to its detriment.*

This chapter will consider security interests. Outright collateral transfers will be considered in Chapter 6. **5.01**

A. Types of Security Interest

English law recognises four types of security interest. These are pledge, mortgage, charge and lien.[1] **5.02**

---

* *Treatise on the Laws and Customs of the Realm of England commonly called Glanvill* (Hall (trans), Oxford: Clarendon Press, 1965) 121.

[1] The different types of security interest are summarised by Millett LJ in *Re Cosslett (Contractors) Ltd* [1997] 4 All ER 115: 'There are only four kinds of consensual security known to English law: (i) pledge; (ii) contractual lien; (iii) equitable charge and (iv) mortgage. A pledge and a contractual lien both depend on the delivery of possession to the creditor. The difference between them is that in the case of a pledge the owner delivers possession to the creditor as security, whereas in the case of a lien the creditor retains possession of goods previously delivered to him for some other purpose. Neither a mortgage nor a charge depends on the delivery of possession. The difference between them is that a mortgage involves a transfer of legal or equitable ownership to the creditor, whereas an equitable charge does not'.

(1) Pledge[2]

5.03 A pledge is the delivery of possession by way of security.[3] The pledge is a strong form of security interest. At a pragmatic level, because the collateral taker has possession of the collateral assets, it is readily able to enforce its security interest by selling the asset. Importantly, the pledge is not registrable under the Companies Act 1985; as will be seen later, this is a major advantage. Further, because it is based on common law possession, the pledge is a legal (as opposed to an equitable) form of security interest. The general rule is that legal interests take priority over competing equitable interests.[4] Priorities will be discussed later in this chapter.

5.04 As discussed in Chapter 3, possession involves the physical control of a tangible asset. Because it is based on possession, a pledge can only relate to tangible assets. The pledge has historically been used in the securities markets in relation to bearer bonds and other negotiable instruments, which are categorised as tangible assets or chattels.[5]

5.05 Because a pledge cannot relate to intangible assets, interests in securities cannot be pledged. A purported pledge over interests in securities may be recharacterised as a charge. Priorities between competing security interests in the same asset are discussed below. Broadly, an equitable security interest is weaker than a legal security interest. A charge is equitable, and is therefore generally weaker in priority than a pledge. More importantly, certain charges are registrable, as discussed below. Failure to register a registrable charge will render it void. Pledges are never registrable, but a purported pledge over interests in securities may be treated as a charge that is void for want of registration. This is a legal risk associated with mistaking interests in securities for securities, as indicated in Chapter 4.

5.06 If the collateral giver wishes to give a collateral taker a security interest in bearer securities in their traditional form, but does not want to entrust the securities to the collateral taker, a possible solution is to place the securities with a trusted third party such as a custodian bank. Before the pledge takes effect, the custodian holds

---

[2] See the excellent discussion in N Palmer and A Hudson, 'pledge' in N Palmer and E McKendrick (eds), *Interests in Goods* (2nd edn, London: LLP, 1998) 621.

[3] '[A pledge] . . . was the fourth type of bailment described by Holt CJ in *Coggs v Bernard* [(1703) 2 Lord Raym 909 at 919], and was identified by him thus: "The fourth sort is, when goods or chattels are delivered to another as a pawn, to be a security to him for money borrowed of him by the bailor; and this is called in Latin vadium, and in English a pawn or pledge". Pledge has been described as both the earliest and the most powerful form of security interest known to English law': N E Palmer, *Bailment* (2nd edn, London: Sweet & Maxwell, 1991) 1379.

[4] The pledgee of a negotiable instrument can take them free of defects in the title of the pledgor, provided the pledgee took possession of the negotiable instrument for value and in good faith: *London Joint Stock Bank v Simmons* [1982] AC 201, 222.

[5] See Chapter 2. The courts have also recognised pledges of share certificates. However, the pledged asset in such a case was the certificate itself, and not the underlying shares; see *Colonial Bank v Cady and Williams* (1890) 15 App Cas 267.

the instruments for the collateral giver as bailee. When the pledge takes effect, the collateral giver delivers constructive possession[6] to the collateral taker, by having the custodian acknowledge that henceforth it holds the instruments as bailee for the collateral taker. This acknowledgement by the custodian is called attornment.[7] However, constructive possession as well as actual possession can only relate to tangible assets,[8] and attornment cannot be used to deliver collateral consisting of interests in securities.

(2) Mortgage

A mortgage is the delivery of title by way of security.[9] The mortgagor delivers title **5.07** to the mortgaged asset to the mortgagee, subject to the equity of redemption, which the mortgagor retains.[10] As discussed in Chapter 4, the equity of redemption is the property right of the collateral giver, which attaches to the collateral assets, to the return of those assets upon the discharge of the secured obligation. As its name suggests, the equity of redemption is always equitable and not legal. The interest of the mortgagee can be legal or equitable. With a legal mortgage, the mortgagor delivers full legal and equitable title (subject only to the equity of redemption). With an equitable mortgage, the mortgagor delivers equitable title (subject to the equity of redemption). The mortgagor can only give a legal mortgage where its interest is legal and not equitable.[11]

Where bearer securities in traditional form are delivered by way of security, it is **5.08** more natural to characterise the arrangement as a pledge rather than a mortgage.[12] Moreover characterising the security interest as a pledge has the advantage of avoiding registration requirements; as indicated below, some mortgages are registrable. Thus, mortgages are more relevant in relation to registered (interests in) securities than bearer securities.

Legal title to registered securities is determined by registration. Thus, in order to **5.09** create a legal mortgage of registered securities it is necessary to reregister them in the name of the collateral taker.

---

[6] See Chapter 2.

[7] This arrangement is used in the Central Moneymarkets Office when instruments are delivered as collateral within the system with the Bank of England acting as bailee. As discussed in Chapter 9, the CMO is proposed to be merged with CREST.

[8] See Chapter 2.

[9] 'A mortgage is a conveyance of land or an assignment of chattels as a security for the payment of a debt or the discharge of some other obligation for which it is given': *Santley v Wilde* [1899] 2 Ch 474 per Lindley MR at 474.

[10] The mortgage has its origins in land law. Originally the mortgage was a form of outright collateral transfer, and involved the outright delivery of the land subject to a mere personal right of redelivery. In time, equity came to treat the right of redelivery as proprietary, in order to protect distressed landowners against rapacious moneylenders.

[11] This is because only a legal asset can be transferred at law; an equitable asset can only be transferred in equity.

[12] See *Carter v Wake* (1877) 4 Ch D 605.

5.10   In the past, reregistration involved significant delay and inconvenience.[13] In many cases therefore, the collateral giver would not reregister the securities, but merely deliver to the collateral taker the share certificates together with a transfer form, which was signed but not dated, and on which the name of the transferee was not stated. This meant that although the collateral taker did not acquire legal title, it was in a position to obtain it, by completing the transfer form and sending it together with the certificates to the registrar.

5.11   The effect of the deposit of certificates and blank transfers is to create an equitable mortgage. The arrangements indicate an intention to create a mortgage, which intention cannot take effect at law for want of reregistration.[14] Because equity regards that as done which ought to be done, the arrangements take effect as a mortgage in equity.[15]

5.12   Because they are informal and rapid, such equitable mortgages were very widely used in the past to give collateral for securities lending transactions. However, today securities lending is collateralised by outright collateral transfer arrangements, as will be discussed in Chapter 6.

5.13   An equitable mortgage has weaker priority than a legal mortgage. As discussed below, the general rule of priorities is that subsequent legal interests for value take priority over prior equitable interests in the absence of notice. This may expose the equitable mortgagee to double-dealing, as a subsequent good faith purchaser or legal mortgagee of the shares would take priority.[16]

5.14   Where a mortgage is taken it is customary to execute the mortgage agreement as a deed and to provide that the mortgagee can sell the (interests in) securities at any

---

[13]   The introduction of CREST has done much to overcome this. See Chapter 9.

[14]   'The deposit of the certificate by way of security for the debt seems to me to amount to an equitable mortgage, ie, in other words, to an agreement to execute a transfer of the shares by way of mortgage': *Harrold v Plenty* [1901] 2 Ch 314, per Cozens-Hardy J at 316.

[15]   'If a man executes a document transferring all his equitable interests, say, in shares, that document, operating and intending to operate, as a transfer, will give rise to and take effect as a trust; for the assignor will then be a trustee of the legal estate in the shares for the person in whose favour he has made an assignment of his beneficial interest. And for my part, I do not think that the case of *Milroy v Lord* is an authority which compels this court to hold that in this case—where . . . the settlor did everything which, according to the nature of the property comprised in the settlement, was necessary to be done by him in order to transfer the property—the result necessarily negatives the conclusion that, pending registration, the settlor was a trustee of the legal interest for the transferee': *Re Rose* [1952] 1 Ch 499, per Evershed MR, at 510–511.

[16]   However, because the equitable mortgagee has the certificates this could only happen if the mortgagor obtains duplicate certificates by fraudulently representing to the issuer that the original certificates were lost. Further protection may be obtained by serving a stop notice on the issuing company. This prevents the company from transferring the shares without giving the equitable mortgagee 14 days' notice. However, the procedure is seldom used because it involves formalities including the swearing of an affidavit. A greater danger is that there may be equitable prior interests because the rule for priorities is that, between equitable interests the first in time prevails. See *Coleman v London County and Westminster Bank Ltd* [1916] 2 Ch 353.

time if the mortgagor does not repay the debt on demand. In the absence of provision, the restrictions (under section 103 of the Law of Property Act 1925) on the exercise of mortgagee's statutory powers of sale (in section 101) apply. These require three months notice to repay.[17]

A mortgage is registrable under Companies Act 1985 registration requirements if it amounts to a fixed charge on book debts, as discussed below. In general, (interests in) securities are not book debts for this purpose, although cash accounts may be.   **5.15**

(3) Charge

If a pledge is the delivery of possession by way of security and a mortgage is the delivery of title by way of security, a charge is less substantial. It is the right of the chargee to appropriate the charged asset to satisfy its indebtedness. While a pledge can only be legal and a mortgage can be either legal or equitable, a charge can only take effect in equity.[18] In the past there was even doubt that the charge conferred any sort of property interest,[19] but now it is clear that the chargee acquires a form of equitable property interest in the charged assets.[20] No formalities are required to create a charge.[21] A charge can arise in relation to assets whenever there is an effective agreement to create a charge, and in many circumstances charges arise by operation of law. This lack of formality makes the charge useful in the securities markets.   **5.16**

An important distinction is that between fixed charges and floating charges.   **5.17**

Fixed charge

A fixed charge attaches to particular assets, which are identified or ascertainable, so that the chargor is not free to dispose of them without the consent of the chargee.[22] The term 'fixed charge' is sometimes used interchangeably with the   **5.18**

---

[17] See the discussion in Milnes Holden, *The Law and Practice of Banking* (8th edn, London: Pitman, 1993) vol 2, 166, at para 15-14.

[18] See R M Goode, *Legal Problems of Credit and Security* (2nd edn, London: Sweet & Maxwell, 1988) 14–15 and the Law of Property Act 1925, ss 86, 87, in relation to legal charges of land.

[19] See the discussions in *Swiss Bank Corporation v Lloyds Bank Ltd* [1979] Ch 548, [1982] AC 584.

[20] 'It is of the essence of a charge that a particular asset or class of assets is appropriated to the satisfaction of a debt or other obligation of the chargor or a third party, so that the chargee is entitled to look to the asset and its proceeds for the discharge of the liability. This creates a transmissible interest in the asset. A mere right to retain possession of an asset and to make use of it for a particular purpose does not create such an interest and does not constitute a charge': *Re Cosslett (Contractors) Ltd* [1997] 4 All ER 115, per Millett LJ at 125.

[21] However, a charge is usually made by deed in order to facilitate enforcement.

[22] 'The essence of a floating charge is that it is a charge, not on any particular asset, but on a fluctuating body of assets which remain under the management and control of the chargor, and which the chargor has the right to withdraw from the security despite the existence of the charge. The essence of a fixed charge is that the charge is on a particular asset or class of assets which the chargor

term 'equitable mortgage'. A fixed charge may be registrable if it amounts to a charge on book debts as discussed below.

Floating charge

5.19 In contrast, a floating charge relates to a changing class of present and future assets, but does not attach to any particular assets (unless and until it is converted into a fixed charge, ie crystallised by attachment to specific assets, either by notice from the chargee or automatically in certain circumstances in accordance with the drafting of the charge document). This means that the chargor is free to dispose of the assets subject to the floating charge without the consent of the chargee. The floating charge was developed in order to permit the chargor to grant a security interest over its entire stock in trade or undertaking while carrying on its business in the normal course.

Romer LJ famously commented[23]

> I certainly think that if a charge has the three characteristics that I am about to mention it is a floating charge. (1) If it is a charge on a class of assets of a company present and future; (2) if that class is one which, in the ordinary course of the business of the company, would be changing from time to time; and (3) if you find that by the charge it is contemplated that, until some future step is taken by or on behalf of those interested in the charge, the company may carry on its business in the ordinary way so far as concerns the particular class of assets I am dealing with.

5.20 On appeal in the same case, Lord Macnaghten commented:[24]

> I should have thought that there was not much difficulty in defining what a floating charge is in contrast to what is called a specific charge. A specific charge, I think, is one that without more fastens on ascertained and definite property or property capable of being ascertained and defined; a floating charge, on the other hand, is ambulatory and shifting in its nature, hovering over and so to speak floating with the property which it is intended to effect until some event occurs or some act is done which causes it to settle and fasten on the subject of the charge within its reach and grasp.

5.21 However, the crucial test is not so much whether the collateral assets change from time to time, because it would be possible to create a fixed charge over a changing pool of assets.[25] The crucial test is whether or not the chargor is free to dispose of the charged assets without the consent of the chargee. In other words, the test is

---

cannot deal with free from the charge without the consent of the chargee': *Re Cosslett (Contractors) Ltd* [1998] 2 WLR 131, per Millet LJ at 143.

   [23] *Re Yorkshire Woolcombers Association Ltd* [1903] 2 Ch 284 at 295.
   [24] *Illingworth v Houldsworth* [1904] AC 355 at 358.
   [25] It would be possible in effect to create a fixed charge over a changing pool of assets, by creating a fixed charge over specific assets, together with provisions for substituting different assets. However, the chargee's consent would be needed each time old assets were released from the pool (and others substituted), and this would be cumbersome in practice.

control. The case of *Re Cosslett (Contractors) Ltd* [26] indicates that, in order to avoid creating a floating charge, it is not sufficient merely to *restrict* the freedom of the chargor to deal with the charged assets.

> The chargor's unfettered freedom to deal with the assets in the ordinary course of his business free from the charge is obviously inconsistent with the nature of a fixed charge; but it does not follow that his unfettered freedom to deal with the charged assets is essential to the existence of a floating charge. It plainly is not, for any well-drawn floating charge prohibits the chargor from creating further charges having priority to the floating charge; and a prohibition against factoring debts is not sufficient to convert what would otherwise be a floating charge on book debts into a fixed charge. [27] The essence of a floating charge is that it is a charge, not on any particular asset, but on a fluctuating body of assets which remain under the management and control of the chargor, and which the chargor has the right to withdraw from the security despite the existence of the charge. The essence of a fixed charge is that the charge is on a particular asset or class of assets which the chargor cannot deal with free from the charge without the consent of the chargee. The question is not whether the chargor has complete freedom to carry on his business as he chooses, but whether the chargee is in control of the charged assets. [28]

In addition to registrability, a number of other disadvantages are associated with **5.22** floating charges. In terms of priorities a floating charge will in general rank after fixed security interests created after the floating charge but before it was converted into a fixed charge by crystallisation. [29] (A floating charge is invariably accompanied by a negative pledge, ie an agreement not to create further security interests ranking in priority, but this may not be effective to prevent subsequent fixed charges from taking priority.) [30] On insolvency, a floating charge ranks not only after a fixed charge but also after preferential creditors. [31] Floating charges are subject to special insolvency invalidation provisions. [32] The chargor's administrator has power to dispose of property subject to a floating charge to cover the expenses of administration free from the charge without leave of the court. [33] Moreover the

---

[26] [1997] 4 All ER 115.

[27] See *Re Brightlife Ltd* [1986] 3 All ER 673 at 676, [1987] Ch 200 at 209 per Hoffmann J.

[28] At 127.

[29] Crystallisation occurs automatically on the appointment of a receiver or the commencement of winding up, and when the company ceases to be a going concern.

[30] If the negative pledge is broken, it will not affect the subsequent fixed chargee unless it had notice of the negative pledge at the time the fixed charge was created. It is prudent to assume that, although registration of a floating charge constitutes notice to the world of the existence of the charge, it does not automatically constitute such notice of the *contents* of the floating charge (including any negative pledge), even if such contents were registered. See the discussion in *Farrar's Company Law* (4th edn, London: Butterworths, 1998) 648 and R M Goode, *Commercial Law* (2nd edn, London: Penguin, 1995) 717, 718.

[31] Insolvency Act 1986, s 40.

[32] See ibid s 245.

[33] Although the security interest attaches to the proceeds of sale, the expenses and liabilities of the administration can be met out of the proceeds.

Financial Services Authority does not permit banks regulated by it to grant float-ing charges.

5.23 The only type of floating security is a floating charge. A mortgage, whether legal or equitable, can only relate to ascertained property. In other words, a mortgage is always a fixed security.

(4) Lien

5.24 A lien is a security interest based on possession.[34] It entitles the lienee to retain pos-session of assets until the secured obligation is discharged.[35] Liens can arise either by agreement or by operation of law.[36] For example, a solicitor has a lien over her client's papers in respect of unpaid fees. Also, a banker has a lien over its clients' documents of title in respect of sums due.[37]

5.25 Although a lien confers the right to retain possession of the assets until the secured obligation is discharged, it generally does not confer a power of sale.[38] By way of exception to this rule, a banker's lien does confer a power of sale. The role of cus-todians is discussed in Chapter 10. Custodians are generally banks, and standard custody documentation describes the security interest of the custodian as a lien. However, the banker's lien does not extend to (interests in) securities held by banks as custodian for clients, and custody liens do not confer automatic rights of

---

[34] 'A lien is a right conferred by law . . . upon a person to retain possession of, or to have a charge upon, the real or personal property of another, until certain demands are satisfied': *Fisher & Lightwood's Law of Mortgage* (10th edn, London: Butterworths, 1988). A possessory lien (which is based on physical possession of goods) must be distinguished from a maritime lien (which relates to ships) and an equitable lien, which arises for example on the exchange of contracts for the sale of land, and is independent of possession. See Schmitthoff and Sarre, *Charlesworth's Mercantile Law* (London: Stevens & Sons, 1984) 476–480.

[35] A pledge involves the delivery of possession by way of security. In contrast, with a lien, posses-sion is delivered otherwise than by way of security (for example, by way of custody) and the lien con-fers only the right to *retain* possession by way of security.

[36] 'though a "lien" is sometimes used in practice to describe a right which arises by way of express contractual agreement of the interested parties, it is more commonly used, in a narrower sense, to refer to a right arising by operation of law': *Re Bond Worth* [1980] Ch 228, per Slade J at 250. See also Sykes and Walker, *The Law of Securities* (5th edn, Sydney: The Law Book Company Limited, 1993) 737: 'Although the lien arises by implication of law, it is possible to create a "lien" by agree-ment'.

[37] 'A banker, in the absence of agreement to the contrary, has a lien on all securities in his hands for the general balance owing to him on all accounts of his customer': *Charlesworth's Mercantile Law* (n 34 above) 477.

[38] 'A possessory lien is enforced only by a right of retention . . . There is no general right of sale": *Charlesworth's Mercantile Law* (n 34 above) 478. However, a lienee can apply to the court for sale.

[39] 'The position with regard to bankers was sufficiently stated by Lord Campbell LC in *Brandao v Barnett*: "Bankers most undoubtedly have a general lien on all securities deposited with them as bankers by a customer, unless there be an express contract, or circumstances that show an implied contract, inconsistent with lien". The lien is based upon commercial custom which is part of the law merchant, and need not be specifically proved. It is doubtful, however, whether it would extend to articles deposited with a bank for safe-keeping': Palmer, *Bailment* (n 3 above) 879. See also Penn, Shea and Arora, *The Law Relating to Domestic Banking* (London: Sweet & Maxwell, 1987) 132 and

sale.[39] A security interest without a power of sale is of little use in the securities markets: if the value of the collateral is falling, the ability to exercise a power of sale immediately upon default is crucial to the collateral taker, as discussed in Chapter 4. For this reason, it is customary in custody documentation to add a contractual power of sale in the drafting concerning the lien.

This raises the following concern. If a lien does not confer a power of sale, a con-   **5.26**
tractual provision that does confer a power of sale may cause the security interest to be recharacterised as a charge, which in turn may be a registrable floating charge, void for want of registration. Recent case law has indicated that the addition of a power of sale to a lien over tangible assets does not create a charge.[40] However, it would be unsafe to assume that the same rule applies to intangible collateral assets such as interests in securities.[41]

B. Registration Requirements

As briefly indicated above, certain types of security interest have to be registered.   **5.27**
The policy considerations behind registration requirements relates to publicity.

(1) Publicity[42]

As discussed in Chapter 13, property rights are distinguished from personal rights   **5.28**
by their ability to bind third parties. Thus personal rights (such as a right arising under contract) bind only particular persons (such as the contractual obligor),[43] whereas a property right (such as a perfected security interest) bind third parties (such as unsecured creditors of the collateral giver). Because property rights affect third parties, natural justice requires that such rights should only arise in circumstances where they are apparent to third parties.[44] In other words, property rights

---

M Hapgood, *Paget's Law of Banking* (11edn, London: Butterworths, 1996) 527: 'The deposit of securities for safe custody is normally inconsistent with a right of lien. This was the position in *Brandao v Barnett* [(1846) 12 Cl & Fin 787, 8 ER 1622], where exchequer bills were deposited with bankers and kept in a tin box of which the depositor kept the key. In those circumstances the bills could not be considered as having been deposited with the bankers *as bankers*, but as bailees'.

[40] *Re Hamlet International plc (in administration)* (1998) 2 BCLC 1 at 172, on appeal as *Trident International Ltd v Barlow* (1999) BCLC 506 at 514.

[41] The jurisprudential basis of the judgment may have been that the natural characterisation of a security interest over tangible assets that confers a power of sale, is as a pledge. A pledge is not registrable. However, a pledge cannot relate to intangibles, and the natural characterisation of a security interest over intangibles that confers a power of sale may remain as a charge. The author is grateful to Mark Evans, partner, Travers Smith & Braithwaite for this point.

[42] See P Wood, *Comparative Law of Security and Guarantees* (London: Sweet & Maxwell, 1996) 4, 5.

[43] The Contracts (Rights of Third Parties) Act 1999 does not change the position; this permits contractual rights to be conferred on third parties, but not for contractual burdens to be imposed on third parties. Therefore a contract can only be enforced *against* a party to it.

[44] Such publicity is particularly important where the transferor remains in possession.

should be public.[45] A wide range of rules of commercial law are based on this principle, including the requirement that certain company charges should be registered.[46]

5.29   It was seen above that a security interest places the secured creditor ahead of unsecured creditors in insolvency. The secured creditor is able to take the assets in which it has a security interest out of the pool of assets available to unsecured creditors. This might be thought to be unjust to unsecured creditors. A counter-argument is that, provided unsecured creditors know about the security interest, they can make informed decisions about the credit-worthiness of the company. For this reason, most systems of commercial law require that certain types of security interest be public in order to be effective.

(2) Companies Act 1985, section 395

5.30   In relation to security interests created by companies incorporated in England the relevant provisions are in section 395 and the following sections of the Companies Act 1985.[47] Particulars of a registrable charge must be delivered to the registrar of companies within 21 days after the date when the charge is created, or the charge will be void against the liquidator, administrator or any creditor of the company.[48] This sanction has the effect of reducing the status of the secured creditor to that of an unsecured creditor. It does not mean that the debt which had been intended to be secured is not payable. Indeed, the avoidance of the charge makes the debt immediately payable.[49]

5.31   The section applies to charges *created* by a company. It does not apply to charges arising by operation of law.

5.32   The requirements apply to companies registered in England and Wales irrespective of where the charged property is located[50] and to overseas companies having

---

[45] Barry Nicholas refers to 'the sound though inarticulate principle that rights *in rem* [or property rights], since they potentially affect everyone, should not be secretly created or transferred, whereas there is no such objection to the secret creation of rights *in personam*. Hence it is that the Roman conveyance is essentially a visible and public act': *An Introduction to Roman Law* (Oxford: Clarendon Press, 1962) 103.

[46] 'The only wholly effective method [to ensure publicity for the creation and transfer of property rights] is registration. The method is increasingly used in the modern world . . . it was quite unknown to Roman law': ibid 104. Registered charges are visible to persons advancing credit to the chargor, so that they will not be misled into believing that the charged assets would be available to them in the insolvency of the chargor, and thus make an informed credit decision.

[47] Equivalent provisions are made for overseas companies having an established place of business in the United Kingdom under s 409. See ss 410 and 424 in relation to the registration of charges in Scotland. (There were proposals to amend the detail of these provisions and prospective amendments were introduced by the Companies Act 1989. However, no date was ever set for these proposed changes to come into effect and probably they never will.)

[48] Companies Act 1985, s 395(1).

[49] ibid s 395(2).

[50] ibid s 395(1)

an established place of business in the jurisdiction, but only in relation to charges on property located in the jurisdiction.[51] Thus, where an overseas company operating in London through a branch delivers to a third party interests in English eurobonds held through Euroclear under a security interest, the security interest will only be registrable if the collateral assets are treated as being located in London.[52] If the collateral assets are treated as being located in Belgium, the registration requirements do not apply. These issues are discussed in more detail in Chapter 7. Because in practice security interests often remain unregistered (for the reasons given below), the answer to the debate about the location of such assets may determine whether such a security interest is enforceable, or void for want of registration.

(3) Reluctance to Register

There is generally a great reluctance among institutions in the international finan- **5.33**
cial markets to register charges. The paperwork involves an administrative burden that may be impracticable where collateral is turned over rapidly. Further, registration involves publicity which may be unwelcome.

Not all categories of security interests are registrable, and much legal effort is **5.34**
devoted in practice to supporting the view that clients' security interests can be characterised as falling within one of the non-registrable categories.

(4) Registrable Security Interests

A charge is a candidate for registration[53] and so is a mortgage.[54] Pledges and liens **5.35**
are not. Pledges and liens are based on possession and therefore can only relate to tangible assets. Legal risk arises when old documentation, which was drafted for use with tangible securities and which creates pledges or liens, is applied to intangible interests in securities; as indicated above, such security interests may take effect as registrable charges.

Not all types of registrable security interest are relevant for the securities markets. **5.36**
Two, however, may be relevant. These are floating charges[55] and charges (or mortgages) on book debts.[56]

Floating charges

Collateral takers in the securities markets are generally concerned to ensure that **5.37**
their security interest does not amount to a floating charge for a number of reasons

---

[51] ibid s 409(1).
[52] See Chapter 7 for further discussion.
[53] Companies Act 1985, s 396(1).
[54] ibid s 396(4).
[55] ibid s 396(1)(f).
[56] ibid s 396(1)(e).

indicated below, the chief of which is in order to avoid the need for registration. Two customary aspects of securities collateral are of particular concern in the light of *Re Cosslett* (discussed above). The first is substitution. Collateral givers generally offer as collateral (interests in) securities which they do not expect to wish to deliver elsewhere in the short term. However, it is always possible, particularly in medium and long term collateral arrangements, that a need or opportunity will arises that the collateral giver wishes to retrieve the original collateral (interests in) securities and substitute other ones having an equal market value, for example because the original collateral (interests in) securities are falling in value and the collateral giver wishes to cut its losses by selling them.[57] Such substitution provisions are customary. However, if they are so drafted that the collateral taker can withdraw (interests in) securities from the collateral pool without restriction, this may render the security interest a floating charge, particularly in the light of the Court of Appeal judgment in *Re Cosslett (Contractors) Ltd.*[58] For this reason, market standard documentation provides that the ability of the collateral giver to substitute assets is subject to the consent of the collateral taker.[59]

5.38 Another concern relates to margin calls. As will be discussed in Chapter 6, under many arrangements (including swaps, repos and stock loans) the value of the collateral and in some cases the value of the collateralised exposure fluctuates from time to time. In order to preserve the original ratio between exposure and collateral during the life of the transaction, it is necessary to make constant adjustments. These adjustments take the form of releases of collateral or calls for more collateral as the case may be. This process is called margining or marking to market. In some cases, these collateral arrangements are structured as security interests

---

[57] Alternatively, their value may have risen, and the collateral giver may wish to sell the assets on the basis of the view that they are at the top of the market.

[58] See paragraph 5.21, above.

Also, in order to establish a fixed charge, the chargee must exercise control *in its capacity as chargee*: *Re Double S Printers Ltd (in liquidation) The Times*, 2 June 1988, Leeds District Registry. A debenture over a company's book debts which purported to create a fixed charge was held to create a floating charge. This was because the debenture holder did not have control in its capacity as chargee. It was intended that the company should get in its book debts and use the proceeds to assist in its cash flow. The chargee was also a director who did have de facto control over the book debts as director; however, this did not suffice. In order for the debenture to create a fixed charge it was necessary to show that the debenture holder had control in that capacity.

[59] However, it might be argued that the risk of recharacterisation as a floating charge because of substitution rights only arises where the collateral is held under a security interest, and is not present where the collateral has been delivered outright. This is on the basis that, under outright transfer arrangements, the collateral taker is not required to retain the original collateral securities, and could therefore meet a substitution call with securities equivalent to the original securities; therefore the right of substitution does not imply that the collateral giver retains a continuing interest in the original collateral securities.

and sometimes as outright collateral transfers. Clearly, it is desirable that a security interest should not be characterised as a registrable floating charge. Even outright collateral transfer arrangements may run the risk in some circumstances of being recharacterised as security interests, in which case the same concern to avoid a floating charge arises.

The concern is that, if the collateral giver has an unfettered contractual right to **5.39** call for the return of excess collateral, this might amount to sufficient control over the collateral assets to create a floating charge. This concern is addressed in standard documentation as follows: the collateral giver has a right to the release of collateral to a value equal to the value of the collateral excess, but it is the collateral taker and not the collateral giver who decides which assets should be released. [60]

Thus, departures from standard drafting that remove the consent requirement to **5.40** substitution, or permit the collateral giver to determine the type of excess collateral to be returned, may present the risk of recharacterisation.

Charges on book debts

A fixed security can be registrable if it amounts to a charge on book debts. As indi- **5.41** cated above, the term charge is defined to include mortgages. There is authority that a book debt for this purpose is an asset that would appear in the well-kept books of a company under the heading 'debts'.[61] Debt securities would not appear as debts but as investments.[62] Therefore the better view is that fixed charges on debt securities are not registrable as charges on book debts.

However, many settlement systems and custodians seek to take a security interest **5.42** over the positive balances of the cash accounts which they maintain for clients. The question therefore arises whether such a security interest may be a registrable charge on a book debt.

Until 1997 the view was taken that these were not registrable because of the judg- **5.43** ment of Millett J in *Re Charge Card Services Ltd.*[63] This judgment related to a purported charge over the balance of a bank account *in favour of the bank*. These arrangements are referred to in the financial markets as 'charge backs'. It was held that such an arrangement could not take effect as a charge because the positive

---

[60] For the reasons outlined in the previous section, it might be argued that this is unnecessarily cautious in the case of outright transfers.

[61] *Independent Automatic Sales Ltd v Knowles & Foster* [1962] 1 WLR 974, per Buckley J at 983.

[62] See the Companies Act 1985, Sch 4, in which separate sections are given for debts and investments.

[63] [1987] 1 Ch 50.

balance on the bank account represented the debt of the bank to the depositor. It was a conceptual impossibility for a bank to have a charge over its own liability.[64] However, it was indicated[65] that a purported 'charge back' may take effect as a right of set off. In other words, the bank is able to set off the debt of the depositor to the bank against the bank's obligation to repay the deposit.

5.44 The later case of *Re BCCI (No 8)* supported *Charge Card* at first instance [66] and in the Court of Appeal.[67] However, in the House of Lords[68] the decision in *Charge Card* was reversed by Lord Hoffmann. He held that a charge back could take effect as a charge. 'The courts should be very slow to declare a practice of the commercial community to be conceptually impossible.'[69]

5.45 This decision appears to assist the banking community. However, in relation to existing charges on cash balances, it may be a source of legal risk. Where existing collateral arrangements involving cash balances relied on *Charge Card* to escape registration, that escape route is no longer available. The question therefore arises whether such arrangements amount to registrable charges on book debts. While there was some indication that they may not in the judgment,[70] the cautious view is to assume that such arrangements are registrable as charges on book debts. In practice, charge backs have traditionally been documented using the so-called 'triple cocktail' of belt, braces and another belt, namely, charge, set off and flawed asset arrangements.[71] It may be prudent for this practice to continue.

---

[64] Blackstone writes of 'the palpable absurdity of a man's bringing an action against himself': *Commentaries*, vol 3, 23.

[65] 'It does not, of course, follow that an attempt to create an express mortgage or charge of a debt in favour of the debtor would be ineffective to create a security. Equity looks to the substance, not the form, and while in my judgment this would not create a mortgage or charge, it would no doubt give a right of set-off which would be effective against the creditor's liquidator or trustee in bankruptcy, provided it did not purport to go beyond what is permitted by [the restrictions on insolvency set off]': [1987] 1 Ch 50, per Millett J at 177.

See also *Re BCCI (No 8)* [1996] 2 All ER 121 per Rose J at 134: 'Since a charge-back is incapable of vesting a proprietary interest in the chargee, its effect is purely contractual . . . If the charge-back secures a pre-existing obligation of the depositor, as in *Re Charge Card Services Ltd*, the bank is entitled, and may be bound, to set off the amount of the deposit against it under r 4.90'.

[66] [1994] 3 All ER 565.

[67] [1996] 2 All ER 121.

[68] [1998] AC 214.

[69] At 228. In the light of the analysis of property rights in Chapter 13, the author agrees with the decision in *Charge Card*, and not with the House of Lords decision in *BCCI (No 8)*. This is on the basis that a debt can be subject to property rights, but only as against a party *other than the debtor*.

[70] 'There is a suggestion in the judgment of the Court of Appeal that the banking community has been insufficiently grateful for being spared the necessity of registering such charges. In my view, this is a matter on which banks are entitled to make up their own minds and take their own advice on whether the deposit charged is a 'book debt' or not. I express no view on the point, but the judgment of my noble learned friend, Lord Hutton in *Northern Bank Ltd. v Ross* [1990] BCC 883 suggests that, in the case of deposits with banks, an obligation to register is unlikely to arise': [1998] AC 214 per Lord Hoffmann at 227.

[71] These provide that the right of the depositor to be repaid by the bank (its asset) is subject to the precondition that the depositor repays its debt to the bank (ie is 'flawed').

C. Rehypothecation of Collateral[72]

The same institutions which receive collateral for their exposures under certain **5.46** transactions are also required to deliver collateral for their obligations under other transactions. As discussed above, (interests in) securities collateral are a relatively scarce commodity, and the commercial pressure on an institution to use the collateral it receives to meet its obligation to deliver collateral, is tremendous. Where the counterparty in both types of transaction is the same, this result may be achieved by netting.[73] Where the counterparties delivering and requiring collateral differ, the result is achieved by rehypothecation.

Rehypothecation is the term which is applied in the securities industry to the **5.47** arrangement where A delivers assets as collateral to B, and B delivers the same assets as collateral to C.

Under most systems of law, the rehypothecation of collateral assets which are **5.48** delivered to B under a security interest, is narrowly restricted.[74]

In general, where B wishes to use the collateral assets it receives from A to collat- **5.49** eralise its own exposures to C, the transaction between A and B should be structured as a outright collateral transfer.

(1) Restriction on Rehypothecation under Security Interests

Under English law, where the collateral taker receives collateral under a security **5.50** interest, its ability to rehypothecate is restricted under equitable rules designed to protect the giver of a security interest.

(2) The Equitable Rules

The equitable rules restricting rehypothecation are traditionally referred to as the **5.51** rule, 'once a mortgage, always a mortgage', the related rule against clogs on the equity of redemption, and the rule against collateral benefits. These will be referred to together as 'the Rules'.[75]

---

[72] See the excellent analysis of the restrictions on rehypothecation in K Artmann, 'The Principles of the Equity of Redemption as Demonstrated in relation to a specific Repackaging Structure' JIBFL (forthcoming).

[73] Industry standard master agreements provide for netting across like transactions, such as repos, stock loans and swaps. Further efficiencies are sought by netting across transaction types under cross product netting agreements.

[74] However, the US Uniform Commercial Code takes a liberal view towards rehypothecation, where the collateral agreement provides for it (except in relation to consumer goods): see article 9-207(4).

[75] 'The first doctrine to which I refer is expressed in the maxim, "Once a mortgage always a mortgage". The second is that the mortgagee shall not reserve to himself any collateral advantage outside the mortgage contract; and the third is that a provision or stipulation which will have the effect of clogging or fettering the equity of redemption is void': *Noakes v Rice* [1902] AC 24, per Lord Davey at 32.

5.52 The Rules are developed in a long line of case law and derive from old cannon law restrictions on usury.[76] The Rules were originally developed to protect distressed mortgagors from hardship, so that they should not lose their land to moneylenders.[77]

5.53 The Rules were developed for legal mortgages, but there is persuasive authority that the Rules also apply to other types of security interest.[78]

(3) Once a Mortgage, Always a Mortgage, and the Equity of Redemption

The principle invoked by the Plaintiff is summed up in the epigrammatic formula 'once a mortgage always a mortgage'. Whenever a transaction is in reality one of mortgage, equity regards the mortgaged property as security only for money, and will permit of no attempt to clog, fetter, or impede the borrower's right to redeem and to rescue what was, and still remains in equity his own.[79]

5.54 As discussed above and in Chapter 4, where a mortgage or other security interest is given, the mortgagor enjoys an equity of redemption, or the right to the return of the mortgaged asset upon discharge of the secured obligation. 'Redemption is of the very nature and essence of a mortgage, as mortgages are regarded in equity.

---

[76] See *Krelinger v New Patagonia Meat and Cold Storage Co* [1914] AC 25, HL, per Viscount Haldane LC at 35. This passage indicates that, interestingly, at common law mortgages were originally a form of outright collateral transfer. The equity of redemption was developed in the late medieval era as a form of equitable recharacterisation by the courts, whereby an outright transfer was reduced to a mere security interest on the grounds that outright transfer was unfair to the collateral giver. This anticipates the modern recharacterisation of outright collateral transfers as mere security interests, on the ground that outright transfers are unfair to the collateral giver's creditors.

[77] There is much colourful judicial language betraying indignation at the ravages of the commercial classes upon the representatives of the old feudal order: 'for being once redeemable and once a mortgage, the negative words shall not make it otherwise; and should this be suffered, the scriveners would get this way, and cozen mortgagors out of their estates': *Newcombe v Bonham* (1681) 22 ER 1063; 'This court will not suffer, in a deed of mortgage, any agreement in it to prevail, that the estate becomes an absolute purchase in the mortgagee upon any event whatsoever; and the reason is, because it puts the borrower too much in the power of the lender, who, being distressed at the time, is too inclinable to submit to any terms proposed on the part of the lender': *Toomes v Conset* (1745) 26 ER 952, per the Lord Chancellor at 952, 953; 'a man will not be suffered in conscience to fetter himself with a limitation or restriction of his time of redemption. It would ruin the distressed and unwary, and give unconscionable advantage to greedy and designing persons . . . For Mr Collier, to prevent the redemption, corrupts the son to rob the father of the deed of defeasance (which was the foundation of it) and to put it into his hands; and he procures the man to be imprisoned, first in a gaol, and next illegally in Carr's house, to prevent his looking into his affairs. I have therefore no doubt that a redemption ought to be decreed as against Collier': *Spurgeon v Collier* (1758) 28 ER 605, per the Lord Keeper at 606; 'And there is great reason and justice in this rule, for necessitous men are not, truly speaking, free men, but to answer a present exigency will submit to any term that the crafty may impose upon them': *Vernon v Bethell* (1761) 28 ER 838, per Lord Henley at 839.

[78] The applicability of the Rules to floating charges was called into doubt by the Earl of Halsbury in *De Beers Consolidated Mines v British South Africa Company* [1912] AC 52, HL, at 71 and by Lord Gorrell at 73. However, in *Krelinger v New Patagonia Meat and Cold Storage Co* [1914] AC 25, HL, Viscount Haldane comments, 'Speaking for myself I do not see why the doctrine should not apply to a floating charge just as much as to any other mortgage security' (at 31, interjecting in counsel's arguments).

[79] *Marquess of Northampton v Pollock* (1890) 45 Ch D 190, per Bowen LJ at 215.

It is inherent in the thing itself.'[80] Generally speaking, the Rules provide that it is not possible for the mortgagor to renounce this right by contract. 'The right of redemption is considered in equity as inseparably incident to a mortgage, and cannot be restrained by any clause or agreement whatever, it being a rule, that what was once a mortgage must always continue a mortgage.'[81] Agreement made at the time that the mortgage is entered into, giving the mortgagee an option to purchase the property, will not be effective, as it will be treated as a clog on the equity of redemption.[82] Offending contractual provisions will simply be struck down.[83] This ancient principle is consolidated in a long line of authority spanning the seventeenth, eighteenth, nineteenth and early twentieth centuries.[84]

(4) Collateral Advantage

Some commentators have suggested that a further challenge to rehypothecation **5.55** arises in the form of the rule against collateral advantages. This rule restricts the ability of the mortgagee to obtain in the mortgage agreement an advantage in addition to the payment of interest, costs and principle.[85] This rule also derives from the old usury laws, and originally restricted the mortgagee to obtaining a lawful rate of interest.[86] Since the abolition of the usury laws the rule has relaxed somewhat,[87] to

---

[80] *Noakes v Rice* [1902] AC 24, per Lord Macnaghten at 30.

[81] *Spurgeon v Collier* (1758) 28 ER 605, footnote in the law report, at 607.

[82] 'And it is, I think, as firmly settled now as it ever was in former times that equity will not permit any device or contrivance designed or calculated to prevent or impede redemption': *Noakes v Rice* [1902] AC 24, per Lord Macnaghten at 30.

[83] 'The doctrine "Once a mortgage always a mortgage" means that no contract between a mortgagor and a mortgagee made at the time of the mortgage and as part of the mortgage transaction, or, in other words, as one of the terms of the loan, can be valid if it prevents the mortgagor from getting back his property on paying off what is due on his security. Any bargain which has that effect is invalid, and is inconsistent with the transaction being a mortgage': *Samuel v Jarrah* [1904] AC 323, HL, per Lord Lindley at 329.

[84] For key judgments, see for example *Newcombe v Bonham* (1681) 22 ER 1063; *Spurgeon v Collier* (1758) 28 ER 605; *Vernon v Bethell* (1761) 28 ER 838; *Northampton v Pollock* (1890) 45 Ch D 190; *Noakes v Rice* [1902] AC 24; *Samuel v Jarrah* [1904] AC 323, HL; *De Beers v British South Africa Company* [1912] AC 52, HL; *Fairclough v Swan Brewery* [1912] AC 565, PC.

[85] Many cases in which this rule is discussed concern 'ties', whereby the mortgagor is bound, as part of the mortgage, to buy or sell a commodity such as tea, wool, beer or petrol, only to or from the mortgagee. See for example *Vernon v Bethell* (1761) 28 ER 838; *Noakes v Rice* [1902] AC 24; *Bradley v Carritt* [1903] AC 253, HL; *Fairclough v Swan Brewery* [1912] AC 565, PC; *Kreglinger v New Patagonia Meat and Cold Storage Co* [1914] AC 25, HL; *Re Petrol Filling Station, Vauxhall Bridge, London, Rosemex Service Station v Shell Mex and BP Ltd* (1968) 20 P & CR 1; *Alec Lobb (Garages) Ltd v Total Oil GB Ltd* [1983] 1 All ER 944. See also *De Beers v British South African Company* [1912] AC 52, HL.

[86] See *Noakes v Rice* [1902] AC 24, per Lord Davey at 32; *Bradley v Carritt* [1903] AC 253, HL per Lord Shand at 263; *Kreglinger v New Patagonia Meat and Cold Storage Co* [1914] AC 25, HL, per Viscount Haldane LC at 37. The original rule may be cited as another early example of equitable recharacterisation, whereby the courts defeat the intention of the parties to evade formal restrictions, by calling arrangements by their true names.

[87] See, eg, *Santley v Wilde* (1889) 2 Ch 474, per Lindley MR at 478,479.

preclude only collateral advantages which are unfair and unconscionable.[88] An unconscionable collateral advantage is avoided.[89]

5.56 It is probably safe to assume that a right of rehypothecation would not be treated as unconscionable, particularly where the collateral giver is a financial institution. The other Rules remain a challenge to rehypothecation under English law.

(5) Techniques for Managing the Rules

5.57 A number of techniques may be available to manage the impact of the Rules on rehypothecation.

5.58 Rehypothecation would not conflict with the Rules if it were so structured that the third party received the (interests in) securities under a sub-mortgage. However, this will not often be a practical solution, as the collateral taker will generally require a first security interest in respect of its commercial exposures.[90]

5.59 Another technique for reconciling rehypothecation with the Rules is to provide that the rehypothecator acts as agent of the original mortgagor in granting a security interest to the third party.[91] However, in most cases the commercial aspects of many rehypothecation arrangements would be difficult to reconcile with such an agency. The collateral taker may not share in the profits of rehypothecation (except indirectly, by the payment of a discounted rate of interest to the collateral taker).[92] More importantly perhaps, the contract between the collateral taker and the third party will generally provide that the collateral taker deals as principal and not as agent. In any case, such an arrangement would deprive the original collateral taker of its security interest.

5.60 A third technique that would theoretically serve to reconcile rehypothecation with the Rules is the use of a separate agreement. There is no prohibition in dealing with the equity of redemption in an agreement separate from the mortgage agreement.[93] (Equally, collateral advantages arising under separate agreements are

---

[88] See *Multiservice Bookbinding Ltd v Marden* [1978] 2 All ER 489, per Browne-Wilkinson J at 502. This departs from earlier judicial indication that collateral advantages need to be reasonable: per Browne-Wilkinson J at 497; see *Cityland and Property (Holdings) Ltd v Dabrah* [1967] 2 All ER 639, per Goff J at 647.

[89] See, eg, *Fairclough v Swan Brewery Co Ltd* [1912] AC 565, PC.

[90] Where the (interests in) securities are delivered by way of an outright transfer, the transferor will be required to give an unencumbered title under representations and warranties given in standard dealing contracts, and under the terms of participation in settlement systems.

[91] This approach is adopted by clearing brokers providing collateral to the London Clearing House which has in turn been provided to them by their clients: see Chapter 8.

[92] See the discussion of prime brokerage in Chapter 10.

[93] See the note at 607 in the report of *Spurgeon v Collier* (1758) 28 ER 605; *Reeve v Lisle* [1902] AC 461, HL; and *Alec Lobb (Garages) Ltd v Total Oil GB Ltd* [1983] 1 All ER 944, per Millett QC at 963.

permitted,[94] and the prohibition only applies to collateral advantages forming a term of the mortgage agreement.)[95] However, this is not a practical solution as in commercial reality rights of rehypothecation will be negotiated as part of the collateral agreement as a whole.

(6) Policy Considerations

There may be policy considerations in favour of the view that rehypothecation should now be freely permitted under English law. **5.61**

The original purpose of the Rule was to avoid oppression, and early decisions are available in which the courts have declined to enforce the Rule in the absence of an intention to oppress[96] or mislead.[97] On occasions where the Rule has been held to be technically applicable, it has been applied with great judicial regret.[98] **5.62**

It might be argued that the case of *Ellis & Co*[99] serves to reconcile rehypothecation in the securities markets with the Rules. In this case, it was held that, where the **5.63**

---

[94] See *De Beers Consolidated Mines v British South Africa Company* [1912] AC 52, HL, per Lord Atkinson at 66. Indeed the two agreements may be contained in the same document: *Kreglinger v New Patagonia Meat and Cold Storage Co* [1914] AC 25, HL, per Lord Mersey at 45.

[95] *Re Petrol Filling Station, Vauxhall Bridge Road, London, Rosemex Service Station v Shell Mex and BP Ltd* (1968) 20 P & CR 1.

[96] See, for example, *Mellor v Lees* (1742) 26 ER 698, per the Lord Chancellor at 699: 'If, indeed, any fetters had been laid upon redeeming the mortgaged estate, by some original agreement, either in the mortgage deed, or a separate deed, it would not avail, where it is done with a design to wrest the estate fraudulently out of the hands of the mortgagor. But where is the fraud, or the inconvenience, in the present case?'

[97] See *Melbourne Banking Corporation Ltd v Brougham* (1888) 7 App Cas 307, PC. There is no general prohibition on the purchase of the equity of redemption by the mortgagee, which will only be set aside if there has been fraud, duress or other circumstances that would generally enable a transaction to be impeached: *Alec Lobb (Garages) Ltd v Total Oil GB Ltd* [1983] 1 All ER 944, per Millett QC at 965. (However, it must be acknowledged that this is not the invariable approach of the courts.) On the other hand, the Rules were applied in the case of *Lewis v Frank Love* [1961] 1 All ER 446 so as to defeat a commercial option, on the basis that it is a technical doctrine which applies irrespective of oppression: 'I pause there simply to observe that the doctrine of a clog on the equity is a technical doctrine which is not affected by the question whether in fact there has been oppression, and which applies just as much where the parties are represented, as they were here, by solicitors': per Plowman J, at 454.

[98] See, eg, *Salt v Northampton* [1892] AC 1, HL, per Lord Bramwell at 21. 'I think the equitable rule unreasonable, and I regret to have to disregard the express agreement of a man perfectly competent and advised by competent advisers'. See also *Samuel v Jarrah Timber and Wood Paving Corp* [1904] AC 323, HL, per Earl of Halsbury LC at 325, 327: 'A perfectly fair bargain made between two parties to it, each of whom was quite sensible of what they were doing, is not to be performed because at the same time a mortgage arrangement was made between them . . . Speaking for myself, I should not be sorry if your Lordships could see your way to modify [the Rule] so as to prevent its being used as a means of evading a fair bargain come to between persons dealing at arms' length and negotiating on equal terms'.

[99] *Ellis & Co's Trustee v Dixon-Johnson* [1924] 2 Ch 451. See also *Crearer v Bank of Scotland* (1922) SC (HL) 137, in which it was held that equivalent redelivery of shares by a legal mortgagee was usual business practice, and therefore involved no breach of the mortgagee's obligations to the mortgagor. See also *Dixon v London Small Arms Co* (1876) 1 App Cas 632. The author is grateful to Karin Artmann for this reference.

mortgaged property consists of (interests in) securities available in the secondary markets, the mortgagee may return (interests in) securities equivalent to the (interests in) securities delivered to it under the mortgage, and not the same ones.[100] Of course, such equivalent redelivery is a feature of rehypothecation; where the original (interests in) securities have been delivered to a third party, they are not available for redelivery to the original mortgagor, so equivalent (interests in) securities must be provided.

5.64 However, a further feature of rehypothecation is credit risk. The equity of redemption is a proprietary right retained by the collateral giver and attaching to the collateral assets. It represents the ownership by the collateral giver in the excess of the value of the collateral over the value of the secured exposure. If the collateral agreement permits the collateral taker to deliver the collateral (interests in) securities to a third party free of the equity of redemption, this property right can no longer attach to the original collateral (interests in) securities. After rehypothecation and before equivalent redelivery to the collateral giver, the collateral taker may happen to hold equivalent (interests in) securities, and if so it is arguable that the equity of redemption would attach to them. However, it is not customary to require the collateral taker to hold equivalent (interests in) securities during this period. If it does not hold them, the rights of the collateral giver are likely to be reduced to a mere personal right to require the delivery of equivalent (interests in) securities. This is because there is no continuing fund of collateral assets in the hands of the collateral taker against which the collateral giver can assert its property rights. If the collateral taker is insolvent these rights may be worthless. If the value of the collateral (interests in) securities delivered by the client significantly exceeds the collateralised exposure, the equity of redemption has significant value, and rehypothecation may involve a significant credit exposure for the collateral giver.

5.65 It would be prudent to assume that this credit exposure is not compatible with the Rules.

---

[100] Sargant LJ discusses the 'once a mortgage' rule (at 469–471): 'But obviously, . . . [the rule's] application to a case where the mortgaged property or property identical in all material respects therewith is readily purchasable on the market may very well be different to its application to an ordinary mortgage of land. It would be absurd to insist on a retransfer of the identical shares mortgaged when other shares of the same nature are available . . . in a case like the present, where the security that has been wrongly disposed of in part by the mortgagees consisted of freely marketable shares which can readily be replaced by others of precisely similar value, there is no necessity for insisting on the restoration of the particular shares charged'. This approach was approved in the House of Lords [1925] AC 489, per Viscount Cave LC at 491.
  See, however, *Langton v Waite* (1868) LR 6 EQ 165, in which a stockbroker was held to have no implied power of rehypothecation, and was obliged to account for the profits of rehypothecation to the collateral giver.

(7) Conclusions

It would be prudent to assume that rehypothecation may be incompatible with the Rules. Therefore, where the collateral taker wishes to use the collateral, the appropriate route is outright transfer. **5.66**

Historically, the Rules have not been burdensome in English law, because English law has always recognised outright transfers of collateral, and permitted insolvency set off, so that (as between an English collateral giver and an English collateral taker) the outright transfer route has always been available. However, with the rise in cross border financial transactions, English market participants now regularly enter into collateral arrangements with foreign counterparties. Under the foreign law that would govern the insolvency of the counterparty, insolvency set off may not be available, and recharacterisation risk may be present. In these circumstances, outright transfer is not appropriate, as discussed in Chapter 6. Thus, globalisation has rendered the Rules commercially burdensome. **5.67**

A further problem is posed by intermediation. Where the collateral consists of securities (and not interests in securities), the consequences of a breach of the 'once a mortgage' rule may not be unduly grave. The effect of the Rules is to invalidate contractual provision that conflicts with them. However, even if the contractual right of rehypothecation is ineffective, the property rights of the third party to whom the collateral giver rehypothecates may not be affected. This is because, under English priority rules, a prior equitable encumbrance on the collateral securities (the equity of redemption) will not bind (broadly) the good faith purchaser of a subsequent legal interest without notice of the prior equity. Of course, if the third party is given a mere equitable interest, for example one under a charge, it will not have priority. However, if the rehypothecation delivers a legal interest to the third party (under a legal mortgage or outright transfer), the equity of redemption may be overreached. Thus, historically, the impact of the Rules on rehypothecation may have been more theoretical than real.[101] **5.68**

However, as discussed in Chapter 2, the effect of intermediation in the securities markets has generally been to reduce the interest of investors and collateral takers to interests in securities, which are equitable. It is impossible to deliver a legal interest in an equitable asset, so that the third party will arguably always take the collateral subject to the equity of redemption. **5.69**

---

[101] Some practitioners have argued that rights of rehypothecation in breach of the 'once a mortgage' rule might have the effect of undermining the collateral taker's security interest. This seems unlikely. The effect of the rule is to invalidate contractual provision that conflicts with it (and not to undermine the rights of the mortgagee). Even if breach of the rule prompted the courts to recharacterise the collateral arrangements as an outright transfer (which would not conflict with the rule), the collateral taker would enjoy rights as the outright transferee of the collateral.

5.70 For these reasons, the Rules have not only outlived their usefulness, but become a burden. Law reform permitting rehypothecation would assist the competitive position of London as an international financial market.

6

OUTRIGHT COLLATERAL TRANSFERS

According to the rabbinic understanding of 'and there shall be no leavened bread be seen with thee' (Exod.12:20) . . . the procedure . . . is for the Jew to sell his leaven to a non-Jew before Passover but with a tacit understanding tht he will buy it back after Passover.[1]

A. Overview

As was seen in Chapter 4, there are two broad legal structures whereby (interests in) securities may be delivered as collateral. First, the collateral taker may be given a security interest in (interests in) securities. This security interest may be a mortgage, pledge, charge or lien. In this case, property rights in the collateral assets are divided between the collateral taker (who acquires a limited property interest under the security interest) and the collateral giver (who retains the equity of redemption).[2] Secondly, (interests in) securities may be transferred outright to the

6.01

---

[1] Louis Jacobs: *A Tree of Life* (Oxford University Press, 1984) 141.
[2] In the case of a legal mortgage, the only property right retained by the collateral taker is the equity of redemption. In the case of other security interests, the collateral taker may retain

119

collateral taker, on the basis that the collateral taker assumes an obligation ('the redelivery obligation') to deliver equivalent assets to the collateral giver on the discharge of the collateralised obligation, and on the further basis that the redelivery obligation will be set off against the collateralised obligation in the event of either party's default.

6.02 Chapters 4 and 5 considered certain disadvantages which are associated with security interests, namely the possible need for registration, the requirement for perfection under lex situs, restrictions on rehypothecation and possible restrictions on enforcement. Outright collateral transfers do not suffer from these disadvantages,[3] and for this reason the 1990s saw a major trend in the international financial markets away from security interests and towards outright collateral transfers.

6.03 The central feature of outright collateral transfers (as their name suggests) is that the collateral assets are transferred outright to the collateral taker, so that the collateral giver retains no residual interest in them. Registration requirements do not apply, because these relate to assets of the collateral giver which are subject to a security interest, and the collateral assets are no longer the assets of the collateral giver. Equally, there is no restriction on the collateral taker's use of the collateral assets, because they belong to the collateral taker outright from the moment of delivery, whether or not the collateral giver has defaulted. These comments are subject to recharacterisation risk, as discussed below.

6.04 Increasing volumes of (interests in) securities are being delivered as collateral under outright transfer arrangements, which are widely emerging as the preferred structure for collateral takers.[4] Outright transfer is widely used to provide collateral in the international financial markets for repurchase agreements (repos),[5] securities lending[6] and swaps,[7] as discussed below.

6.05 Settlement systems, global custodians and prime brokers (see Chapters 9 and 10) are active intermediaries in these markets, and serve a number of functions. They provide their clients with access to cheap finance by delivering their (interests in) securities as agent to market counterparties under outright collateral transfers.

---

additional property rights. For example, under a pledge, it retains legal and equitable title, and under an equitable mortgage or charge, it retains legal title.

[3] Provided they are not recharacterised as security interests; see below.

[4] For a discussion of outright transfer as an alternative to security interests, see Philip Wood, *Title Finance, Derivatives, Securitisations, Set-off and Netting* (London: Sweet & Maxwell, 1995) ch 1.

[5] In economic effect, the obligation of the seller to pay the repurchase price is collateralised in the hands of the purchaser by the outright transfer of the purchased (interests in) securities.

[6] The obligation of the borrower to redeliver (interests in) securities equivalent to the loaned (interests in) securities is collateralised either by cash or the outright transfer of collateral (interests in) securities. This discussion is relevant to the latter.

[7] As discussed below, under English market standard documentation, collateral for exposures arising under swaps can be provided by way of outright transfer or alternatively by way of security interest.

They enable their clients to fill their short positions by lending the (interests in) securities of other clients to them, also as agent. Thirdly, they act as administrative agents for their client's collateral programmes under tri-party repo programmes, as discussed below. Some market commentators have identified collateral management as the most important future role for such intermediaries.

B. Outright Transfer

The legal principle underlying these arrangements is that the (interests in) securi- **6.06** ties originally delivered to the collateral taker ('original securities') are transferred outright to the collateral taker ('the outright transfer principle'). The collateral taker acquires the entire property rights of the collateral giver in the original securities, and the collateral giver retains no residual interest in them. Any compromise of the Outright Transfer Principle may raise recharacterisation risk, as discussed below.

C. Contractual Redelivery of Equivalent Securities

In accordance with the outright transfer principle, the redelivery obligation is **6.07** only enforceable by the collateral giver as a personal right against the collateral taker, arising under contract. It is not enforceable as a property right, attaching to the original securities. (As indicated below, the collateral giver is protected in the insolvency of the collateral taker by insolvency set off).

The redelivery obligation is reconciled with the outright transfer principle by **6.08** careful drafting in market standard documentation, which provides that the redelivery obligation relates, not to the original securities, but rather to equivalent securities.[8] Equivalent securities mean (interests in) securities of the same number and type as the original securities.[9] Of course, it may be that in practice the

---

[8] Strictly, it is not a *re*delivery obligation, but a delivery obligation, because the original assets are not returned in specie.

[9] See the definition of 'Equivalent Credit Support' in para 10 of the International Swaps and Derivatives Association English Law Credit Support Annex; the definition of 'Equivalent Securities' in para 2(o) of the Public Securities Association/International Securities Markets Association Global Master Repurchase Agreement (GMRA); and the definition of 'Equivalent' in para 2.1 of the International Securities Lenders Association Global Master Securities Lending Agreement (GMSLA).

See also Justinian's discussion of the Roman law concept of *mutuum*: 'This arises only with things identified by weight, number or measure, such as wine, oil, corn, money, bronze, silver, and gold. When we lend such things by number, measure, or weight, we intend that they should become the property of the recipient and that when the time comes for getting them back we should receive not the very things we gave but others of the same kind and quality': *Institutes* III.14 pr (Birks and McLeod (trans), London: Duckworth, 1987) 105, 107.

collateral taker returns the original securities in specie.[10] However, it is important that it should be under no contractual or operational obligation to do so, in order to avoid recharacterisation risk.

D. The Benefits and Burdens of Ownership

6.09 Even though the original securities are transferred outright, the economic effect of the transaction is intended to be that the collateral giver retains the both the benefits and burdens of ownership. At the end of the transaction it will receive equivalent securities (of the same number as the original securities, irrespective of their market value at the time of redelivery). For this reason, it continues to have a position in the collateral (interests in) securities, making a gain if their market value rises and a loss if it falls. Therefore, the outright transfer arrangement should be 'balance sheet neutral', in the sense that the collateral assets remain on the balance sheet of the collateral giver, and do not appear on the balance sheet of the collateral taker.[11] In addition, if the collateral (interests in) securities generate income during the term of the transaction, it is provided that the collateral taker will pay to the collateral giver a sum equal to the income it receives. However, it is normal for the collateral giver to forfeit the right to direct voting.[12]

---

[10] As discussed below, this is fairly unlikely where the collateral taker trades actively in the financial markets, as it may wish to use the collateral it receives as collateral for its own exposures, or otherwise; see below.

[11] In the United Kingdom, the criteria for balance sheet neutrality are indicated in Financial Reporting Standard 5 (FRS 5) of the Accounting Standards Board, entitled 'Reporting the Substance of Transactions': 'To determine the substance of a transaction it is necessary to identify whether the transaction has given rise to new assets or liabilities' (para 16). For this purpose, 'assets' and 'liabilities' are defined in economic and not legal terms (paras 2 and 4). In relation to repos, 'the seller will retain all significant rights to benefits relating to the original asset and all significant exposure to the risks inherent in those benefits . . . The seller should account for this type of arrangement by showing the original asset on its balance sheet' (para B4).

For US persons who are required to account under US Generally Accepted Accounting Principles (GAAP), the position is governed by the Statement of Financial Accounting Standards No 125 (FAS 125) of the Financial Accounting Standards Board of the Financial Accounting Foundation, entitled 'Accounting for Transfers and Servicing of Financial Assets and Extinguishment of Liabilities': 'This statement provides consistent standards for distinguishing transfers of financial assets that are sales from transfers that are secured borrowings'. Broadly, transactions treated as secured borrowings are balance sheet neutral, whereas sales are not. (It will be seen in Chapter 12 that the concern with securitisations is that the transaction be characterised as a sale, whereas the converse is generally the position for repos.) Assets will only be treated as sales and removed from the balance sheet of the collateral giver if (very broadly) (i) the transfer is isolated from the insolvency of the collateral giver; (ii) the collateral taker is free to rehypothecate; and (iii) the transferor does not maintain effective control over the transferred assets (see para 9). In relation to repos, see also paras 27–29.

An annex is available to the London standard documentation for repos (GMRA) adapting it in order to comply with the criteria set out in FAS 125 for balance sheet neutrality.

[12] See para 6.3 of GMSLA. However, in equity repos, the collateral taker agrees to use its best endeavours to arrange for voting in accordance with the collateral giver's instructions, provided it holds the relevant securities at the time. See para 3.6 of the GMRA Equity Annex (n 9 above).

E. Credit Risk

It is useful to contrast the methods by which credit risks are managed in security **6.10** interests and in outright collateral transfers.

Under any collateral arrangement, both parties are likely to have potential credit **6.11** exposures. The exposure of the collateral taker is the debt or other obligation of the collateral giver; this exposure is addressed by taking collateral. The collateral giver usually has a credit exposure also, because the value of collateral assets usually exceeds the value of the collateralised exposure by a significant margin.[13] The collateral giver is concerned to ensure that, in the insolvency of the collateral taker, it receives back the whole of this excess value and is not obliged to prove for it as an unsecured creditor.

Where a security interest is given, each party has a concurrent interest in the col- **6.12** lateral assets. The collateral taker has the security interest, and the collateral giver has the equity of redemption. These interests serve to elevate each party above the status of unsecured creditor in the insolvency of the other, and thus address credit risk.

The position differs with outright collateral transfers. The credit risk of the col- **6.13** lateral taker is addressed by its outright ownership of the collateral. The credit risk of the collateral giver is only incompletely addressed. In the insolvency of the collateral taker, the collateralised exposure will be set off against the redelivery obligation. However, the collateral giver must prove for any surplus value as an unsecured creditor in the insolvency of the collateral taker.

F. Master Agreements

The collateralisation of financial exposures has significantly increased during the **6.14** last decade, and accordingly market standard collateral documentation has been developed. Standard outright transfer collateral documentation has been prepared by leading trade associations. Of particular importance in the London and international securities markets are the standard documentation for repos (the Global Master Repurchase Agreement endorsed by PSA[14]/ISMA);[15] securities

---

[13] Broadly speaking, a 5 per cent margin is normal. The most important factor affecting margin is the quality and volatility of the collateral (interests in) securities. The credit standing of the counterparty is also a factor. Margin might vary from perhaps 1 per cent or 2 per cent (for short term OECD treasury securities) to 10 per cent for corporate bonds, 20 per cent for equities and 25 per cent for emerging market securities. Margin is colloquially referred to as 'haircut'.

[14] The Bond Market Association, formerly, the Public Securities Association, based in New York.

[15] The International Securities Markets Association, based in Zurich.

lending (the Global Master Securities Lending Agreement, prepared by ISLA);[16] and swaps (the Credit Support Annex (Transfer—English Law) (prepared by ISDA).[17]

6.15 In each case, the parties enter into a master agreement setting out the terms on which they will enter into particular transactions from time to time.[18] Each transaction is incorporated into a single agreement governing the whole programme of transactions between the two parties. Master agreements generally envisage that either party may enter into a transaction either as collateral giver or as collateral taker.

6.16 The key trade associations have obtained legal opinions for use by their members on the enforceability of the close-out netting and set off provisions (known as netting opinions) from independent counsel practising in a large number of jurisdictions.[19]

6.17 A more recent trend is the development of cross-product master netting agreements.[20] These permit the netting of exposures between the same parties arising under different transaction types.

G. Marking to Market

6.18 Changes in market values affect both the value of (interests in) securities collateral and also (in the case of swaps and securities lending)[21] the value of collateralised exposures. In order to avoid the risk that the value of the collateral should rapidly fall short of the collateralised exposure, the collateral taker specifies a margin by which the collateral value should exceed the exposure, as discussed above.[22]

---

[16] The International Securities Lenders Association, based in London. See their website at www.isla.co.uk

[17] The International Swaps and Derivatives Association New York and London. See their website at www.isda.org

[18] After the conclusion of the master agreement, trades are characteristically concluded over the telephone and recorded by a simple confirmation. Each trade is consolidated into the master agreement to form a single agreement. (The arrangements for securities loans differ in minor respects.)

[19] ISDA, PSA/ISMA and the Stock Lending and Repo Committee of the Bank of England have each obtained dozens of such opinions. Also, in relation to foreign exchange, deposit and derivatives netting, similar opinions have been obtained by the British Bankers Association and the Futures and Options Association.

[20] The Cross-Product Netting Agreement of the British Bankers Association was finalised in February 2000. Such an agreement has also been produced by the Bond Market Association.

[21] In the case of repos, the collateralised exposure increases daily as 'price differential', or interest element, accrues.

[22] However, in 'the precipitous decline in the value of Russian GKO securities in 1998. . .[n]o institution's haircut on these securities proved sufficient cushion against the 80% value decline they suffered over a short period': *ISDA 1999 Collateral Review* 13 (see the ISDA website at www.isda.org).

Throughout the collateral arrangement, the parties seek to preserve this margin by marking to market, as follows. If at any time the value of the collateral should fall short of the agreed margin, a collateral shortfall is said to arise. This entitles the collateral taker to call for the delivery of additional collateral to restore the agreed margin. In the event of a collateral excess, the collateral giver is entitled to call for the release of margin so as to restore the agreed margin. In calculating whether there is a margin shortfall or excess, the position on all outstanding transactions is calculated on a net basis.[23]

Marking to market serves to address the market risk that in turn presents credit **6.19** risk for the parties to the transaction. Active marking to market is important in managing these risks, and in practice several calls may be made daily.

H. Netting

As discussed above, in outright collateral transfers, the collateral giver has a credit **6.20** exposure to the collateral taker equal to the margin, or the excess of the value of the collateral assets over the value of the collateralised exposure. This credit exposure represents a commercial risk, and also attracts regulatory capital requirements. For these reasons, it is desirable for the collateral giver to minimise such exposures as much as possible. The size of the margin on each transaction is a matter for negotiation with the collateral taker. However, it is often the case that two financial institutions enter into a large number of outright collateral transfer transactions with each other, with each institution acting as collateral giver in some transactions, and collateral taker in others. Such transactions are documented together under a single master agreement. In these cases, an important technique for reducing credit risk is netting under the master document, whereby collateral shortfalls arising on one transaction are set off against collateral surpluses arising on another transaction. This is an important argument in favour of the use of master agreements.

Another (related) level of netting comes into operation upon the default of a party. **6.21** After default, close-out netting arrangements serve as a preliminary stage to insolvency set off, converting the mutual obligations of the parties into obligations which can be set off in insolvency.

The market standard master agreements set out a list of events of default, which **6.22** include insolvency events, and other defaults such as failure to deliver margin in response to a mark to market call.[24] An event of default may be defined so as to

---

[23] However, when the parties rely on automatic marking for market within CREST (the UK settlement system), this takes place on a transaction by transaction basis. See Chapter 9 for a discussion of CREST.

[24] Failure to deliver the repoed securities on time is not itself an event of default, because late deliveries are not uncommon in the international settlement systems.

require the service of notice by the non-defaulting party, or may be automatic.[25] In most cases, default triggers a close out netting mechanism as follows. First, all outstanding transactions between the parties are accelerated, so that all duties to discharge the collateralised obligations and to redeliver equivalent collateral become immediately due and performable.[26] Secondly, redelivery obligations are converted into obligations to pay a sum equal to the current market value of the equivalent securities.[27] (Such provision is necessary because the defaulting party may be insolvent, and insolvency set off is only available in respect of payment obligations.)[28] Thirdly, any payment obligations in currencies other than the base currency specified in the master agreement are converted into the base currency.[29]

I. Set Off

6.23 Following default, once the exposures of each party have been reduced to a single net sum under close out netting provisions, these two net sums are set off against each other, so that only a single net sum is payable. If marking to market has operated effectively, this net sum should be payable by the collateral taker to the collateral giver, and should be equal to the margin that was initially agreed.

6.24 Under English law, set off is available even when one's counterparty is affected by administration (which places a general moratorium on the enforcement of claims) and (subject to the limits of rule 4.90 of the Insolvency Rules, discussed below) in liquidation.

(1) Nature

where a creditor claims a debt from his debtor and the debtor has a cross-claim on the creditor, then, if the debtor can reduce or extinguish the amount of the creditor's claim by his cross-claim, the debtor is said to set-off. The set-off operates as a double payment or discharge of the reciprocal claims . . . Note that the debtor uses his asset to pay his liability.[30]

6.25 The rules relating to set off differ depending on whether or not one of the parties is in insolvent liquidation.

---

[25] The appointment of a liquidator is automatically an event of default, in order to avoid the risk of post-insolvency dispositions.

[26] Such provision is necessary, because counterparty insolvency does not release a person from performing her obligations under a contract in accordance with its original terms.

[27] Somewhat different provision is included under ISDA; this is often amended to reflect market value.

[28] See the discussion of rule 4.90 of the Insolvency Rules 1986, SI 1986/1925, below.

[29] See para 10 of GMSLA (n 9 above) and para 10 of GMRA (n 9 above).

[30] P R Wood, *English and International Set-Off* (London: Sweet & Maxwell, 1989) 5.

(2) Insolvency Set Off

The central purpose of outright collateral transfers is to protect the collateral taker **6.26** in the event of counterparty insolvency. Therefore it is crucial for the collateral taker to establish that insolvency set off would be available if its counterparty became insolvent. If the counterparty is a foreign entity whose insolvency would be governed by a foreign system of law, the availability of insolvency set off must be established under that system of law. As indicated above, opinions are available for market standard documentation in a range of jurisdictions.

Very broadly speaking, the availability of insolvency set off is narrowly restricted **6.27** under general legal principles in civil law jurisdictions.[31] However, some civil law jurisdictions have introduced special statutory regimes which permit insolvency set off in the context of repos and certain other types of transaction widely used in international finance.

Under English law, set off is available and indeed mandatory in liquidation. Rule **6.28** 4.90 of the Insolvency Rules 1986 applies where there have been mutual dealings between a company and a counterparty, and the company subsequently goes into liquidation. Where such dealing has given rise to mutual debits and credits, there is mandatory set off between such debits and credits under rule 4.90(2):

> Under r 4.90 of the 1986 rules, . . . all mutual credits and debits are set-off so that only the net balance is provable in, or payable to, the liquidation. An account must be struck as at the commencement of the liquidation between the company and the creditor/debtor whereby all credits and debits are set-off regardless of the jurisdiction in which any credit or debit arose. In *Stein v Blake* [1995] 2 All ER 961 at 964, 967, [1996] AC 243 to 251, 255 Lord Hoffman (with whose speech the other members of the House agreed) said: 'Bankruptcy set-off . . . affects the substantive rights of the parties by enabling the bankrupt's creditor to use his indebtedness to the bankrupt as a form of security', and that bankruptcy set-off 'is mandatory and self-executing and results, as of the bankruptcy date, in only a net balance being owing'.[32]

Rule 4.90 provides that set off is mandatory in the event of insolvent liquidation. **6.29** It is not possible to disapply or modify the operation of Rule 4.90, and contractual provision purporting to do so will be ineffective.[33]

---

[31] Philip Wood has identified creditor-friendly jurisdictions, which readily permit insolvency set off, and debtor-friendly jurisdictions, which do not.

[32] *Re BCCI (No 10)* [1996] 1 All ER 796, per Sir Richard Scott VC at 812.

[33] *British Eagle International Airline Ltd v Compagnie Internationale Air France* [1975] 2 WLR 758. This House of Lords decision concerned a clearing system set up by the International Air Transport Association (IATA). Member airlines incurred debts to each other, for example by accepting each other's tickets. Rather than settle these debts on a gross basis it was agreed that a multilateral netting arrangement would be implemented so that, where at the end of the month an airline overall was owed money by the system, it would receive a payment from IATA and where an airline owed money to the system it would make a payment to IATA. British Eagle went into liquidation owing money overall to the system on a net basis but on a gross basis being owed money by Air France. Its liquidators sought to recover the debt from Air France arguing that the multilateral

6.30 As indicated above, market standard documentation provides for set off upon default, and events of default are defined to include insolvency and non-insolvency events. With non-insolvency related events of default, the contractual provisions will generally take effect in accordance with their terms. In insolvent liquidation, rule 4.90 will apply on a mandatory basis in place of the contractual set off provisions. Therefore the set off provisions of market standard documentation have been drafted to mirror as closely as possible the effect of rule 4.90, so that the substitution of statutory for contractual provision in the event of insolvency liquidation should not defeat the contractual expectations of the parties.[34]

6.31 In some cases, market participants adapt their agreements to extend the contractual set off provisions beyond the scope of insolvency set off.[35] While useful in non-insolvency default, it is important to understand that such provisions will not be effective in insolvency.

6.32 The requirement for mutuality in rule 4.90(1) means in effect that one person's claim cannot be used to pay another person's debt.[36] Issues may therefore arise where one party contracts as agent or trustee.

6.33 Where one party contracts as agent, set off will apply between the principal and the counterparty, and not between the agent and the counterparty.[37] In practice, securities lending and repo agreements are routinely entered into by custodians and fund managers as agent for their clients. Where an agreement is entered into by the agent for a single client, insolvency set off should operate so as to mirror the contractual set off provisions, by taking effect between the single principal and the counterparty. However, in many cases a custodian or fund manager will enter into a single agreement with a particular counterparty in respect of a number of different clients. In this case, the operation of insolvency set off may not accord with the contractual provisions.[38] Whereas the contract provides for a single set off (with all outstanding exposures being reduced to a single net sum) insolvency set off will apply separately between each principal and the insolvent counterparty (producing as many net sums as there are counterparties).[39]

---

netting agreement was not effective against them as it contravened the pari passu rule and the mandatory provisions of statutory insolvency law. They won.

[34] One minor point of mismatch between contractual and insolvency set off relates to the rate of exchange in which foreign currency obligations will be converted into base currency; see the discussion below.

[35] For example, contractual set off provisions may seek to include sums owed to associated companies.

[36] See P Wood, *Law and Practice of International Finance, Outright Collateral Transfer, Derivatives, Securitisations, Set-Off and Netting* (London: Sweet & Maxwell, 1995) 125.

[37] See para 16 of GMSLA (n 9 above).

[38] Unless, of course, the contract is drafted to reflect the fragmented set off that will apply in insolvency. Some agreements do contain such drafting.

[39] The position is more complex in some prime brokerage arrangements, in which the prime broker commingles the assets of a number of clients, and lends (interests in) securities from that pool as

There has been a debate in the London legal community about the application of insolvency set off between a trustee and a counterparty. The concern has been raised that mutuality may not be present because of the different treatment of trust assets and trust liabilities under the general principles of trust law. Where the trust assets include a debt owed by a counterparty, that asset will be held on trust by the trustee for the beneficiaries. However, where a debt is owed to the counterparty, the trustee is personally liable for it (although it is entitled to be indemnified out of the trust fund in respect of such liabilities provided they were incurred without breach of trust). In other words, the debt is the debt of the trustee, but the asset is not the asset of the trustee, so that mutuality is, arguably, absent.[40] Others[41] are understood to have taken a more robust approach, and argued that set off is available in these circumstances. **6.34**

Rule 4.90(3) excludes from set off any debts of the company if, at the time they became due, the creditor had notice of a petition for the winding up of the company (or of the summoning of a creditors meeting in the case of a voluntary winding up). **6.35**

Under rule 4.91 foreign currency debts are converted into sterling at the official rate of exchange prevailing at the date when the company went into liquidation. It is important to note that both the rate and the timing of the conversion may differ from contractual provision, and this currency exposure remains a shortcoming of set off provisions in industry standard documentation.[42] **6.36**

(3) Cherry Picking

In English law, section 178 of the Insolvency Act 1986 gives the liquidator power to disclaim onerous property, including any unprofitable contract.[43] Executory (or unperformed) contracts are vulnerable to such disclaimer, and therefore master agreements (which rely on the insolvency set off of all transactions entered into them) provide upon default for unperformed trades to be immediately accelerated and closed out, as discussed above. Further protection is provided by the 'single agreement' language in the master agreements. Where a foreign counterparty is involved, it is necessary to establish that close out netting and insolvency set off is **6.37**

---

agent to third parties. In these circumstances, it may not be straightforward to identify the principal to any particular trade. See Chapter 10 for a discussion of prime brokerage.

[40] See the discussion in P Wood, *English and International Set-Off* (London: Sweet & Maxwell, 1989), para 21-32 et seq.

[41] Including, anecdotally, Leading Counsel.

[42] See the Opinion of Mr Sykes QC on GMRA dated 8 November 1995. It is advisable to hedge against the consequent currency risk.

[43] Insolvency Act 1986, s 178(3)(a). A person suffering loss in consequence of such a disclaimer is deemed to be a creditor of the company to the extent of such loss (s 178(6)), and this debt is eligible for set off: see P Wood, *English and International Set-Off* (n 40 above) para 7-80.

not disturbed by the liquidator of one party exercising such disclaimer power, so as to enforce some contracts but disclaim others ('cherry picking').

(4) Interveners

6.38 A potential danger for the debtor (A) who relies on insolvency set off is that, if the creditor (B) assigns B's claim against A to a third party (C), this assignment to C (the intervener) may disturb A's rights of set off. Similar concerns arise where a third party judgment creditor attaches the claim of B against A. Under English law, the position is broadly that, provided the collateral agreement contains provisions against interveners,[44] and A has no notice of any intervener at the time the collateral agreement and the transactions in question are entered into, its rights of set off take priority over the rights of the intervener.[45] It is important for collateral takers to establish the position under foreign systems of law that would govern the insolvency of their counterparties.

J. Recharacterisation Risk[46]

6.39 Recharacterisation risk is the risk that the label which parties apply to their transaction is rejected by the courts. Under English law, recharacterisation relies on the principle that equity looks to the substance, not the form.[47]

6.40 Chapter 5 considered the risk that a purported fixed charge might be recharacterised as a floating charge. This section will consider the risk that a purported outright collateral transfer is recharacterised as a security interest.[48]

---

[44] Market standard documentation contains prohibitions on assignment.

[45] See P Wood, *English and International Set-Off* (n 40 above) 854, para 16-16.
See also para 1–86 at 25 for a discussion of interveners generally. This rule is the corollary of the rule that equitable assignments (such as those without notice) are vulnerable to set off; see Chapter 3.

[46] Recharacterisation as it is discussed in this section should not be confused with characterisation for the purposes of private international law.

[47] 'There are in principle two ways for a court to discard the parties' expressed description of the nature of a transaction into which they enter. One is by a finding that some or all of the agreement does not reflect what the parties did agree. That is a state of affairs which is commonly labelled a sham, although there are other words used. The other separate means whereby the court discards the parties' expressed intention is by a finding that the transaction entered into by the parties is on analysis of a different nature from the description that they have given to it. If the transaction is a cow and has cloven hooves, the parties cannot turn it into a horse by using equine terminology or saying that it is a horse': per Knox J in *Re New Bullas Trading Ltd* [1993] BCLC 1389, at 1394.

[48] The effect of recharacterisation risk is broadly the same as the effect of the unavailability of insolvency set off in the insolvency of the collateral giver, ie that the collateral taker is required to perform its side of the transaction but is deprived of the benefit of its interest in the collateral, and is reduced to the status of unsecured creditor. However, the legal reasoning behind the two misfortunes for the collateral taker are different. In the former, courts reject the provisions of the contract as contrary to the mandatory provisions of insolvency law. In the latter, they reject the express provisions of the contract as not reflecting the true agreement between the parties.

A number of disadvantages are associated with such recharacterisation, as dis- **6.41**
cussed below. In many cases the most significant of these is that such a security
interest may be void for want of registration.

The English courts take a robust approach, and recharacterisation risk is not con- **6.42**
sidered to be present when parties use London industry standard documentation
in accordance with its terms. However, recharacterisation risk is significant, particularly in civil law jurisdictions, in the absence of special statutory regimes in
favour of repos and certain other transactions. In cross border arrangements, this
is an important limit on the use of outright transfer.

As indicated above, the key advantages of outright transfer arrangements include **6.43**
freedom from the rules concerning rehypothecation, registration, perfection and
enforcement that apply to security interests ('the Rules'). The Rules were developed to protect unsecured creditors (in the case of registration and perfection)[49]
and the debtor (in the case of rehypothecation and enforcement).[50] Collateral takers seek to avoid the Rules by characterising their arrangements as outright transfers and not as security interests. However, the same policy concerns that lie
behind the Rules may lead the courts in some circumstances to attack the outright
transfer arrangements that purport to remove collateral arrangements from their
scope. The courts may do this by recharacterising outright transfer arrangements
as security interests.

In practice, an action for recharacterisation is likely to be brought by the liquida- **6.44**
tor of an insolvent collateral giver wishing to reclaim the collateral and reduce the
position of the collateral taker to that of unsecured creditor.[51]

(1) Disadvantages of Recharacterisation

Recharacterisation may have the following disadvantages under English law; **6.45**
many of these are the converse of the advantages of outright transfer arrangements
discussed above. Similar concerns are likely to arise in cross border arrangements
where outright transfers are recharacterised in other jurisdictions. Additionally, in
some jurisdictions there are onerous restrictions on the enforcement of a security
interest, involving delays and possibly court proceedings.

A security interest may be avoided for want of registration under section 395 of **6.46**
the Companies Act 1985, if it amounts to a floating charge (for example where the

---

[49] If security interests are made public by registration and perfection, unsecured creditors will not
be misled into believing that the encumbered assets would be available to them in the insolvency of
the collateral giver, and so advance credit on this mistaken basis.

[50] See the discussion of rehypothecation in Chapter 5.

[51] Even where the likelihood of recharacterisation is remote, the liquidator may feel obliged to
litigate where large sums of money are involved in order to avoid criticism and potential liability for
failing to do all it could to maximise the insolvent's assets. It may not be deterred by the expense of
litigation, as its costs will come out of the insolvent estate.

collateral giver retains a measure of control over the collateral pool) or a charge on book debts (for example where cash balances are used as collateral).

6.47 If an outright collateral transfer is recharacterised as a security interest, the application of close out netting and set off may amount to the enforcement of a security interest. If the collateral giver is in administration, there is an automatic freeze on the enforcement of security interests granted by it and breach of this freeze may involve criminal contempt of court.[52] (However, there is indirect authority that this restriction does not apply to assets located overseas.)[53]

6.48 If the collateral arrangements are recharacterised as creating a floating charge, special insolvency invalidation provisions may apply.[54]

6.49 The collateral giver may not have had power under its constitution to grant security interests. The individual who executed the agreement may not have had authority to execute a security interest.

6.50 If the parties had contemplated the creation of a security interest, different provisions would have been included in the documentation.[55]

6.51 The collateral giver may have given a negative pledge to a third party, of which the collateral taker may have constructive notice (because it formed part of a registered charge). This may expose the collateral taker to tortious liability to the third party for inducing breach of contract.

6.52 A security interest may be postponed to other competing security interests having priority over it.

(2) Recharacterisation under English Domestic Law

6.53 A very long line of cases deals with this type of recharacterisation under English domestic law. The more important of these are indicted in the footnote below

---

[52] There is no specific statutory offence contained in the Insolvency Act 1986 of taking steps to enforce a security interest over the property of a company in administration. However, any act preventing an officer of the court from carrying out its official duties is generally a criminal contempt of court: see *Halsburys Laws* (4th edn) vol 9, para 31. An administrator is an officer of the court: *Re Atlantic Computer Systems plc* [1992] Ch 505, per Nicholls LJ at 529, and *Barclays Mercantile v Sibec Ltd* [1992] 1 WLR 1253, per Millett J at 1259. While the mens rea necessary for criminal contempt is in some respects unclear, it appears that recklessness is generally necessary. See C J Miller, *Contempt of Court* (Oxford: Clarendon Press, 1989) 4–14.

[53] See *Re Vocalion (Foreign) Ltd* [1932] All ER 519. See also *Re Maudslay* [1900] 1 Ch 602, per Cozens-Hardy J at 610 and *Schemmer v Property Resources Ltd* [1974] Ch D 45, per Goulding J at 458.

[54] See the Insolvency Act 1986, s 245.

[55] eg, standard outright transfer documentation does not contain language relating to further assurances, negative pledge, appropriate representations, modification of the Law of Property Act 1925 and other enforcement language.

('the Cases').[56] The Cases concern financing arrangements under which collateral assets are purported to be transferred outright to the person providing finance. Such arrangements include sale and lease back,[57] tri-party sale and lease back,[58] block discounting[59] and sale and buy back transactions.[60] In each of the cases, it was asserted that the purported outright transfer did not succeed in conferring outright title to the collateral on the collateral taker, but only a security interest. In most of the cases it was argued further that this security interest was avoided or rendered unenforceable for want of compliance with statutory requirements.[61]

In only approximately one-third of the cases were the arrangements recharac- **6.54**
terised. Most of these were recharacterised because the written agreement was a sham which did not truly reflect the intention of the parties.[62] Others were recharacterised because the arrangements, although not a sham, included features which were inconsistent with outright transfer (for example, provision that the collateral taker is not free to dispose of the collateral;[63] and mortgage language).[64]

In general, the English courts take a robust approach and seek to avoid recharac- **6.55**
terisation. A range of legitimate financing techniques is available under English law, including the provision of collateral by outright transfer.[65] The fact that the economic motive behind the transaction is the provision of collateral does not

---

[56] *Alderson v White* (1858) 2 De G & J 95; *Ed p Odell* (1878) 10 Ch D 76; *Yorkshire Railway Wagon Co v MaClure* (1882) 31 Ch D 309; *Manchester, Sheffield & Lincolnshire Railway Co v North Central Wagon Co* (1888) 13 App Cas 554; HL; *Re Watson, ex p Official Receiver in Bankruptcy* (1890) 25 QB 27; *Mandell v Thomas & Co* [1891] 1 QB 230; *Beckett v Lower Assets Co Ltd* [1891] 1 QB 1; *McEntire v Crossley Bros Ltd* [1895] AC 457, HL; *Maas v Pepper* [1905] AC 102, HL; *British Railway Traffic v Kahn* [1921] WN 54; *Re Inglefield (George) Ltd* [1933] Ch 1; *Staffs Motor Guarantee Ltd v British Wagon Co Ltd* [1934] 2 KB 305; *Re Lovegrove, ex p George Lovegrove & Co (Sales) Ltd* [1935] Ch 464, CA; *Palette Shoes Ptd Ltd v Krohn* (1937) (unreported); *Olds Discount Co Ltd v John Playfair Ltd* [1938] 3 All ER 275; *Polsky v S & A Services Ltd* [1951] WN 136; *Chow Yoong Hong v Choong Fah Rubber Manufactory Ltd* [1961] 3 All ER 1163, CA; *Spencer v North Country Finance Co, The Guardian*, 20 February 1963; *Stoneleigh Finance Ltd v Phillips* [1965] 2 QB 537, CA; *Re Curtain Dream plc* [1990] BCLC 148; *Welsh Development Agency v Export Finance Co Ltd* [1992] BCLC 148; *Lloyds & Scottish Finance Ltd v Cruil Lord Carpets Sales Ltd* [1992] BCLC 609, HL; *Orion Finance v Crown Financial Management Ltd* (1994) (unreported); *Re G E Tunbridge ltd* (1995) 1 BCLC 34.

[57] *Alderson, Odell, Yorkshire, Manchester, Watson, Madell, Beckett, Maas, Kahn, Staffs, Polsky, Spencer* and *Stoneleigh.*

[58] *Inglefield, Orion.*

[59] *Olds v Cohen, Olds v Playfair, Lloyds.* See also *Lovegrove, Palette, Chow, Welsh Development Agency.*

[60] *Curtain.*

[61] For example, the Bills of Sale Act 1878 registration requirements (*Odell, Manchester, Watson, Madell, Beckett, Maas, Kahn, Staffs, Polsky*), the Companies Acts registration requirements (*Inglefield, Palette, Stoneleigh, Curtain, Welsh Development Agency, Lloyds, Orion*) or the Moneylenders Act 1927 (*Olds v Cohen, Olds v Playfair, Chow*).

[62] For example, see *Watson, Madell, Maas* and *Polsky.*

[63] *Curtain.*

[64] *Odell.*

[65] See *Beckett, Kahn, Chow.*

indicate that recharacterisation is appropriate.[66] Provided London market standard documentation is used in accordance with its terms, recharacterisation risk is not considered to be present under English domestic law.[67] This view is supported by the opinions of Leading Counsel.[68]

6.56 However, concerns may arise in practice if parties to outright transfer arrangements wish either to amend market standard documentation, or to implement arrangements which conflict with its provisions. For example, the collateral giver may wish to restrict the ability of the collateral taker to remove the (interests in) securities from a particular account[69] or to reserve an absolute right to withdraw (interests in) securities and substitute others. This may raise recharacterisation risk, by indicating that the collateral giver retains a proprietary interest in the collateral (interests in) securities.

(3) Conflict of Laws

6.57 Another route whereby recharacterisation risk arises for outright collateral transfers made under by English law documentation, is under the rules of conflict of laws. Where arrangements documented under London market standard documentation include a foreign element, English domestic law may not determine the question of recharacterisation. This may be either because, under the rules of English private international law, the English courts would apply foreign law to the question, or alternatively because another court may assume jurisdiction and itself apply foreign law.

Foreign counterparty

6.58 If the insolvency of the collateral giver is governed by foreign law, the outright transfer collateral arrangements will have to pass the test of any local law insolvency displacement rules (such as rules avoiding preferences).[70] Assuming it does not fall within the scope of such rules, it could be argued in theory that the local courts conducting the liquidation should recognise property rights arising prior

---

[66] *Olds v Playfair*. See also *Bank of Tokyo v Karoon* [1986] 3 All ER 468, per Goff LJ at 486, and *Re Polly Peck International plc (in administration) (No 3)* [1986] 1 BCLC 428, per Robert Walker J at 439, after a discussion the judgment of Staughton LJ in *Welsh Development Agency*: 'the general proposition that when the law is looking for the substance of a matter, it is normally looking for its legal substance, not its economic substance (if different)'.

[67] For a robust approach in refusing to recharacterise a repo transaction, see the full (unreported) judgment of Millet J in *Macmillan v Bishopsgate Investment Trust plc* (December 1993) 113, 114, 144, 145. (These comments do not appear in the abbreviated, reported version of the judgment at [1995] 3 All ER 747.)

[68] See the opinions of Mr Sykes QC to the PSA and ISMA on GMRA (November 1995); and to the Bank of England on the Gilt Annex to the GMRA (November 1995). Following Mr Sykes' retirement, Clifford Chance is producing an opinion on GMSLA.

[69] Unfortunately, this is the case in certain tri-party repo documents, as discussed below.

[70] See Chapter 4.

to the onset of the insolvency,[71] and therefore not recharacterise. However, it may be unwise to assume that such an argument would prevail in practice. Broadly speaking, recharacterisation involves the question of whether collateral assets may be retained by the collateral taker (under outright transfers), or whether they are returnable to the liquidator (under void security interests). If the result of recharacterisation would be significantly to increase the assets available to general creditors, and if the domestic law of the forum would recharacterise, insolvency courts may be unable to resist the temptation to recharacterise foreign law outright collateral transfers.

For these reasons, where outright transfer arrangements are entered into with a   **6.59** foreign counterparty, recharacterisation risk should always be considered under the law that would govern the insolvency of that counterparty. (This is covered in standard collateral enforceability opinions obtained by trade associations.)

Foreign collateral

Where the collateral consists of assets other than English (interests in) securities   **6.60** ('foreign collateral'), foreign law may become relevant to the question of recharacterisation risk, for two reasons. First, foreign courts may assume jurisdiction where third parties seek to claim the foreign collateral through them. Secondly, where the English courts have jurisdiction[72] the question arises whether the English courts might apply foreign law under the lex situs rule. The two possibilities will be considered in turn.

A liquidator or third party creditor of the collateral giver ('third party') may seek   **6.61** to recover the collateral (interests in) securities from the collateral taker through the local courts in the jurisdiction where those assets are held, on the basis that the title of the collateral taker is defeated by recharacterisation, and the local courts might apply their own law to the question. The prospects of success of any such action (and therefore the likelihood of it being brought) may depend on the ability of the third party to identify the assets in question. This may prove difficult, particularly where the collateral assets are held through an international settlement system which uses more than one local depositary in the relevant jurisdiction; in such a case, the third party may be unable to identify which depositary to sue. However, in jurisdictions and circumstances where the benefit of the Settlement Finality Directive (discussed in Chapter 7) is not available, the risk of such local attachment should be considered.

In the English courts, the question arises whether foreign law would be applied to   **6.62** the question of recharacterisation under the lex situs rule. As indicated in Chapter 7, this rule of private international law provides that rights of property are

---

[71] See Art 5 of the European Bankruptcy Regulation (1999/C221/06).
[72] eg because of the presence in England of the defendant.

determined by the law of the place where the asset in question is located, or lex situs; the rule applies alike to land, chattels and choses in action.[73]

6.63 There has been an active debate in the English legal community as to whether the lex situs rule applies to recharacterisation. As indicated above, English domestic law generally does not recharacterise, but recharacterisation risk is significant in a number of commercially important jurisdictions. Enormous volumes of foreign collateral are delivered under English law outright transfer documentation. It would therefore be commercially desirable to conclude that the lex situs rule would not cause an English court to apply foreign (and potentially recharacterising) law to these arrangements.[74] This section will argue that the better view is that the lex situs rule does not apply, but that the risk that it may cannot be absolutely excluded.

6.64 The arguments in favour of applying the lex situs rule are as follows. There are potentially two aspects to recharacterisation. The first is contractual: whether an agreement purporting to transfer property outright is, on true construction, an agreement to create a security interest ('the first issue'). The second is proprietary: whether an agreement to transfer property outright can take effect in accordance with its terms, or whether its effect will be to deliver a security interest (irrespective of the intention of the parties) ('the second issue'). Only the first issue is considered in the Cases.

6.65 Under normal conflict of laws principles, the approach of the English courts would be to apply the governing law of the contract to the first issue (as a contractual matter)[75] and lex situs to the second issue (as a proprietary matter).[76]

6.66 However, there is no support for the application of lex situs in the Cases. The Cases concern the correct construction of collateral agreements. In some of the Cases, the court considered whether the agreement between the parties was a sham in that it did not record their true agreement.[77] In some, the court considered whether the agreement was altered by a subsequent course of action.[78] In others the court considered whether the substance of the agreement was at odds with the legal label given to it by the parties.[79] In all the Cases, the criterion for recharacterisation is contractual construction.[80] This would tend to indicate that

---

[73] See *Macmillan v Bishopsgate Investment Trust plc (No 3)* [1996] 1 WLR 387, CA, per Staughton LJ at 399.

[74] A further problem with applying the lex situs rule is that collateral delivered under a single master agreement may consist of a mixed portfolio of international (interests in) securities.

[75] See Article 12 of the Rome Convention on the Law Applicable to Contractual Obligations 1980, implemented in the United Kingdom by the Contracts (Applicable Law) Act 1990.

[76] See the discussion of the lex situs rule in Chapter 7.

[77] See, for example, *Watson, Madell, Mass* and *Polsky.*

[78] eg *Cyril Lord.*

[79] eg *Welsh Development Agency* and *Palette Shoes.*

[80] See, for example, *Curtain* per Knox J at 937, *McEntire v Crossley* per Lord Watson at 834 and *Alderson v White* per Lord Cranworth LC at 928.

recharacterisation as it is considered in the Cases is a contractual matter and (where London market standard documentation is used) is governed by English law as the governing law of the collateral agreement.

It is true that the Cases did not involve foreign assets,[81] and therefore governing **6.67** law and lex situs coincided. However, it seems to be most unlikely that the English courts would recharacterise an English law agreement under private international law under the lex situs rule, in circumstances where it would not do so under domestic law. The English courts are very reluctant to defeat legitimate commercial intentions, particularly where they accord with English (domestic) law and practice.

Nevertheless, the position is not beyond doubt. Therefore, where foreign collat- **6.68** eral is delivered under outright transfer arrangements, it would be prudent to establish that the lex situs of collateral is not a recharacterising jurisdiction.[82]

(4) Litigation Risk

At a pragmatic level, the disadvantages of recharacterisation may be limited by the **6.69** following point. The collateral taker under a security interest needs to take positive steps involving third parties in order to enforce its security interest (by selling the collateral), and any restriction on its ability to take these steps may prevent it from realising the benefit of its collateral. In contrast under an outright transfer, the recourse of the collateral taker in the event of default is simply to apply set off. Set off is merely a mathematical calculation, and does not involve any positive steps involving third parties. In practice, the collateral taker will apply set off whether or not the agreement is recharacterisable. If it is subsequently recharacterised, the risk for the collateral taker is that the liquidator of the collateral giver will sue it for the return of the collateral. In other words, recharacterisation risk is litigation risk. The collateral taker is not prevented from applying the assets; it is sued for their return. This may be a significant comfort to collateral takers, because 'it is far better to be possessor than to be plaintiff'.[83]

---

[81] While foreign assets were involved in *Chow Yoong*, the case was not relevant to the lex situs issue as it did not concern the status of the collateral assets in the hands of the collateral taker, but rather the status of the transfer of cash.

[82] A very significant part of the foreign collateral which is delivered under outright transfer arrangements consists of interests in securities held through Euroclear. In the past, there was doubt as to the willingness of the Belgian courts to recognise outright transfers of collateral. However, the matter has now been put beyond doubt by legislation. In the case of interests held through Clearstream, it is understood that while recharacterisation risk may be present, in practice the requirements for perfecting a security interest may be satisfied by the customary arrangements for delivering collateral outright (crediting of the collateral to the account of the collateral taker).

[83] Justinian, *Institutes* IV.15.4 (Birks and McLeod (trans), London: Duckworth, 1987) 143.

K. Transaction Types

6.70 As indicated above, three major types of transaction in the securities markets rely on outright collateral transfers.

(1) Repos[84]

6.71 The term 'repo' is an abbreviation of 'repurchase agreement', which is in turn an abbreviation of 'sale and repurchase agreement'.[85] A transaction which is described as a repo from the point of view of the collateral giver is described as a reverse repo from the point of view of the collateral taker. Repos are very widely used by institutions such as investment banks as a technique for obtaining short-term finance from commercial banks and other institutions with surplus cash. Although outright collateral transfers have a very long history in England, repos in their current form originated in the USA, and were introduced into the United Kingdom in the mid-1980s. Traditionally repos involve the delivery of (interests in) fixed income sovereign debt securities,[86] although more recently other forms of (interests in) securities, including equities, have been delivered under repos. As indicated in Chapters 1 and 4, repos are also widely used by central banks in their money market operations.

6.72 Repos form a convenient and informal alternative to secured lending.[87] Instead of chargee or mortgagee, the collateral taker is the purchaser of the collateral (interests in) securities; cash is provided to the collateral giver as the purchase price of the collateral (interests in) securities, and not as a loan. At the end of the arrangement, equivalent (interests in) securities are repurchased. The repurchase price exceeds the purchase price by a sum of money (called the price differential) which

---

[84] 'The European repo market is essential to the operation of both the cash and securities markets. The European system of Central Banks (the 'Eurosystem') focuses on repo transactions as the main instrument of monetary policy. Repos and similar transactions are widely used in the EU markets, but have developed on a national basis. EMU and other European Single market developments, as well as the general internationalisation of the EU markets, mean that repo activity is now increasingly undertaken cross border': *EU Repo Markets: Opportunities for Change* (Brussels, October 1999) Report of the Giovannini Group, 5.

See generally C Browne, 'How to Spot a Repo in the Financial Jungle', IFLA (February 1997), H Motani, 'Legal Aspects of Repos', *The Euromoney Multi-Currency Repo Handbook* (London: Euromoney, 1997) and Jane Bush, 'PSA/ISMA Agreement: An Analysis of the Principal Terms', JIBFL (January 1997).

[85] The author is grateful to Habib Motani, partner, Clifford Chance, for this point.

[86] Treasury securities are considered more suitable than corporate securities because of the lower risk of issuer default.

[87] An advantage for the collateral giver is that the repo rate, or the sum of money equal to interest that it must pay to the collateral taker, is lower than the market rate for unsecured borrowing. An advantage for the collateral taker is that, because repos are collateralised, it can use them as a source of revenue even where it is not free to engage in more unsecured lending because its credit limits have been exceeded.

is calculated at an annual rate, and which is economically equivalent to an income payment on the principal sum which was advanced to the collateral giver.[88]

More recently, repos and reverse repos are used for a wide range of purposes. As **6.73** well as a means of raising collateralised finance, repos are used to finance positions in (interests in) securities[89] and for tax arbitrage.[90] Reverse repos (like securities loans; see below) are used to cover temporary short positions in (interests in) securities, which may arise inadvertently because of settlement failures or deliberately for arbitrage reasons. Reverse repos are also used as an alternative to bank lending.[91]

The London market standard repo document is the PSA/ISMA Global Master **6.74** Repurchase Agreement (GMRA).[92] The first draft of GMRA was developed[93] in 1992 by adapting the PSA Master Repurchase Agreement (MRA) (which is used in the US markets) for use under English law. The most important change made to the MRA was to include English law close out netting and set off provisions, modelled on those used since 1990 in London securities lending documents (see below). GMRA was revised in 1995.[94] A new version is expected in late 2000. The London repo market in gilts was liberalised in 1996, and a Gilt Annex prepared for use with GMRA in gilt repos.[95] In 1998 an Equities Annex was produced for use in equity repos.[96] GMRA is now widely used in the international repo markets, and a range of country annexes have been developed.[97]

---

[88] The repurchase price is wholly unrelated to the market value of the (interests in) equivalent securities on the repurchase date.

[89] If an investment bank wishes to hold a position in ABC securities, it might buy them in the market and repo them out to a third party. The purchase price paid to the bank by the third party under the repo is used to fund the market purchase price of the securities. This is a cheaper source of funding for the market purchase.

[90] In some jurisdictions, there are cases where securities pay income net to one type of holder and gross to another type of holder. Under repo tax arbitrage arrangements, a holder to whom income is paid net may repo the securities to a holder to whom income is paid gross over the income payment date, and split the profits of avoiding withholding tax between them.

[91] Corporate treasurers may place their cash out on reverse repos rather than on deposit. The credit risk is better because of the use of collateral.

[92] The 1995 version of GMRA was somewhat misleadingly entitled 'Version 1'. When it was written, a second version for use with net paying securities was intended. This never materialised, and net paying securities were dealt with under an annex to GMRA, rather than in a second version.

[93] By a team of lawyers including the author.

[94] Changes included the calculation of marking to market provisions on a global basis.

[95] This was prepared by a working party established by the Bank of England, which also produced a Code of Best Practice.

[96] Equities were not originally addressed under GMRA because of the taxation of equity repos is more complex than that of debt securities repos, and also because of the challenge of handling corporate actions. However, the annex was drafted in response to market demand.

[97] For a fuller discussion, see Guy Morton, 'The PSA/ISMA Global Master Repurchase Agreement' in Tyson-Quah (ed), *Cross-Border Securities Repo, Lending and Collateralisation* (London: FT Law & Tax, 1997).

6.75 An active repo programme can involve a significant administrative burden,[98] and smaller market participants often delegate the administration to a third party. Many global custodians administer repo programmes on behalf of their clients, identifying counterparties and entering into transactions with third parties as their clients' agent. The profits of such programmes are generally shared between the custodian and client. As indicated above, where the custodian contracts with a third party as agent for more than one principal under a single agreement, the impact of these agencies on insolvency set off must be carefully considered.

6.76 A number of custodians and settlement systems offer a tri-party repo service, whereby the bank or system operator acts as administrative agent for both parties to a master repurchase agreement, and administers the programme on behalf of both of them.[99] Tri-party repo services have opened the repo markets to many smaller investment houses and corporate treasury operations which do not have the necessary capacity to mark to market a repo programme in-house.

6.77 In agency and tri-party repo arrangements, it is important to ensure that the ability of the collateral taker (purchaser) to remove the purchased (interests in) securities from the hands of the agent is in no way restricted. Any such restriction may be considered by a court to be incompatible with outright ownership, and therefore to raise recharacterisation risk.

6.78 Hold-in-custody repos, whereby the collateral giver does not deliver (interests in) securities under the repo to the collateral taker, but holds them for it in custody, obviously expose the collateral taker to the fraud of the collateral giver.[100]

6.79 A clearing service has been introduced for European repos by the London Clearing House (see Chapter 8 for a discussion of clearing).

(2) Securities Lending

6.80 In the London markets, the fundamental legal structure of securities lending transactions is now[101] the same as that for repos, although certain differences

---

[98] Administrative tasks include settlement, valuation and margining, handling substitutions and income payments.

[99] The repo transactions are still entered into on a bilateral basis between the parties under a standard form GMRA. A tri-party administration agreement is entered into as a separate document.

[100] The Bank of England, under its Code of Best Practice, suggests strict procedures to limit this risk.

[101] Prior to 1990, the drafting of market standard agreements was ambiguous, and suggested that the interest of the collateral taker in the collateral securities might be a security interest. In that year Tim Herrington, partner in Clifford Chance, expressed the view that this documentation was not legally robust, largely because of problems under English law with rehypothecation. Such was his influence that securities lenders ceased lending securities until the matter was resolved. This caused an acute shortage of lendable securities, and affected prices on the London stock market more than the resignation of Margaret Thatcher. Mr Herrington redrafted London market standard documentation on the basis of outright transfer. The new drafts were introduced at the end of 1990.

remain. Collateral under a securities loan may consist of either cash or securities.[102]

Traditionally, the economic purpose of a securities loan has been different from **6.81** that of a repo. Where traditionally a repo serves as an alternative to a secured loan, and is driven by the need of the collateral giver to raise finance, the traditional purpose of a securities loan is to cover a short position in (interests in) securities. Securities lending is an important source of liquidity in securities settlement.[103]

As discussed in Chapter 9, the need for securities lending arises because of the **6.82** impact of failed (ie delayed) settlement on short sales. Suppose B sells 100,000 ICI shares to C. At the time of the sale, B does not hold 100,000 ICI shares, but has agreed to buy 100,000 ICI shares from A for delivery in time to settle the sale to C. The delivery from A is delayed for two days. B therefore has a temporary short position, and needs to borrow 100,000 ICI shares from D for two days. B will deliver to C the securities it borrows from D. When A makes its late delivery to B, B will deliver these shares to D in order to bring the securities loan to an end.

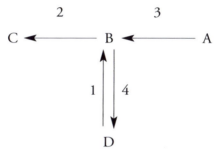

1 = Securities loan from D to B
2 = Delivery from B to C
3 = Late delivery from A to B
4 = Redelivery of loaned securities from B to D

Figure 6.1: Securities loan to cover short position following failed settlement

---

[102] With a repo, the repayment obligation of the purchaser is always collateralised with securities, so that the value of the securities exceeds the value of the payment by the agreed margin. With a securities loan, the redelivery obligation for the loaned securities may be collateralised either with cash or with other securities. If it is collateralised with cash, the value of the cash will exceed the value of the securities delivered by the agreed margin. Collateral takers place cash collateral on deposit, and this is an important source of revenue. However, collateral givers are reluctant to give cash collateral because it is expensive.

A more recent development is 'Bond for Bond' repos, where no cash changes hands, and (interests in) securities are delivered by both parties.

[103] See the discussion in the G30 Report, *Clearance and Settlement Systems in the World's Securities Markets* (1989) 47.

6.83 Securities lending is particularly important in quote-driven markets, which rely for liquidity on the ability of market makers to buy and (importantly) sell larger volumes of (interests in) securities than they hold at any time.[104] Market makers are able to sell short in this way because securities lending enables them to settle their trades in a timely manner.

6.84 In addition to facilitating settlement and short sales, securities lending is used today for hedging. For example, where a firm (B) wishes to acquire a long position (ie a holding of) in particular (interests in) securities (XYZ), it may seek to hedge its position (or protect itself from losses in respect of that holding) by taking a short position in related (interests in) securities (ABC) (ie agreeing to sell them to C at a time it does not hold them). The firm may use the proceeds from the short sale to pay the purchase price of XYZ to the vendor, A. ABC can then be borrowed under a securities loan from D, and XYZ can be delivered as collateral for the loan of ABC.

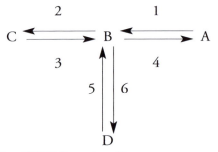

1 = Sale of XYZ from A to B
2 = Short sale of ABC from B to C
3 = Proceeds of sale of ABC securities from C to B
4 = B pays purchase price of XYZ to A
5 = Loan of ABC from D to B (which B delivers to C)
6 = B delivers XYZ to D as collateral for securities loan

Figure 6.2: Securities loan for hedging

6.85 Securities lending is also used for arbitrage. For example, if a firm (B) believes that the price of particular (interests in) securities will fall in the medium or long term, it could sell them to C and meet its delivery obligations to C by borrowing the (interests in) securities from a third party (A) under a medium or long term securities loan. At the end of the securities loan, it can meet its redelivery obligation by buying the (interests in) securities cheaply in the market from D.

---

[104] See Chapter 1.

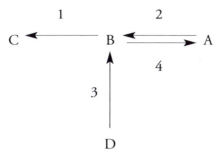

1 = Short sale from B to C
2 = Securities loan from A to B (which B delivers to C)
3 = B buys securities from D
4 = B redelivers loaned securities to A

Figure 6.3: Securities lending for arbitrage

Securities lenders comprise institutional investors such as insurance companies, **6.86** pension funds and managed funds.[105] As fund managers come under increasing competitive pressure, securities lending fees offer an important technique for generating additional revenue for their funds under management. In practice, securities lending in London operates on an intermediated basis.[106]

London securities lending documentation is widely used in the international mar- **6.87** kets. Until recently a number of different versions of market standard documentation were available for use with different types of loaned (interests in) securities.[107] In May 2000, the Global Master Securities Lending Agreement was issued by ISLA, which consolidates the previous agreements. The Stock Lending and Repo Committee of the International Securities Lenders Association publish a Code of Guidance, indicating the procedures which market participants should observe as a matter of good practice.[108]

As indicated above, custodians and settlement systems operate securities lending **6.88** programmes on behalf of their clients on an agency basis.

---

[105] Index tracking funds are particularly reliable securities lenders, as their portfolios always include securities comprised in the index, which are available for lending (ie not required to be sold by the lender) as long as they remain in the index.

[106] Although requirements in the rules of the London Stock Exchange relating to Stock Borrowing and Lending Intermediaries (SBLIs) were deleted with effect from October 1977

[107] For overseas securities, the Overseas Securities Lender's Agreement (OSLA) was prepared by the International Stock Lenders Association (ISLA). In relation to UK loaned securities, the London Stock Exchange prescribed the Gilt Edged Stock Lending Agreement (GESLA) for gilts and the Equity and Fixed Interest Stock Lending Agreement (EFISLA) for equities and fixed rate securities.

[108] At the time of writing, the latest version of the Code of Guidance was dated 1995; it is currently under review.

(3) Swaps[109]

6.89 A swap transaction is a form of derivative transaction.[110] The simplest, and original form of swap is an interest rate swap.[111] An example of an interest rate swap might be as follows. A enters into a five-year interest rate swap with B. Under the terms of this swap, A agrees annually to pay B an agreed fixed rate of interest on a notional capital amount of £1,000,000, and B agrees annually to pay A an agreed floating rate of interest on the same notional capital amount. The interest payments will be netted, so that in a year when the floating rate exceeds the fixed rate, B will make a net payment to A, and in a year when the floating rate falls short of the fixed rate, A will make a net payment to B.

6.90 The calculation of credit exposures under a swap is more complex than under a repo or a securities loan, and the following represents a simplification.[112] Future floating interest rates on each of the five annual payment dates are estimated. To the extent that these estimated rates exceed the fixed rate, the swaps contract is valuable to A, which would lose money if B failed to perform. A therefore bears B's credit risk. Conversely, to the extent that estimated future floating rates fall short of the fixed rate, B bears A's credit risk. The extent of these credit risks are calculated on the basis of the discounted present value of the future payment obligation. Because of the relative complexity of these calculations, mark-to-market valuations are usually undertaken by a valuation agent.[113]

6.91 In recent decades, participants in the swaps markets have increasingly sought to collateralise these credit exposures.[114] In the 1990s, this practice had become so widespread that the International Swaps and Derivatives Association (ISDA) pro-

---

[109] See the discussion of swaps in Simon James, *The Law of Derivatives* (London: LLP, 1999) 6–9.

[110] See the definition of swap transaction in Article 1, section 1.1 of the 1991 ISDA definitions.

[111] For a discussion of the use of swaps in the Eurobond markets, see the section on asset swaps in Chapter 12.

[112] See Michael C Clarke, 'Collateralisation in the OTC Derivatives Markets', in *Cross-Border Securities Repo, Lending and Collateralisation* (n 97 above).

[113] As explained above, marking to market involves valuing both the credit exposure and the collateral, ie identifying the current market value of the collateral assets, and applying a discount or hair cut. Under a swap transaction, either party may from time to time have a credit exposure to the other, so that collateral may be required to be delivered to either party.

[114] 'Poor credit quality is the most obvious reason for employing collateral. A client may have a weak credit rating or be in a deteriorating state, and this may lead to collateralisation. Unrated clients (who may be of good credit quality but simply unrated) provide a similar application for collateralisation. There are several reasons to use collateral which we could categorise as providing access to some service or facility. Collateral might permit access to riskier transactions, such as very long maturity deals (typically over ten years but sometimes well over 30 years), very large size transactions, and other types of transaction with higher risk factors such as leverage and optionality. Quote commonly, collateral is employed with well-rated, long-established clients where there is absolutely no credit quality concern, but simply a view on one or both sides that enough exposure is enough. In these cases collateral may be used to decrease outstanding exposure levels and thereby

duced standard form collateral documentation under New York,[115] English and Japanese law[116] to be used to collateralise credit exposures arising under ISDA master agreements. The English law collateral documentation comprises the 1995 Credit Support Deed (Security Interest—English Law) and the 1995 Credit Support Annex (Transfer—English Law).[117] The English Law Deed provides for collateral to be taken under a security interest, and the English Law Annex provides for the outright transfer of collateral.[118]

Typical swaps collateral comprises cash (ideally US dollars) and (interests in) G10 **6.92** treasury securities (ideally US treasuries).[119]

A clearing service has been introduced for European swaps by the London **6.93** Clearing House (see Chapter 8 for a discussion of clearing).

L. Pros and Cons of Outright Collateral Transfers

Broadly speaking, outright collateral transfers are more favourable to the collateral **6.94** taker, for a number of reasons, the chief of which are as follows. They involve a minimum of formality, and (unlike security interests) are usually entered into without the assistance of independent lawyers. They are not registrable, or perfectible under lex situs. They permit the collateral taker freely to deal with the collateral assets. They are enforceable without formality or delay and (under English law) enforcement is not affected by an insolvency freeze affecting the collateral giver.

However, outright collateral transfers are not always suitable. They would only be **6.95** taken where the close out netting and insolvency set off is available under the

---

facilitate the continuance of a valuable relationship. This applies to end-user clients as much as to a bank's professional liquidity partners . . . Prior to 1990 there was very limited use of collateral, but around this time many of the swap market professionals whose business was constrained by the relatively poor credit ratings of their client base and their own limited credit capital began to pioneer the use of collateral. The trend was accelerated greatly by the explosive growth in unregulated investment funds (the hedge funds and leveraged funds) which began in 1992/93 and continues still. Nearly all of the funds are unrated or of very low credit quality. . . . Since 1995/96, another trend has emerged as a driver for growth, which is the advent of commercial collateral services, such as those offered by Cedel Bank, Euroclear and others': Clarke (n 112 above) 185, 186.

[115] New York Law Credit Support Annex (1994).

[116] Japanese Law Credit Support Annex (1996).

[117] For a discussion of these documents, see E Murray, 'The ISDA Credit Support Documents', in *Cross-Border Securities Repo, Lending and Collateralisation* (n 97 above).

[118] The English Law Annex relies on the netting and set off provisions in the ISDA Master Agreement (section 6(e)). It is understood that ISDA is considering consolidating all the credit support documentation into one document.

[119] With increasing volumes of collateral being taken, these assets are not always available. Although less common, some swaps are collateralised with non-G10 treasuries, eurobonds, and even (rarely) equities.

insolvency law of the collateral giver, and where recharacterisation risk is absent. It is also important to establish that the balance sheet,[120] regulatory capital[121] and taxation[122] treatment of outright collateral transfers is appropriate under the taxation and regulatory regimes affecting the collateral taker.

6.96 For the collateral giver, security interests are preferable to outright transfers, because the latter involve a credit exposure equal to the surplus value of the collateral; see the discussion in Chapter 5. The shift over recent years from security interests to outright transfers reflects the relative commercial bargaining strengths of those who need collateralised finance, and those who can provide it.

---

[120] Market participants generally wish outright collateral transfer arrangements to be balance sheet neutral. This means that the collateral securities should remain on the balance sheet of the collateral giver and not appear on the balance sheet of the collateral taker. Balance sheet neutrality is justified by the fact that the collateral giver retains, and the collateral taker does not acquire, the economic risks and rewards of ownership. As discussed above, because the collateral taker is required to deliver equivalent securities having the same number as the original securities, and not the same value, the collateral giver profits from any increase in value of securities of that type, and suffers loss from any diminution.

As indicated above, in the United Kingdom, the criteria for balance sheet neutrality are indicated in FRS 5 and the US position by FAS 125.

[121] At the time of writing, many parties to outright transfer arrangements are subject to the regulatory capital requirements in the rulebook of the Securities and Futures Authority (SFA). Rule 10-173 generally governs the counterparty risk requirement (CRR) of firms engaging in securities lending and repo transactions. Only the margin, as marked to market, attracts CRR. Netting between transactions is permitted where the firm uses a written agreement supported by legal opinion, provided both the agreement and the opinion comply with certain specified requirements. These include the absence of a 'walkaway' clause, releasing the non-defaulting party from making any net payment. The requirements for the agreements are satisfied by the standard London market documentation prepared by the leading trade associations. The opinion must relate to the law of the jurisdiction in which the counterparty is organised, the law of the jurisdiction in which any branch involved is located, and the governing law of the agreement (and, if different, any transaction) together with the law governing the legal status of the counterparty. Opinion of in-house counsel is not acceptable, and any opinion must also be satisfactory to the regulator of the counterparty. The standard opinions obtained by the leading trade associations are designed to satisfy these requirements.

It was argued above that recharacterisation risk may be present under the lex situs of the collateral assets. This issue is not addressed in these regulatory opinions.

[122] Among other things, it should be established under the applicable taxation regimes that the delivery and redelivery of collateral will not attract either transfer tax nor capital gains tax. Where the arrangement will span a date on which income will be paid on the collateral securities so that the collateral taker pays to the collateral giver a sum equal to the income it receives, the collateral taker should be able to make that payment without deduction of withholding tax, and to pass on the benefit of any tax credit for any withholding made by the issuer on the income payment; furthermore, the collateral taker should not pay profit tax on the income. The UK taxation position for outright transfer arrangements under market standard documentation is broadly speaking favourable, following a series of deregulatory changes introduced in the late 1990s.

7

THE CONFLICT OF LAWS AND SECURITIES COLLATERAL[1]

> ... the poet's pen
> ... gives to airy nothing
> A local habitation and a name[2]

A. Background

This chapter will consider the conflict of laws in relation to the use of interests in **7.01** securities as collateral. In the space available only an extremely brief introduction to the conflict of laws is possible. A number of excellent textbooks on the conflict of laws are available; readers are particularly referred to the new edition of *Dicey and Morris*.[3]

---

[1] The author is grateful to Professor Ian Fletcher, Director, The Centre for Commercial Law Studies, Queen Mary & Westfield College, for reviewing this chapter. The opinions expressed in it and any errors are her own.

[2] *A Midsummer Night's Dream*, V.i. (The author is grateful to Lesley Benjamin for finding the local habitation of this quotation.)

[3] L Collins (ed), *Dicey and Morris on the Conflict of Laws* (13th edn, London: Sweet & Maxwell, 2000).

7.02   Conflict of laws is marked by a high level of abstraction in its theory, and intense pragmatism in its practice. There is an active debate in the legal community concerning the correct conflict of laws treatment of securities collateral. This chapter will address both the theoretical aspects of the debate, and also suggest how risks may be addressed pragmatically.

7.03   The emphasis is on English conflict of laws rules. However, market participants operating in, from and into London must also consider the circumstances in which other systems of private international law may become relevant.[4] While not attempting an exhaustive analysis, this chapter will seek to point out key concerns in practice.

(1) Cross Border Nature of the Securities Markets

7.04   Many factors have contributed to the rise of cross border securities investment in recent decades. Chapter 1 referred to the growth of the eurosecurities markets in the later part of the twentieth century. The relaxation of exchange controls from the end of the 1970s greatly increased the cross border flow of capital, and the deregulation of the financial markets has facilitated institutional cross border investment. For demographic reasons, pension funds have experienced exponential growth in recent years; as the domestic markets become no longer able to meet their demands, pension funds have been forced to turn abroad for new investment opportunities. Political change in the former Soviet Union and, over the medium term, rapid economic growth in the Far East[5] have encouraged investment in the emerging markets. The introduction of the euro is a further factor facilitating cross border investment, as foreign exchange risk is removed within Euroland. For all the above reasons, participants in the securities markets regularly deal with foreign assets, foreign counterparties and foreign intermediaries.

7.05   Of course, cross border securities investment is not new and certain conflict of laws rules relating to the securities markets are very well established. For example, it has been settled since the Victorian era that the negotiability of an instrument for the purposes of any transaction is determined by the law of the jurisdiction in which the delivery of the instrument under that transaction took place.[6] More

---

[4] Foreign conflicts rules are most likely to be relevant when a foreign court may assume jurisdiction. The principle of *renvoi* (under which the English courts might apply foreign conflicts rules) is most unlikely to apply in commercial matters: see *Macmillan Inc v Bishopsgate Investment Trust plc (No 3)* [1995] 3 All ER 747, per Millett J at 766. See also *Dicey and Morris* (n 3 above) 4-019.

[5] The crash of 1998 notwithstanding.

[6] *Alcock v Smith* [1892] 1 Ch 238, in which this rule (lex loci actus) is clearly stated, eg per Lopes LJ at 266. In other types of transaction, where no physical instrument is delivered, the lex loci actus rule begs the question, as it is not always straightforward to identify the locus of a transaction in circumstances where the parties have dealt at a distance.

The lex loci actus rule might be considered as an aspect of the lex situs rule, discussed later in this chapter. The lex loci actus of the transaction and the lex situs of the instrument delivered in a transaction necessarily coincide, and lex loci actus may be construed as the lex situs at the time of the

recently, however, the rapid rate of change in the securities markets has taken practice beyond the scope of settled law for many purposes. A particular challenge is the computerisation of the securities markets. As discussed in Chapters 1 and 2, the effect of computerisation has in many cases been to convert securities which are tangible, allocated and held direct from the issuer, into intangible, unallocated assets held indirectly, which the author has called interests in securities. These changes raise novel conflict of laws issues, which this chapter will consider. The need to address these issues with certainty is rendered urgent by the use of interests in securities to collateralise vast financial exposures in cross border arrangements.

(2) Role and Nature of Conflict of Laws

'The branch of English law known as the conflict of laws is that part of the law of **7.06** England which deals with cases having a foreign element.'[7] Because of the cross border nature of the securities markets, conflict of laws is an essential part of their legal analysis.

Systems of domestic commercial law differ from each other

Where a legal question arises in a cross border situation, a number of different sys- **7.07** tems of law may potentially be relevant to it. If the answer to the question under each of such legal systems is the same, there is no conflict of laws. There is no need to determine which system applies because the answers under all of them coincide. However, there are profound differences in the domestic commercial laws of the jurisdictions involved in the securities markets, and therefore conflicts of laws arise regularly. These differences are present for historic and political reasons. Generally speaking, the legal systems of continental Europe are civil in nature, and based on the principles of Roman law. However, England largely resisted the influence of Roman law for a range of political and cultural reasons (including the schism from Rome and the establishment of the Church of England in the sixteenth century), and a system of common law operates in England and in jurisdictions influenced by it.[8] Civil law differs profoundly from common law in

---

transaction in question. In the relevant case law, the rule in favour of lex loci actus is discussed as an aspect of the lex situs rule, on the basis that negotiable instruments are a species of chattel, and that the lex situs rule applies to chattels. The decision in *Alcock* is clearly based on the authority of the lex situs rule in relation to chattels, as stated in *Cammell v Sewell* (1858) 3 H & N 617 and a line of subsequent cases (see eg Kay LJ at 268). The assimilation of negotiable instruments to chattels (and therefore the proposition that the lex loci actus rule is an aspect of the lex situs rule) is discussed further in *Embiricos v Anglo-Austrian Bank* [1904] 2 KB 870 (see Walton J at 874 and, on appeal [1905] 1 KB 677, per Vaughan Williams at 683, 684).

[7] *Dicey and Morris* (n 3 above) 1-001.

[8] Leading common law jurisdictions include New York, Australia, New Zealand, and Hong Kong.

matters relevant to the international securities markets, such as the recognition of trusts and the requirements for a valid contract.[9]

7.08   Politics is also relevant, as national insolvency regimes reflect the current concerns of each jurisdiction.[10] Insolvency law determines which groups of people will bear the misfortune of commercial failure. Philip Wood has pointed out[11] that some jurisdictions' insolvency laws are creditor-friendly; they facilitate the use of collateral techniques whereby lenders to insolvent companies can limit their losses by escaping the status of unsecured creditor. In contrast, other jurisdictions are debtor-friendly, and restrict the use of such collateral techniques in order to maximise the pool of assets available to unsecured creditors. In practice, these legal differences reflect such political choices as whether the bank of an insolvent company or its workforce is to be paid. Continuing differences of political outlook between different countries may in part explain the slow progress of international initiatives to harmonise insolvency law.[12]

7.09   Thus, conflict of laws rules in the securities markets are necessary because the domestic commercial laws of the relevant jurisdictions differ. Sadly, the conflict of laws rules of such jurisdictions also differ. This means that the outcome of any particular dispute may differ according to the forum in which it is heard, with the result that the cross border legal aspects of the international securities markets are to some extent inherently unpredictable.

Categorisation and connecting factors

7.10   The first issue in any cross border matter that comes before an English court is whether or not the court has jurisdiction to hear it. The rules of jurisdiction are beyond the scope of this book.

7.11   After establishing that it has jurisdiction, it is necessary for the court to choose which system of law to apply. The matter before the court may involve a number of different questions, and different systems of law may be applicable to each.[13]

---

[9] These conceptual differences present a real challenge to the project of EU harmonisation.

[10] 'there is a profound and intimate correlation between insolvency—whether individual or corporate—and the very wellsprings of policy and social order from which national law ultimately draws its inspiration. For this reason, despite numerous general resemblances, national insolvency laws and procedures differ from one another almost infinitely in ways both great and small': I Fletcher *Insolvency in Private International Law* (Oxford: Clarendon Press, 1999) 4.

[11] See P Wood, *Principles of International Insolvency* (London: Sweet & Maxwell, 1995) 3, 4.

[12] See the discussion of the EU Convention on Insolvency Proceedings, Fletcher, *Insolvency in Private International Law* (n 10 above) ch 6. The Convention Project, which lapsed in 1996, was revived in 1999 as a Regulation (1999/C 211/06), which was adopted in May 2000, and will automatically come into force on 31 May 2002 (except in Denmark, where it will require to be implemented separately).

[13] See *Macmillan v Bishopsgate* [1996] 1 WLR 387 per Staughton LJ at 399.

The rules of the conflict of laws are, traditionally, expressed in terms of juridical concepts or categories and localising elements or connecting factors. Typical rules of the conflict of laws state that succession to immovables is governed by the law of the *situs*; that the formal validity of a marriage is governed by the law of the place of celebration; and that capacity to marry is governed by the law of each party's antenuptual domicile. In these examples, succession to immovables, formal validity of marriage and capacity to marry are the categories, while *situs*, place of celebration and domicile are the connecting factors.[14]

The categorisation of an issue can be crucial to the outcome of a dispute, as illustrated in the case of *Macmillan v Bishopsgate*.[15]   **7.12**

B. The Lex Situs Rule

A connecting factor which is crucial to cross border collateral arrangements, is lex   **7.13** situs. The lex situs rule provides that property rights in an asset are determined by the law of the place where the asset is located, or lex situs. 'If personal property is disposed of in a manner binding according to the law of the country where it is, that disposition is binding everywhere.'[16] Thus, for example, the English courts will apply Norwegian law to a question concerning property rights in a cargo of wood located in Norway.[17]

In the relevant case law, the chief policy reason which is given for the lex situs rule   **7.14** is commercial convenience. 'I do not think that anybody can doubt that with regard to the transfer of goods, the law applicable must be the law of the country where the movable is situate. Business could not be carried on if that were not so.'[18] A number of cases stress the importance of the rule in enabling the purchaser of goods to establish title with certainty.[19] In this way, the lex situs rule also serves to protect the courts from unnecessary litigation: 'A little imagination will show that any different rule might produce a multiplicity of claims and confusing and unnecessary questions of competing priorities'.[20] Some cases justify the rule on the

---

[14] *Dicey and Morris* (n 3 above) 1-074.

[15] *Macmillan v Bishopstage Trust (No 3)* [1995] 1 WLR 978, per Millett J at 988.

[16] *Cammell v Sewell* (1858) 3 H & N 617, per Pollock CB at 624.

[17] ibid.

[18] *In re Anzziani* [1930] 1 Ch 407, per Maugham J at 420.

[19] See for example, *Cammell v Sewell* (1860) 5 H & N 728, per Crompton J at 1374 (if the rule did not apply, 'A purchaser would have no secure title, and consequently a fair price would not be obtained'), and 1378; *Winkworth v Christie* [1980] 1 Ch 496, per Slade J at 512 ('Commercial convenience may be said imperatively to demand that proprietary rights to movables shall generally be determined by the lex situs under the rules of private international law. Were the position otherwise, it would not suffice for the protection of a purchaser of any valuable movables to ascertain that he was acquiring title to them under the law of the country where the goods were situated at the time of the purchase'). See also *Embraces v Anglo-Austrian Bank* [1904] 1 KB 677, per Vaughan Williams LJ at 684, in which the lex situs rule is compared with the market overt rule.

[20] *Schemer v Property Resources Ltd and others* [1974] Ch D 451, per Gelding J at 458.

basis of the comity of nations; it would be incompatible with the United Kingdom's recognition of a foreign state as sovereign for the English courts to seek to interfere with property rights in assets located in that foreign state.[21]

7.15 In cross border situations, third parties are most likely to assess the availability of assets under the law of the place where the assets are located, and hence the lex situs rule.

7.16 The rule may in part be attributable to the pragmatic desire of judges to avoid making futile orders. Because an order relating to, for example, French land can only be enforced in France with the co-operation of the French judiciary, such an order which is at odds with the mandatory provisions of French law will be unenforceable in practice.

7.17 In matters before the English courts, the identification of the situs of an asset will be determined by English law as the law of the forum.[22]

(1) Applicability of the Rule

7.18 There is an active debate in the legal community concerning application of the lex situs rule to securities collateral. This debate concerns two questions. The first is whether the rule applies to intangibles such as interests in securities. The second question (which becomes relevant if the answer to the first question is positive) concerns the identification of the situs of interests in securities. The first question will be considered in this section, and the second question will be considered thereafter.

---

[21] Any other approach 'is contrary to all the rules of the comity of nations': *Norton v Florence Land and Public Works Company* (1877) 7 Ch D 332, per Jessel MR at 337. See also *Cammell v Sewell* (1858) 3 H & N 617, per Pollock CB at 627; *Castrique v Imrie* (1870) LR4 HL 414, per Blackburn J at 437; *In re Maudslay* [1900] 1 Ch 602, per Cozens-Hardy J at 609; and *Winkworth v Christie* [1980] 1 Ch 496, per Slade J at 513.

Many of the relevant cases concern the nationalisation of private property by the Soviet Government following the Russian revolution. See *Askionairenoye Obsechestvo A M Luther v James Sagor & Co* [1921] 3 KB 532, per Scrutton LJ at 556: 'But it is impossible to recognise a government and yet claim to exercise jurisdiction over its person or property against its will'. 'It is no business of mine to criticise the decrees or to express any view as to their propriety': *Re Bank de Marchands de Moscou* [1952] 1 All ER 1269, per Vaisey J at 1275. (See also *Re Helbert Wagg* [1956] Ch 323, per Upjohn J at 346.) The lex situs rule also defines when such an nationalisation order will not be effective: see *Sedgwick Collins v Rossia Insurance Co of Petrograd* [1925] 1 KB 1, per Sargant LJ at 15. (See also *The El Condado* (1939) 63 Lloyds Rep 83 and 330, per Lord Jamieson at 87, per Lord Mackay at 338.)

[22] *Rossano v Manufacturers' Life Insurance Co* [1963] 2 QB 352, at 379–380. See *Dicey and Morris* (n 3 above) 1-076.

Extension of the lex situs rule to intangible assets

The lex situs rule has long been applied to tangible assets such as land and chat- **7.19**
tels.[23] More recently, the Court of Appeal decision in the case of *Macmillan v
Bishopsgate*[24] has confirmed that the rule applies to tangible and intangible assets
alike.[25] Case law provides further authority that the lex situs rule applies to intangibles. In *re Maudslay*[26] the question of whether a debt owed by a French firm was
subject to a debenture was determined by the lex situs;[27] in *New York Life Insurance
Company v Public Trustee*[28] lex situs was applied to the question of whether insurance policies were subject to a charge; and in *Jabbour v The Custodian*[29] lex situs
was applied to determine whether an insurance policy was subject to an expropri-
ation order.[30]

Relevance for collateral

This issue has clear relevance where interests in securities are used as collateral. If **7.20**
property rights in intangibles are determined by lex situs, it follows that security
interests require to be perfected under lex situs.[31] Arguably it also follows that,
where interests in securities are delivered under outright transfer arrangements,
recharacterisation risk must be considered under lex situs (as well as under the
governing law of the collateral contract and the law of the insolvency jurisdiction
of the counterparty).[32]

---

[23] See for example *Inglis v Usherwood* (1801) 1 East 525 (chattels) and *Norris v Chambers* (1860)
29 Beav 246 (land).

[24] *Macmillan v Bishopsgate (No 3)* [1996] 1 WLR 387.

[25] ibid at 404, 405 (per Staughton LJ), 410, 411, 412 (per Auld LJ) and 423, 424 (per Aldous
LJ). This complex judgment indicates overall that lex situs is relevant, rather than lex loci actus,
which was favoured by Millett J in the first instance decision [1995] 1 WLR 978. (It would be interesting if the issue came before Lord Millett again in the House of Lords.)

[26] [1900] 1 Ch 602.

[27] 'It seems to me that I must treat the debt due from Delaunay & Cie as being situate in France,
and subject to French law, and I cannot therefore prevent the claimants, at the suit of the debenture-
holders, from taking any proceedings the law of France allows from recovering their debt out of this
French asset': per Cozens-Hardy J at 609.

[28] [1924] 2 Ch 101.

[29] [1954] 1 All ER 145.

[30] per Pearson J at 151: 'It is established by the decided cases that not only debts, but also other
choses in action, are for legal purposes localised and are situated where they are properly recoverable
and are properly recoverable where the debtor resides'.

[31] A long line of cases applies lex situs to determine the validity or perfection of security interests.
See, eg (lien on land) *Norris v Chambers* (1860) 29 Beav 246, per Sir John Romily MR at 253; on
appeal 3 De G F & J 583, per the Lord Chancellor at 548; (pledge of goods) *City Bank v Barrow*
(1880) 5 App Cas 664, per Lord Blackburn at 677; (pledge of share certificates) *Williams v Colonial
Bank* (1888) 38 Ch D 388, CA, per Lindley LJ at 403; (pledge of documents of title to goods) *Inglis
v Robertson* [1898] AC 616, per Earl of Halsbury LC at 625; (charge on real property under a debenture) *Mount Albert Borough Council v Australasian Temperance and General Mutual Life Assurance
Society Ltd* [1937] 4 All ER 206, per Lord Wright at 213, 217.

[32] See Chapter 6 for a further discussion.

7.21 Of course, in cross border collateral arrangements, the English law position is not the end of the matter, as the courts of other countries may assume jurisdiction in relation to the collateral arrangements. However, for the London financial markets, English law is a very important part of the picture. In particular, clarity on this issue will offer a significant advantage to lawyers in drafting the English legal opinions routinely sought by clients.

The governing law argument

7.22 Some commentators have argued that the Court of Appeal decision in *Macmillan* was mistaken. This is on the basis that the lex situs rule properly applies to tangible things (which have physical locations) and not to claims (which do not). It is unhelpful (they argue) to reify claims by artificially attributing locations to them.

7.23 Rather, such commentators argue, questions concerning assets that arise under contract are properly answered by the law of contract. The Rome Convention[33] applies 'to contractual obligations in any situation involving a choice of the laws of different countries'.[34] Article 12(2) relates to assignments of contractual rights, and indicates (broadly) that the position of the assignee is governed by the governing law of the assigned right (and not by the law of its notional situs).[35] It follows analogously from this (it is argued), that the perfection of a security interest over interests in securities should be governed by the governing law of that asset. This argument will be called 'the governing law argument'.

7.24 There is persuasive authority that the Rome Convention does not apply to property rights.[36] However, this does not hinder the governing law argument, because that argument rests on the premise that contractual claims are not subject to property rights; it is argued that personal rights bind persons, and this distinguishes them from property rights, which relate to things. On this basis (it is argued) contractual claims (which bind persons) cannot be subject to property rights. Therefore (it is argued) the lex situs rule (which relates to property rights) cannot

---

[33] The Convention on the Law Applicable to Contractual Obligations 1980, implemented in the United Kingdom by the Contracts (Applicable Law) Act 1990.

[34] See Article 1.

[35] See Article 12: 'Voluntary Assignments. . . . 2. The law governing the right to which the assignment relates shall determine its assignability, the relationship between the assignee and the debtor, the conditions under which the assignment can be invoked against the debtor and any questions whether the debtor's obligations have been discharged'.

[36] 'since the Convention is concerned only with the law applicable to contractual obligations, property rights . . . are not covered by these provisions': see M Guiliano and P Lagarde, *Council Report on the Convention on the Law Applicable to Contractual Obligations*, OJ L266 9.10.80, comments on Article 2 of the Convention. However, the contrary view has been expressed. For discussion of the relevant issues, see Strucken, 'The Proprietary Aspects of International Assignment of Debts and the Rome Convention, Article 12' [1998] LMCLQ 345.

apply to intangibles such as contractual claims, and the Court of Appeal decision in *Macmillan* was wrong.[37]

The counter argument

The author's counter argument to the governing law argument is set out at length   **7.25**
in Chapter 13. Briefly, contractual and other claims have been treated as things in Western law since Justinian. They may be subject to property claims (and therefore property rights) in the hands of third parties (ie persons other than the obligor). The client holding interests in securities through an intermediary is able to recover its asset in the insolvency of that intermediary because *as against the intermediary* its interests are proprietary. If the client grants a security interest to a collateral taker over its interests in securities, the collateral taker is able to enforce its security interest in the insolvency of the client because *as against the client* its interest is proprietary. Therefore it is clear (to the author at least) that interests in securities are legal things, and may be subject to property rights.

In this connection the author has long argued in favour of the approach now   **7.26**
endorsed by the 13th edition of *Dicey and Morris*. In its discussion of dealings in immobilised securities, the new edition rejects the governing law argument.[38]

The question remains whether it is helpful artificially to attribute locations to   **7.27**
claims by legal fiction. The author would argue that it is. Legal fictions have a long and successful history in English law. More fundamentally, Western law has always dealt with intangible things by analogy with tangibles. The use of analogy has long served as a powerful technique for extending settled rules to new circumstances. This has contributed to the flexibility of the common law, which has enabled it to remain alive for a millennium. Law is a system of ideas, and provided the attribution of a situs to a claim is helpful, it matters not that it is notional.[39]

Whether or not it is helpful to confer a situs on a claim, must be assessed at a prac-   **7.28**
tical level. As briefly indicated in the introduction to this Chapter, conflict of laws is abstract in its theory, but in practice often turns on pragmatic considerations of enforcement. The rules for attributing a situs to an intangible are based on enforcement; broadly speaking, a claim is located where it may in the ordinary

---

[37] See the discussion in *Dicey and Morris* (n 3 above) 24-048, 24-059.
[38] 'If the investor seeks to enter into a transaction such as a loan, and purports to transfer title to, or pledge or charge, his interest in the securities as security for the loan, a question arises to determine which law governs . . . the purported assignment of such interest as he may have. In analysing the proprietary aspect of such facts, it . . . seems improbable that Article 12 of the Rome Convention was designed to be applied': *Dicey and Morris* (n 3 above) 24-064. A further argument for not applying Article 12 to deliveries of interests in securities as collateral, is that book entry transfers of interests in securities do not take effect by assignment, but rather by novation; see Chapter 4.
[39] Because the subject matter of financial law largely comprises notional things such as corporations and debts, financial law is a metaphysical subject. The tendency to mistake it for an empirical subject has always been a source of confusion.

course be enforced.[40] Herein lies the usefulness of applying the lex situs rule to intangibles. The English courts apply French law to the perfection of a security interest in a debt owed by a French-resident person, because France is the situs of the debt. In practice the chargee sees the sense of obtaining the opinion of a French lawyer in relation to the charge, because it knows that in practice it is likely it will need the co-operation of the French courts to enforce its interest. In this way the application of the lex situs rule to intangibles permits theory and practice to coincide. Further arguments in favour of the lex situs rule in this context are given in Chapter 13.

(2) Identifying the Situs of Interests in Securities

7.29 As indicated above, the first part of the current debate about the lex situs rule in relation to securities collateral is whether the rule is applicable. On the basis that it is, the second part of the debate is how one should identify the situs of interests in securities.

The situs of securities

7.30 The theme of this chapter is the rule that property rights in assets are determined by the lex situs. The situs of assets is also relevant for a number of other legal rules, particularly those relating to jurisdiction,[41] probate[42] and taxation.[43]

7.31 The physical location of a tangible asset at any time is a question of fact. Its situs is a question of law. In most cases,[44] situs and physical location coincide. Of course, intangible assets have no physical existence and therefore no physical loca-

---

[40] 'Choses in action generally are situated in the country where they are properly recoverable or can be enforced': *Dicey and Morris* (n 3 above) 22R-023, rule 112(1).

[41] See for example *Deutsche Schachtbau v Shell International Petroleum Co Ltd* [1900] 1 AC 295; *Swiss Bank Corporation v Boehmische Industrial Bank* [1923] 1 KB 673 (relating to the making of a garnishee order).

[42] See eg *Payne v King* [1902] AC 552, PC; *In re Clark* [1904] 1 Ch 294; *McMonagle v Westminster City Council* [1900] 1 All ER 993; *Brassard v Smith* [1925] AC 371, PC; *In the estate of Alberti (dec'd)* [1955] 3 All ER 730; *Callwood v Callwood* [1960] AC 659; *Re Osoba* [1978] 2 All ER 393 and 1099; *Vervaeke v Smith* [1982] 2 All ER 144. The application of the lex situs rule in probate was criticised in *Re Collens* [1986] 1 All ER 611, per Browne-Wilkinson VC at 616. Arguably, the probate cases involve a version of the lex situs rule, ie whether an English probate can take effect in relation to foreign property.

[43] See, for example, *Attorney General v Bouwens* (1838) 4 M & W 171; *Commissioner of Stamps v Hope* [1891] AC 476; *Commissioners of Inland Revenue v Muller & Co's Margerine Ltd* [1900] AC 217; *London and South America Investment Trust v British Tobacco Co (Australia)* [1927] 1 Ch 107; *Erie Beach Company Ltd v Attorney General for Ontario* [1930] AC 161, PC; *English Scottish and Australian Bank v IRC* [1932] AC 238; *Alloway v Phillips* [1980] 1 WLR 888; *Kwok Chi Leung Karl v Cmmr Estate Duty* [1988] 1 WLR 1035.

[44] There are exceptions for casual and transitory situs; see the rules for ships and aircraft in *Dicey and Morris* (n 3 above) 22E-057 and 22E-060.

tion. However, in probate cases from the nineteenth century onwards[45] and later[46] in taxation and jurisdiction cases, the courts developed rules whereby a legal location or situs might be conferred on an intangible asset by virtue of a legal fiction.[47] 'But debts do, in one form or another, represent property of very considerable value in the modern world, and it appears to me it is desirable that they should possess a locality, even if they are invested with it by means of a legal fiction.'[48] The general rule is that a debt is located where it is payable and recoverable in the normal course.[49] In the case of simple contract debts, this is where the debtor is resident.[50] For a bank debt payable at a particular branch, this is where the branch is located,[51] and for a debt under a letter of credit this is located where it is payable under the terms of the documentation.[52] The proposition that an intangible is

---

[45] Indeed, older ancestry is claimed for the probate rules: 'That for the purposes of probate and estate duty a simple contract debt is assumed to be situated where the debtor resides is established by a long series of authorities that stretch far back into the mists of antiquity': *English Scottish and Australian Bank v IRC* [1932] AC 238, per Lord Buckmaster at 242.

[46] The probate rules provided guidance in these new areas: 'The authorities which bear upon the locality of incorporeal personal property for purposes of probate appear to me to afford the best guides for the solution of the case before us': *Commissioners of Inland Revenue v Muller & Co's Margarine Ltd* [1901] AC 217, per Lord Lindley at 236, 237.

[47] An intangible may have more than one situs: 'It may perhaps be true that property which has no physical existence may, if necessary, be treated for some purposes in one locality, and for other purposes in some other locality': *Commissioners of Inland Revenue v Muller & Co's Margarine Ltd* [1901] AC 217, per Lord Lindley at 237.

[48] *English Scottish and Australian Bank v IRC* [1932] AC 238, per Lord Buckmaster at 245.

[49] *Re Russian Bank for Foreign Trade* [1934] 1 Ch 745, per Maugham J at 767: 'Its locality must be taken to be the place where the debt was in the ordinary course recoverable'. See also *Alloway v Phillips* [1980] 1 WLR 888, per Waller LJ at 894.

[50] In *Commissioner of Stamps v Hope* [1891] AC 476, it was necessary to determine the situs of a debt for probate purposes. 'Now a debt per se, although a chattel and part of the personal estate which the probate confers authority to administer, has, of course, no absolute local existence; but it has been long established in the Courts of this country, and is a well-settled rule governing all questions as to which Court can confer the required authority, that a debt does possess an attribute of locality, arising from and according to its nature, and the distinction drawn and well settled has been and is whether it is a debt by contract or a debt by speciality. In the former case, the debt being merely a chose in action—money to be recovered from the debtor and nothing more—could have no other local existence than the personal residence of the debtor, where the assets to satisfy it would presumably be, and it was held therefore to be bona notabilia within the area of the local jurisdiction within which he resided': *Commissioner of Stamps v Hope* [1891] AC 476, per Lord Field at 481, 482. See also *Payne v King* [1902] AC 552, PC, per Lord Macnaghten at 559, 560 and *Sedgwich Collins v Rossia Insurance Co of Petrograd* [1925] 1 KB 1, per Sargant LJ at 15; *AG der Manufacturen IA Woronin v Frederick Huth* (1928) 79 Lloyds Rep 262, per Wright J at 266; *English Scottish and Australian Bank v IRC* [1923] AC 238; *New York Life Insurance Company v Public Trustee* [1924] 2 Ch 101, per Pollock MR at 112, 116, per Atkin LJ at 119; *In re Fry* [1946] Ch 312, per Scrutton LJ at 430, 431; *Kwok Chi Leung Karl v Commr Estate Duty* [1988] 1 WLR 1035, per Lord Oliver at 1040.

[51] *Martin and Nadel* [1906] 2 KB 26, at 31 and other cases referred to in *Dicey and Morris* (n 3 above), 22-029, n 73.

[52] 'a debt under a letter of credit is different from ordinary debts. They may be situate where the debtor is resident. But a debt under a letter of credit is situate in the place where it is in fact payable against documents': *Power Curber International Ltd v National Bank of Kuwait* [1981] 1 WLR 1233, per Lord Denning at 1240.

located where it is payable and recoverable in the normal course accords with the observation made above that the lex situs rule is based partly on pragmatic considerations of enforcement.[53]

7.32   The rules for attributing a situs to the traditional forms of securities are discussed at length in *Dicey and Morris*,[54] and might very broadly be summarised as follows. The situs of a traditional bearer security is the physical location of the instrument constituting it.[55] The situs of registered securities is generally determined by the location of the register[56] as this is the place where dealings in them must be recorded in order to confer title.[57] This is usually the same as the place of incorporation, but in cases where share transfers are required to be recorded in a branch register, the location of the branch register and not the residence of the issuing corporation prevails as situs.[58]

The challenge of identifying the situs of interests in securities

7.33   The rules for attributing a situs to a *security*, which were very broadly summarised above, are well settled. In contrast, the question of how a situs should be attributed to an interest in securities has generated a fierce and continuing debate in the international legal community. Chapters 1 and 2 argued that securities and interests in securities are different types of assets, having different legal characteristics. Therefore it would be incorrect to assume, for example, that the situs of a physical bearer bond is the same as the situs of an unallocated, indirect and intangible interest in such a bond.

The account-based approach[59]

7.34   This section considers the situs of the interest of a participant in an international settlement system such as Euroclear, Clearstream and DTC ('the settlement sys-

---

[53] Rule 112(1) of *Dicey and Morris* (n 3 above) provides that 'Choses in action generally are situate in the country where they are properly recoverable or can be enforced'. See the discussion in *Dicey and Morris* at 22-024 et seq.

[54] At 22-040 for bearer securities and 22-044 for shares in companies.

[55] *Alcock v Smith* [1892] 1 Ch 238. See however the more complex treatment of this issue in *Dicey and Morris* (n 3 above) at 22-040, 22-041.

[56] See the Court of Appeal decision in *Macmillan* (n 24 above) at 411 (per Auld LJ).

[57] *Brassard v Smith* [1925] AC 371, at 376 (per Lord Dunedin); *Erie Beach Co v Attorney General for Ontario* [1930] AC 161, at 168 (per Lord Merrivale).

[58] *Brassard v Smith* (n 57 above).

[59] The following discussion represents the author's views, as they were developed with a group of leading lawyers practising in this area during discussions that took place in the course of 1998. The assistance of the following in the preparation of this discussion is gratefully acknowledged: Luigi De Ghenghi, formerly Vice President and Resident Counsel, Morgan Guaranty Trust Company of New York, Brussels Office, as operator of the Euroclear System; Randall Guynn, Partner, Davis Polk & Wardwell; Tim Herrington, Partner, Clifford Chance; Guy Morton, Partner, Freshfields; Ed Murray, Partner, Allen & Overy; Richard Potok, formerly of Davis Polk & Wardwell; Richard Slater, Partner, Slaughter & May; Larry Thompson, Senior Vice President and Deputy General

tems'), to whose account interests in securities are credited. It will argue that the situs of such interest is the local law of the office where the settlement system maintains the participant's account, ie Belgium in the case of Euroclear, Luxembourg in the case of Clearstream, and New York in the case of the DTC. This approach accords with existing customary practice in the securities markets, whereby security interests in such assets are perfected under, for example, Belgian law in the case of a Euroclear account.[60] It is consistent with the provisions of Article 9(2) of the Settlement Finality Directive, which is discussed below.

This discussion addresses the position where, in proceedings before an English **7.35** court, the court is required to identify the law under which a security interest granted by a participant in a settlement system over its interests in securities requires to be perfected. The discussion does not address questions of foreign law or proceedings that may be brought in foreign courts.[61] Nor does it address the law applicable to other stages in the creation and defence of a robust security interest, such as registration or priorities, which are considered later in this chapter.

As indicated in Chapter 2, in the case of each settlement system, a local statutory **7.36** regime affects the rights of participants in respect of securities held through those systems.[62] In each case, by virtue of this regime, the contractual arrangements with the relevant settlement system and the practical arrangements put in place by the settlement system, the asset of the participant takes on a special character, and is different from the underlying securities. As discussed in Chapters 1 and 2, the interest of the participant is unallocated, indirect and intangible. However, this asset is not at risk in the insolvency of the operator of the settlement system. In accordance with the local law of each settlement system's jurisdiction, participants' interests in securities would not be available to the creditors of the operator

---

Counsel, Depository Trust Company of New York; Francoise Verbiste, Lawyer, Clearstream (formerly Cedel Bank); Philip Wood, Partner, Allen & Overy. See Benjamin [1999] JIFM 68–71. See also Benjamin (1995) 10 JIBFL 253–357; *The Law of Global Custody* (London: Butterworths, 1996) 79–84; (1997) JIBFL 6; (1998) 13 JIBFL 85; (1998) 47 ICLQ 923. See also *The Oxford Colloquium on Collateral and Conflict of Laws* (London: Butterworths, September 1998).

There is a measure of consensus in the City that the account-based approach is correct. See eg P Wood, *Comparative Law of Security and Guarantees* (1995) 190. It has now been cautiously taken up in *Dicey and Morris* (n 3 above) 22-042, as discussed below. A leading contributor to this debate, Richard Potok of Potok & Co, London, calls this approach the 'place of the relevant intermediary approach', or 'PRIMA'. For an interesting discussion of the position under Netherlands law, see Rick Verhagen, 'Book-Entry Securities and the Conflict of Laws' EBLR (March/April 2000) 1.

[60] ie, security interests over interests credited to Euroclear accounts are perfected under Belgium law, or Luxembourg law in the case of Clearstream, or New York law in the case of DTC. The local law requirements for perfection in these systems of law are convenient.

[61] Collateral takers will have to consider the likelihood that participants' interest might be attached by third parties in the jurisdiction of the depositary. It is understood that the settlement systems have obtained local opinion to the effect that such attachment would not be possible.

[62] Belgian Royal Decree No 62 of November 1967; Luxembourg Grand-Ducal Decree of February 1971; article 8 of the New York Uniform Commercial Code.

in its insolvency. Accordingly, such settlement arrangements do not expose participants to the credit risk of the operator.

7.37 Of course, participants might be affected by any fraud or negligence on the part of the operator; in the case of settlement systems which are recognised by the UK regulatory authorities, the risk of this might be considered remote. On this basis, the fact that the rights of a participant are indirect and not direct does not affect the balance sheet, credit rating or taxation treatment of the collateral assets in the hands of the participant.

7.38 It was seen above that the rules for attributing a situs to an intangible asset are informed by a pragmatic concern for the practicalities of enforcement. Broadly speaking, claims are legally located where they are enforceable in the normal course of dealing; this often coincides with the place where they are recorded and delivered. Now the interests of the participant are recorded and deliverable only in the accounts of the settlement system and, in the normal course (ie in the absence of default by issuer or settlement system operator) enforceable only against the operator.[63] On this basis, it is argued that the situs of the interests of the participant is the location of the office of the settlement system where the accounts are maintained.[64] This will be called 'the account-based approach'. The author is delighted that this view finds support in the 13th edition of *Dicey and Morris*.[65]

7.39 The account-based approach is consistent with the position under the rules of private international law of Belgium, Luxembourg and New York[66] respectively.

---

[63] See Chapter 2 for a discussion of the use of deed polls, conferring direct rights on participants in the event of issuer default. However, these direct rights are not rights arising under interests in securities, but rather rights arising under the deed poll.

[64] An alternative argument, that supports the same conclusion, is as follows. Chapter 2 argued that the local statutory relationship between the operator of each settlement system and the participant is akin to an English law trust. (Of course they are not trusts but sui generis local statutory regimes; indeed in Belgium and Luxembourg, the trust is not recognised under domestic law.) The interests of the participant as beneficiary under this trust is unallocated. A line of case law considers the situs of another type of unallocated trust interest, namely interests in unadministered estates; the situs of such interests is the location of the trustee (which equates analogously with the operator of the settlement system). See *Lord Sudeley v Attorney General* [1897] AC 11; *Re Smyth* [1898] 1 Ch 89; *Stamp Duties Comr (Queensland) v Hugh Duncan Livingstone* [1965] AC 694; *Baker v Archer-Shee* [1927] AC 844; *Archer-Shee v Garland* [1931] AC 212. See also *Marshall v Kerr* [1994] 3 WLR 299, per Lord Browne Wilkinson at 312.

[65] 'the better view would be that the investor's proprietary rights are located at the place where his account with the depository is maintained, and that the law which governs dealings with these rights is the law which governs his relationship with the broker. This will be the law governing the relationship between the investor and broker, under which the rights of the investor arose, and it will often be the *lex situs* of the rights the investor has against the broker': *Dicey and Morris* (n 3 above) vol II, 986, para 24-064.

[66] In the case of the DTC, this is achieved contractually under the documentation entered into between participants and the DTC, in accordance with article 8.110 of the New York Uniform Commercial Code.

While (in the absence of *renvoi*)[67] foreign conflicts rules have no direct authority in English law, the English court will be assisted in adopting the account-based approach by the knowledge that relevant foreign courts will do the same, thus reducing the incidence of conflicts of law in the international securities markets.

Also, the governing law argument points to the same result. Because participants' **7.40** rights arise under special local law statutory regimes and local law contractual arrangements, they are governed by local law.[68]

The author has argued above that the Court of Appeal decision in *Macmillan* was **7.41** correct, and that the governing law argument is mistaken. However, the success of this argument is not a necessary premise of the account-based approach, for the governing law argument also leads to it. As indicated above, participants are protected in the insolvency of the operator in accordance with local law legislation. Participants' rights in respect of interests in securities arise under and are dependent upon local statute, together with contractual arrangements with the operator, which are governed by local law. Because participants' rights are creatures of local law, the English courts may properly treat these rights as being determined locally.

Thus, a number of different legal arguments are available to address this question, **7.42** and happily they all point to the same conclusion, namely that perfection is determined by the local law of the office of the settlement system where the participant's account is maintained.

Reject depositary jurisdiction

In the case of interests in immobilised securities, where a physical global instru- **7.43** ment constituting the underlying securities is held by a depositary for the clearing system, some might seek to argue that the property rights of participants are determined by the law of the jurisdiction in which such instrument is located. The bulk of immobilised securities take the form of bearer instruments. When such securities are held outside immobilisation systems, they constitute negotiable instruments.[69] It is established that, for taxation purposes at least, the situs of a negotiable instrument is the physical location of the paper that constitutes it.[70] However, it has been argued in Chapter 3 that interests in securities cannot be negotiable instruments.

---

[67] *Renvoi* is expressly excluded from the Rome Convention by Article 15.

For a similar conclusion in relation to units in unit trusts, see Kam Fan Sin, *The Legal Nature of the Unit Trust* (Oxford: Clarendon Press, 1997) 330, 331.

[68] In the case of the DTC, article 8.10 of the New York Uniform Commercial Code permits the governing law to be determined by contract. The documentation entered into by the DTC with participants chooses New York law.

[69] See eg *Edelstein v Schuler* [1902] All ER Rep 884.

[70] See *Dicey and Morris* (n 3 above) 22-040.

7.44 More fundamentally, the interest of the participant must be distinguished from the underlying instrument. The argument that the interest of the participant is located with the depositary of the underlying instrument involves conflating the interest of the participant with the underlying securities. As shown in Chapters 1 and 2, the two are distinct. At a practical level, global instruments are in many cases held with depositaries in the jurisdiction in which the closing of the issue took place. Many global instruments are held for Euroclear and Clearstream by depositary banks in London. However, participants will not know (nor have any contractual right to discover) the location of the global instrument. Accordingly, this approach reveals no straightforward way of perfecting a security interest.[71] Moreover, where international portfolios of securities are used as collateral, the relevant global instruments may be held in a range of different jurisdictions. In practice it may not be feasible for participants to consult a range of foreign lawyers in respect of one collateral arrangement. Many collateral arrangements permit substitution, and here the challenge would be more acute because a changing class of jurisdictions would be involved. Thus, this approach is wrong in principle, and unworkable in practice.

7.45 The account-based approach avoids this uncertainty and fragmentation. The courts have shown a strong desire to develop rules of private international law which are convenient to business people, and to support the secondary markets by enabling transferees to establish title without having to enquire into more than one system of law. These are all reasons to avoid disturbing existing market practice (whereby security interests over entitlements held through Euroclear are, for example, perfected in accordance with Belgian law) and to reject reference to the jurisdiction of the underlying depositary.

The Settlement Finality Directive

7.46 The Settlement Finality Directive[72] was introduced with a view to reducing risk in payment and securities settlement systems within the EU.[73] (Much of the impetus for the Settlement Finality Directive came from the introduction of TARGET,

---

[71] Because participants do not have accounts with the depositary, and because the depositary does not take instructions from participants, a participant cannot perfect any security interest at that level.

[72] Directive 98/26/EC of the European Parliament and the Council of 19 May 1998 on Settlement Finality in Payment and Securities Settlement Systems. Member States were required to implement the Directive by 11 December 1999. It was implemented in the United Kingdom by the Financial Markets and Insolvency (Settlement Finality) Regulations 1999, SI 1999/2979.

[73] See recitals 1 and 2 to the Directive: '(1) . . . whereas the reduction of legal risks associated with participation in real time gross settlement systems is of paramount importance, given the increasing development of these systems; (2) whereas it is also of the utmost importance to reduce the risk associated with participation in securities settlement systems, in particular where there is a close connection between such systems and payment systems'.

the real time large value euro payment system.) Article 9(2) supports the account-based approach. It provides as follows:

> Where securities (including rights in securities) are provided as collateral security to participants and/or central banks of the Member States or the future European central bank . . . and their right (or that of any nominee, agent or third party acting on their behalf) with respect to the securities is legally recorded on a register, account or centralised deposit system located in a Member State, the determination of the rights of such entities as holders of collateral security in relation to those securities shall be governed by the law of that Member State.

The term 'collateral security' is defined in Article 2(m) as follows: **7.47**

> 'collateral security' shall mean all realisable assets provided under a pledge (including money provided under a pledge), a repurchase or similar agreement, or otherwise, for the purpose of securing rights and obligations potentially arising in connection with a system, or provided to central banks of the Member States or to the future European central bank.

There has been an active debate in Europe as to the correct interpretation of this **7.48**
Article.

> Under one view—the narrow view—Article 9(2) would only [benefit] certain collateral takers:
> — central banks of member states;
> — the European central bank; and
> — those participants providing liquidity to an EU payment or securities settlement system to which the Finality Directive applies (for example, a European system operator taking securities as collateral in return for extensions of credit that allow participants of that system to complete transactions relating to securities in the system).
> Under another view—the broad view—Article 9(2) would [benefit] all participants in an EU settlement system. Among proponents of the broad view, some argue that Article 9(2) should apply to indirect participants as well as to direct participants of EU payment or securities settlement systems. Others argue that the principle in Article 9(2) should apply to direct and indirect participants of all payment and securities systems, whether or not they are EU systems.[74]

The broad view received widespread support in the financial community and is **7.49**
reflected in the implementing legislation adopted by most Member States.[75]
Unfortunately, the narrow view was adopted in the United Kingdom. The
Directive was implemented by regulation under the European Communities Act
1972, and because of the restrictive terms of that statute,[76] HM Treasury did not
consider that it had vires to adopt the broad view.

---

[74] Richard Potok of Potok & Co, *Providing Legal Certainty for Securities Held as Collateral* (London: IFLR, December 1999) 12–16.
[75] For a full discusssion, see Potok (n 74 above).
[76] See s 2(2).

7.50 As mentioned above, the Settlement Finality Directive was implemented in the United Kingdom by the Financial Markets and Insolvency (Settlement Finality) Regulations 1999.[77] Article 9(2) of the Directive was implemented by regulation 23, which tracks the terms of Article 9(2) with minor amendments.[78] The narrow view is reflected in the definition of the term 'collateral security'.[79] Therefore, it would appear that the regulations do not apply to commercial collateral arrangements, where the collateralised exposure is not associated with the operation of payment and settlement systems.

7.51 This chapter has argued that the position that would have pertained under a wide implementation of the Directive in the United Kingdom, arises in any case by the general principles of conflicts of laws under the record-based approach. However, it is clearly unsatisfactory for both a statutory and non-statutory regime to apply in circumstances which are legally alike. It is hoped that HM Treasury will take the earliest opportunity to rectify this anomaly, by legislation that clarifies the application of the account-based approach for all collateral arrangements involving interests in securities.

Other foreign legislation

7.52 In some jurisdictions, other statutory provisions either replicate or anticipate the effect of a wide implementation of the Settlement Finality Directive. Important examples are New York (under the UCC);[80] Belgium and Luxembourg.

---

[77] SI 1999/2979.

[78] 'Applicable law relating to securities held as collateral security.

23. Where—

(a) securities (including rights in securities) are provided as collateral security to a participant or a central bank (including any nominee, agent or third party acting on behalf of the participant or the central bank) and

(b) a register, account or centralised deposit system located in an EEA State legally records the entitlement of that person to the collateral security,

the rights of that person as a holder of collateral security in relation to those securities shall be governed by the law of the EEA State or, where appropriate, the law of the part of the EEA State, where the register, account, or centralised deposit system is located.'

[79] Regulation 2(1): ' "collateral security" means any realisable assets provided under a charge or a repurchase or similar agreement, or otherwise (including money provided under a charge)—(a) for the purpose of securing rights and obligations potentially arising in connection with a designated system ("collateral security in connection with participation in a designated system"); or (b) to a central bank for the purpose of securing rights and obligations in connection with its operations in carrying out its functions as a central bank ("collateral security in connection with the functions of a central bank")'. Again, this tracks the terms of Article 2(m) of the Directive, with minor amendments.

[80] See in particular article 8-110.

C. Insolvency

(1) Property Rights and Insolvency

As discussed in earlier chapters, a number of arrangements in the securities mar- **7.53**
kets involve the assertion of property rights. In each case, such rights serve to
address the risk of counterparty insolvency. Thus, it is in order to escape the status
of unsecured creditor that the collateral taker claims property rights in collateral
assets, the custody client claims property rights in custody securities, and the purchaser claims property rights in the purchased securities in the course of settlement. It is therefore crucial to these persons that their purported property rights
should stand up in their counterparty's insolvency.

Sadly, the insolvency laws of the different commercial jurisdictions are very far **7.54**
from harmonised.[81] Therefore, a person asserting property rights in relation to a
counterparty is obliged to identify the law that would govern the insolvency of its
counterparty, in order to ensure that its property rights will be recognised under
that law. In theory, property rights arising under foreign law prior to the onset of
insolvency should be recognised in insolvency proceedings, providing of course
that they are not avoidable under preference rules or other mandatory provision
of insolvency law.[82] In practice, however, if a pre-existing foreign law property
right would not be recognised under the domestic law that governs the insolvency,
the danger arises that the courts of certain jurisdictions may decline to give effect
to such rights.[83] It is therefore standard practice for collateral takers and others
asserting property rights to seek the opinion of counsel in the jurisdictions whose
laws are most likely to govern the insolvency of the counterparty, to the effect that
the property rights will survive local insolvency proceedings.[84]

(2) Insolvency Jurisdiction

The first step in practice is to establish the nationality of the courts that are likely **7.55**
to assert jurisdiction over the insolvency of a counterparty. Clearly, the courts of
the country of incorporation may be likely to do so. In addition, if the counterparty acts through a branch office, the courts of the jurisdiction where the branch

---

[81] The slow progress of initiatives to harmonise insolvency laws such as the European
Bankruptcy Convention may be due in part to the profound political and social differences that
underlie the different provisions of national insolvency regimes. See generally Fletcher, *Insolvency in
Private International Law* (n 10 above).

[82] See Article 5 of the European Bankruptcy Regulation (1999/C 221/06), and the discussion in
Fletcher (n 10 above) 272.

[83] Anecdotally this has presented problems for collateral takers seeking to enforce their interests
in certain Latin American countries.

[84] Collateral is routinely taken under market standard documentation prepared by trade associations such as ISDA, PAS/ISMA and ISLA. As discussed in Chapter 6, such trade associations
obtain standard form legal opinions in favour of their documentation from key jurisdictions.

is established may assert jurisdiction, particularly if there are significant local assets.[85] The English courts have statutory jurisdiction to wind up companies registered in England and Wales,[86] and also to wind up companies which are not registered under the Companies Act 1985, in circumstances which include the court being of the opinion that it is just and equitable that the company should be wound up.[87] A liberal approach has been taken to interpreting this statutory provision, and in practice the English courts may assume jurisdiction to wind up a foreign company if either the company has assets in England, or at any time carried on business in England, provided there is a reasonable possibility of benefit accruing to creditors.[88]

(3) Applicable Law

7.56 The next question is, what system of law will the court having jurisdiction apply to insolvency proceedings? As a general rule, insolvency is governed by the law of the jurisdiction in which it is conducted.[89]

> It has long been regarded as conclusively settled that in any winding up conducted pursuant to the English legislation relating to insolvent companies, English law will apply both as to matters of substance as well as to matters of procedure.[90]

7.57 This remains the case even where English proceedings are ancillary to foreign proceedings.[91] (However, under section 426 of the Insolvency Act 1986 the English courts may apply foreign law if so requested by certain (mainly) Commonwealth courts.)[92]

7.58 The mandatory provision of insolvency law will override contractual provisions that are incompatible with them.[93]

---

[85] See Article 3 of the European Bankruptcy Convention.

[86] Insolvency Act 1986, s 117(1).

[87] '(a) if the company is dissolved, or has ceased to carry on business, or is carrying on business only for the purpose of winding up its affairs; (b) if the company is unable to pay its debts; (c) if the court is of the opinion that it is just and equitable that the company should be wound up': Insolvency Act 1986, s 221(5).

[88] See the discussion of relevant case law in Fletcher (n 10 above) 127–139. In theory, the jurisdiction of the English court extends to the worldwide assets of the company in liquidation: Insolvency Act 1986, s 144. However, in practice, enforcement of English insolvency rules against foreign assets may be limited, and the co-operation of foreign courts is required in relation to foreign assets. Where insolvency proceedings in other jurisdictions are also involved, the English courts will in general seek some form of co-operation.

[89] See the European Bankruptcy Convention, Article 4.1.

[90] Fletcher (n 10 above) 152.

[91] See Fletcher (n 10 above) 153 and the discussion of *BCCI (No 10)* below.

[92] See the discussion in Fletcher (n 10 above), 187 et seq. 'Although section 426 was conceived as an instrument to further the cause of international cooperation, its bemusing and elliptical drafting has proved an obstacle to ready understanding and application': at 196.

[93] See, for example, *British Eagle International Airlines Ltd v Compagnie Nationale Air France* [1975] 1 WLR 758.

D. Steps in Taking Collateral

Chapter 5 considered the various steps that must be taken to protect the position **7.59** of the collateral taker. In cross border situations, where either foreign counterparty or foreign collateral is involved, it is important to identify which system of law will govern each step of the process. The following is a very summary discussion of the rules that are likely to be applied by the English courts; for a full discussion, see *Dicey and Morris*.

As discussed in Chapter 5, collateral arrangements rest on the establishment of **7.60** collateral contracts. Any professionally drafted collateral agreement will have a governing law clause. In proceedings in one of the EU states in which the Rome Convention applies,[94] as a general rule the courts will give effect to such clauses under Article 3(1) of the Rome Convention, which is implemented in the United Kingdom by the Contracts (Applicable Law) Act 1990.[95] However, in proceedings outside the EU the position may differ. Therefore a choice of forum clause is also advisable in the collateral agreement to support the contractual choice of law.[96] However, although the governing law of the collateral contract governs many issues, it by no means governs all of them, as discussed below.

The material validity of a contract is generally determined by its governing law.[97] **7.61** Thus, for example, where a floating charge is taken, it is important to ensure that that form of security interest is recognised under the law that governs the charge document. A contract is formally valid if it complies with the formal requirements of its governing law or, alternatively with the law of the place where it is concluded.[98] As constitutional questions, power and authority will generally be determined by the law of incorporation.[99]

Compliance with any necessary regulatory authorisations should be considered **7.62** under the regulatory regimes that may be applicable to the business of the collateral giver. While certain states[100] claim extra-territorial regulatory jurisdiction, it is customary to address the question of regulatory authorisations only under the laws where the collateral giver carries on business. These would include the jurisdiction where it is incorporated and/or operates through a branch.

---

[94] Convention on the Law Applicable to Contractual Obligations.
[95] See *Dicey and Morris* (n 3 above) rule 173(1), at 32R-059.
[96] This is especially true as the Rome Convention 1980 excludes *renvoi*: see Article 15.
[97] See Article 8 of the Rome Convention 1980 and *Dicey and Morris* (n 3 above) rule 176(1) at 32R-151.
[98] See Article 9 of the Rome Convention 1980 and *Dicey and Morris* (n 3 above) rule 177, 32R-172.
[99] See for example *Carl Zeiss Stiftung v Rayner & Keeler (No 2)* [1967] 1 AC 853 at 972E and at 919G. See *Dicey and Morris* (n 3 above) rule 154, at 30R-020.
[100] Notably the USA.

7.63 Very broadly, the due execution of a document on behalf of a corporation is a matter for the law of incorporation.[101] Attachment and perfection involve the acquisition of property rights, and therefore are determined by the lex situs of the collateral assets. Also, any registration requirements imposed by the law of the place of incorporation or branch of the collateral giver should be complied with.

7.64 Where a question of priority arises because of double-dealing (eg where both the plaintiff and the defendant are collateral takers) the rule is generally that priority is determined by the law of the forum.[102] However, where a question of priority arises from breach of fiduciary duty (eg a tracing claim, where the plaintiff is or represents a defrauded beneficiary) priorities will be determined by the lex situs.[103]

7.65 In ascertaining that the collateral giver either is the beneficial owner of the collateral assets, or is authorised by the beneficial owner(s), the collateral taker should consider the law that governs the relationship between the collateral giver and any clients for whom it beneficially holds (interests in) securities. However, the collateral taker will in practice not be in a position to determine with certainty what law or laws governs any such relationship. Since it is customary to document client relationships under the local law of the service provider, in most circumstances practitioners would address the question of beneficial ownership under the law of the jurisdiction in which the collateral is established or operates a branch.

7.66 As a practical matter, collateral takers should consider the enforcement requirements of the jurisdiction in which enforcement action would need to be taken; in practice this will depend on the location and manner in which the collateral assets are held. As a general rule, the English courts will permit the enforcement of a security interest over English securities arising under a foreign law agreement, provided the perfection requirements of English law as lex situs have been met.

7.67 The question of exchange control should be considered under the laws of the jurisdiction *from* which the collateral taker would wish to remit proceeds of sale. Identifying this jurisdiction will depend on the payment arrangements that are in place in the market in which the collateral taker would sell the collateral securities.

7.68 The rules of insolvency displacement should be considered under the law or laws that are likely to govern the insolvency of the collateral giver; the law of incorporation and of any branch should be considered. Under the principle in *Macmillan v Bishopsgate*, the English courts will treat tracing claims as governed by the lex situs.

---

[101] See *Dicey and Morris* (n 3 above) 30-023.

[102] ie English law in the English courts. See *Le Feuvre v Sullivan* (1855) 10 Moo PC 1, at 13; *Kelly v Selwyn* [1905] 2 Ch 117 at 122 and *Republica de Guatemala v Nunez* [1925] 1 KB 669, CA. See also *Dicey and Morris* (n 3 above) 7-032.

[103] In such a case, the plaintiff's argument is based on an undestroyed proprietary claim. See *Macmillan v Bishopsgate* [1995] 1 WLR 978 at 989.

E. Conflict of Laws and Insolvency Set Off

As discussed in Chapter 6, outright collateral transfers rely on insolvency set off. **7.69**
In cross border outright transfer arrangements it is therefore necessary to establish
which system of law will govern the availability of set off in the insolvency of the
counterparty.

(1) English Law

The case of *Re Bank of Credit and Commerce International SA (No 10)*[104] held that **7.70**
rule 4.90 of the Insolvency Rules 1986, SI 1986/1925, which provides for mandatory insolvency set off, applies under English law irrespective of the governing law
of the debt. Moreover, the English courts have no power to disapply the rule even
where the English liquidation is ancillary to a foreign liquidation and where the
law governing that foreign liquidation does not permit insolvency set off.[105] The
application of an ancillary English liquidation will in practice be limited to
English assets, but nonetheless English law will apply.[106] Professor Fletcher refers
to '[t]he unhappy breakdown of international comity over the matter of set-off'
in the context of this case.[107]

(2) Foreign Law

In relation to any proposed outright collateral transfer arrangement, it would be **7.71**
prudent in practice to confirm that insolvency set off is available both under the
law that would govern the insolvency of the counterparty and also under the

---

[104] [1996] 4 All ER 796.

[105] 'The courts have, in my judgment, no more inherent power to disapply the statutory insolvency scheme than to disapply the provisions of any other statute': ibid 814.

[106] '(1) Where a foreign company is in liquidation in its country of incorporation a winding-up
order made in England will normally be regarded as giving rise to a winding up ancillary to that
being conducted in the country of incorporation.

(2) The winding up in England will be ancillary in the sense that it will not be within the power
of the English liquidators to get in and realise all the assets of the company worldwide. They will necessarily have to concentrate on getting in and realising the English assets.

(3) Since in order to achieve a pari passu distribution between all the company's creditors it will
be necessary for there to be a pooling of the company's assets worldwide and for a dividend to be
declared out of the assets comprised in that pool, the winding up in England will be ancillary in the
sense, also, that it will be the liquidators in the principal liquidation who will be best placed to
declare the dividend and to distribute the assets in the pool accordingly.

(4) None the less, the ancillary character of an English winding up does not relieve an English
court of the obligation to apply English law, including English insolvency law, to the resolution of
any issue arising in the winding up which is brought before the court. It may be, of course, that
English conflicts of law rules will lead to the application of some foreign law principle in order to
resolve a particular issue.

Rule 4.90 of the 1986 rules is a substantive rule of English law. *Stein v Blake* [1995] 2 All ER 961,
[1996] AC 243 establishes that that is so': ibid 820.

[107] Fletcher (n 10 above) 366, n 4. See also the note on this case by Fletcher [1997] JBL 471.

governing law of the contract.[108] A further potential obstacle to the availability of insolvency set off arrangements is recharacterisation risk, discussed in Chapter 11. There is a debate as to whether it is necessary to consider recharacterisation risk under lex situs as well as under the governing law of the collateral agreement; this is discussed in Chapter 6.

F. Conclusions

7.72 It will be seen from the above that cross border collateral arrangements involve complex questions of conflict of laws, and this accounts for much of the legal expense of such arrangements. Trade associations have done much to reduce the expense of legal risk management in cross border collateral by obtaining standard foreign law opinions for the use of their members. However, these opinions only apply where industry standard documentation is unamended, and may not assist in bespoke arrangements.

7.73 Therefore there is a tremendous commercial need for measures that serve to harmonise the legal aspects of cross border collateral.

---

[108] Interestingly, the position under Netherlands law is understood to be that, outside insolvency, the availability of set off should be determined by the governing law of the claim and counterclaim, where this is the same.

8

COLLATERALISING CLEARING EXPOSURES[1]

A. Clearing

As briefly indicated in Chapters 1 and 9, clearing is a process that takes place after **8.01** trading and before settlement. Its purpose is to manage the credit exposures that arise during this interval between the parties to a trade. The core function of clearing is the novation of market contracts, whereby a clearing house[2] is interposed between the original trade counterparties. Trades are novated so that the original contract between the buyer and the seller is replaced by two new contracts, one between seller and the clearing house and buyer, one between the buyer and the clearing house as seller. The clearing house is contractually required to perform on one contract even if its counterparty defaults on the other. Thus the original parties to the trade continue to bear credit risk, but the quality of the credit risk is improved from that of original counterparty to that of the clearing house. Because clearing houses have significant financial resources, novation upgrades the quality of the credit exposures of participants. An additional function of clearing is the netting of obligations of market participants, so that the requirements to deliver

---

[1] The author is grateful to Dermot Turing, Partner, Clifford Chance and Monica Sah and Nishi Shant, Senior Associates, Clifford Chance, for their comments in relation to this chapter.

[2] In some cases, the clearing house is a separate legal person from the exchange. For example, The London Clearing House (LCH) provides clearing services for a number of markets. In other cases, the exchange itself provides clearing. Examples are the Chicago Mercantile Exchange, Deutsche Terminborse and the Singapore International Monetary Exchange.

collateral in respect of such exposures may be calculated on a net basis. Netting reduces the sum of credit exposures borne by participants and by the clearing house.

8.02 Historically only the on exchange derivatives markets benefited from clearing. However, more recently, clearing is being extended to off exchange derivatives business.[3] A further development is the provision of clearing services in relation to the cash securities markets. The settlement interval for derivatives is usually very long (three months or more). This makes post-trade, pre-settlement counterparty risk commercially onerous for market participants. However, as indicated above, recently the non-derivatives securities markets (known as the cash securities markets)[4] have become intolerant of counterparty risk even during their shorter settlement cycles, and a wide range of initiatives are introducing clearing to the cash securities markets. In the United Kingdom, there are proposals for the clearing service provided by LCH to be extended to equity trades executed on SETS (the London large value order-driven market) and settled in CREST, the UK dematerialised settlement system, in the near future, as discussed further in Chapter 9.[5]

8.03 The clearing house bears the credit risk of its clearing counterparties, and requires collateral in respect of these credit exposures. In general, collateral accepted by clearing houses comprises certain types of (interests in) securities and cash.

8.04 In general, clearing houses are only willing to provide clearing services to well-capitalised market participants which are admitted to membership of the clearing house.

(1) LCH

8.05 The following discussion will consider the use by the London Clearing House ('LCH') of collateral in respect of its exposures to it members.

8.06 At the time of writing, details of the proposed clearing service for equity trades concluded on the London Stock Exchange and settled through CREST are not available, so this discussion will consider the role of LCH in clearing trades made on LIFFE. LCH is a recognised clearing house for the purposes of section 38 of the Financial Services Act 1986 (FSA). As such it is required to have arrangements for ensuring the performance of transactions effected on LIFFE and the other

---

[3] Examples are services provided by LCH to the OTC repo market through Repoclear and the swap market through Swapclear.

[4] The term 'cash securities markets' is used to indicate the markets where securities are bought and sold for present delivery (or delivery as quickly as available settlement systems permit) as opposed to the derivatives markets.

[5] For a detailed discussion of these proposals, see *Central Counterparty for SETS, Service Outline* (LCH, CREST and LSE, March 2000).

recognised investment exchanges for which it provides clearing services.[6] LCH is also required to have default rules designed to enable LCH to ensure that the open contracts of defaulting members are settled, thus addressing systemic risk. Part VII of the Companies Act 1989 provides special statutory protection to LCH as a recognised clearing house. Accordingly, security interests taken by LCH and the exercise by LCH of its powers under the default rules are not vulnerable to challenge by the administrator or liquidator of a defaulting member.

The role of LCH in modifying the contractual arrangements affecting members will be considered first; a discussion of margin arrangements will follow. **8.07**

(2) Credit Exposures

From the time that an exchange member enters into a derivatives trade, to the time that the trade is settled[7] or alternatively closed out,[8] the member is said to have an open contract.[9] At any time, an open contract will be either profitable or unprofitable. Where a person's contract is unprofitable, the risk arises that that person will not perform on the contract. **8.08**

During the currency of a derivatives transaction, fluctuations in market values give rise to credit exposures between the parties. This is illustrated by an example given by LIFFE:[10] **8.09**

> On 1 December, company ABC plc buys a futures contract which states that on 31 March, ABC will buy one lot (5 metric tonnes) of coffee of an agreed quality, for $75,000 ($1,500 per metric tonne) from company XYZ plc. This means that whatever the actual market price of coffee on 31 March ABC will still only pay $7,500.
>
> As 31 March approaches, the price of coffee could start to rise above $1,500 per metric tonne. If this happens, then ABC's futures contract has a positive value as the future contract price agreed is lower than the current market price.
>
> Alternatively the price could start to fall and in this instance ABC's contract has a negative value.

ABC's contract has a negative value where the future contract price is higher than the current market price, because in those circumstances settlement[11] of the contract would involve loss for ABC. Thus ABC has the prospect of future loss. **8.10**

---

[6] FSA 1986, s 39(4)(c) and Sch 4, para 2(4).

[7] Settlement may be by cash settlement or delivery on expiry: see LCH Procedures 2.7.5.

[8] A member closes out a contract when it enters into a contract on the same terms, except that where it was acting as seller in the original contract, it acts as buyer in the closing-out contract, and vice versa.

[9] See the definition section in The London Clearing House General Regulations for London Markets ('the General Regulations'). (That definition also excludes contracts which have been invoiced back.)

[10] *Introduction to LIFFE* 4.

[11] On LIFFE, all futures contracts are settled by a cash payment, except for LIFFE government bond futures (other than Japanese Government Bond futures), which are settled by delivery of the underlying asset.

The corollary for XYZ is the risk that ABC will fail to settle the contract, thus depriving XYZ of its profit. A way of expressing this risk is to say that XYZ bears ABC's credit risk.

8.11 The parties are required to deliver collateral in respect of such credit exposures. At any time that ABC's contract has a negative value, LCH must hold collateral from ABC.

B. Contractual Arrangements

8.12 Clearing through LCH involves modifying the contractual arrangements between market participants, in the manner outlined below.

(1) Principal Trading

8.13 Under LIFFE's rules, all LIFFE members are obliged to trade as principal and not as agent.[12] In cases where the LIFFE member is trading in order to fill a client's order, the member will enter into a principal to principal trade with another member, and will also enter into a back to back trade in like terms with its client. Clearing members of LIFFE are also members of LCH. Because clearing involves LCH in credit exposures to its members, LCH imposes significant financial resources requirements on its members. It is therefore concerned to avoid agency trades, which would involve it in credit exposures to the clients of its members, whose financial standing it is not able to control.

(2) Members of LCH

8.14 LIFFE contracts are cleared through LCH. Members of LIFFE who have clearing member status may clear their trades directly with LCH. As indicated above, LIFFE clearing members are also members of LCH.[13] Only some members of LIFFE have clearing member status. Non-clearing members must arrange to have their trades cleared with LCH through clearing members.[14] For the sake of simplicity, this discussion will consider only the position of members of LCH.

---

[12] See rule 4.11.4 in the LIFFE Rules.

[13] There are different categories of LCH membership, permitting different types of business to be cleared, and having corresponding different levels of financial resources requirements.

LCH also clears trades on IPE, LME and Tradepoint. There has been discussion of extending its clearing service to London Stock Exchange trades settled through CREST.

[14] 'Those "firms" permitted to trade on the floor of the exchange or on its trading system, which are not Members, must conclude a Clearing Agreement with the exchange, LCH and a Member who agrees to clear on their behalf': LCH Procedures 2.4.2. See also LIFFE Rules, rule 3.4.9.

(3) Novation

Trades concluded on LIFFE are matched and then automatically registered with **8.15**
LCH.[15] Upon registration of the trade between member A as seller and member B
as buyer, the original contract between A and B is novated and replaced by two
new contracts, one between A as seller and LCH as buyer, and the other between
B as buyer and LCH as seller. Each party contracts as principal.[16] In this way, LCH
acts as central counterparty, and assumes contractual liability for the performance
of the obligations owed to both parties.[17] This means that neither A nor B has to
bear each other's credit risk, and each is only exposed to the credit risk of LCH. If
A defaults, LCH is still bound to perform its contract with B, and vice versa. LCH
therefore bears the potential credit risk of both A and B.

C. Collateral

In respect of these exposures, LCH requires members to deliver collateral.[18] In the **8.16**
LCH documentation, the collateral requirement is called the margin requirement, and collateral is called margin cover. LCH can require the delivery of margin cover as a condition of the registration of a trade.[19] LCH's ability under the
default rules to deal with the margin cover in the event of member default has special statutory protection under Part VII of the Companies Act 1989, as discussed
in more detail below.

(1) Calculation of Margin Requirement

The margin requirement is made up of two parts, namely initial margin and vari- **8.17**
ation margin.

---

[15] Trade matching, presentation of trades to LCH for registration and the allocation and designation of trades to an account is done automatically by the Trade Registration System (TRS).

[16] 'Upon registration of an original contract by the Clearing House, such contract shall be
replaced by novation . . . by two open contracts, one between the seller and the Clearing House as
buyer, as principals to such contract, and one between the buyer and the Clearing House as seller, as
principals to such contract': General Regulations, reg 3(a). The General Regulations contractually
bind the member by virtue of its Clearing Membership Agreement with LCH (clause 2.10). A number of other provisions have the same effect: 'The benefit of the performance by the Clearing House
of such obligations is conferred upon Members as principals and upon no other persons whatsoever': General Regulations, reg 1(c). See also reg 3(a); reg 4(b); clauses 2.12 and 2.15 of the Clearing
Membership Agreement; and the Client Consent Form.

[17] General Regulations, reg 1(b).

[18] General Regulations, regs 9(b) and 12(a). In addition, financial resources are available to LCH
in order to address the risk that margin cover should be insufficient to meet the costs of default by
any member. The members of LCH provide £150 million in respect of exchange-traded business,
and beyond that insurance cover is available up to £100 million.

[19] See LCH Procedures, 2.5.3.

Initial margin

8.18 The initial margin requirement arises when a trade is concluded. It is calculated by LCH in liaison with LIFFE[20] with reference to the risks associated with the contract in question.[21] It takes into account a range of factors including recent daily price movements, the volatility of the contract in question and anticipated future events that may affect the contract. LCH has a discretionary power to call for additional initial margin at any time.[22] This power is exercised to reflect additional risks arising upon changing market conditions or circumstances that may otherwise affect the member's ability to perform.[23] 'For example, LCH raised initial margin rates on certain contracts in anticipation of increased volatility at the outbreak of the Gulf War, during the 1992 UK election and prior to the French referendum on Maastricht.'[24]

Variation margin

8.19 Whereas initial margin is calculated in the discretion of LCH to reflect risk factors affecting the market and the member, and thus to reflect anticipated future losses on the close out of a contract, variation margin is calculated on a formulaic basis, to reflect changes in market prices for the contract in question. Variation margin is calculated throughout the life of the open contract on a daily basis at the close of business or intra day.[25] For each open contract, the daily variation margin is the difference between that day's closing market settlement price and the previous day's closing market settlement price, as discussed below.[26]

Daily settlement or marking to market

8.20 At the end of every day, LCH in general closes out each open contract of every member.[27] It does this by opening and registering a settlement contract between itself and the member. The settlement contract is on the same terms as the open contract, other than price, and except that where a member acts as buyer in the open contract, it acts as seller in the settlement contract.

---

[20] General Regulations, reg 12(d).
[21] In practice, the initial margin requirement is calculated using a software system called London SPAN.
[22] General Regulations, reg 12(e).
[23] General Regulations, reg 12(f).
[24] *LCH Risk Management in Operation* (London Clearing House) 6.
[25] LCH routinely calculates margin requirements daily, and has powers to make intra-day calculations and calls when appropriate.
[26] General Regulations, reg 15(c). Different rules apply to the calculation of variation margin on equity options.
[27] The reasons for this practice are largely historic. The daily closing out of open contracts is not the invariable practice. For example, London Metal Exchange (LME) open contracts are not closed out daily and different rules apply to equity options.

The official market quotation[28] for a contract at the close of the business day is **8.21** called its settlement price. Each day LCH checks the settlement price for the member's open contract.[29] If this quotation is more favourable to the member than yesterday's quotation, LCH will make a credit to the member's financial account.[30] If it is less favourable, LCH will make a debit to the financial account of the member.[31]

The next day, LCH will re-open the member's positions, by registering in the **8.22** member's name new open contracts on the same terms as the settled open contract.[32]

(2) Delivery of Margin Cover by Member

Members may meet their initial margin requirements with cash, (interests in) **8.23** securities[33] or guarantees from banks approved by LCH. Most cover is provided in the form of cash.[34] A range of (interests in) securities are currently acceptable as initial margin.[35]

Variation margin must in general be met with cash cover.[36] Cash cover may be pro- **8.24** vided in a number of different currencies.[37]

Cash

The arrangements for the delivery of cash cover are as follows. **8.25**

Payment

Cash cover is delivered and released to and from LCH through the Protected **8.26** Payments System (PPS). All LCH members are required to maintain accounts with a bank which participates in PPS. A separate account is maintained for each currency in which cash cover is paid. As discussed in more detail below, a member

---

[28] 'Official quotations are based on "closing settlement prices", "closing quotations" or "closing prices" and are supplied by the exchanges at the close of business each day': LCH Procedures, 2.8.

[29] ie the price for entering into a new contract on that day on the same terms as the open contract in question.

[30] See LCH Procedures, 2.7.

[31] General Regulations, reg 15(b). See also LCH Procedures, 2.7.5.1. In effect, the variation margin called from one member under a cleared contract is paid out to another member who was the counterparty to the original market contract.

[32] General Regulations, reg 15(d).

[33] If any (interests in) securities delivered as cover become unacceptable to LCH for any reason, LCH may demand replacement cover in the form of cash: General Regulations, reg 12(j).

[34] At the time of writing, acceptable currencies include sterling, euros, US dollars, Japanese yen and Canadian dollars.

[35] At the time of writing these include (interests in) UK treasury bills and gilts, certain sterling CDs, US treasury bills, certain US dollar CDs, Eurozone government securities, and UK FTSE 100 equities as well as equities underlying LIFFE equity options.

[36] See LCH Procedures, 2.7.4.

[37] See fn 34 above.

may provide clearing services to 'segregated clients', and in this case the member must open one house account and one client account for each currency.

8.27 The PPS bank debits and credits the member's account in accordance with LCH's instructions,[38] and makes corresponding credits and debits in an account which it maintains for LCH. The effect of these book entries is that the cash cover is paid outright by the member to LCH.

8.28 Because LCH is not authorised to carry on deposit-taking business, LCH can only accept cash cover in respect of current or anticipated obligations.

Documentation

8.29 Under the terms of a PPS Agreement in the form of a letter between LCH and each PPS bank, the PPS bank agrees to operate the PPS in relation to each member which the PPS bank has approved by notice to the LCH.

8.30 The member must complete a mandate to its PPS bank ('Mandate for the London Clearing House Limited Clearing Operations') authorising the PPS bank to debit its account at the instance of LCH and to rely on the information provided by LCH.

Enforcement

8.31 As indicated above, cash cover is paid outright to LCH through the PPS system. The member has a right of repayment to the extent that there is a cover surplus.[39] In the event of member default, LCH has power under its Default Rules to set off this repayment obligation against the member's liabilities.[40]

(Interests in) securities

8.32 The arrangements for the delivery of (interests in) securities as margin cover are as follows.

Delivery

8.33 LCH Procedures[41] specify different delivery methods for the different categories of acceptable (interests in) securities as margin cover.[42] Where LCH is a direct participant in the relevant settlement system, it requires the (interests in) securities to be transferred (free of payment) into its account. Thus, UK treasury bills and ster-

---

[38] These instructions are sent via SWIFT.

[39] See General Regulations, reg 12(k).

[40] Default Rules, rule 8 (c). The requirements of rule 4.90 of the Insolvency Rules 1986 (which generally govern insolvency set off) do not apply here; default netting by LCH is governed by a special regime under the Companies Act 1989, s 163, Sch 29.

[41] The Procedures are contractually binding on members by virtue of clause 2.10 of the Clearing Membership Agreement.

[42] See LCH Procedures, 4.2.

ling CDs must be delivered to LCH's CMO account;[43] UK gilts must be delivered to its CGO account;[44] and (interests in) securities held through Euroclear must be credited to its Euroclear account.[45]

Where LCH is not a direct participant, indirect delivery is taken. (Interests in) **8.34** Italian and Spanish securities may be delivered into Euroclear's account in the local settlement system (Banca d'Italia's Gestiona Centralizzate in the case of Italy, and Banco de Espania's Central de Anotaciones in the case of Spain); they will in turn be credited to LCH's Euroclear account.[46] Equities must be registered in the name of a depositary nominee authorised by LCH,[47] which will hold the equities for LCH as custodian. (Interests in) US treasuries are delivered via Fed Wire into the account of Citibank NA, New York, which will hold them for LCH. US CDs must be delivered physically to Citibank in New York,[48] which acts as LCH's custodian.

A number of these methods of delivery confer legal title to the securities on LCH. **8.35** This is the effect of a delivery through the CMO and the CGO. In the case of UK equities and US treasuries and CDs, legal title is conferred on the custodian of LCH. The delivery of legal title is helpful, both because a legal security interest is stronger than an equitable security interest, and also because it assists LCH in defending any adverse claims that might arise.

Documentation

Members wishing to provide cover in the form of (interests in) securities must exe- **8.36** cute a document in standard form granting a security interest to LCH over the collateral securities specified in a schedule. This document is entitled 'Charge by Member' and indicates that it serves to confer a fixed charge on LCH.[49] A charge is an equitable form of security interest,[50] but the delivery arrangements required by LCH often involve the delivery of legal title as indicated above. Therefore in these cases the correct interpretation may be that the documentation confers not a fixed charge (or equitable mortgage) but a legal mortgage, which is a stronger form of security interest. The use of the term 'charge' to include a mortgage is not uncommon.[51]

---

[43] See ibid 4.3.
[44] See ibid 4.4.
[45] See ibid 4.7.
[46] See ibid 4.7.2.4.
[47] See ibid 4.5.
[48] See ibid 4.6.
[49] See ibid 4.2.1.
[50] 'a charge on [personal property] is necessarily equitable, since the charge is the creation of equity and the statutory provision by which a charge by way of legal mortgage creates a legal interest (Law of Property Act 1925, s 87(1)) is confined to land': R Goode, *Commercial Law* (2nd edn, London: Penguin, 1995) 38.
[51] See Companies Act 1989, s 190(5) and Companies Act 1985, s 396(4).

8.37 In addition, members must execute and deliver a collateral lodgement form. In this they acknowledge that the (interests in) securities may be held by any custodian in any depositary, securities clearing or settlement system in accordance with the rules of the relevant settlement system or depositary, and that LCH will not be responsible for the performance of such custodian, system or operator. If the securities in question are delivered to the LCH by a member on behalf of a client, a client consent form must be delivered in which the client consents to the arrangement. (A collateral release form, or an equity collateral release form in the case of equities, must be delivered to request the release of securities margin cover in the event of a margin cover surplus.)

Enforcement

8.38 In the event of member default,[52] LCH has power under its Default Rules to sell securities cover.[53] Its default procedures enjoy special statutory protection under Part VII of the Companies Act 1989, so that they are not vulnerable to the actions of administrators or liquidators of defaulting members.[54] In particular, the rules against the enforcement of security interests during administration[55] and disposition of property after the commencement of winding up[56] are disapplied.

Conflict of laws and perfection of security interests in (interests in) securities

8.39 Certain (interests in) securities which are acceptable as margin cover are held through international settlement arrangements. This raises the question of which system of law governs the perfection of security interests over such assets. In relation to (interests in) bonds issued from a foreign jurisdiction (Erewhon) and held through Euroclear, it might be argued that LCH's security interest requires to be perfected in accordance with Erewhon law as well as in accordance with Belgian law. This would be on the basis that the Erewhon courts may consider that asset which is subject to the charge is legally located in Erewhon and therefore permit creditors of the collateral giver to attach the assets in Erewhon free of LCH's security interest if it had not been so perfected. As discussed in Chapter 7, the implementation of Article 9(2) of the Securities Finality Directive addresses this issue in relation to EC settlement systems.

---

[52] LCH is able to exercise its default powers 'In the event of a Member appearing to the Clearing House to be unable, or to be likely to become unable, to meet his obligations in respect of one or more contracts': Default Rules, rule 3.

[53] Default Rules, rule 6(e).

[54] But not administrative receivers, who do not have any relevant powers, except the power to dispose of charged property free of the charge (overreaching powers) under the Insolvency Act 1986, s 43(1).

[55] See Companies Act 1989, s 175(1)(a), disapplying the Insolvency Act 1986, s 11(3)(c).

[56] See Companies Act 1989, s 175(4), disapplying the Insolvency Act 1986, s 127.

Valuation and revaluation of margin cover

In calculating whether available margin cover meets daily its margin require- **8.40**
ments, LCH values cover as follows: cash balances and guarantees are valued at
100 per cent. The calculation for (interests in) securities is more complex. The
valuation of (interests in) treasury bills and CDs is based on their nominal value,
whereas the calculation for (interests in) gilts, bonds and equities is based on their
market value. To these base values, LCH applies a discount or 'haircut', so that the
value of the securities for the purpose of meeting margin requirements is less than
100 per cent of their nominal or (as the case may be) market value. LCH may vary
these haircuts at its discretion.[57] UK equities suffer a haircut of 20 per cent of market value, and short term UK treasury bills suffer a haircut of 5 per cent of nominal value. Haircuts address the risk of intra day falls in market value.

Securities margin cover is revalued daily by LCH. Margin cover shortfalls arising **8.41**
because securities margin cover has fallen in value entitles LCH to call for additional margin cover, and it may demand that such additional margin cover takes
the form of cash.[58]

A margin cover excess may arise because margin requirements have dropped, or **8.42**
because the value of securities margin cover has risen. In the event of a margin
cover excess, the member is entitled to call for the return of excess margin cover.

Client cover delivered to LCH

As indicated above, LCH imposes margin requirements on members. In turn, **8.43**
where open contracts have been entered into on behalf of clients, the rules of
LIFFE[59] require members to impose corresponding margin requirements on their
clients.[60] These client margin levels must at least equal the margin levels imposed
on members by LCH in respect of the back to back trades entered by members on
their client's behalf. This client margin must be calculated at least daily and col-
lected promptly.

Use of client cover as clearing member cover

In some cases, members of LCH charge (interests in) securities to LCH as **8.44**
agent for their client.[61] LCH takes a charge over securities directly from clients of

---

[57] See LCH Procedures, 3.3.
[58] General Regulations, reg 12(j).
[59] LIFFE Rules, rule 3.35.1.
[60] Including clients who are non-clearing members of LIFFE.
[61] In the Client Consent Form, the client authorises the member to grant a security interest in
the securities to LCH 'on our behalf'. The natural reading is that the member grants the security
interest to LCH *as agent* for the client.

members. In these cases the client warrants that the security interest it gives to LCH constitutes a first security interest in the securities.[62]

8.45 This is entirely compatible with secured obligations being owed to LCH by the member as principal,[63] as there is no requirement in commercial law that a security interest must be granted by person who owes the secured obligation. It is also consistent with the wording of the Charge by Member.

8.46 It may be the case that the same (interests in) securities are delivered first by the client to the member under a charge in favour of the member, and then by the member (as agent for the client) to LCH under a charge in favour of LCH. This practice is consistent with the documentation. The securities are delivered to LCH subject to the equity of redemption in favour of the client.[64] The equity of redemption is in turn subject to the security interest in favour of the member.

8.47 It is important to ensure that LCH receives good title to the (interests in) securities under its security interest, which will not be subject to adverse claims from the client or from any third party. Accordingly, in the Charge by Member, the member warrants (broadly) that it has the necessary power to enter into and perform the Charge by Member[65] and that its execution does not violate any obligation to which it is subject.[66] It is also indicated that the member acts so as to give full title guarantee.[67]

8.48 The client agrees in the Client Consent Form to the use of its (interests in) securities to secure the obligations of the member to LCH.[68] Additionally, in the Charge by Member, the member warrants that the member may give the security interest to LCH free of adverse interest, so that LCH is free to enforce the security in

---

[62] Clause 6(iv) of the Charge by Member. The first priority of the charge in favour of LCH is supported by a Client Consent Form, in which the client agrees as follows: 'We authorise the granting by the Member on our behalf to LCH, as collateral for the Member's obligations to LCH, a security interest in the above-mentioned securities . . . ranking prior to any security interest from time to time granted by us to the Member or any other person'. See also clause 7(2) of the Charge by Member.

[63] In the Client Consent Form, the client acknowledges and consents that 'all transactions between the Member and LCH are effected by the Member and LCH as principals'.

[64] In the Charge by Member, the member does not warrant that the securities are delivered to LCH subject to no interest of the client, but rather that they are delivered subject to no interest that is *adverse* to the interest of LCH: see below. It is only in respect of cash cover that the member undertakes that it is the sole beneficial owner (Clearing Membership Agreement, clause 2.15). Regulation 4(b) of the General Regulations provides that LCH will take no account of the right of any person other than the member in cover, but not that such a right does not exist. See also reg 12(c)(aa).

[65] Clause 6(iii) of the Charge by Member.

[66] ibid clause 6(vi).

[67] See clause 2(1), and the definition of 'acting in due capacity' in clause 2(1).

[68] 'We authorise the granting by the Member on our behalf to LCH, as collateral for the Member's obligations to LCH, a security interest . . . We acknowledge and consent that: if there occurs a default by the Member in its obligations to LCH . . . LCH may sell or otherwise dispose of the securities and apply the proceeds in or towards satisfaction of the Member's obligations to LCH.'

accordance with its terms. The member warrants (broadly) that it has agreed with each of the beneficial owners of the (interests in) securities that the member may deliver the (interests in) securities as collateral on the terms required by LCH, and in particular on terms that LCH may apply the (interests in) securities to satisfy the obligations of the member to it, free from any adverse interest.[69]

Further protection is provided by section 177(2) of the Companies Act 1989, which provides in effect that LCH will not be affected by adverse claims of which it does not have notice.[70]   **8.49**

Net margining

In practice, LCH calculates margin requirement and applies margin cover on a net basis within the house and client accounts of members, as explained below. This practice will be referred to as 'net margining'.   **8.50**

The clients for whom members perform clearing services fall into two categories. First, there are 'segregated clients'. These are clients who have the benefit of Client Money Regulations, so that when the member receives money from them which is not immediately due and payable to the member for its own account, it receives it as trustee for its client. Secondly, a member may have non-segregated clients, who do not have the benefit of the Client Money Regulations. The difference between segregated and non-segregated clients is relevant to the manner in which LCH maintains accounts, which in turn informs net margining.   **8.51**

LCH maintains accounts in which a member's open contracts (or 'positions') are recorded. These are known as 'position accounts'.[71] In addition, LCH maintains accounts in which cash and securities margin cover is recorded. These are known as 'financial accounts'.[72]   **8.52**

The balances from the position accounts and financial accounts are recorded together in consolidated accounts known as 'member accounts'.[73] While position accounts and financial accounts are maintained by LCH merely for administrative purposes, the member accounts are significant for the operation of net margining.[74]   **8.53**

---

[69] Clause 6(vii) of the Charge by Member.

[70] 'So far as necessary to enable the property to be applied in accordance with the rules of the . . . clearing house, it may be so applied notwithstanding any prior equitable interest or rights or any right or remedy arising from a breach of fiduciary duty, unless the . . . clearing house had notice of the interest, right or breach of duty at the time the property was provided as margin.' Such adverse rights are overreached; see Companies Act 1989, s 177(4). Notice for this purpose includes, broadly, constructive notice: see s 190(5).

[71] LCH Procedures, 2.6.2.

[72] ibid 2.7.

[73] ibid 2.6.1.

[74] The key provisions are contained in the General Regulations, reg 5, which only applies to member accounts; see LCH Procedures, 2.6.1.

8.54   Separate 'house' and 'client' member accounts are maintained. Positions and margin cover in respect of contracts entered into by the member on its own account, and also for the account of non-segregated clients, are recorded in the house member account. However, positions and margin cover in respect of segregated clients must be recorded in the client member account. (To support the maintenance of separate member accounts, separate position and financial accounts are also maintained.)[75]

8.55   When LCH calculates the initial margin requirements for contracts within any particular member account, it does so on a net basis. This means that, 'if long and short positions are held in the same delivery month/prompt date for futures . . . or the same series for options, initial margin is charged on the net position'.[76] In effect variation margin is also netted. As indicated above, variation margin is effected by debits and credits to the financial account of the member. These book entries are in turn reflected in the member account. The effect of recording the variation margin for a number of different contracts in a single running account is that profits arising on one contract are automatically set off against losses arising on another.[77] Thus margin is calculated on a net basis within house and client member accounts respectively.

8.56   Moreover, if a member opens more than one member's account, LCH is entitled to set off balances between the different member's accounts[78] and if a member opens more than one client account, LCH is entitled to set off balances between the different client accounts.[79]

---

[75] For position accounts, see LCH Procedures, 2.6.2.1. When each contract is presented for registration with LCH, the member must indicate whether the contract should be posted to the house or the client account: General Regulations, reg 8. For financial accounts, see LCH Procedures, 2.7.1. In relation to cash cover, as indicated above, members with segregated clients must maintain separate house and client accounts for cash cover with their PPS banks. Equally, in relation to securities cover, if (interests in) securities are lodged as cover for both house and client accounts, the member must execute two separate charges. 'Any collateral lodged with LCH will be applied as cover against the Members (house or client) margin liabilities as per the relevant documentation . . . Collateral charged in respect of a Member's client account will not be applied by LCH to his liabilities on a house account': LCH Procedures, 4.2.1. This accords with the provisions of the Companies Act 1989, s 187. (For the converse position, see the Companies Act 1989, Sch 21, para 14.) The author is grateful to Dermot Turing for these references.

[76] LCH Procedures, 2.11.

[77] This netting takes place in the books of LCH. Of course, the member will also maintain books, and when the value of cover provided by a client to the member falls short of the margin requirement imposed by LCH on the member in respect of open contracts entered into by the member of that client's behalf, the member will in practice require the client to provide more cover. However, there will be a delay between the time when LCH adjusts the member's account and the time when the member makes a margin call on its client in consequence of the adjustment to its member account, and during this interval netting may occur. Also, in practice, margin calls by the member will not exactly correspond to margin calls from LCH.

[78] General Regulations, reg 5(b).

[79] ibid reg 5(c).

However, separate margin calculations are made in respect of house and client **8.57** accounts, and no set off is made between them.[80] This segregation of house and client accounts reflects the regulatory requirements imposed on members under the rules of the Securities and Futures Authority.[81] The segregation is preserved in the netting provisions under the default rules.[82]

The maintenance of separate house and client financial accounts (and corre- **8.58** sponding member accounts) serves to divide the margin cover provided by a member into two categories, namely house and client. Within those categories, there is no further subdivision.[83] The financial account does not link debits and credits of margin cover to particular contracts. Thus, a fall in the value of securities margin cover originally provided in relation to one contract, is automatically set off against an increase in the value of securities margin cover originally provided in relation to another contract. Thus, margin cover is applied on a net basis within (but not across) house and client accounts.

Net margining achieves real economies for members, because it reduces the value **8.59** of margin cover that requires to be delivered. Because of netting, the value of margin cover received by the member is likely to exceed the value of the margin cover that the member is required to deliver to LCH, so that a margin cover surplus will arise in its hands. Where margin cover takes the form of cash, the member may deposit this surplus with an affiliate bank.[84] The calculation of margin on a gross basis would introduce significant expense. Of course, the client of the member of LCH may be a non-clearing broker, which in turn acts for a client, which in turn may act for its clients. Net margining may apply at every link in the chain. If so, the value of cover that is passed up the chain from the ultimate client to the clearing house will be smaller at each point in the chain. In the event of default, where it is sought to transfer positions from a defaulting member to a non-defaulting member, net margining means that insufficient cover may be available to permit such transfers. This was illustrated in the Far Eastern markets in the Barings crisis.[85]

The effect of this on clients is that cover provided by one client to a member **8.60** (which is passed by the member up to LCH) may be applied by LCH to discharge obligations owed by the member in respect of the business of another client.

---

[80] See ibid reg 5(d) and LCH Procedures, 2.11.
[81] See SFA Rules, rules 4-62 and 4-63.
[82] Default Rules, rule 10.
[83] See LCH Procedures, 2.7.1.
[84] This can lead to problems for clients where a member and its group is affected by insolvency, as was seen in the Barings crisis.
[85] If some but not all positions within the client account are transferred, the full efficiencies of net margining may not be available, and it may be necessary to put up further cover.

8.61   This potential cross-collateralisation is expressly acknowledged and consented to by the client in the Client Consent Form.[86] Given it is not possible to transact business on LIFFE on another basis, such consent by the beneficial owner of (interests in) securities should be enforceable.

8.62   However, special concerns arise where the client is not the beneficial owner of the (interests in) securities. Where the client holds the (interests in) securities as a fiduciary for third parties, it is not entirely clear that consent to cross-collateralisation would not amount to a breach of fiduciary duty. Therefore LCH will not accept (interests in) securities which were received by members from trustee clients. In the Client Consent Form, the client is required to confirm that it is the absolute beneficial owner of the securities.[87] Also, the member is required to give a warranty to the same effect in the Charge by Member,[88] together with a further warranty that the arrangements will not involve the member, the client or any third party in breach of trust or any other fiduciary duty.[89]

---

[86] 'We acknowledge and consent that . . . the Member's obligations to LCH which are secured by the LCH security interest in the securities are not directly related to our obligations to the Member (or any other person) and may in part reflect obligations to the Member of persons with which the Member is affiliated . . . on the Member's default, LCH may well enforce the LCH security interest in the securities . . . irrespective of whether or not we have satisfied our obligations to the Member (or any other person).'

[87] 'We confirm that, save for the security interest in favour of LCH and any security from time to time permitted by LCH in favour of the Member or any other person, we are entitled to the entire beneficial interest in the securities, and that the securities are not subject to any trust, sale agreement or security.'

[88] See clauses 6(i) and 6(vii) of the Charge by Member.

[89] ibid clause 6(viii).

PART III

INFRASTRUCTURE PRODUCTS AND SERVICES

9

INTERNATIONAL AND UK SECURITIES SETTLEMENT[1]

The medium is the message[2]

Settlement is the process whereby (interests in) securities are delivered from per- **9.01** son to person, usually against payment, in order to fulfil contractual delivery obligations such as those arising under contracts of sale and collateral arrangements. Chapter 1 provided a brief overview of settlement, and considered the different types of electronic arrangements that have been developed in order to facilitate settlement. It argued that where the interests of participants in settlement systems are intermediated and commingled in the course of electronic settlement, such arrangements alter the nature of the asset of the participant. This asset consists, not of securities held directly from the issuer, but rather of unallocated and indirect interests constituting intangible assets, which the author has called interests in securities. Chapter 2 considered the legal nature of interests in securities. Chapter 13 will argue that they confer property rights as against the intermediaries through whom they are asserted.

This chapter will consider the legal and commercial reasons for the introduction **9.02** of electronic settlement, which have brought about such profound changes to the

---

[1] The author is grateful to Mark Kirby, Head of Legal Affairs, CRESTCo for kindly reviewing this chapter. The opinions expressed in it, and any errors are her own.

[2] Marshall McLuhan, *Understanding Media: The Extensions of Man* (London: Routledge, 1964) 15.

legal nature of assets in the securities markets. Broadly speaking, the purpose of electronic settlement, with its incidents of fungibility and, usually, intermediation,[3] is to reduce settlement risk and improve efficiency. The first part of this chapter will give a general discussion of the different types of settlement risk and the techniques used to address them. After a brief note of developments in European settlement, these risk management techniques will be considered in the context of the UK settlement industry.

A. Managing Risk in Securities Settlement

9.03 For over a decade, the risks that arise in the course of securities settlement have received very significant attention from market participants and their regulators, and sophisticated models of operational risk analysis have been developed. The analysis that follows in this discussion has been kept simple, in order to clarify the legal aspects of risk management in securities settlement, which have sometimes been a source of confusion.

(1) Counterparty Credit Risk: Loss of Countervalue

9.04 The fundamental premise of settlement risk is that one's counterparty may become insolvent before it discharges its delivery or payment obligations. Suppose A agrees to sell shares to B. If A delivers the shares to B before receiving payment, and if B then becomes insolvent without making payment, A will be an unsecured creditor in respect of the purchase price.[4] A has given value, but may not receive countervalue.

DVP

9.05 The answer to this risk is delivery versus payment or DVP.[5] The G30 Report[6] defines DVP as 'the simultaneous exchange of securities (the delivery side) and cash value (payment) to settle a transaction. (Also called Cash On Delivery.)'.

---

[3] CREST is not intermediated: see below.

[4] The converse position, if B pays the purchase price before the shares are delivered, is similar. If A fails to perform its delivery obligation, B would have a right of action for breach of contract, for which it could prove as unsecured creditor. (This claim would be quantifiable by the liquidator under rule 4.86 of the Insolvency Rules 1986.) The author is grateful to Adrian Cohen, Partner, Clifford Chance for clarifying this point.

[5] The idea of DVP is derived from the idea of PVP, or payment versus payment. PVP was identified as an objective in the foreign exchange markets in the late 1970s and early 1980s when the failure of Bank Herstatt, and consequent disruption of the wholesale dollar settlement system, illustrated the danger of giving value before receiving value. See *Settlement Risk in Foreign Exchange Transactions* (Bank for International Settlements, 1996).

[6] *Clearance and Settlement Systems in the World's Securities Markets* (G30, 1989). See Chapter 1 for a discussion of this report.

With DVP the giving of value on both sides should not only be simultaneous, but should also (as far as possible) be final and irreversible.

Although DVP is conceptually simple, the achievement of true DVP in practice **9.06** can be a real challenge. This is so for legal and operational reasons, including the highly intermediated nature of the securities and cash settlements systems. Operationally, the links between some international settlement systems and the payment systems or local settlement systems on which they rely, do not yet permit the final (gross) delivery of value during the business day. With enhancements to the operation of settlement and payment systems, these problems are being rapidly addressed in practice, as discussed below.[7]

Legally, the objective of irreversibility runs counter to the policy considerations **9.07** that lie behind the insolvency displacement and tracing rules that render certain transactions reversible in the event of insolvency and fraud. Under such rules, which are discussed in Chapter 3, the liquidator of an insolvent transferee may challenge transactions that represent a fraud on general creditors, and defrauded clients of a fraudulent transferor may trace their assets into the hands of third parties who (broadly) are not good faith purchasers. As indicated in Chapter 3, special statutory regimes[8] seek to address the risk of insolvency displacement (and therefore systemic risk) within key settlement systems. However, these protections do not apply to fraud risk, as discussed below.

Different models

The Bank for International Settlements in Basle has identified three models of **9.08** DVP.[9] The differences between them relate to timing. The least desirable is model 3, in which both (interests in) securities and funds are delivered on a net basis at the end of the business day. During the day, transferees' and payees' entitlements are recorded by book entry, but because value is not finally given until the end of the day, intra day the risk remains that credits to securities and/or cash accounts might be reversed. Model 2 DVP presents less risk, because it involves the real time gross delivery of (interests in) securities[10] followed by end of day net

---

[7] However, in a cross border settlement, where the vendor and purchaser participate in different national systems, DVP cannot occur simultaneously in both systems: 'it is technically impossible to ensure that both securities and payments are delivered simultaneously for both parties involved in a cross-border transfer': *A Report on DVP Links Between ECSDA Members* (ECSDA, September 1998), ('the *DVP Report*') 17.

[8] Such as those under Part VII of the UK Companies Act 1989, and the Settlement Finality Directive (98/26/EC).

[9] See *Delivery Versus Payment in Securities Settlement Systems* (Basle: Bank for International Settlements, 1992).

[10] 'This implies that final settlement of individual transactions takes place on a continuous basis during the processing day rather than periodically at pre-determined times': *Report on the Infrastructure for Securities Settlement: Collateral Management for the purposes of the ESCB Credit and Monetary Policy Operations* (ECSDA, 1998) ('the *Infrastructure Report*') 13.

payment. Although delivery of (interests in) securities takes place throughout the business day, cash entitlements remain provisional until the end of the day. The most desirable type of DVP is model 1, which involves real time gross delivery and payment. At the time of writing, UK settlement offers model 2 DVP.[11] However, it is proposed to be upgraded to model 1, as discussed below.

Different qualities of delivery and payment

9.09   In assessing any DVP arrangement, it is not enough to identify the timing model. One also needs to consider the quality of the assets which are delivered and of the payment which is made at the time when a payment event and a delivery event are synchronised.

(Interests in) securities

9.10   On the securities side, the best delivery is of legal title, and not merely of an equitable interest. At the time of writing, as discussed below, in UK settlement the deliveries that are synchronised with the payment event are equitable only (with legal title being delivered shortly thereafter). However, it is proposed to upgrade deliveries so that they confer immediate legal title, as indicated below.

Cash

9.11   On the cash side, it is important to remember that in the financial markets money is debt. When A is said to have paid £1,000 to B, in practice A has arranged for a bank or other credit institution to make a credit entry to an account recorded in its books in favour of B. This credit entry has the effect that A creates or increases an existing debt to B to the extent of £1,000. The quality of the 'payment' of A to B depends on the credit rating of the credit institution which maintains this account. The credit institutions with the best credit ratings are central banks (and in particular the central banks of OECD countries). Therefore the best quality of payment is a credit to an account maintained in the books of such a central bank, or 'central bank money'. As discussed below, payment in UK settlement (at the time of writing) involves commercial bank money. There are proposals to upgrade this to central bank money. However, these proposals will not remove the credit exposures of participants to their own settlement banks, although it does remove the credit exposures of participants to their counterparties' settlement banks.[12]

---

[11] Except in cases where, as a contractual matter, a settlement bank agrees to provide intra-day finality of payment to its clients.

[12] 'From the perspective of a CREST member, it reduces their double claim on both their chosen settlement bank and that of their counterparty, to a single claim on their own bank': CREST *Newsletter* (April 2000) 9.

Vendor/purchaser trusts

This section will briefly consider vendor/purchaser trusts. These are arrangements **9.12**
that serve to achieve a form of DVP, either by operation of law or by express statutory provision. In some circumstances, when A has agreed to sell assets to B, A is
treated as holding those assets on trust for B. Thus, although A has not delivered
the assets to B, they become B's assets in equity. This means that the assets are not
available to the creditors of A if A becomes insolvent while still holding them.

The general rule is that equity will only impose a vendor/purchaser trust in rela- **9.13**
tion to contracts of sale that are specifically enforceable.[13] Specific enforcement is
a discretionary equitable remedy whereby a person is ordered to act in a certain
way.[14] For example, a person in breach of contract might be ordered to perform
the contract and not merely to pay damages for breach of contract. The approach
of the courts is not to order specific performance where damages would be an adequate remedy.[15] Contracts for the sale of land are specifically enforceable, on the
basis that a piece of land is unique and damages would not be an adequate remedy
for breach of such a contract. Contracts for the sale of shares in a private company
are specifically enforceable, and thus give rise to vendor/purchaser trusts.[16] In contrast, damages generally provide an adequate remedy for breach of contracts for
the sale of (interests in) securities which are generally available in secondary
markets. The general rule is therefore that contracts for the sale of (interests in)
securities are not specifically enforceable, and therefore not subject to vendor/pur-
chaser trusts.[17]

However, the case of *Chinn v Collins*[18] establishes that a vendor/purchaser trust **9.14**
will arise even if the contract of sale is not specifically enforceable, if and when the
purchaser pays the purchase price prior to delivery.[19] Once the vendor has been

---

[13] 'So long as the vendor enters into a specifically enforceable contract for the sale of property he
becomes a constructive trustee thereof for the purchaser until the contract is completed by the transfer of the property to the purchaser or to the order of the purchaser': D J Hayton, *Underhill and
Hayton, Law Relating to Trusts and Trustees* (15th edn, London: Butterworths, 1995) 399.

[14] 'Specific performance is a decree of the court which compels the defendant personally to do
what he promised to do': G Jones and W Goodhart, *Specific Performance* (2nd edn, London:
Butterworths, 1996) 1.

[15] *Specific Performance* (n 14 above) 1, 2. See also *Chitty on Contracts* (28th edn, London: Sweet
& Maxwell, 1999) 1357.

[16] This is established by *Oughtred v IRC* [1960] AC 206.

[17] 'Although the court will not order the seller of Government stock actually to deliver the stock,
because Government stock is always obtainable in the market [*Cuddee v Rutter* (1720) 5 Vin Abr
538, 21] it will order specific performance of an agreement for the sale and purchase of stock or
shares which cannot always be bought in the market. [*Duncuft v Albrecht* (1841) 12 Sim 189]':
J McGhee, *Snell's Equity* (London: Sweet & Maxwell, 2000) 651.

[18] [1981] AC 533 at 548, [1981] 2 WLR 14 at 20, HL.

[19] 'As soon as there was an agreement for their sale accompanied or followed by payment of the
price, the equitable title passed at once to the purchaser' per Lord Wilberforce at 20. For a discussion of the same principle in relation to an assignment of future debts, see also *Palette Shoes Pty Ltd*

paid then, if she has not yet delivered the purchased assets, she holds them on trust for the purchaser.

9.15   In practice it would be unusual for a purchaser of (interests in) securities to pay the vendor in advance of delivery, because of the efforts of market participants to achieve DVP.[20]

9.16   A modified form of vendor/purchaser trust is created by statute in relation to UK settlements, as discussed below.[21]

(2) Counterparty Credit Risk: Loss of Bargain

9.17   Even in a DVP environment, a party to a bargain (A) may still be exposed if her counterparty (B) becomes insolvent before settlement. As a party to an executory (ie unperformed) contract and the unsecured creditor of an insolvent company, A will be unable to compel B to perform the contract.[22] If the bargain would have been profitable to A, she may therefore risk losing that profit.[23]

Short settlement cycles

9.18   One simple but effective way of addressing this risk of loss of bargain is to shorten the period of time during which this arises arises, ie to shorten the settlement cycle.

9.19   The length of the settlement cycle is expressed as a number of business days after trade date. Thus settlement on the third business day after trade date is 'T+3', and settlement on the first business day after trade date is 'T+1'. At the time of writing, the eurobond markets settle T+3 and UK equities settle T+5. Considerable

---

v Krohn (1937) 58 CLR 1, per Dixon J at 27: 'Because value has been given on the one side, the conscience of the other party is bound when the subject comes into existence, that is, when, as is generally the case, the legal property vests in him. Because his conscience is bound in respect of a subject of property, equity fastens upon the property itself and makes him a trustee of the legal rights or ownership for the assignee'. For a similar point in relation to assignments of after acquired property, see *Re Lind* [1915] 2 Ch 345, per Phillimore LJ at 365, 366.

[20]   A further possible difficulty in relying on the principle in *Chinn v Collins* in the secondary securities markets is the requirement for certainty of subject matter in establishing a trust. In practice a vendor would be unlikely to segregate the purchased securities prior to delivery. However, under the principle in *Hunter v Moss* (discussed in Chapter 2), this problem may not arise, provided of course the vendor holds securities of the relevant type.

[21]   This is under reg 25 of the Uncertificated Securities Regulations 1995, SI 1995/3272, which governs settlement within CREST. Arguably, this regulation was unnecessary in the light of *Chinn v Collins* and *Hunter v Moss*. This vendor/purchaser trust will be replaced by immediate deliveries of legal title under proposals for electronic transfer of title or ETT, as discussed below.

[22]   See the powers of the liquidator to disclaim onerous unprofitable contracts under the Insolvency Act 1986, s 178.

[23]   Where a contract is disclaimed under s 178, any person sustaining loss in consequence of the operation of the disclaimer is deemed to be a creditor of the company to the extent of that loss under s 178(6). Of course, this right will only be of value to the extent that the claims of unsecured creditors are met.

effort is being devoted to the project of achieving T+1 in New York,[24] London[25] and other leading markets.

Clearing

Another technique for addressing loss of bargain risk is clearing. The collateralisation of clearing exposures was discussed in Chapter 8. Because a clearing house assumes liability for the performance of cleared trades, each party's credit risk during the settlement interval is upgraded, from that of the counterparty to that of the clearing house. As discussed in Chapter 8 and below, there is trend towards the introduction of clearing in the settlement of securities transactions. **9.20**

(3) Late Deliveries

The term 'settlement failures' is generally used in the securities markets to mean occasions on which vendor or collateral giver fails to ensure that the (interests in) securities are credited to the account of the purchaser or collateral taker on the contractually agreed settlement date. In practice, most settlement failures involve late deliveries, whereby the (interests in) securities arrive eventually, but not on time; in these cases the problem generally relates to liquidity and not to credit. Delays in the settlement of (interests in) securities are not uncommon, particularly in cross border settlement. **9.21**

The practice of selling short raises the potential for illiquidity to spread within the settlement system. Market makers[26] and others[27] regularly sell (interests in) securities which they do not hold at the time of the sale, in the expectation that they will receive the (interests in) securities from third parties in time to make delivery. Of course, if delivery from a third party fails, settlement of the short sale may also fail in consequence. **9.22**

The traditional technique for addressing illiquidity in the securities markets is securities lending. Securities lending was considered in Chapter 6. **9.23**

---

[24] The project is being co-ordinated in New York by the Securities Industry Association's T+1 Steering Committee. See www.sia.com/tradedateplusone. It is understood that the goal of T+1 by 2002 has been identified.

[25] See the discussion of the GSTPA in Chapter 10. UK gilts currently settle T+1, but considerable effort will be needed to achieve T+1 in relation to UK equities.

[26] As discussed in Chapter 1, a market maker is a participant in a securities markets who (in return for certain market privileges) agrees to provide liquidity by making continuous offers to buy and sell (interests in) securities. Such a market is called a quote-driven market, as opposed to order-driven markets, in which buyers' and sellers' orders are matched.

[27] An investment bank might deliberately assume a short position, and rely on securities lending to make delivery in the expectation that the price of (interests in) securities will fall by the end of the securities loan. In this case, the securities loan is not a response to a bad delivery, but part of the original plan. See Chapter 6 for a fuller discussion.

(4) Bad Deliveries[28]

9.24 The previous section considered late deliveries, where a credit to the transferee's securities account in a settlement system is not made on the due date; late deliveries are common, but are readily addressed by securities lending. This section considers bad deliveries, where an existing credit to a securities account is reversed. Although much less common than late deliveries, the consequences of bad deliveries may be more difficult to manage.

9.25 All settlement systems[29] reserve the right to reverse credits which they have made to participants' accounts in certain circumstances.[30] Naturally, credits made in error are reversible.[31] Further, the need to reverse credits may arise for systemic reasons, relating to insolvency and fraud.

9.26 As discussed briefly above, and in more detail in Chapter 3, the insolvency of a transferor may compromise the security of a transfer, because of provisions of insolvency law including liquidator's insolvency displacement powers. Certain statutory provisions serve to modify the general rules of insolvency law, including these displacement powers, in the interests of security of transfer within key settlement systems. In the United Kingdom, Part VII of the Companies Act 1989 modifies the general the law of insolvency in favour of recognised markets and settlement systems, so as (inter alia) to disapply insolvency displacement provisions. Broadly comparable provisions are introduced at European level by the Settlement Finality Directive[32] (implemented in the United Kingdom by the Financial Markets and Insolvency (Settlement Finality) Regulations 1999).[33]

9.27 As indicated above, these provisions do not affect the ability of the operator of a system to reverse a credit entry to correct an error or in response to a court order providing redress in the event of fraud.

---

[28] In relation to bad deliveries in CREST, see reg 23 of the Uncertificated Securities Regulations 1995, SI 1995/3272, CREST Rules, rule 18 and CREST *Reference Manual* ch 5 section 7.

[29] And all well advised custodians.

[30] In CREST these circumstances are narrowly restricted by reg 23 of the Uncertificated Securities Regulations.

[31] Erroneous credits may be divided into two classes. First, 'balancing errors' are those that can be corrected by debiting one account and crediting another in the same amount. Secondly, 'shortfall errors' are corrected by a simple debit. Shortfall errors arise where the quantity of a certain type of (interests in) securities held by or through the settlement system falls short of the sum of credits in respect of such (interests in) securities made in the accounts of the settlement system, so that a shortfall arises.

[32] 98/26/EC. The conflict of laws provisions of the Directive were discussed in Chapter 7.

[33] SI 1999/2979.

(5) Systemic Risk[34]

The efficiencies of electronic settlement have helped to address credit risk, by **9.28** permitting forms of DVP and shorter settlement cycles. However, the same efficiencies may themselves be a source of systemic risk in some circumstances. Systemic risk, also known as the domino effect, is the risk that the liquidity and/or credit problems of one participant in a market or settlement system are transmitted to other participants, because of the interdependencies involved in the market or system.

This can be illustrated by an example. B buys 1,000,000 (interests in) securities **9.29** from A and they are credited to B's account at 10.00 am. B held no such (interests in) securities prior to this credit, so at 10.00 am B has a credit balance of 1,000,000. At 12.00 noon B transfers 500,000 (interests in) securities to C and 500,000 to D, leaving B with a zero balance. At 1.00 pm the settlement system is informed that the 1,000,000 (interests in) securities in question (which were introduced into the settlement system by A) were forgeries. A is required by the settlement system to introduce new (interests in) securities to make up the shortfall, but A is insolvent and unable to comply with this requirement.[35] Therefore the settlement system debits B's account in respect of the bad (interests in) securities, creating a debit balance of 1,000,000, and requires B immediately to restore the account to zero by introducing 1,000,000 (interests in) securities, buying them in from the market if necessary.[36] If B is unable to comply (for example because the requirement has the effect of putting B into insolvency), the settlement system may have recourse against C and D. If the (interests in) securities have been delivered on several times before the problem is spotted, significant numbers of participants may be affected and the problem becomes systemic.[37]

Different systems adopt different methodologies for distributing the burden of **9.30** such systemic risk among participants. Most systems[38] reserve the right to share the loss pro rata among all participants having positions in the relevant (interests in) securities.[39]

---

[34] There is an interesting discussion of systemic risk in *Cross-Border Securities Settlement* (BIS, March 1995) ch 4.

[35] At this stage there is a shortfall error.

[36] An alternative approach would be to share the losses associated with bad (interests in) securities rateably among all participants having that type of (interests in) securities credited to their accounts.

[37] The benefit of electronic settlement is that it facilitates the delivery of securities and cash; its burden is that it facilitates the delivery of illiquidity and shortfall or credit risk.

[38] Including Euroclear.

[39] CREST reserves the right to select particular victims; see the references in n 28 above.

(6) Managing Risk in European Settlement

9.31 At the time of writing, the European securities settlement industry is in a state of rapid change.

Competitive pressures

9.32 This is largely in response to tremendous competitive pressures, which have a number of causes. The volume and value of securities trades continues to increase. Market participants and their regulators have developed a more sophisticated awareness of the risks associated with inefficient settlement, particularly following the market disturbances of 1998. The demand for securities to collateralise financial exposures is greater than ever, as discussed in Chapter 4. Settlement inefficiencies inhibit the rapid delivery of collateral and therefore limit the volumes of profitable business that firms are able to undertake. A direct connection is made between settlement efficiency and profitability. Quicker securities settlement enables securities houses better to compete, and the pressure on the settlement industry in part reflects the increased climate of competition among market participants.[40]

Enhancements

9.33 Another factor driving enhancements in European securities settlement is the role of the European Central Bank (formerly the European Monetary Institute), which was the original force behind ECSDA, the European Central Securities Depositories Association. The ECB's need for the efficient cross border delivery of collateral to support its money market operations generated the original demand for new settlement efficiencies. In response to this, and the competitive pressures discussed above, European securities settlement is being enhanced in a number of respects.

9.34 First, a number of the recent and proposed developments in European securities settlement relate to improving the quality of DVP, for example by the achievement of model 1 DVP,[41] and the introduction of central bank money on the payment side.[42]

9.35 Secondly, securities settlement is becoming quicker. While at the time of writing, the eurobond markets settle on T+3 and the UK equity markets on T+5, it is pro-

---

[40] With the deregulation of the financial markets, financial institutions are offering a wider range of products, following the continental model of the financial supermarket. This development erodes the traditional segmentation of the markets in securities, commercial banking and insurance services. Relative inefficiencies are more visible in an unsegmented market. Also, the introduction of the euro has increased the number of potential service providers, and highlights pricing inefficiencies across jurisdictions.

[41] See the proposals for model 1 DVP in the United Kingdom, discussed below.

[42] Again, see the proposals for the United Kingdom discussed below.

posed to move to T+3 by 2001.[43] T+1 will not be achievable until the pre-settlement processing of trades is automated, without manual intervention at any stage. Such 'straight through processing' raises a number of legal issues, which are discussed in Chapter 10.

Increasingly, DVP and short settlement cycles are supplemented by the further **9.36** risk management technique of clearing, as indicated above.[44] A number of initiatives have the objective of introducing clearing into the European settlement of securities transactions.[45]

In order to assist market participants and their regulators in assessing the man- **9.37** agement of risk in particular settlement systems, the Bank of International Settlements, in collaboration with IOSCO,[46] has published a Disclosure Framework for Securities Settlement Systems.[47] This takes the form of a standard questionnaire, to which key settlement systems have published answers.[48]

In the context of the development of cross border settlement within Europe, the **9.38** European Central Securities Depository Association (ECSDA)[49] has formulated standards with which a European national settlement system must comply in order to be eligible to participate in a series of bilateral settlement links. The initial purpose of this project is to permit the cross border delivery of collateral to central banks providing Euro liquidity through the TARGET system;[50] these

---

[43] Some commentators suggest that the London Stock Exchange should move directly from T+5 to T+1.

[44] However, central securities depositaries are themselves precluded from acting as clearing houses by standards for cross border links, specified by the European Central Securities Depositories Association (ECSDA): *Infrastructure Report* (n 10 above) 14.

[45] For example, in the United Kingdom it is proposed to link CREST with the London Clearing House, as discussed below. There are also proposals for clearing in Euroclear and Clearstream. There have also been proposals for the merger of the London Clearing House with another clearing house, in order to permit greater collateral netting efficiences. Trades on COREDEAL, a screen-based order-driven exchange in international debt securities developed by ISMA, will benefit from clearing through a central counterparty. See www.isma.org.brochure/breakingnewground.htm

[46] IOSCO is the International Organization of Securities Commissions.

[47] 'The present Disclosure Framework for Securities Settlement Systems . . . [provides] a protocol for the review of a securities settlement system's operation and its allocation of risks': BIS website at www.bis.org/publ/cpss20.htm

[48] With, arguably, varying degrees of frankness.

[49] www.ECSDA.com. ECSDA was formed in May 1997. At the time of writing it is composed of the national settlement systems of 15 European countries; Iain Saville of CREST was elected Chairman of ECSDA in 1998.

[50] 'The ESCB credit and monetary policy operations require that cash transfers are effected only if they are covered by credit balances or by intraday credit facilities. To provide such credit facilities or to carry out monetary policy, national central banks will require eligible securities as collateral. When the single currency is introduced, many credit institutions are expected to hold eligible securities issued in several EU countries. They may wish to use them as collateral in their credit relations with their local central bank': *Infrastructure Report* (n 10 above) 8.

deliveries will be on a free of payment basis.[51] The further purpose of the ECSDA project is to permit the cross border delivery of collateral in private commercial arrangements on a DVP basis,[52] as discussed below. ECSDA specifies certain minimum standards as a precondition of participation.[53] These standards include the real time gross settlement of securities,[54] finality of settlement[55] and the use of central bank money.[56]

Cross border links

9.39 With the rise in cross border investment and collateralisation, there is a new level of demand for cross border settlement.[57] Market participants wish to access the international settlement from one point of entry, and to be able to use excess collateral in one jurisdiction to cover exposures in another. Some commentators have argued that the introduction of the euro has accelerated the trend towards cross border investment and collateralisation within Europe,[58] which in turn has emphasised the need to overcome fragmentation in European securities settlement. There are currently a relatively large number of national settlement systems, and relatively few links between them.[59] This is changing rapidly, as the European settlement industry is consolidated.

---

[51] This is because the corresponding payments will be made through TARGET. 'At first the ECSDA infrastructure will be used to make cross-border transfers of securities for use as collateral in ESCB credit operations between credit institutions and central banks and has therefore been based on cross-border transfers *free of payment*': *Infrastructure Report* (n 10 above) 7.

[52] 'The next step in the ECSDA's development is to address and respond to the needs of the private sector participants in an environment where cross border securities trades have increased remarkably during recent years': *DVP Report* (n 7 above) 4.

[53] 'In order to ensure the safety and the efficiency of securities settlement some minimum standard requirements for cross-border operations have to be established among EU-CSDs . . . These principles are in line with the standards developed by the EMI [See the Standards for the Use of EU Securities Settlement Systems in ESCB Credit Operations, published January 1998]': *Infrastructure Report* (n 10 above) 13. See also the *DVP Report* (n 7 above) 12 et seq.

[54] *Infrastructure Report* (n 10 above) 13.

[55] ibid 14.

[56] ibid 14.

[57] Another major source of new volumes of cross border settlement is corporate actions such as rights issues in the context of international takeovers.

[58] 'One of the triggers for this turn of events [the consolidation of European settlement systems] has been the introduction of the Euro and the desire of the European Central Bank to be able to mobilise collateral across Member State borders in the context of its monetary policy operations. This has probably been superseded in importance by the growing realisation among major international securities houses that maintaining multiple interfaces to different European CSDs and different sub-custodians is both costly and inefficient': M Kirby, *CREST and Securities Law Reform* (January 2000) 1.

[59] 'It is well known to investment bankers that clearing and settlement costs in Europe exceed those in the US by between 6 and 10 times for a typical trade. If Europe is ever to compete on equal terms with the United States in the market for raising equity capital for tomorrow's entrepreneurs, its capital markets must be both liquid and efficient. The main reason that they're not is that there are far too many clearing systems in Europe (26 at last count)': Andrew Muir, 'Technobabble', *Global Investment Services* (March 2000) 13.

At the time of writing, a number of different initiatives are competing to bring **9.40** about this consolidation.[60] New alliances, links and mergers are announced with striking frequency.[61]

In this context, several competing models for consolidated European settlement **9.41** have emerged. A model of international settlement advocated by Euroclear is the hub and spoke model. This involves a central settlement system or hub in which participants have accounts. The hub has links (equated with the spokes of a wheel) with a large number of national settlement systems. Thus, international settlement is centralised in the hub, which offers a single point of access for participants.

In an alternative model (advocated by ECSDA) a large number of national sys- **9.42** tems form a series of bilateral links with each other.[62] This model has no single central hub, and has been called 'the spider's web'.[63] A settlement network is proposed having linked multiple hubs whereby, for example, an Italian investor holding (interests in) US securities may access the DTC through, first, its account at the Italian system, Monti-Titoli, which would in turn have an account at CREST, which would in turn have an account at the DTC. Of course, such 'relayed links' serve to increase the number of intermediaries involved, and therefore the number of different levels of interests in securities. As will be discussed below, CRESTCo is proceeding rapidly to establish such bilateral links, and its success demonstrates the plausibility of this model of consolidation.[64]

---

[60] At the time of writing, three candidates for the future leadership of European settlement appear to be (in no particular order) Euroclear (in alliance with Sicovam), Clearstream (which is the product of the merger between Cedel and Deutsche Börse Clearing) and CREST (in alliance with the Swiss SIS SegaInterSettle). In the Spring of 2000 CREST and SIS SegaInterSettle launched the Settlement Network, a co-operative programme of cross border settlement and custody services.

[61] Important recent developments include the mergers that at the time of writing had been announced between London Clearing House and the French Clearnet, and also between Euroclear and Sicovam (to be known as Euroclear France) Of course, Clearstream is the product of the merger between Cedel and Deutsche Börse Clearing.

These developments have been compared to a Darwinian struggle for existence, on the basis that consolidation will also mean a shake out of the industry.

[62] See generally the *Infrastructure Report* (n 10 above) and the *DVP Report* (n 7 above).

[63] 'The key principle of the infrastructure is that the CSD of an investor's country provides a single point of entry that allows the investor to hold securities issued at any other participating CSD and to use those securities as collateral within its own country. This will generally be achieved by the CSD in which the investor has its account . . . holding securities in the primary CSD . . . , usually in an omnibus account': *Infrastructure Report* (n 10 above) 6. The ECSDA model involves DVP settlement in the settlement system of the buyer, with subsequent book entries in the system of the seller ('realignment'). See the *DVP Report* (n 7 above) 6 and 36.

[64] In the April 2000 *CREST Newsletter*, Iain Saville discusses the development of DVP links between the Settlement Network (made up of CREST and SIS SegaInterSettle) and Euroclear), to 'allow the integration of European settlement': at 5.

Like the Internet, the ECSDA model is less vulnerable to failure than a system having a central hub, without which no part can operate.

9.43   To some extent the above two models may complement[65] each other, by serving different elements of the securities markets. It has been suggested that the spider's web model may be more suitable for small brokers and other minor participants wishing to use their local depositary to access the European market, and that the hub and spoke model may be more suitable for major institutions.

9.44   A further alternative is provided by alternative markets such as Jiway, the new trading platform for European and US equities, discussed briefly in Chapter 1. Jiway offers consolidated settlement for its international trades through a series of links to local depositaries.

9.45   The trend towards cross border settlement raises important questions of conflict of laws. As discussed in Chapter 4, a major use of (interests in) securities is as collateral; the effectiveness of collateral arrangements depends on the collateral taker acquiring property rights in the collateral assets. As indicated in Chapter 7, the general rule of conflict of laws is that property rights can only validly be acquired in accordance with the law where the asset in question is located, or lex situs. With the use of cross border settlement systems, the interest of the participant is indirect, and the intermediaries through which it is held are located in different countries.[66] In order to ensure that collateral arrangements are legally robust, it is crucial to establish which account represents the situs of the interest of the collateral taker.[67] As discussed in Chapter 7, the Settlement Finality Directive has assisted in providing clarity on the issue in relation to certain collateral arrangements, and it is hoped that a further European Directive will shortly be introduced to put the matter beyond doubt in all European collateral arrangements.

B. Securities Settlement in the United Kingdom[68]

9.46   Securities settlement in the United Kingdom is undergoing a number of profound changes, which reflect the broad themes discussed above in relation to European settlement. First, it is being consolidated. At the time of writing, two different systems operate in London; it is proposed these should be merged into

---

[65] In a press release of 3 May 2000, CRESTCo and Clearstream welcomed the proposed merger of the London Stock Exchange and Deutsche Börse, and confirmed their commitment to co-operating in providing settlement for the merged trading platform.

[66] The chain of ownership between the issuer and the participant involves a series of accounts maintained in different jurisdictions.

[67] Another important consequence of the location of (interests in) securities serving as collateral is their eligibility for Eurozone monetary operations. In the *CREST Newsletter*, Iain Saville comments 'on the decision of the Irish authorities to issue Irish government debt into Euroclear. In my view, this primarily reflects the requirement of the European Central Bank that collateral must be located in the Eurozone to be eligible for Eurozone monetary operations': (April 2000, Issue 73) 3.

[68] See generally *CREST: The Legal Framework* (CRESTCo, March 1998). See also the CREST website at www.crestco.co.uk

one system, named CREST. Secondly, risk management in CREST is being enhanced to set international standards in a number of ways. In particular, it is proposed to improve the quality of DVP, to reduce settlement cycles and to introduce clearing. In a third and related development, international settlement is being facilitated. A series of bilateral links are being established between CREST and foreign systems; these permit the cross border settlement of interests in securities by CREST members.

(1) Introduction to CREST

CREST is a securities settlement system operating in London. CREST is operated **9.47** by CRESTCo, a special purpose vehicle owned by participants in the securities markets. Equities, corporate registered debt securities, warrants, depositary receipts, and units in unit trusts are eligible for settlement in CREST.[69] Following its merger with the Central Gilts Office (CGO) on 3 July 2000, CREST also settles gilts[70] and on its proposed merger with the Central Moneymarkets Office (CMO)[71] it will settle money market instruments.[72] Only registered securities may be settled in CREST.[73] Currently, only UK, Irish, Isle of Man and Jersey securities are eligible to be settled in CREST. Other foreign securities can only be brought into CREST through depositary receipt (DR) programmes, under which UK CREST-eligible DRs are issued in respect of them.

Securities settled through CREST are known as uncertificated securities, and are **9.48** in dematerialised form. This means that no paper is issued in respect of them.[74] The legal basis for dematerialisation in CREST is the Uncertificated Securities Regulations 1995.[75]

---

[69] Shares in open-ended investment companies (see Chapter 11) were intended to be CREST eligible, but at the time of writing a technical obstacle to their admission into CREST was still being addressed.

[70] Gilts are UK treasury securities in registered form.

[71] It is proposed that this merger will take place at a later date.

[72] Money market instruments (MMIs) are short term bearer debt instruments such as bills of exchange and certificates of deposit. Dematerialisation in CREST will change the legal nature of MMIs, as discussed below.

[73] Bearer securities must be repackaged into registered (interests in) securities in order to be CREST-eligible.

[74] No certificates are issued in respect of them, and transfer forms are not required for their transfer. Dematerialised securities in CREST may be removed from CREST and recertificated, with the exception of CDIs in respect of foreign securities and (it is proposed), treasury bills when they are introduced into CREST (see below) which may not be removed from CREST or recertificated. In addition, amendments made to the Uncertificated Securities Regulations 1995 by the Uncertificated Securities (Amendment) Regulations 2000, SI 2000/1682, permit issuers to issue new securities which cannot be certificated.

[75] SI 1995/3272 (as amended by the Uncertificated Securities (Amendment) Regulations 2000, SI 2000/1682). These regulations disapply the provisions of company law that require the issue of share certificates, and the provisions of company law and the law of property that require written instruments of transfer (regs 14 and 15, in effect disapplying the Companies Act 1985, ss 183, 185, and reg 32(5), disapplying the Law of Property Act 1925, ss 53(1)(c) and 136).

Holding and delivery

9.49 As discussed in Chapter 2, legal title to registered securities is determined by entries in the register maintained by the issuer (or a registrar on its behalf).[76] At the time of writing, the arrangements for holding and delivering securities in CREST are as follows. CREST maintains securities accounts in the names of members[77] in respect of their holdings of uncertificated securities. In the normal course, entries in these securities accounts accord with entries in the register,[78] so that if CREST member A holds 100 uncertificated ICI shares, it has 100 such shares credited to it, both in its CREST ICI securities account and on the register of ICI.

9.50 If CREST receives matching instructions[79] to deliver 40 of A's ICI shares to B, then provided certain conditions are satisfied,[80] CREST will effect settlement by debiting A's securities account so that it shows only 60 ICI shares, and at the same time crediting B's securities account so that it shows 40 ICI shares which A holds on trust for B.[81] The legal effect of this is to confer an equitable interest on B equivalent to 40 ICI shares.[82] Because B's equitable interest is proprietary, B should not lose its bargain if A becomes insolvent at this stage.

9.51 At the same time as it makes these book entries, CREST automatically instructs the registrar of ICI to amend its register so as to reduce A's holding of shares by 40, and to enter B as holding 40 shares. The registrar is required[83] to update the register within two hours, and in practice usually does so within 45 minutes.[84] Such registration has the effect of transferring legal title to 40 ICI shares from A to B.[85]

---

[76] In the case of equities, see the Companies Act 1985, s 361.

[77] CREST refers to participants for whom CREST maintains securities accounts as members (see CREST *Reference Manual* ch 2, sections 2 and 5); that terminology is adopted in this discussion.

[78] CREST reconciles its securities accounts with register entries; see CREST *Reference Manual* ch 5 section 5.

[79] Matching instructions from A and B will require to be received for deliveries; see CREST *Reference Manual* ch 4 sections 2 and 3.

[80] See CREST *Reference Manual* ch 4 section 10. The normal conditions are that sufficient securities are available in the transferor's account and that sufficient credit or headroom is available in the transferee's account in relation to any specified consideration; see the discussion of debit caps below.

[81] See CREST *Reference Manual* ch 4 section 10. This discussion assumes that B held no ICI shares prior to this transfer.

[82] See reg 25 of the Uncertificated Securities Regulations 1995, SI 1995/3272 and CREST *Reference Manual* ch 5 section 1. A holds an unallocated part of its holding of ICI shares equal to 40 shares on trust for B in accordance with reg 25 of the Uncertificated Securities Regulations. Regulation 25(6) addresses the risk that this trust might otherwise fail for want of certainty of subject matter. Arguably, the decision in *Hunter v Moss* rendered reg 25(6) unnecessary; see Chapter 2.

[83] This requirement is contained in the Registrars Service Standards, which form part of the CREST Rules; see *CREST: The Legal Framework* (n 68 above) 29.

[84] A few registrars are understood to register CREST deliveries within ten minutes.

[85] At this stage, A is no longer a trustee, and B's equitable interest is merged with legal title. Of course, in relation to units in an authorised unit trust scheme, the transferred asset consists of an equitable interest under a trust, so that registration has the effect of conferring beneficial and not legal title.

These arrangements will be simplified under the proposals for electronic transfer **9.52** of title, discussed below.

It will be seen that CREST differs from many other settlement systems in that it **9.53** is not, and does not use, a depositary[86] in relation to UK securities.[87] Securities are not immobilised in CREST, and CRESTCo does not stand in the chain of ownership between members and the issuers of the securities which it settles. CREST members hold UK securities directly from the issuer, and do not hold interests in securities through an intermediary.[88]

Payment and DVP

It was seen above that CREST does not act as a depositary holding title to (inter- **9.54** ests in) securities for members. Neither does it act as a bank holding cash deposits for members. Payment entitlements and payment obligations in respect of CREST deliveries are recorded in members' cash memorandum accounts.[89] Payments are effected through the assured payment system, which involves settlement banks.[90] Each CREST member is required to appoint a settlement bank as a precondition of membership.[91] Each settlement bank is required to enter into contractual arrangements[92] under which it assumes assured payment obligations in respect of members for whom it acts as settlement bank. The effect of this is that when CREST member X settles a purchase, secured loan or outright collateral transfer under which it is obliged to make payment to another CREST member (Y, the vendor or collateral giver) the payment obligation is recorded by debiting the cash memorandum accounts of X and crediting that of Y.[93] Under the assured

---

[86] CREST is not a depositary, but a securities settlement system. CREST is a 'a relevant system' for the purposes of the Uncertificated Securities Regulations; these regulations define 'a relevant system' as 'a computer-based system, and procedures, which enable title to units of a security to be evidenced and transferred without a written instrument, and which facilitate supplementary and incidental matters': reg 2(1).

[87] However, in relation to foreign securities, an associated CREST entity does provide a depositary service in order to repackage foreign securities into CREST-eligible interests, as discussed below.

[88] The nature of the asset of clients of CREST members who act as custodian is considered below.

[89] These are not bank accounts, and positive balances in them do represent the debt of CREST to the member. A separate CMA is maintained for each currency. See CREST *Reference Manual* ch 6 section 2.

[90] See CREST *Reference Manual* ch 6. Payments may be made in sterling, euros and US dollars.

[91] CREST *Reference Manual* ch 6 section 1.

[92] A CREST Assured Payment Agreement and a CREST Settlement Bank Agreement.

[93] 'Subject to any agreement between the member and its payment bank, the balance on the CMA at any time during the settlement day represents the net amount which each member owes to (or is owed by) its payment bank in respect of assured payment obligations or entitlements in the relevant designated currency arising during the settlement day': CREST *Reference Manual* ch 6 section 2.

payment system, the settlement bank of X is irrevocably[94] obliged to make payment to the settlement bank of Y.[95]

9.55 At the time of writing, payment is made between the settlement banks on a net basis at the end of the business day, by debiting and crediting their accounts at the Bank of England.[96] Because payment is made net end of day, this is model 2 DVP. It is proposed to upgrade CREST to model 1 DVP, as discussed below.

9.56 The arrangements for Y's settlement bank to make payment to Y are a private commercial matter, outside the scope of the rules of the assured payments system.[97] Usually such payments are made at the end of the business day. There is no proposal for this to change.[98]

9.57 In order to manage their credit exposures to their member clients, settlement banks may impose credit limits or caps on the value of net purchases their clients are permitted to make.[99] These are called debit caps, and at any particular time the available unused credit of a member within a debit cap is called headroom. Before accepting instructions to settle a trade, CREST checks that the purchaser (or borrower) has sufficient available headroom.[100] It is customary for settlement banks to take security interests over securities held in CREST (and beneficially owned by the member)[101] in order to secure these exposures.[102] CREST permits settlement

---

[94] It must make payment even if its client (X) defaults, so that it has no prospect of being reimbursed by X.

[95] See CREST Rules, rules 7–9.

[96] See CREST *Reference Manual* ch 6, section 5.

[97] 'The arrangements which exist between each CREST member and its settlement bank(s) are a matter for them to agree bilaterally and CRESTCo does not prescribe any particular form of agreement. As a general matter, however, these agreements contain provisions requiring the CREST member (when, at the end of the business day, he is a net buyer of securities) to discharge his obligations towards his settlement bank . . . either by putting his settlement bank in funds before settlement takes place or by doing so within a certain period afterwards or by operating within the limits of an overdraft or other credit facility agreed by the settlement bank. Where the CREST member is a net seller of securities, his agreement with his settlement bank will also specify the timing and circumstances in which the settlement bank will credit the CREST member's bank account . . . Some settlement banks undertake to credit the bank account of a CREST member who is a net seller in all circumstances; others will not do so if they themselves do not receive end of day funds from the counterparty settlement bank': *CREST: The Legal Framework* (n 68 above) 34, 35.

[98] This is a normal banking arrangement.

[99] See CREST *Reference Manual* ch 6, section 3.

[100] It also checks that the vendor or collateral giver has sufficient available securities in its free balance, or the part of its securities account that represents securities available for delivery. See CREST *Reference Manual* ch 4, section 10, ch 6, section 3. If a member has insufficient headroom, no further purchases may be possible until a sale goes through, thereby freeing up some headroom.

[101] It is not customary for settlement banks to take a security interest over securities held by members for clients; this is understood to be because of the difficulty of establishing that the beneficial owners consent to the arrangements. See Chapter 3 for a discussion of the tracing rules which apply where the beneficial owner does not consent.

[102] These take effect as floating charges over securities credited to member's securities accounts. They are registrable under the Companies Act 1985, s 395. Protection from insolvency

banks to calculate debit caps by reference to the value from time to time of charged securities (collateralised debit caps).[103]

Client accounts

CREST members who hold securities in CREST as custodian for their clients may do so in three different ways. **9.58**

The most normal arrangement is for the custodian CREST member to operate a pooled client account. This means that, for example, in respect of all ICI shares held by the custodian member for its various clients, the custodian has only one account in CREST (which will be designated an omnibus client account). Because the register of the issuer reflects the CREST securities accounts, there is a single entry in the register of ICI in the member's name for the omnibus client holding.[104] The respective interests of the individual clients are recorded only in the books of the custodian member. Because the custodian member acts as an intermediary holding its clients' assets on a commingled basis, pooled custody clients hold interests in securities, and not securities. **9.59**

Where the custodian member offers individual client designation to a custody client, a separate account in CREST is opened in respect of the securities held by the member for that client. A separate entry is also made on the register of ICI. Both the CREST account and the register entry is in the name of the custodian member, but so designated (often with an alpha numeric code) that it is earmarked for the client. Some custodians may find these arrangements cumbersome.[105] Designated custody clients have allocated rights in particular securities; the custodian acts as intermediary, but does not hold their interests on a commingled basis. Accordingly such clients hold securities and not interests in securities. **9.60**

Sponsored membership is a third option, which permits clients to avoid intermediation.[106] A client may hold legal title to uncertificated securities by becoming a **9.61**

---

displacement is available to these charges as 'system charges' under the Financial Markets and Insolvency Regulations 1996 and Part VII of the Companies Act 1989.

[103] See *CREST: The Legal Framework* (n 68 above) 36.

[104] Custodians are required by the rules of equity and by UK regulation to segregate client assets from assets they own beneficially. Therefore, if the custodian member also owns ICI shares beneficially, there will be two CREST ICI accounts and two entries on the ICI register, one in each case for the client position and one for the house position.

[105] Because there is a single debit cap, one client's sale cannot provide headroom for another client's purchase. Other drawbacks for custodians are the administrative burden of maintaining separate CREST accounts, and the fact that such surplus balances in such accounts are not available to meet shortfalls attributable to the business of other clients. (Of course, such arrangements amount to securities lending and are not lawful without the express consent of the clients whose securities are being lent.) Nevertheless, large numbers of designated accounts are provided by custodians.

[106] See CREST Rules, rules 1–6.

CREST member (and therefore a registered shareholder of ICI shares) without maintaining the electronic link to CREST, by asking a custodian or other CREST member to sponsor its CREST membership. The sponsor maintains the electronic link with CREST and operates the CREST accounts on the client's behalf.[107] Sponsored members need their own settlement banks, and custodians often offer this facility as well. Sponsored members have separate debit caps.[108] Clearly, because they hold securities directly on an allocated basis, the asset of the sponsored member is securities and not interests in securities.[109]

(2) Collateral in CREST

9.62 A number of arrangements are available in CREST to facilitate the delivery of uncertificated securities as collateral. It is important to note that these arrangements are not in themselves effective to confer security interests on collateral takers, and that collateral agreements must be appropriately documented in order to clarify the legal effect of collateral deliveries through CREST.

Outright transfer (DBV)[110]

9.63 Outright transfers of collateral may be made within CREST using a normal member to member delivery of the collateral securities. However, participants normally make use of the delivery by value (DBV) facilities for overnight outright collateral transfer arrangements.

9.64 Under the DBV facility, CREST automatically selects securities to be delivered as collateral under outright transfer arrangements. The value of the collateral is specified, but not the individual securities.[111] The corresponding payment is synchronised with the DBV by debiting and crediting the parties' cash memorandum accounts, thus offering DVP. DBVs are registered,[112] and therefore confer legal

---

[107] Acting as sponsored member is regulated as a form of investment business under the Financial Services Act 1986, Sch 1, para 16A (as amended). Sponsors who are members of IMRO are subject to special conduct of business requirements under the IMRO Rulebook.

[108] Further, a sponsored member may specify a limit on the net value of transfers that a sponsor may make on their behalf in any one day. See CREST *Reference Manual* ch 4, section 11. However, in practice this option is generally not used.

[109] Sponsored members may perceive the arrangement as tying them to the particular broker which acts as sponsor.

[110] See CREST *Reference Manual* ch 7, section 2.

[111] The collateral giver specifies the value of collateral to be delivered, but not the particular securities. Different categories of securities may be specified for a DBV: see CREST *Reference Manual* ch 2, section 6. When giving DBV instructions, parties must specify a number of items including: (i) Securities category type: whether category 1 (based on FT-SE 100), category 2 (based on FT-SE 250) or Category 3 (other securities); (ii) a margin (default margin is 5 per cent); and (iii) whether a 10 per cent concentration limit should apply. Collateral takers may instruct CREST to exclude certain securities from DBVs.

[112] ie the delivery appears on the registers of the relevant issuers, as well as on the CREST accounts of the parties to the arrangement.

interests in the collateral securities. DBVs are automatically returned to the collateral taker, and the collateralised payment repaid, on the business day following the delivery.[113] DBVs are widely used to deliver collateral for securities loans[114] and equity repos. Enforcement merely involves notifying CREST of default, so that they disable the automatic return of DBVs. A tri-party repo service is proposed for 2001.

Legal mortgage

Uncertificated securities may be delivered under a legal mortgage. This involves moving them into the general CREST account of the collateral taker. Under the collateral documentation, the collateral giver retains the right to receive the securities back upon the discharge of the secured obligation. As discussed in Chapter 5, this right is known as the equity of redemption, and is a property right. In order to avoid ad valorem stamp duty reserve tax, a standard form letter of direction is required by the Inland Revenue.   **9.65**

Equitable mortgage (escrow balance)

It was argued in Chapter 5 that an equitable mortgage is the same as a fixed charge. Where a CREST member wishes to grant an equitable mortgage over uncertificated securities to another CREST member, it may do this by transferring the securities to a sub-account known as the escrow balance within its general securities account. Here the securities are blocked from the control of collateral giver and subject to the control of the collateral taker. The collateral taker may instruct CREST to release the securities back into the general account of the collateral giver (which it will do on discharge of the secured obligation) or alternatively instruct CREST to transfer them to its own account (which it will do on the default of the collateral giver, in order to enforce its security interest). CREST does not monitor whether such enforcement action is authorised under the terms of the collateral agreement.   **9.66**

In the past, where the collateral giver was affected by insolvency, enforcement difficulties arose. In practice CREST would freeze the account of an insolvent member, and would not allow the collateral taker automatically to enforce its interest   **9.67**

---

[113] DBV securities are automatically 'redelivered' on the next business day (unless countermanding instructions are given by the collateral taker wishing to enforce the collateral). New DBV collateral must be put up by the borrower daily; the amount of daily DBV collateral will need to be adjusted to reflect the margining requirements of the securities lending arrangement. Where DBVs are serving to collateralise a securities loan, there is no automatic margining as the CREST system does not link the DBV with the delivery of loaned securities, but treats the two as separate transactions.

[114] DBVs are also used to deliver loaned securities. Where uncertificated securities are agreed to be loaned against cash collateral, the assured payment obligation generated by the delivery of securities serves as the cash collateral.

where the collateral giver's account has been frozen. In practice, CREST might unfreeze accounts of insolvent members by agreement with the insolvency official within a few days.[115] While the account was frozen, the collateral taker could only enforce its security interest with the consent of the insolvency official. Now these enforcement difficulties have been addressed as follows. A transfer from the escrow balance of an insolvent member can still be settled at the request of the chargee (provided this is legally permissible, eg the chargor is not in administration). CRESTCo considers each such request on a case by case basis. Nevertheless, escrow balances are still not widely used for collateral.[116] Escrow balances are made free of consideration so that DVP is not available.

Floating charge

9.68 It is open to a CREST member to grant a floating charge over the balances of its CREST securities accounts from time to time. As discussed in Chapter 5, this is a relatively weak form of security interest. Because the securities remain in the account of the collateral giver, the position on enforcement is the same as with escrow balances.

9.69 The security interests customarily taken by settlement banks from their client members take effect as floating charges, because the member retains the freedom to deal with the securities in the ordinary course of its business. Lawyers representing the settlement banks have been in discussions with CRESTCo with a view to overcoming the enforcement problems. To facilitate enforcement, CRESTCo has prepared a form of power of attorney whereby the member authorises the settlement bank to act as its sponsor and to give instructions for the realisation of the security interest on the member's behalf. CRESTCo's ability to act on such instructions has been strengthened by regulation 36A of the Uncertificated Securities Regulations, introduced by the Uncertificated Securities (Amendment) Regulations 2000, SI 2000/1682.[117]

(3) Developments

9.70 A number of existing and proposed developments will serve to enhance the management of risk in CREST.

---

[115] In practice CRESTCo will enter into dialogue with the chargee as well as the insolvency official of the chargor.

[116] Part VII of the Companies Act 1989 provides settlement banks with insolvency protection in relation to their floating charges, but enforcing the same charges remains problematic, as discussed above. This may appear inconsistent from a policy point of view. Escrow balances were originally designed by CREST for use in relation to take-over elections.

[117] See section 6 of the *CREST Reference Manual* and the CREST *Guidance Note on Realisation of a Settlement Bank's Security* (28 June 2000) for more details.

Securities Settlement Priorities Review

In 1998, the Bank of England undertook its Securities Settlement Priorities **9.71**
Review in order to consider the future development of securities settlement in the
United Kingdom. In its report on the review,[118] a number of key recommenda-
tions were made.

First, UK settlement should be consolidated. Prior to July 2000, two settlement **9.72**
systems in addition to CREST operated in London. The Central Gilts Office (the
CGO) settled gilts,[119] and the Central Moneymarkets Office (the CMO) settled
(and at the time of writing still settles) money market instruments (MMIs).[120] The
report recommended that the CGO should merge with CREST, and that the
CMO should be integrated with CREST as far as possible.

Secondly, the quality of DVP in CREST should be enhanced, both on the pay- **9.73**
ment side (with central bank money) and on the delivery side (with the immediate delivery of legal title) in order to meet international standards.

Thirdly, cross border links should be developed between CREST and foreign set- **9.74**
tlement systems. As a lower priority, the introduction of clearing was considered.

Less than three years later, very significant progress has been made in implement- **9.75**
ing these recommendations.

Integration of the three systems

Interestingly, a key reason given by the market for desiring the integration of the **9.76**
three systems was the need for new efficiencies in collateral management.[121] The
Bank of England previously operated the CGO and the CMO, but in preparation
for their merger with CREST, CRESTCo took over responsibility for their operation in 1999.

---

[118] *Securities Settlement Priorities Review* (September 1998).
[119] As discussed in Chapter 1, gilts are UK registered treasury securities. Prior to the merger, as at
31 March 2000, the daily average settlement value was £46,224,000,000 in CREST and
£153,580,000,000 in the CGO. See *CREST Newsletter* (April 2000, Issue 73) 21. Gilts settle T+1,
whereas at the time of writing equities settle T+5, with the objective of T+1 settlement by 2003.
[120] As discussed in Chapter 1, MMIs are highly liquid short term bearer instruments. The CMO
currently settles sterling-denominated treasury bills, local authority bills, certain types of bank bills,
trade bills, certain bank certificates of deposit, building society certificates of deposit and commercial paper.
[121] 'A view expressed particularly strongly (but not exclusively) by the settlement banks was that
the ability to maximise the efficiency with which credit and collateral are allocated and utilised is
critical': *Securities Settlement Priorities Review* (Bank of England, September 1998) 9. 'Gilts and
money market instruments could be held within a single pool of collateral, subject to a single debit
cap, and potentially interchangeable on a Delivery versus Delivery (DvD) basis': ibid 16.

CGO

9.77   The merger of CGO and CREST took place on 3 July 2000. The legal aspects of this exercise were relatively straightforward because the two original systems were very similar. Since the upgrade of the CGO (to 'CGO2') in 1997, CGO had adopted the same software as CREST.[122] More importantly, the legal structure of the CGO was fundamentally the same as that of CREST, which was modelled on it. The CGO, like CREST, settled registered securities on a fungible basis, with legal title being delivered by registration and an equitable interest arising upon book entry transfer (but see the proposals for electronic transfer of title in CREST, discussed below).[123] The CGO also offered an assured payments system.[124]

CMO

9.78   The proposed merger of the CMO with CREST will involve a number of legal and operational changes, and at the time of writing it has not yet taken place. The legal structures of the two systems, and the legal nature of the securities settled through them, are fundamentally different from each other. Whereas CREST securities are registered and dematerialised, CMO securities take the form of bearer tangible instruments.[125] Whereas CREST is not a depositary, so that participants are in a direct legal relationship with the issuer of securities, the CMO is an immobilisation system in which participants securities are held by a depositary[126] as bailee[127] for participants. Whereas securities are settled in CREST on a

---

[122]   There were some differences relating to different functionality, eg the strips market peculiar to the CGO. However, the core software was the same.

[123]   Whereas the transferee's equitable interest arises in CREST under a statutory trust by virtue of reg 25 of the Uncertificated Securities Regulations 1995, SI 1995/3272, the basis for the transferee's equitable interest in the CGO was contractual; see section 8.2.4 and 8.2.8 of the former CGO *Reference Manual,* and section 4(1) of the former CGO Membership Agreement.

[124]   There are a significant number of minor functional differences between the two original systems, which are detailed in *Gilts Settlement in CREST* (CREST, September 1999).

However, something of a challenge was posed by 'bulldogs' within the CGO, ie sterling sovereign securities issued by foreign issuers, as it was necessary to establish in each case that the terms of issue were compatible with the Uncertificated Securities Regulations, by amending those terms if necessary.

[125]   Since 1994, sterling CDs have been dematerialised in the CMO, but other securities remain in physical form.

[126]   The Bank of England provides this depositary service.

[127]   Unlike the CGO and CREST, the legal structure of the CMO has no statutory basis and rests on general legal concepts based on common law possession. These are set out in the contractual framework in which the CMO operates made up of the CMO *Reference Manual* and the various agreements signed by members. The Bank holds CMO securities as bailee for the members to whose accounts they are credited. When member A transfers its securities to member B by the debiting and crediting of the relevant accounts the legal effect is that the Bank ceases to hold the securities as bailee for member A and instead holds them for member B. The process of acknowledging the change of bailor is known as attornment. The CMO *Reference Manual* provides for CMO securities to be used as collateral. It describes these arrangements as pledge. Thus, the CMO is legally based on common law possession, and the possessory concepts of bailment, attornment and pledge.

fungible basis, the CMO is non-fungible and allocates particular securities to particular participants.

Physical MMIs in the CMO enjoy the status of negotiable instruments. The **9.79**
merger of the CMO with CREST will involve settling MMIs on a dematerialised
and fungible basis. An important consequence of this will be the loss of negotiable
status.[128] The Bank has consulted widely on whether there is any need to preserve
the negotiability of money market instruments. In a paper prepared by Guy
Morton of Freshfields and appearing as Appendix II to the Bank's consultation
paper, *The Future of Money Market Instruments*[129] it identified the various benefits
of negotiability, and concluded that the key benefit is security of transfer.[130]
However, the Bank went on to conclude that the merger will not reduce security
of transfer. This is on the basis that regulation 29 of the Uncertificated Securities
Regulations creates a level of security of transfer equal to that conferred by negotiable status. This robust view is based on the opinion of Leading Counsel.[131]

---

[128] See Appendix II to *The Future of Money Market Instruments* (Bank of England, November
1999), and Benjamin, 'Negotiability and Computerisation' (1995) 10 JIBFL 253–357.

[129] ibid.

[130] 'A number of parties stressed the great importance of certainty of title': *The Future of Money
Market Instruments: Next Steps* (Bank of England, March 2000) 11. 'Negotiable instruments have
four main legal features: they can be transferred solely by physical delivery, they provide the holder
with unchallengeable title, they provide certain benefits in the event of a court action, and they may
include rights against two or more parties': *The Future of Money Market Instruments* (n 128 above)
12.

[131] 'These views were confirmed by Richard Sykes, QC, when the Bank and CRESTCo sought
his advice on the questions regarding the benefits of negotiability. Mr Sykes' advice supported the
view that there is no reason to replicate negotiability for dematerialised MMIs. In his opinion there
is no respect in which a holder of a security in CREST is worse off than a holder of a negotiable
instrument': *The Future of Money Market Instruments* (n 128 above) 13. A note of the consultation
with Mr Sykes appears in Appendix II to that document.

A more cautious approach (which, it should be stressed, is the view of the author and not necessarily of anyone else) would be that reg 29 does not have the effect of making CREST transfers irreversible, but rather of making them reversible only after registration. CREST was originally built for
registered securities, which have never been negotiable. The Companies Act 1989, s 207, under
which the Uncertificated Securities Regulations 1995, SI 1995/3272 were made, provides that
rights are to be changed as little as possible. On this basis, reg 29 might be interpreted, not as converting equities in effect into negotiable instruments, but rather as providing only that CREST
transfers should proceed to registration, in order to avoid systemic risk. If so, the owner of securities
that have been fraudulently transferred to a third party is as free to bring a tracing action within
CREST as without it. If successful, such a tracing action could not result in the original CREST
transfer being interrupted (because of reg 29), but could result in an order for the retransfer of the
securities through CREST to the original owner. On this narrower interpretation of reg 29, the
effect of the merger will be to reduce security of transfer in relation to money market instruments.
Of course, it would not affect the integrity of the CREST system, as any tracing action would be
against the transferee and not CRESTCo.

9.80 It is therefore proposed that MMIs should be settled through CREST on a dematerialised[132] and fungible basis.[133]

Higher quality DVP

9.81 As indicated above, the proposals to enhance the quality of DVP in CREST relate to both the payment and the delivery side of CREST settlements.

Electronic transfer of title

9.82 Amendments to the Uncertificated Securities Regulations are proposed[134] to enable CREST to operate as a sub-register of participating companies.[135] This will mean that a credit entry in a CREST account will confer legal title and not merely an equitable interest.[136] The delivery of immediate legal title is the highest possible quality delivery. It is hoped that these arrangements will be in place by the end of 2000.[137] In outline, it is proposed that, for issues having both certificated and

---

[132] Although 'Treasury bills should be dematerialised, with no paper option' (*The Future of Money Market Instruments: Next Steps* (n 130 above) 2), in respect of other MMIs 'Issuers could continue to issue MMIs in physical form, but such issues would be wholly separate from dematerialised MMIs in CREST': ibid 6.

[133] See generally *The Future of Money Market Instruments* (n 128 above) and *The Future of Money Market Instruments: Next Steps* (n 130 above). 'Issues of dematerialised MMIs should be fungible so that holdings of the same issue can be interchanged and divided into smaller holdings. Fungible MMIs could also bring benefits for the wider market including: —Enabling MMIs to be identified by ISINs which would assist greater efficiency in back office systems (most of which are based on ISINs) and could help in the development of straight-through processing . . .—A deeper and more liquid market; and—Fungibility could facilitate the introduction of assured payment (as it would reduce the number of identifiers which settlement banks would need to track as collateral': *The Future of Money Market Instruments: Next Steps* (n 130 above) 19. See also, ibid 8. Indeed, it is proposed that MMIs should be undivided: 'MMIs should be issued as "issues" (rather than as separate physical instruments)': *The Future of Money Market Instruments* (n 128 above) 7 and *The Future of Money Market Instruments: Next Steps* (n 130 above) 7.
See the discussion in Appendix VI to *International Securities in CREST*.

[134] See HM Treasury, *The Uncertificated Securities Regulations 1999; A Proposal for Consultation* (15 July 1999).

[135] 'Under this proposed change, the CREST records of uncertificated securities would become an electronic sub-register (ESR), so that full legal title was conferred on the investor at the point of settlement': Appendix VI to *International Securities in CREST* 22.

[136] 'There has been some comment in UK legal circles about what this equitable interest might be and, for example, how it might compete with any other equitable interests. Those from civil law jurisdictions have found it still more confusing being unfamiliar with (and frequently distrusting of) concepts of equity; indeed one or two overseas organisations have taken the opportunity to cite this as evidence of weakness in the UK legal infrastructure': Kirby, *CREST and Securities Law Reform* (n 58 above) 3.

[137] 'However, it is not intended that there should be any wider business implications for registration practice, which should continue very much as at present. Issuers and their registrars will remain responsible for processing corporate actions, providing public access to the register and managing the relationship with holders of their securities. In order to achieve this, the new regulations will need to go further than simply designating CREST as a central register and will separate the respective responsibilities which are to be assumed by CRESTCo from those which will remain with registrars. To this end, there will be a new concept of the 'Record' of uncertificated securities which is to be maintained by the issuer reflecting the entries in the uncertificated register maintained by

uncertificated securities, there will be three records of shareholdings. First, for certificated securities, a certificated share register will be maintained independently of CREST. Secondly, in respect of uncertificated securities, securities accounts maintained by CREST will constitute the register. In addition, in respect of uncertificated securities, the issuer will maintain a record. Although not part of the register, this record will be used to determine entitlements to corporate actions. Both the issuer and CRESTCo will be obliged to reconcile their records, as they do at present. The real significance of the proposals is to alter the legal status of the records of CRESCTCo and the issuer, so that the former (and not as at present the latter) determines legal title.

Central Bank Money[138]

It was seen above that CREST currently offers model 2 DVP; payments are made between settlement banks on a net basis at the end of each business day. The size of the intra day exposures of one settlement bank to another has been a source of concern.[139] Moreover, the relatively greater payment risks in CREST than in other systems amounted to a competitive disadvantage.[140] The Bank of England is therefore working with CRESTCo and APACS[141] to develop a system of DVP involving real time gross payments. It is proposed that facilities will be introduced for sterling and euro payments[142] between settlement banks to be discharged on a real time gross basis across their accounts at the Bank of England. **9.83**

The Bank of England will provide the necessary intra day liquidity to enable these payments to be made.[143] In order to collateralise the exposures of the Bank of England, the settlement banks will deliver uncertificated securities to the Bank of **9.84**

CRESTCo. It will be this Record which forms the basis of establishing record date entitlement and to which public viewing rights will be given': Kirby (n 58 above) 4.

[138] See generally the *Report of the DVP Steering Group* (February 2000), available on the Bank of England's website at www.bankofengland.co.uk/dvpsteergrp.htm

[139] 'Settlement banks control their exposure to their customers through application of credit limits but cannot limit the growth of their exposures to other settlement banks during the day': CREST *Newsletter* (April 2000) 8.

'The daily payment value flowing through CRESTCo's services regularly exceeds £200 billion per day': CREST *Newsletter* (April 2000) 9.

[140] See *Securities Settlement Priorities Review* (n 118 above) 19.

[141] APACS is the Association for Payment Clearing Services; in this context it represents the settlement banks.

[142] 'The process should be applicable to euro settlement as well as sterling, [self-collateralisation should not apply to euro transactions for Bank of England settlement banks while the Bank's access to euro liquidity remains restricted.] transfers between settlement banks which hold accounts at the Central Bank of Ireland and, as far as possible, to settlements requiring cross-border payments between Bank of England and Central Bank of Ireland accounts': *Report of the DVP Steering Group* (n 138 above) 13. A link between the RTCS systems of the Bank of England and the Bank of Ireland is planned for early 2001.

[143] At present, CREST checks the availability of two resources prior to making a delivery. These are available securities and 'headroom' (ie settlement bank credit). With the new arrangements, a third resource will be checked as a precondition of settlement, namely liquidity.

England under repo transactions; these securities will have been delivered to the settlement banks by their member clients under back to back repos. These repos facilities will operate automatically.[144] Securities which have been so delivered under repos will appear in separate balances in CREST members' accounts.[145]

9.85   In some cases,[146] purchased securities can serve to collateralise the liquidity required to fund their purchase, under 'self-collateralisation' arrangements.[147] Where securities which have been delivered from a member's account under such a repo are required for delivery, they will be returned.[148] It appears that, under the proposals for self-collateralisation, title to purchased securities would travel intra day as follows: from vendor to purchaser (through CREST); from purchaser to its settlement bank (under the first repo); from the purchaser's settlement bank to the Bank of England (under the second repo); from the Bank of England to the purchaser's settlement bank (as the second repo is reversed at the end of the day); and from the purchaser's settlement bank to the purchaser (as the first repo is reversed).

9.86   These arrangements are described by the Bank of England as 'central bank money', and it is hoped that they will be implemented in 2001.[149] When they are implemented, the settlement bank of a vendor of uncertificated securities will be paid by the settlement bank of the purchaser in real time. This protects both the vendor and its settlement bank from the credit risk of the settlement bank of the purchaser.[150] However, the proposals do not protect the vendor from the settlement risk of its own settlement bank.[151] The arrangements for payment by the

---

[144]   See the discussion in CREST *Newsletter* (April 2000) 11–13.

[145]   *Report of the DVP Steering Group* (n 138 above) 13.

[146]   Self-collateralisation will only be permitted for principal trades for sterling consideration. See *Report of the DVP Steering Group* (n 138 above) 5.

[147]   See the discussion in the *Report of the DVP Steering Group* (n 138 above) 5 et seq.

[148]   'Where the securities being sold by a CREST member have already been used for self-collateralisation that day, they should be repurchased by the selling member prior to the transfer to the buyer and on-repo to the Bank of England (ie the Bank's account should be credited and then debited, rather than the securities simply remaining on its account)': *Report of the DVP Steering Group* (n 138 above) 14.

[149]   'We remain confident of achieving our original objective to implement settlement in central bank funds for sterling and euro by end 2001': CREST *Newsletter* (April 2000) 5. If and when the United Kingdom joins EMU, these arrangements will assist it in participating in the ECB's open market operations: see the discussion ibid at 9, and *Report of the DVP Steering Group* (n 138 above) 3: 'Payment in central bank money in real time . . . is increasingly seen, both in the UK and internationally and by users and providers alike, as a component of settlement "best practice". The ECB has specified that, from January 2002, only Securities Settlement Systems (SSS) offering intraday finality in central bank money will be eligible for use in the provision of euro credit in ESCB monetary policy operations. Payment in central bank money may well be a strategic requirement should the UK join the single currency'.

[150]   Of course, the existing assured payment system protects them from the credit risk of the purchaser.

[151]   As would be the case if, eg, cash accounts in the settlement system constituted central bank accounts, as in Sicovam, the French settlement system.

vendor's settlement bank to the vendor are a commercial matter between the parties, and payment is usually made at the end of the day, so that the vendor takes the intra day credit risk of its settlement bank. This will not change.[152]

Clearing[153]

In a joint project between CRESTCo, the London Clearing House (LCH) and the London Stock Exchange (LSE), arrangements are being developed whereby LCH will provide a clearing service, initially[154] for trades executed on the LSE's order-driven market, SETS[155] and settled through CREST. This clearing service will be called the central counterparty, or CCP service.[156] It is proposed to be introduced in the first quarter of 2001.[157] Under the CCP service, trades between buyers and sellers will be novated at the point of execution and replaced by two new trades, one between the buyer and LCH as seller, and one between the seller and LCH as buyer. Trades will automatically be passed on to CREST for settlement; settlement in CREST will be between the buyer and LCH as seller, and the seller and LCH as buyer.

9.87

The use of LCH as central counterparty protects both buyer and seller from market risk, as their trade will still settle even if their original counterparty becomes insolvent post-trade and pre-settlement. The market risk is borne by LCH, because it is obliged to settle one side of the original transaction even if the other side will not settle due to the insolvency of one of the original parties. In order to collateralise these exposures, which arise post-trade and pre-settlement, LCH will take cash and securities collateral in the form of initial and variation margin.[158]

9.88

---

[152] See also the discussion in CREST *Newsletter* (April 2000) 8, 9.

[153] See generally *Central Counterparty for SETS, Service Outline* (March 2000), published by the LCH, CREST and the LSE, and CREST *Newsletter* (March 2000) 6–9.

[154] 'The objective of this work is to deliver an effective central counterparty, in two phases; first the LSE's SETS trading system; and for the trading facilities to be provided to the Irish Stock Exchange by the German XETRA trading system . . . We expect that it may well prove of use to the Swiss market, with whom we are exploring its development': CREST *Newsletter* (April 2000, Issue 73) 4.

[155] The Stock Exchange Electronic Trading Service. 'SETS is the LSE electronic order book for trading leading equity shares': *Enhancing CREST: The Central Counterparty (Part One)* (CRESTCo, April 2000) 4. The service is proposed to be extended to SEAQ auctions, when they are introduced during the course of 2000: see *Central Counterparty for SETS, Service Outline* (n 153 above) 8.

[156] 'The primary objectives of the CCP service in the first phase of implementation [to be introduced in the first quarter of 2001] are to introduce post trade anonymity for trading on the Stock Exchange Electronic Trading Service (SETS), to improve the management of counterparty risk and to provide the infrastructure for introducing optional multilateral settlement netting as part of the second phase of implementation anticipated to go live 9–12 months after the first phase': *Enhancing CREST: The Central Counterparty (Part One)* (n 155 above) 1. See also *Enhancing CREST: The Central Counterparty (Part Two)* (CRESTCo, May 2000).

[157] *Central Counterparty for SETS, Service Outline* (n 153 above) 12.

[158] See *Central Counterparty for SETS, Service Outline* (n 153 above) sections 9 and 10.

The CCP service will made directly available to clearing members of LCH;[159] CREST participants who are not clearing members will be able to access the service via a clearing member, with whom they will need to enter into a clearing agreement.

9.89 A detailed discussion of the existing arrangements whereby LCH provides a clearing service in other markets,[160] and collateralises its clearing exposures, is given in Chapter 8. On a related point, proposals are being developed for the netting of equity trades in the course of clearing.

Cross border links in CREST

9.90 In order to facilitate cross border settlement, CREST is forming a series of bilateral links with settlement systems in other jurisdictions, so that CREST participants may settle interests in foreign securities through their CREST accounts. At the time of writing, links exist between CREST and the Swiss SIS SegaIntersettle AG settlement system, NECIFEF in the Netherlands, VPC in Sweden and DTC in New York.[161] These links are designed to comply with ECSDA standards, discussed above.

9.91 Because UK legislation does not generally purport to have extra-territorial effect, the Uncertificated Securities Regulations (which render securities eligible for settlement within CREST) are only effective in the United Kingdom. It is not possible generally[162] to admit foreign securities directly into CREST. Therefore, cross border settlement involves forming links with foreign settlement systems.

9.92 As discussed in Chapter 1, many settlement systems operate on an indirect basis, so that either the operator of the system and/or its depositary stand in the chain of ownership between the issuer of the underlying securities and participants. In such cases, the customary method of forming a cross border link between two systems is very simple; a sub-custodian of the operator or depositary of the first sys-

---

[159] A general clearing member (GCM) clears trades for itself and its customers, and also for non-clearing members. An individual clearing member (ICM) clears trades only for itself and its customers. See *Central Counterparty for SETS, Service Outline* (n 153 above) 14, 15. LCH imposes financial and other criteria on clearing members, including net capital of £5 million for ICHs and £10 million for GCMs. See *Central Counterparty for SETS, Service Outline* (n 153 above) 16.

[160] LCH provides a clearing service for trades executed by its members on the London International Financial Futures and Options Exchange (LIFFE), the London Metal Exchange (LME), the International Petroleum Exchange (IPE) and Tradepoint, as well as OTC trades (cleared through RepoClear and SwapClear).

[161] In relation to Nasdaq and S&P 500 Index securities.

[162] It is possible directly to admit Irish, Isle of Man and Jersey securities because those jurisdictions have passed regulations modelled on the Uncertificated Securities Regulations, namely (in Ireland) the Companies Act 1990 (Uncertificated Securities) Regulations 1996, SI 68/1996 and (in the Isle of Man) the Companies Act 1992 Transfer of Securities Regulations 1996.

tem becomes a participant in the second system.[163] However, this option is not available for CREST, which is a direct system in the sense that (in relation to UK securities) neither CRESTCo nor any depositary stands between the issuer and the participant. A special structure was therefore needed to form cross border links.

This structure involves two subsidiaries of CRESTCo, which were formed as spe- **9.93** cial purpose vehicles for the purpose of establishing cross border links. These are CREST International Nominees Limited ('the Nominee') and CREST Depositary Limited ('the Depositary').[164] These entities serve to establish cross border links between CREST and foreign systems as follows. The Nominee becomes a participant in the foreign system (so that it acquires title to the foreign securities settled through that system). The Nominee holds its title to the foreign securities on bare trust for the Depositary under the terms of a nominee agreement between it and the Depositary.[165]

The Depositary in turn issues a new form of security known as a CREST Depositary **9.94** Interest (CDI) in favour of CREST members under the terms of a deed poll. The Depositary holds its interest in the foreign securities on bare trust for holders of CDIs;[166] CDIs therefore represent a beneficial interest in the foreign securities. CDIs are a form of depositary receipt; depositary receipts are discussed in Chapter 11. The CDIs are issued under English law in the form of registered securities,[167] and they are therefore eligible for settlement in CREST.[168] When one CREST member wishes to deliver its interest in foreign securities to another CREST member, a member to member delivery of the CDIs is made within CREST.

When a CREST member wishes to receive an interest in foreign securities from a **9.95** participant in the foreign system, the securities are delivered through the foreign system to the Nominee, and the Depositary issues new CDIs in favour of the CREST participant. Conversely, when a CREST participant wishes to deliver interests in foreign securities to a participant in the foreign system, its CDIs are cancelled and the Nominee delivers foreign securities to the foreign participant.

---

[163] Generally speaking, Euroclear, Clearstream and the DTC form their cross border links in this way.

[164] In some cases, the Depositary may itself act as Nominee; see section 3.3 of the Global Deed Poll.

[165] The Depositary holds securities, and not merely interests in securities, because there is no commingling (ie the nominee has only one client).

[166] The holders of CDIs are the CREST members to whose accounts they are from time to time credited; see below.

[167] A register of CDIs is maintained by the Depositary.

[168] Unlike existing UK securities settled in CREST, CDIs cannot be recertificated, and are in effect 'locked into' CREST. See section 2.5 of the Global Deed Poll, the text of which appears in section 3 of ch 13 of the CREST *Reference Manual*.

9.96 As discussed above, in relation to UK securities, CREST is a direct system in the sense that it does not involve intermediation, and members hold securities (and not merely interests in securities) directly from issuers. However, in relation to foreign securities, CREST members hold interests in securities, because their assets are intermediated by and commingled in the hands of the Depositary.[169]

9.97 This is an elegant solution to the legal challenge of forming cross border links, borrowing a repackaging technique that has been developed in the depositary receipt industry. As with all DR holders, two particular legal issues arise for holders of CDIs. The first involves irreconciliations, and the second involves conflict of laws.

9.98 In active DR programmes under which DRs are regularly issued and cancelled, it is not unusual for irreconciliations to arise through operational error, whereby the number of DRs in issue may exceed the number of underlying securities held by the depositary. In this case, until the shortfall is eliminated, the asset of the DR holders is less valuable than it purports to be. If cross border links in CREST are very active, so that CDIs are regularly issued and cancelled, similar irreconciliations may be possible (although this is considered unlikely because reconciliations will be made daily). Another potential source of shortfall is bad deliveries, whereby a credit to the Nominee is reversed because of a defect in title, or operational problems in the foreign settlement system.[170] The risk of shortfall is drawn to members' attention in section 3(4) of the Terms and Conditions for International Settlement Links, in Schedule 3 to the CREST *Reference Manual*.

9.99 Secondly, the CDI arrangements are effective *as a matter of English law* to confer property rights on CREST members in the underlying securities. Whether they are so effective as a matter of the law of the foreign system is left to the member to determine. CREST comments on the complexity of the conflict of laws position,[171] and indicates that it has made certain assumptions in establishing the cross border links, including (heroically) 'that the CSD will not recognise third party claims to securities credited to the CREST Nominee'.[172] This clear statement of the relevant assumptions will help participants to obtain their own legal opinions.

---

[169] See clause 5.1 of the Global Deed Poll, which indicates that the rights of CDI holders arise under equitable tenancies in common. Although foreign securities are also intermediated by the Nominee, they are not commingled in its hands, as the Nominee holds only for the Depositary. Therefore the Depositary holds the same asset as the Nominee.

[170] Members must provide an indemnity in respect of defects in title to foreign securities acquired for their account; see section 4(1)(a) of Sch 3 to the CREST *Reference Manual*. See also section 9.3 of the Global Deed Poll.

[171] 'The legal analysis of acquisitions and transfers between participants in different jurisdictions, or affecting securities outside the jurisdiction of one or both participants, is necessarily complex. It is possible that the same transactions may be analysed in different ways in each particular jurisdiction concerned. CREST *Reference Manual* ch 13, section 6.

[172] CREST *Reference Manual* ch 13, section 6.

As discussed in Chapter 7, where interests in securities are delivered as collateral in one jurisdiction, the risk of adverse claims arising in the jurisdiction of the underlying securities may be difficult to exclude, in the absence of clear statutory provision such as that provided by Article 9(2) of the Settlement Finality Directive.[173]

Shorter settlement cycles[174]

In accordance with the norms of the London equity markets, settlement of equities within CREST is currently T+5 (although gilts in the CGO settle T+1). It is proposed to move to T+3 in 2001.[175] It is understood that the goal of T+1 in 2003 has been informally adopted. However, this is not a firm commitment, and is dependent on the success of the US securities markets in meeting their objective of T+1 in 2002. Achieving T+3 will involve an increase in automation of pre-settlement trade processing,[176] although it may be achievable before the implementation of the GSTPA initiative[177] for straight-through processing, discussed in Chapter 10; however this is likely to be a pre-condition for T+1.

9.100

---

[173] Sadly, this provision has been implemented in the United Kingdom too narrowly to benefit commercial collateral arrangements, as discussed in Chapter 7.

[174] See generally CREST *Newsletter* (March 2000) 9–10.

[175] 'In November 1999, the Bank of England, CRESTCo, the London Stock Exchange and the Association for Payment Clearing Services (APACS) jointly consulted on the proposal that a T+3 settlement standard for UK equities and corporate debt should be adopted with effect from February 2001 . . . a large majority of respondents were in favour of the move. It is therefore proposed to adopt a standard settlement cycle of T+3 in February 2001': CREST *Newsletter* (March 2000) 9.

[176] 'The following key issues were highlighted . . . the ability of all segments of the market to agree trade details in good time ahead of settlement date, particularly in situations where a chain of instructions is necessary, eg involving brokers, fund managers and custodians': CREST *Newsletter* (March 2000) 9.

[177] See CREST *Newsletter* (March 2000) 10.

10

GLOBAL CUSTODY, PRIME BROKERAGE AND STRAIGHT THROUGH PROCESSING

A. Global Custody

It will be seen from the foregoing that many inefficiencies remain in cross border settlement. The global custody industry has developed in order to relieve institutional investors from the burden of these inefficiencies. **10.01**

Global custody is of particular interest because of its fungible nature. It is customary for a custodian to commingle the (interests in) securities which it holds for its respective clients. Because each client's (interests in) securities are held on an intermediated and unallocated basis, global custody clients hold interests in securities and not securities. **10.02**

(1) The Service

Global custody is a service involving the safekeeping, administration and settlement of international portfolios of securities. It is associated with the rise of cross border institutional investment. **10.03**

As discussed in Chapter 6, many factors have contributed to the rise of cross border institutional investment in recent decades. Large international securities portfolios have accumulated in the hands of institutional investors such as pension funds, insurance companies and mutual funds. The settlement and administration **10.04** of international portfolios is a complex matter, particularly where a portfolio spans markets in different jurisdictions, in different time zones, with different currencies and settlement conventions; it also involves significant investment in electronic systems and links. It is therefore convenient for institutional investors to delegate such functions to banks acting as global custodians.[1]

10.05   Of course, banks have provided safekeeping services for their clients' securities for several centuries. However, global custody involving international settlement and administration is more recent. It evolved in the USA in the 1970s, and was introduced to London by US banks in the 1980s.

10.06   Many institutional investors engage fund managers to manage their portfolios on a professional basis.[2] Where fund managers have been appointed, it is customary for the custodian to be authorised to accept settlement instructions directly from the fund manager.[3] It is important for the global custodian to remember that it is receiving instructions from someone other than the beneficial owner of the custody portfolio. If the fund manager's settlement instructions cause loss to the client, the custodian needs to consider its potential liability.

10.07   The core custodial service involves settlement, safekeeping and administration. The global custodian receives its clients' settlement instructions, and delivers and receives cash and (interests in) securities in accordance with them. In most cases settlement takes place through electronic settlement systems in which title to (interests in) securities is recorded, but in which the client does not participate. Therefore, in order to provide the settlement service, the custodian must also provide a safekeeping service, in the sense that it holds or controls title to the client's assets. The custodian also administers the (interests in) securities in the client's portfolio, for example by managing cash flow through income collection and claiming tax credits where income is paid net of withholding tax and (in the case of equities) by voting and handling corporate matters on the client's behalf.

10.08   Many functions relating to foreign (interests in) securities and cash are more safely and conveniently done by participants in the local markets. For example, local banks may participate in local settlement systems, and are more conveniently able to deal with local issuers and tax authorities. Where the global custodian has branches in the jurisdictions in which the client has invested, it will act through them. Where it does not, it will appoint a local bank or other financial institution to act as its sub-custodian, and delegate these services to it. The leading global cus-

---

[1] Most global custodians are banks. There are a few non-bank custodians; they must employ a bank or other credit institution to hold client cash balances.

[2] See the discussion in Chapter 11.

[3] Normally, the fund manager is a party to the global custody agreement. It may enter into this agreement as agent of the client (the institutional investor), or there may be a tri-party agreement between the global custodian, fund manager and client.

todians have extensive networks of sub-custodians. Under normal arrangements, the client has no direct contractual or commercial relationship with the sub-custodian. The global custody agreement is entered into between the client and the global custodian as principals, and the sub-custody agreement is entered into between the global custodian and the sub-custodian as principals also.[4]

As was seen in the previous chapter, cross border securities settlement is being **10.09** enhanced through the development of links between different settlement systems, and improvements to the services offered by such systems. As cross-border securities settlement becomes more convenient, the need for some institutional investors to appoint a global custodian to undertake it may become less clear. In order to attract and retain clients, the recent emphasis in global custody has been on the provision of additional services, known as value-added services.

Because of competitive and regulatory pressures, it is crucial for fund managers to **10.10** receive prompt and transparent information on the performance of their portfolios. Consolidated reporting, so that data from all markets is presented in like form with multi-currency reporting valuation and portfolio analysis, is an important part of the global custodial service. Indeed, global custody has sometimes been described as an information service.

Global custodians also offer a range of financial services to complement the core **10.11** global custody function. These include cash management, whereby surplus cash balances are swept into income-generating accounts. Global custodians also offer foreign exchange (so that, for example, the sterling proceeds of the sale of UK equities can be converted into US dollars to fund the purchase of US treasury bills) and credit services, to fund the intra day cash shortfalls that are common in international securities settlement. These may be formal overdrafts or informal lending in the form of contractual settlement, which is described below. Where settlement inefficiencies give rise to shortfalls in (interests in) securities, the global custodian may help the client to meet these through stocklending services, either as agent of the client or as principal counterparty. It may also help the client increase portfolio returns by delivering (interests in) securities out under securities lending and repo programmes, again either as agent or principal.

These value-added services generate considerable profits for the global custodian. **10.12** Because of the equitable rule against secret profits by fiduciaries, the ability of the

---

[4] In exceptional cases, the global custodian may agree to appoint the sub-custodian as agent of the client, in order to confer on the client direct rights of action against the sub-custodian in the event that the sub-custodian's default causes loss to the client. As discussed below, it is not normal for the global custodian to accept strict liability for such defaults, and the agency arrangement may serve to address the client's concerns. However, global custodians are not normally willing to confer a direct relationship on the client with the sub-custodian, because of the risk that the client might form its own commercial relationship with the sub-custodian, by-passing the global custodian.

global custodian lawfully to retain such profits depends on their disclosure to the client.

(2) Legal Status of the Custodian

10.13 For the purposes of this discussion, it is assumed that the global custodian operates in London, and that the global custody agreement is governed by English law.

10.14 'Global custody' (and indeed 'custody') are commercial and not legal terms. To call someone a global custodian does not of itself denote the nature of the legal relationship between the client and the custodian in respect of the custody assets. A key point is that this relationship has two different parts. The status of the global custodian in relation to cash is different from its status in relation to (interests in) securities.

Cash accounts

10.15 Cash accounts are always associated with the custody of (interests in) securities. The global custodian receives cash in the form of income from (interests in) securities, and the proceeds of their sale and, when its clients buy (interests in) securities, it must pay out the purchase price on their behalf. Most global custodians are banks, and there is long-standing authority that, under normal arrangements, the positive balance on a bank account represents the debt of the bank to the depositor.[5] The bank does not act as trustee, and is free to use money deposited with it as part of its working capital.[6] Thus, if the custodian bank becomes insolvent, the client will be an unsecured creditor and may lose its cash (except to the extent that deposit protection insurance may be available).

10.16 In 1995 Barings Brothers & Co Ltd went into administration. In the event, it was rescued by ING Bank, but prior to the rescue it was widely expected to go into insolvent liquidation. Barings was a global custodian, and held considerable sums of cash on deposit for custody clients including pension funds. Because this cash would have been lost in Baring's insolvency, the episode served to focus attention on the credit risk of institutional investors to their global custodians.

10.17 In the wake of Barings, global custodians and their clients considered techniques for addressing this risk. Some clients asked their custodian banks to hold their cash balances on trust. This raised a problem which is best illustrated by example. If a bank acting as global custodian maintains a sterling cash account for a client with a balance of £100,000, this account records the debt of the global custodian

---

[5] See *Carr v Carr* (1811) 1 Mer 625, *Foley v Hill* (1848) 2 HL Cas 28, *South Australian Insurance Co v Randell* [1869] 16 ER 775, *Joachimson v Swiss Bank Corporation* [1921] 3 KB 110, *Space Investments Ltd v Canadian Imperial Bank of Commerce Trust Co (Bahamas) Ltd* [1986] 3 All ER 75.

[6] This principle is carefully upheld in commercial law; without it, banking business and therefore capitalism would be impossible.

to the client of £100,000. Assuming (for the sake of simplicity) that the global custodian is a clearing bank, its sterling assets will comprise a positive balance in an account in its name maintained by the Bank of England.[7] The balance of this account is £1 million. As discussed in Chapter 2, the traditional rule is that a trust requires certainty of subject matter. If the global custodian is to declare a trust over £100,000, the question arises which £100,000 comprises the trust asset in the hands of the global custodian trustee. The balance of the account maintained by the global custodian cannot be the trust asset, because this account records the liability of the global custodian, and not its asset. The sterling assets of the global custodian are recorded in the account maintained by the Bank of England account. Which £100,000 within that larger pool of £1 million is subject to the trust? Although (as discussed in Chapter 2) the case of *Hunter v Moss* held that the requirement of certainty of subject matter does not apply to trusts of intangibles such as shares, most lawyers practising in London would hesitate to advise that this principle extends to trusts of cash. This is because of the long line of conflicting authority that purported trusts over unsegregated cash balances fail for want of certainty of subject matter.[8]

The Bank of England will not permit the global custodian to open a sub-account on the Bank's books, and it is therefore not straightforward to overcome this problem. One option is for the global custodian to deposit £100,000 with another bank (B), and declare a trust over the debt of B to the global custodian in favour of the client. However, this will be operationally inefficient. The global custodian will be reluctant to place money with a rival bank, and the client will find that, even though its money will be safe in the insolvency of the global custodian, it will be lost in the insolvency of B. Because money in the financial markets is credit institution debt, the client cannot remove credit risk from its cash balances. It can only move credit risk from bank to bank, for example from the custodian to B, or to a number of different banks. **10.18**

An option developed in the USA in the 1970s and introduced to London around the time of Barings, is to invest surplus cash balances in 'near-cash'. Near cash means short term and highly liquid money market instruments such as certificates of deposit. These can be sold so readily that they are almost economically akin to cash. Because the client owns the CDs in the hands of the custodian, it does not bear the custodian's credit risk. (Of course, it does bear the credit risk of the issuer of the CDs, but issuer credit risk may be managed by investing in a mixed CD portfolio.) **10.19**

---

[7] A non-clearing bank would have an account with a clearing bank, which in turn would have an account with the Bank of England.

[8] See *Mac-Jordan Construction v Brookmount Erostin* [1992] BCLC 350 and the other cases discussed in Chapter 2.

Securities accounts

10.20 The position for securities accounts is different. The commercial expectation of the parties is that the (interests in) securities credited to the securities accounts maintained by the global custodian in the name of the client should not be at risk in the insolvency of the global custodian, and that these assets should be beneficially owned by the client and appear on its balance sheet.

10.21 As discussed in Chapter 2, the traditional legal characterisation of the custody relationship in relation to securities was bailment. The custodian took possession of its clients' documents of title as bailee. However, bailment relates to the physical possession of tangible goods and as the securities markets became increasingly computerised, the characteristic subject matter of global custody is not tangible paper but electronic records. This renders the concept of bailment unavailable, and the author has argued therefore that the global custodian is a trustee.[9]

10.22 (Interests in) securities are generally held by the global custodian for clients on a commingled and fungible basis. As discussed in Chapter 2, there is now a large measure of comfort among the London legal community that fungible custody presents no obstacle to the formation of a valid trust in favour of the client under English law.[10]

(3) Risk for the Client

10.23 The client entrusts portfolios of enormous value to the global custodian and is therefore clearly at risk if the custodian defaults. The risk analysis differs in relation to cash and securities respectively.

Cash

10.24 The global custody client is an unsecured creditor of the global custodian in relation to positive cash balances, and may therefore lose its money in the insolvency of the global custodian. The credit rating of the global custodian is therefore important, as is cash management. After the Barings crisis, as indicated above, many custodian clients have called for cash management techniques that sweep surplus cash balances into near cash investments.

10.25 However, the client does not bear the credit risk of the global custodian's foreign correspondent bank. Where the cash balance in the books of the global custodian is denominated in a foreign currency, the global custodian may maintain a corre-

---

[9] Anecdotally, when Barings went into administration, the administrators called up custody clients to reassure them that the bank held their securities as trustee.

[10] This is on the basis that all clients in the fungible account co-own the securities credited to it, or alternatively on the basis of the principle in *Hunter v Moss*, that the requirement for certainty of subject matter does not apply to intangibles. Careful drafting is advisable.

sponding balance in that currency with its correspondent bank in the relevant jurisdiction. Thus, the debt of the global custodian to pay the client US dollars, for example, is matched by the debt of the correspondent bank to pay US dollars to the global custodian. Under standard custody documentation, the debt of the global custodian is not affected by the default of the correspondent. Therefore the custodian bears the credit risk of the correspondent. In theory this risk could be addressed by 'limited recourse' wording in the global custody agreement, so that the custodian is relieved of its obligation to pay the client if the sub-custodian defaults. However, in practice this is unlikely to be commercially acceptable.

(Interests in) securities

The risks for the client differ in relation to (interests in) securities. **10.26**

Insolvency of global custodian

Under English law, trust assets are not available to the creditors of a trustee in its **10.27** insolvency. It was seen that the natural characterisation of the global custody relationship in relation to (interests in) securities is as a trust. Provided that there is a valid trust, the custody (interests in) securities held by the global custodian are not at risk in its insolvency. (Of course, the position may differ where the custody relationship is not governed under English law.)[11]

However, the presence of a valid trust does not necessarily prevent a shortfall from **10.28** arising. The interests of the client in the (interests in) securities is represented by the credit entry in a securities account in favour of the client maintained in the books of the global custodian ('client balances'). The asset to which this credit relates will usually be a credit balance in favour of the global custodian in the books of a sub-custodian, settlement system, depositary or nominee ('third party balance'). This is likely to be an omnibus account to which the entitlements of all custody clients having positions in the relevant (interests in) securities are credited. A danger for clients is that there may be a shortfall, in the sense that the third party balance falls short of the aggregate of the client balances. There are a range of reasons why such a shortfall may arise, including error, bad deliveries, the enforcement of security interests by the operators of settlement systems and custodian fraud.[12]

The question arises how such a shortfall would be borne among the different **10.29** clients. The rules of English law for attributing a loss as between different beneficiaries is discussed in relation to depositary receipts in Chapter 11; that discussion concludes that the better view is that losses will be borne rateably by all clients. The rules of settlement systems such as Euroclear provide for such pro ration.

---

[11] See Chapter 2.
[12] See Chapters 3 and 8.

Such loss-sharing wording is not customary in English law custody agreements, but UK regulated custodians are required to warn their clients that the effect of commingled custody accounts is that shortfalls will be borne rateably. The overall result of this is that with fungible custody, shortfalls attributable to the business of one client may cause loss to other clients participating in the pooled account.

10.30 Regular reconciliations between the custodian's records and those of sub-custodians serve to reduce the risk of shortfalls.

Default of solvent custodian

10.31 If the act or default of a solvent global custodian causes loss to the client, the client may be able to make good its loss by suing the global custodian. However, the liability of the global custodian is not strict. In general terms, in order successfully to sue, the client must show not only that it has suffered loss, but also that either the global custodian was in breach of its duties and that that breach caused the loss, or that the global custodian has been unjustly enriched.[13] Very broadly speaking, in the absence of fraud there are three types of breach of duty that the client might assert, namely breach of contract, tort (and in particular, negligence) and breach of fiduciary duty.

10.32 The global custody contract will characteristically specify the service that the global custodian will offer (with operational details being given in a service schedule) and also the level of care that the global custodian will take in delivering this service (duty defining clauses).[14] A very brief discussion of the duty of securities intermediaries as fiduciaries is given in Chapter 2. UK regulated custodians are required to accept liability for their own negligence and that of their nominees.

10.33 In practice, global custodians often compensate clients for losses caused by their own defaults, even where they are not under a legal duty to do so, in order to preserve their client relationship and professional reputation.

Default of delegate

10.34 In many cases, client loss will be caused not by the default of the global custodian, but by that of the sub-custodian. This risk of sub-custodian default may be higher where the client invests in emerging jurisdictions, where the infrastructure may be underdeveloped and market and regulatory standards may be lower than those in London. It may be difficult for the client to sue the sub-custodian directly, because it has no direct relationship with it.

10.35 The ability of the client to sue the global custodian in relation to sub-custodian default is one of the most intensely negotiated issues in the global custody indus-

---

[13] This is the basis for an action in restitution. This is a developing branch of English law.
[14] For example, it will take reasonable care, or the same level of care as it would take in relation to its own investments.

try. The regulatory regime offers no guidance on the point, merely providing that the question must be addressed in the global custody agreement. The general law is fairly generous to the global custodian. Under the Trustee Bill 2000, clause 23 in effect relieves the custodian from liability for the acts or defaults of the sub-custodian provided the custodian complied with its duty of care in appointing the sub-custodian and keeping the sub-custodial arrangements under review; very broadly, its duty of care is to exercise reasonable care and skill having regard to any special knowledge or experience that it is reasonable to expect a professional custodian to have, and which it holds itself out as having.[15]

There are arguments against the global custodian agreeing to assume a higher level **10.36** of liability. Strict liability for sub-custodian default might be construed as a guarantee, triggering a very significant regulatory capital requirement. The custodian may not be capitalised for such liabilities, and in any case the global custody service is not priced to reflect such a capital burden. A related point involves systemic risk. If the London global custodian assumes strict liability to the client for sub-custodian default, and if a sub-custodian fails to segregate a custody holding having a value of £1 billion, and becomes absolutely insolvent so that the holding is lost,[16] then the global custodian will owe the client £1 billion. This may make the global custodian insolvent. The bank which acts as global custodian to clients in London is likely also to act as sub-custodian to New York global custodians. If a New York global custodian has assumed strict liability to its clients for sub-custodian default, and if the insolvency of the London custodian involves loss to its client's portfolio, the New York bank may then incur a significant exposure, that may put it into insolvency. The credit exposure may extend to foreign global custodians for whom the New York bank acts as sub-custodian. Global custody networks link the major banks in the world's financial centres, and in this way strict liability for sub-custodian default may involve an unacceptable level of systemic risk.

(4) Risk for the Global Custodian

The provision of global custodial services involves a number of risks for the **10.37** global custodian. It was seen above that, in some circumstances, it may incur liability for the defaults of sub-custodians, and that it bears the credit risk of cash

---

[15] Trustee Bill 2000, clause 1, Sch 1, para 3(1)(b). Global custodians' promotional literature and any comments by account officers to clients about the custodian's local expertise should be reviewed in this connection. However, note that under clauses 20(2) and 20(3), a client which is itself a trustee may not permit the custodian contractually to limit its liability 'unless it is reasonably necessary'. Of course, on the basis that the custodian is itself a trustee, this restriction will apply to its appointment of the sub-custodian, if it relies on the power under the Act to appoint sub-custodians. However, it is most likely that the custodian would rely on its express powers of sub-delegation and not on the Act.

[16] This is on the basis that the custodian must prove as a general creditor, and as such receives no dividend because all the assets of the insolvent are taken by preferential and secured creditors.

correspondents. A further potential exposure for the global custodian is the fact that in many cases it will take instructions from the fund manager, and not from the beneficial owner of the custody portfolio. Following the Maxwell scandal, a bank operating in London was sued as custodian of the pension fund for implementing the fraudulent instructions of the fund managers, in circumstances where it would have been a breach of contract to omit to do so; this action was settled.

10.38 However, perhaps the most significant exposure of the global custodian is credit exposure to its custody clients. As a participant in settlement systems, the global custodian will incur significant potential liabilities to the operators of the systems and/or settlement banks in respect of liquidity and credit problems associated with their clients' business. It was seen above that, in the absence of model 1 DVP, significant intra day credit exposures may arise in the course of securities settlement.

10.39 Custodians' credit exposures to clients may be increased by the provision of 'contractual settlement'. Contractual settlement is a service offered by custodians to assist clients in overcoming the disadvantages of late payment and settlement. In many cases, cash payments (such as dividends and proceeds of sale) and deliveries of (interests in) securities are not made to the client on the date agreed by the payor or deliveror under the contractual arrangements pursuant to which the payment or delivery is made ('the contractual date'). With contractual settlement, the custodian agrees to credit the account of the client with cash or (less commonly) (interests in) securities at the contractual date, whether or not the custodian has itself received value at that date. If the payment or delivery is made late, the custodian lends the cash or (interests in) securities to the client until that time. The custodian reserves the right to reverse the credit if the payment or delivery is not made within a reasonable period.

10.40 It is customary for global custodians to seek to collateralise these credit exposures with the custody assets. Thus, standard global custody agreements confer on the global custodian a right of set off in respect of cash balances, and a security interest over the portfolio of (interests in) securities which it holds for the client. As discussed in Chapter 6, insolvency set off is mandatory under English law within the scope of rule 4.90 of the Insolvency Rules 1986.[17]

10.41 The effectiveness of custodians' security interests has generated a debate in London. In many cases, the security interest is described in the global custody contract as a lien, to which a contractual power of sale is added. As discussed in

---

[17] The requirement for mutuality must be considered in relation to clients acting as agent or trustee. With clients whose insolvency would not be governed by English law, the availability of insolvency set off under the law that would govern their insolvency must be considered. See Chapter 6.

Chapter 5, a lien is (broadly speaking) a right to retain possession of assets by way of security, and does not generally confer a power of sale. (Although exceptionally a banker's lien does confer a power of sale, it appears that a banker's lien only arises in relation to securities held by a bank *as banker*, eg to present for payment, and does not extend to securities held by a bank as custodian.)[18] As discussed in Chapter 5, the question arises whether a purported lien with a power of sale would be recharacterised as a charge, which in turn might be avoided as a floating charge, void for want of registration. As discussed in Chapter 5, it would be prudent to assume that a security interest over intangibles which confers a power of sale may be characterised as a charge.[19] Because the client is able at any time to give settlement instructions removing assets from the scope of the security interest, it would be prudent to assume that the security interest may be registrable as a floating charge, if given by an English company. It is not customary for custodians in London to register charges. Where a custodian is particularly concerned about its credit exposures, different options are available, including restricting the client's ability to remove (interests in) securities from the portfolio (so as to characterise the security interest as a non-registrable fixed charge) or even outright transfer arrangements in favour of the custodian.

Another potential challenge to the custodian's security interest arises under the lex **10.42** situs rule, which was discussed in Chapter 7. It might be argued that a charge over that part of the portfolio that consists, for example, of interests in shares held by a sub-custodian in Transylvania, requires to be perfected under Transylvanian law. Of course, it would be impracticable for global custodians to seek to perfect their security interests under the law of the underlying jurisdictions. The counter argument is that the charged assets do not consist of Translyvanian shares, but English interests in such shares. This argument was developed in Chapter 7.

There has been some discussion in the London legal community of the question **10.43** whether a charge by a client in favour of its global custodian involves a merger of interests. A charge of personal property takes effect in equity. On the basis that the global custodian is a trustee, the client's interests in securities is an equitable interest. The question therefore arises, is it possible for a beneficiary to grant an effective charge of its trust interest to the trustee? Because the beneficiary's interest arises under a trust, it might be argued that this is a form of charge back, and that it cannot take effect because it would involve a merger of interests, under the principle in *Charge Card*. However, as discussed in Chapter 5, the decision in *BCCI (No 8)* has overruled *Charge Card*, holding charge backs to be effective. In any

---

[18] See Chapter 5.
[19] The case of *Re Hamlet International plc (in administration)* [1998] 2 BCLC 1, on appeal as *Trident International Ltd v Barlow* [1999] BCLC 506 (which held that a lien with power of sale over tangible goods was recharacterisable as a registrable charge) should be considered to apply only to intangibles, as discussed in Chapter 5.

case, equity is a robust and flexible branch of law, which looks to the substance of transactions and not their form. Provided there was a clear commercial intention to use the portfolio as collateral, the courts may be relied on to give effect to this intention, whether by way of a charge, a right of set off or a trustee's right of indemnity.[20]

10.44 Clause 31 of the Trustee Bill 2000 confers on trustees a right of reimbursement out of the trust fund for expenses properly incurred when acting on behalf of the trust. Provided there is clear and express authority under the custody agreement for the custodian to incur a particular credit exposure on the client's behalf, the custodian should be entitled to be repaid in respect of it out of the custody portfolio even in the absence of a valid security interest, under its statutory right of reimbursement.

(5) Conclusions

10.45 Global custody and electronic securities settlement have developed in order to facilitate cross border delivery. In both, the assets of clients are held on an intermediated and commingled basis. This book has argued that the assets of clients therefore comprise interests in securities and not securities. The asset of the client is proprietary in the sense that it is ring-fenced in the insolvency of the intermediary which maintains the accounts in which the client's assets are recorded; however the client's assets are intangible and unallocated, and confers no direct right of action against the issuer of the underlying securities in the ordinary course.

10.46 As discussed in Chapter 2, the general effect of this is that the asset of the client is intangible; even where the underlying securities are in bearer form, the interests of clients to not attach to them. The legal significance of this is tremendous, both in domestic and private international law. In domestic law, possession-based concepts drop away, and alternatives must be found. As illustrated by the proposed merger of the CMO and CREST, negotiable status does not survive transition, and security of transfer must be reappraised. The status of the custodian can no longer be that of bailee, and becomes that of trustee, so that implied levels of fiduciary duty may require contractual modification. Informal security interests are likely to take effect as charges, raising questions of registration.

10.47 As links are developed between national settlement systems, (interests in) securities issued in one jurisdiction may be recorded and transferred not only in the domestic settlement system but also foreign settlement systems. The proliferation of 'entry points' into international securities settlement begs the question of where these assets are legally located. As discussed in Chapter 7, determining the legal location of interests in securities is necessary in order to establish effective collat-

---

[20] The author is grateful to Professor David Hayton for clarifying this point.

eral arrangements, and thus the need for clarity on this issue is crucial to risk management in the financial markets.

For all these reasons, recent developments in the settlement and custody industries have proved a fertile source of creative development in domestic and international financial law. **10.48**

B. Prime Brokerage[21]

This section will consider the complex proprietary arrangements that arise when the assets of hedge funds are held under prime brokerage arrangements. **10.49**

(1) Hedge Funds and Gearing

Managed funds are discussed in Chapter 12. The term 'hedge fund' is applied to **10.50**
certain unregulated managed funds. Hedge funds seek to offer a high return to participants by a range of mathematically complex investment techniques, with a view to achieving profits in falling as well as rising markets. Hedge funds are heavily geared. Gearing means borrowing. By adding large sums of borrowed cash to participants' investments in the fund, the market exposure of the fund is greatly increased. This in turn greatly increases both the fund's potential profits when its investment strategy is successful, and its potential losses when its strategy is unsuccessful (as became plain in 1998, when Long Term Capital Management failed).[22]

(2) Prime Brokerage

In common with all types of managed funds, hedge funds rely on third parties for **10.51**
brokerage and custodial services. In the case of hedge funds, these needs together with their need for gearing are met by prime brokers. These are banks entering into a complex package of services and reciprocal rights known as prime brokerage. A typical prime brokerage service might be as follows. The hedge fund (through its manager) identifies (interests in) securities ('the assets') which it wishes to purchase. In order to fund the purchase, (i)[23] the prime broker lends the purchase price to the hedge fund.[24] (ii) The prime broker purchases the assets on

---

[21] See generally, M Taylor, 'Hedge Fund Regulation' JIBFL (May 1999); Report of the President's Working Group on the Financial Markets, *Hedge Funds, Leverage and the Lesson of Long Term Capital Management* (April 1999); Warren Holmes, *Starting a Hedge Fund: A European Perspective* (ISI Publications, August 1999).

[22] The risk of failure is increased by the fact that hedge funds are typically thinly capitalised as well as highly geared.

[23] Numbering has been adopted in order to assist the reader.

[24] These arrangements are known as margin trading. The ability of regulated firms to lend cash to their clients in order to fund their deals is restricted in some markets, because of the credit risks involved.

behalf of the hedge fund as broker. As the hedge fund's custodian, the prime broker (iii) settles the purchase by paying the purchase price to the vendor and receiving the assets, (iv) which it holds and administers[25] as global custodian for the hedge fund.[26] (v) The prime broker collateralises the debt of the hedge fund to it in respect of the purchase price by taking a security interest over the assets. (vi) In order to increase the hedge fund's gearing by enabling it to service the largest possible debt, the prime broker agrees to charge a rate of interest below commercial rates. As a quid pro quo for the low rate of interest, (vii) the hedge fund agrees that the prime broker may deliver the assets to third parties under repo, securities lending and other arrangements as part of the prime broker's business, retaining any profits for itself ('onward dealing').[27]

10.52   The above may represent a simplification of the arrangements entered into by the prime broker, who may also provide derivatives and foreign exchange services.[28] Also, the prime broker may enable the hedge fund to access the repo securities lending markets by entering into back to back transaction with the hedge fund and a market intermediary respectively.[29] The highly profitable (and risky) levels of gearing and therefore of market exposure achieved by hedge funds would not be possible without prime brokerage, which enables the hedge fund to raise enormous sums of money very cheaply. However, the commercial risks involved for prime brokers, particularly in adverse market conditions when collateral shortfalls may arise, are significant.

10.53   A number of legal issues also arise for the prime broker. The following discussion is of the position under English law, which is relevant for London prime brokers.

(3) Floating Charge

10.54   The portfolio of the hedge fund in the hands of the prime broker is subject to onward dealing. Accordingly, at any time, particular (interests in) securities might be removed from the portfolio under a repo transaction between the prime broker and a third party, and replaced at the end of that transaction by equivalent (interests in) securities. The portfolio will also be actively traded by the hedge fund's

---

[25] Administration includes the normal custody services of receiving dividends, tax reclamations and handling corporate actions.

[26] In some cases, the hedge fund wishes to use a separate entity as its custodian, in which case the prime broker will act as sub-custodian

[27] On the basis that the prime broker may be a fiduciary, the conflicts of interest involved in these arrangements call for very careful drafting in the prime brokerage agreement.

[28] In these cases, the assets (which serve as margin collateral for the hedge fund's margin trading) are pooled by the prime broker with collateral received from the hedge fund in respect of foreign exchange and derivatives transactions.

[29] 'a loan for which the ultimate borrower is a hedge fund client of an investment bank's prime brokerage business might involve three stock loan transactions within the CREST system [institutional lender to market intermediary; market intermediary to investment bank; investment bank to prime broker]': CREST *Newsletter* (March 2000) 14, 15.

manager.[30] Therefore the prime broker's collateral comprises a changing pool of assets. The question therefore arises whether the security interest in favour of the prime broker is a floating charge. The prime broker would naturally wish to avoid this conclusion, because of the weaknesses associated with floating charges, discussed in Chapter 5.

As indicated in that chapter, a security interest over a changing pool of assets does **10.55** not necessarily constitute a floating charge.[31] The judgement in *Re Cosslett*[32] illustrates that the test of a floating charge is that the collateral giver retains control or freedom to deal in the collateral assets. On this basis, the fact that the collateral assets change from time to time under onward dealing raises no risk of reacharacterisation as a floating charge, because onward dealing takes place at the instigation of the prime broker, and is beyond the control of the hedge fund and its manager.

The question then arises whether the ability of the hedge fund manager to con- **10.56** tinue to manage the portfolio raises such recharacterisation risk. It should not be present provided the documentation and systems supporting the prime brokerage operation give the prime broker the ability to refuse to settle a transaction which would remove assets from the collateral pool. It is understood that this will generally be the case.[33]

(4) Rehypothecation

Rehypothecation was discussed in Chapter 5. As discussed in that chapter, **10.57** English law restricts the ability of a person who has received assets as collateral under a security interest to rehypothecate, or to dispose of those assets to a third party in circumstances where the collateral giver has not defaulted. While a number of techniques have been considered by the London markets with a view to overcoming the restriction of rehypothecation, Chapter 5 concluded that these may not be reliable.

Therefore, where the prime broker holds a security interest in the assets of **10.58** the hedge fund, it would be prudent to assume that the prime broker cannot

---

[30] It is a feature of prime brokerage that the collateral giver continues actively to manage the collateral pool.

[31] It would be possible to create a fixed charge, or a series of fixed charges, over a changing pool of assets, provided the collateral giver was not able to remove assets from the collateral pool without the consent of the collateral taker.

[32] [1997] 4 All ER 115.

[33] Typical documentation specifies a margin by which the value of the collateral portfolio should exceed the value of the debt, and provides that the prime broker is not required to implement a trade if its effect would be to reduce the value of the collateral portfolio below the agreed margin. Since the prime broker is responsible for settlement, it should have the ability to block the settlement of trades in these circumstances. It might be argued that, by implementing a trade, the prime broker expresses its consent to the release of collateral assets. However, it is important to ensure that the practical arrangements support this argument. In particular, it is important to ensure that this ability is not compromised by straight through processing arrangements, discussed below.

rehypothecate without breach of the restrictions on rehypothecation. The important question is whether such a breach would affect the validity of the prime broker's interest in the collateral in the event of the hedge fund's insolvency. As discussed in Chapter 5, the consequences of such breach is that contractual provision permitting rehypothecation is not effective. This might mean that, notwithstanding the terms in the prime brokerage agreement permitting rehypothecation, collateral assets held by the prime broker are so held subject to the hedge fund's equity of redemption. Of course, the equity of redemption is the right of the collateral giver to the return of the collateral assets *upon the discharge of the secured obligation.* Clearly, if the collateral giver defaults, the equity of redemption does not prevent the collateral giver from enforcing its security interest, because in those circumstances the preconditions for the exercise of the equity of redemption have not been satisfied. Thus, rehypothecation should not weaken the position of the prime broker in the default of the hedge fund.

10.59 However, rehypothecation may pose problems for the hedge fund in the event that the prime broker becomes insolvent at a time when collateral assets have been rehypothecated under onward dealing arrangements. If such arrangements are incompatible with the status of the collateral arrangement as a security interest, one possibility is that courts would recharacterise the collateral arrangement as an outright transfer. Under outright transfers, as discussed in Chapter 6, the collateral giver bears the credit risk of the collateral taker to the extent that the value of the collateral exceeds the value of the collateralised debt. In other words, the hedge fund would lose the net value of its portfolio in the insolvency of the prime broker.

C. Straight Through Processing

10.60 For a number of years, straight through processing (STP) has generated a considerable debate in the financial sector, and in particular in the securities industry. [34] Various initiatives in the securities, derivatives and cash markets share the objective of increasing automation in the processing of transactions, with a view to reducing costs, errors and delays. [35] While the operational and business aspects of

---

[34] Important background papers calling for STP include *A New Processing Model for Cross-Border Transactions* (International Depository & Clearing, September 1997) and *The Tower Report*, prepared by a US-based group, calling for STP in 1996.

[35] Important initiatives include the following. In 1991 the Institutional Users Group (IUG) was formed to automate trade confirmations. It merged in 1996 with the Industry Standardisation for Institutional Trade Communications Committee (ISITC). ISITC began in 1991, when some 25 fund managers, custodians and information vendors formed a group to discuss developing standard automated methods for communicating trade instructions between investment managers and custodians. Financial Information eXchange (FIX) is a communications protocol or language providing a standard format for the electronic exchange of pre-trade information between brokers and

STP are the subject of much effort and discussion, the legal implications of processing financial transactions 'straight through' have received relatively little attention, at least in the public domain. This discussion will flag some of the legal implications of STP. While the law is only a small part of the picture, an early consideration of these issues will help to ensure that the STP models that eventually emerge are built on solid legal foundations.

(1) Intermediation

A theme of this book is the intermediation of the financial markets. The heavily intermediated nature of the contemporary securities, cash and derivatives markets arises for a number of reasons. As discussed in Chapter 1, an important reason is that access to large value delivery systems is limited to a small number of large institutions (such as investment banks participating in Euroclear, commercial banks participating in TARGET or clearing brokers participating in the London Clearing House). Medium-sized institutions wishing to participate in these markets must instruct such large institutions to act on their behalf. Small institutions in turn instruct medium-sized institutions, and retail clients instruct small institutions. Thus, chains of intermediaries arise. **10.61**

In the managed funds industry, the chain of intermediaries is lengthened further by the involvement of brokers and fund managers, as discussed in Chapter 12. The potential benefits of STP are particularly clear in this industry, because of the large number of different operational stages entailed in the formation, execution and settlement of securities trades. Trade details (such as the identities of the parties, the number and type of securities, the trade and delivery dates and the consideration) must be transmitted between brokers, fund managers, global custodians, sub-custodians and settlement systems. **10.62**

In the absence of STP, such details have to be recorded afresh at each stage in the processing of the transaction. For example a broker may communicate its bids and offers to a fund manager by fax, and an agreement for a block trade between the broker and fund manager may be concluded by telephone. Then the fund manager may make a telephone call to the broker indicating how the block trade is to be allocated among its various clients. Trade confirmation may well be automated, but regulatory trade reporting may not be. The broker may then send a **10.63**

---

institutional investors. FIX originated from a 1992 project between Fidelity Investments and Salomon Brothers to link their trading systems. The Global Straight Through Processing Association (GSTPA) originates from SWIFT's annual conference, SIBOS, in 1997. Here ISITC and FIX hosted a joint meeting at which the new project was proposed, whereby brokers, fund managers and custodians should share a common transaction record as a platform for T+1. Commercial vendors such as SWIFT and Thompsons as vendors are also involved in developing STP applications.

telex or SWIFT message to the lead custodian giving settlement instructions.[36] If settlement involves a sub-custodian, the global custodian may send a fax to it in respect of the same trade. If settlement involves a settlement system, the global custodian or sub-custodian will need to instruct that system, possibly electronically. Clearly, these cumbersome arrangements involve delay, and also the potential for error, as the same trade details are recorded again and again.

(2) Automation

10.64 The simple idea behind STP is to reduce costs, delays and error by eliminating the repetition of data input. STP involves the communication of transaction data by an intermediary in a format that can be automatically transmitted on to other involved parties, so that rekeying of the data is not necessary.[37]

10.65 Within the finance sector, STP initiatives are perhaps the most advanced in the securities markets.[38] 'We have defined Straight-Through-Processing (STP) as an uninterrupted transmission from the point of trading in one country, through a chain of intermediaries (possibly in several other countries), down to the last entity ultimately involved in the settlement process.'[39] Much of this work is driven by brokers and custodians, in liaison with fund managers and others engaged in securities dealing and settlement. FIX[40] and GSTPA[41] represent major industry-

---

[36] It is understood that in the past, the traditional approach was for the fund manager to give two instructions in relation to each trade, one to the broker and one (the 'Y' copy) to the custodian. Now in practice the instruction goes from the manager to the broker; the broker executes the trade and routes the instruction to the custodian for settlement; the custodian then routes the instruction to the sub-custodian.

[37] 'A significant trend in the industry is a move towards "straight-through processing", or the complete automation of trade processing, from pre-trade indications through post trade processing and on to settlement. A major step towards achieving straight-through processing will be the seamless integration of many different post-trade processes, including allocation, trade comparison, and clearance and settlement. The widespread adoption of the FIX protocol is an important step towards achieving such integration': SEC Report to Congress, *The Impact of Recent Technological Advances on the Securities Markets* (1998) 52.

[38] Currently, custodians' links with settlement systems are largely automated in the United Kingdom. Custodians' communications with the fund managers and brokers involve standard settlement instructions, using SWIFT in many cases.

[39] D Gilks, *The Role of ISITC in Developing Straight Through Processing* (London, Financial Publications International, 1998) 33.

[40] Fund managers prefer passively to receive potential bids and offers, since if they initiated a request for a trade, thereby either indicating a long or a short position, the brokerage community might use this information against them to raise or lower prices as appropriate. Accordingly brokers contact fund managers with indications of interest or IOIs; these are lists of potential bids and offers. IOIs do not amount to contractual offers, but are rather invitations to treat. In the past IOIs were communicated by telephone and fax. The increasing practice is to communicate IOIs electronically.

A group of brokers and fund managers in New York piloted the use of FIX. (Salomans and Fidelity originally developed FIX in 1994; other brokers and fund managers are now participating in the arrangement.) The FIX protocol is a standard format (not a software) for the electronic communication of potential bids and offers. FIX provides a platform from which vendors can develop software applications. Brokers and fund managers wishing to participate may either develop their own software using the FIX format, or may buy such software from specialist vendors. More

based initiatives for automation in the front and middle offices respectively in the wholesale securities markets.[42] In tandem with this, individual institutions are actively collaborating with a number of vendors (including SWIFT and Thompsons) in developing their own in-house STP programmes.

There is no doubt that the simple idea behind STP is a good one. Many feel that **10.66** its implementation is long overdue. However, full STP will involve the industry-wide adoption on a global basis of common message standards. The operational and policy challenge of achieving such harmonisation should not be underestimated. But, just as the Victorians eventually agreed to build railway tracks with a standard gauge, so the securities industry will undoubtedly rise to this challenge.

A number of important legal issues arise in relation to STP. Some, such as finan- **10.67** cial services regulation,[43] data protection and the electronic formation of contracts[44] in domestic and private international law, are beyond the scope of this

recently the use of FIX has been promoted in London. FIX currently relates to the wholesale markets; it may in due course be extended to the retail shares and authorised funds sectors.

[41] The Global Straight Through Processing Association (GSTPA) is an association of brokers, custodians and fund managers having the objective of developing a system to automate the post-trade and pre-settlement processing of cross border securities transactions. The initiative relates to all cash securities (ie not derivatives), including equities, bonds, GDRs and ADRs, and relates to the middle office. Accordingly, confirmations, matching and allocation will be handled, and possibly regulatory transaction reporting. The proposed system will not be an exchange or a settlement system, and will involve neither the formation of the dealing contracts (subject to the comments on agency and allocation, below) nor the delivery of cash or securities.

It is proposed to operate on the basis of a central Transaction Flow Monitor (TFM) to which all participants would be linked electronically. The TFM is a central record of the progress of the transaction. It is proposed that the TFM would act as an intelligent router which, based on the content of the trade, would determine the timing, nature and sequence of operations that need to be performed. The transaction record would be progressively enriched during the progress of the transaction.

[42] Two different models of STP are emerging in the securities markets. In the first, each party in the chain automatically transmits the original message (with or without their own additions) on to the next party in the chain, so that the same parcel of data is passed from hand to hand ('onward transmission STP'). FIX is an example of onward transmission STP. Alternatively, rekeying might be avoided by creating a central record, to which all parties involved in a trade can refer, and in which the progress of the trade is recorded ('central record STP'). GSTPA is an example of central record STP. In either case, the parties may enrich the record (for example, the fund manager adding allocation details and the custodian adding settlement details). However, once recorded, data will not be recorded again. STP involves a process of addition, but not of repetition.

[43] For a discussion of regulatory policy issues in relation to STP, see the FSA Consultation Paper on *Market Infrastructure* (January 2000).

[44] The provisions of the Electronic Communications Act 2000 are relevant to this issue. See also the E-Commerce Directive (Directive 2000/31/EC), which at the time of writing had yet to be implemented. A possible trap for the unwary is the decision in *The Brimnes* [1975] 1 QB 929. In this case, it was held that a notice had been validly given by telex even though the recipient was not aware of it. 'As I have already said, I do not think that the law regards the effective time of the giving of a notice as liable to be postponed because of some failure by the recipient to see it in the ordinary course of a business competently conducted in a normal businesslike way': per Megaw LJ at 967. Clearly, a fund manager or broker would not wish to be bound by a trade in circumstances where it had no notice of that fact, for example because it was unable to download its e-mail.

discussion. However, certain legal issues surrounding STP will be touched on, namely the impact of STP on floating charges, arguments for limits on STP associated with bad transactions and credit risk, and the question of agency.

(3) Floating Charges

10.68   As discussed elsewhere in this book, custodians, settlement systems, prime brokers and other intermediaries regularly incur significant credit exposures on behalf of their clients. In order to collateralise these exposures, they take security interests over (interests in) securities which they hold for clients. As discussed in Chapter 5, such security interests may be registrable under the Companies Act 1985 if they amount to floating charges. In some cases, intermediaries may seek to ensure that these security interests are not so registrable by requiring the client to obtain their consent before removing assets from the collateral pool. In order to be effective, it is not enough that such a restrictions be included in client documentation; it is necessary that the restriction applies in practice. It is important to ensure that STP does not compromise any such practical restriction, and therefore raise the risk that an intermediary's security interests are void for want of registration as a floating charge.

(4) Bad Transactions

10.69   The objective of STP is the rapid and unfailing settlement of transactions. While this is clearly desirable for the majority of transactions, it may be less desirable for bad transactions to go straight through along with the good ones.

10.70   Transactions may be bad for a variety of reasons. They may be erroneous, fraudulent, or otherwise criminal. The requirement for both parties' instructions to match is effective in screening out many input errors, and there is no doubt that STP will reduce erroneous instructions, by limiting the number of occasions on which errors can creep in. However, other forms of bad instruction may be harder to screen.

Fraud

10.71   One of the lessons from the Barings scandal was the importance of two pairs of eyes, so that transactions which are input by the front office are reviewed by an independent back office prior to their implementation. Yet STP reduces the role of the back office, and therefore of independent review.[45]

10.72   As indicated above, following the Maxwell scandal, a custodian was sued by a client who suffered loss because the custodian failed to block fraudulent settle-

---

[45]   In the securities markets, in the absence of STP, a trade is only released for settlement after it has been confirmed and verified. Thus there are two pairs of eyes after the electronic trade confirmation. With the move to STP these two stages are removed.

ment instructions, and the claim was settled. Custodians therefore need to consider how to protect themselves from liability where their settlement of fraudulent instructions causes loss to their clients.

In practice, even outside an STP environment, there is little real opportunity for **10.73** custodians' staff to spot bad instructions before they are implemented. The volume of transaction is so overwhelming that it would be hard for even an experienced settlement clerk to spot a bad instruction or even recognise a pattern. Provided all the mandatory fields are completed in the instruction received by the custodian, it will be automatically implemented.[46] Even where unusual trades are identified, the practice of custodians is often not to block bad trades, but to seek to identify and query them after settlement. Certainly, standard documentation relieves the custodian of any contractual duty to block bad trades.[47] However, where fraud or negligence is alleged, such contractual provision may not be entirely reliable.

If the automation of settlement removes any ability on the part of the custodian **10.74** to assess instructions before they are implemented, it is important to ensure that the custodian is under no residual duty to do so. If there is any risk that the client does not understand and consent to the degree of automation involved, with the fact that no oversight can be exercised by the custodian, the custodian may be at risk. Indeed, it is possible that a judge might hold that a custodian was negligent in giving up the opportunity of exercising oversight by allowing trades to be settled straight through, in the absence of clear disclosures in the custody documentation. If the client is a trustee, the possibility of claims by or on behalf of beneficial owners needs to be addressed.[48]

Custodians may in some cases agree to remove certain client's business from STP **10.75** and assume duties of oversight in relation to settlement instructions, as an additional service for which they would be separately remunerated.

---

[46] Of course, even with STP, some measure of protection against fraud is automatic. For example, the general rule is that instructions must match in order to settle. Instructions for settlement must match with delivery instructions. A free delivery (ie a delivery of securities without consideration) would not match as it is one-sided; the custodian expects both to receive and deliver value. The Maxwell scandal involved the free delivery of securities. To effect this undetected in an STP environment would generally require the collusion of different parties to the settlement.

[47] Limited provision is often contained in the global custody agreement, and more developed provision is often contained in the software licence authorising the customer to use the custodian's software.

[48] Of course, if special wording is included for STP confirming that the custodian will not review instructions, it is important to draft it so as not to raise the implication that the custodian will review instructions where STP is not offered, if this is not the case. Generally, it is important to correct any misconception that the custodian offers a supervisory rule, for example in relation to pension fund clients, where it does not do so.

Other criminality

10.76 Certain securities transactions involve criminal breach of restrictions on insider dealing, money laundering, freeze orders and market abuse. In relation to transactions which are prohibited under certain criminal provisions, criminal liability may attach to parties participating in their implementation, on the assumption that such participation is knowing. If it is automatic, parties need to ensure they are not exposed.

10.77 Criminals endeavour to conceal their activities. Moreover, the definitions of many of the offences discussed above involve subjective factors. For these reasons, it is unrealistic to expect software to be developed which will be able to screen out such transactions from an STP system. Intermediaries therefore should consider whether some brakes on STP would be appropriate with a view to limiting the implementation of criminal transactions. Equally, regulators and prosecuting authorities should consider the impact of STP in their policies on the responsibilities and liability of intermediaries.

(5) Credit Risk

10.78 As STP is introduced into the settlement of trades,[49] important credit issues arise. As discussed in Chapter 8, credit risks associated with settlement are being addressed by a number of developments, including shortening settlement cycles, the move to real time gross settlement, and the Settlement Finality Directive (which assists payment and settlement systems in collateralising their credit exposures). Still, in the course of settlement, custodians, settlement banks and depositaries may continue to take significant credit exposures on behalf of their clients and participants. The willingness of parties to bear these exposures depends on a number of factors, including the identity of the client, its overall trading pattern, and the availability and quality of collateral. Complex credit decisions are involved, based in part on qualitative factors. It will not be possible to replicate all these judgments electronically. Effective credit management may therefore involve some limitation on full STP.[50]

(6) Agency

10.79 Where an intermediary enters into a contract, it may do so either as principal or as agent. The status of intermediaries is often crucial to managing risk in the financial markets. Contractual provision is not always conclusive in determin-

---

[49] In its *Objectives and Principles of Securities Regulation* (September 1988), IOSCO calls for greater automation between trading and settlement (section 13.10).

[50] A similar issue arises for exchanges and clearing houses, which wish to preserve the financial integrity of members and clearing brokers by requiring them to control their credit exposures to their clients. They will be concerned to ensure that STP does not compromise such control.

ing the legal status of an intermediary (particularly if it is at odds with the facts), and the factual details of the arrangement may be highly relevant. Because STP may profoundly alter the factual circumstances of intermediaries' business, it is important to consider any implications of such changes for the law of agency.

In a pre-STP environment, A might deal with B, who in turn deals with C. With **10.80** STP, if B has no active role, the question might arise whether A is dealing directly with C. Market participants therefore need to consider the possible risk that they might find themselves doing business, not with their intended counterparty, but with the counterparty or customer of their intended counterparty.

As discussed above, in the settlement of securities transactions, the global custo- **10.81** dian keeps its sub-custodial network behind the scenes. All the documentation (including the global custody agreement, the sub-custody agreements and the mandates of the global and sub-custodians) contemplate that the global custodian will be instructed by the fund manager (or its broker) and the sub-custodian will be instructed by the global custodian. On this basis, two separate instructions (in like form) are involved. However, if the instruction of the manager (or broker) is automatically transmitted through the software of the global custodian to the sub-custodian, this analysis may break down. It becomes hard to argue that there are two instructions and not one, and that the latter is the instruction of the global custodian, if the global custodian is not aware of it until after it has been implemented. This measure of automation may raise the argument that the global custodian is the mere conduit of the instructions of the manager (or broker). If such an argument succeeded, it might have a number of consequences. First, the documentation would be at odds with reality; the sub-custodian would not have the correct mandates, and the documentation might not be a reliable guide to the potential liabilities of the parties for losses flowing from the implementing or failing to implement instructions. Secondly, compliance with UK regulatory requirements might be compromised.[51]

Clearing houses and large value delivery systems in the securities, cash and deriv- **10.82** atives markets are also generally concerned to ensure that they contract with their members as principal and not as agent. Because they seek to manage systemic risk by carefully regulating the financial standing of their members, they are unwilling to incur credit exposures to the clients of their members, over whose financial standing they have no control. Thus a controversial issue in the on-exchange

---

[51] Under the Financial Services Act 1986 the custody of securities is a form of investment business, which is defined broadly as safekeeping and administering assets belonging to another. It might follow that, with STP, the sub-custodian is providing custody directly to the fund manager; however, the sub-custodian may not be an authorised depositary for regulatory purposes.

derivatives markets is the extent to which members of electronic derivatives exchanges should be permitted to make terminals available to their clients.[52]

10.83   Of course, the traditional law of agency has long been familiar with the passive principal; lack of awareness of a contract at the time it is entered into is perfectly compatible with principal status *where the contract is entered into on its behalf by an agent.* Thus, traditionally, A is bound by the contract which B makes with C on A's behalf. However, the position with STP is different. Here the purported principal is B. B is not aware of the contract with C until after it has been made by A's actions. It is sought to argue that B contracts as principal, and that the contract with A is not the same as the contract with C. This does not appear to the author to accord with the traditional principles of agency. She wonders whether the risk may arise that the courts would recharacterise the arrangement as involving one contract between A and C as principals, with B as an agent. This would be most unhelpful from a regulatory and risk management point of view.

10.84   A possible solution, which may serve to reconcile regulatory and risk management objectives with the traditional law of agency, is to characterise A as the agent of B.[53]

10.85   Conversely, fund managers are concerned to establish that they deal as agent, and recharacterisation of their trades as principal trades would raise major concerns.[54] In this connection, the timely allocation of trades is essential.[55] If the allocation

---

[52] Where derivatives exchanges permit screen-based trading, members may provide a software link to their clients, which allows the clients directly to input their orders under the mnemonic of the member. The member has the ability to intervene so as to stop the trade, but in practice generally does not. Indeed, its staff may not be aware of the deal until after it is executed. Thus, it is important to clarify whether the member 'adopts' the message of the client which it transmits to the exchange. Whether it does may in part depend on whether the broker merely passes the message on, or enriches it with its own data. In the former case, it may be more likely that B is not treated as being responsible for the message any more than British Telecom is treated as being responsible for communications transmitted through its telephone systems. However, if B modifies a message it may be harder to argue that it is a mere conduit for someone else's message. The best approach is to clarify these issues in the contractual documentation that governs the use of these systems. The derivatives exchanges generally require that the software of the member should add a 'thumb print' which attributes the order to the member. The deal is executed in the member's name as principal.

[53] The author is grateful to Stefan Gomoll of Clifford Chance for this elegant piece of lateral thought.

[54] Fund managers are not capitalised to bear the market risk associated with principal positions in securities.

[55] In practical terms, allocation, or shaping, is the process whereby the fund manager requires the settlement of a block trade to be sub-divided into a number of different pieces, relating to the different funds for which it acts. Even where different funds use the same custodian, separate allocation may be necessary for settlement purposes as the different funds may have different tax status.

In legal terms, allocation involves identifying the principals to the trades making up the block trade which the fund manager has formed as agent. The legal analysis of this process is complex; see the Financial Law Panel's paper, *Fund Management and Market Transactions; A Practice Recommendation* (September 1995). Currently allocation is generally communicated by phone or fax.

Allocation may involve a high level of mathematical complexity. This is because there may be

process is disrupted, the risk of principal liability would need to be addressed. Thus, with the automation of allocation with STP, it is important that the legal consequences of any disruption to the allocation process be understood, and clearly addressed by appropriate drafting.

(7) Conclusions

Industry initiatives to develop STP in the financial markets are wholly welcome. **10.86** There is no doubt that STP is the precondition for T+1, and it will undoubtedly be effective in achieving new efficiencies and reducing risk. As part of the project of achieving STP, the legal risk associated with automation should be considered. It should not be assumed that the existing legal and regulatory analysis of the securities markets will continue to serve in an STP environment. Thus the legal impact of STP should be anticipated, and directed towards a commercially appropriate result.

---

considerable delays in filling large orders. In the bond and foreign exchange markets, there is generally sufficient liquidity immediately to fill a large order. However, with equities a large order may take some time to fill. Accordingly it may be necessary to allocate a fractionally fulfilled trade on a pro-rata basis. Alternatively fund managers may 'warehouse'. This involves buying in the market but not booking the securities to the client for an interval. At the end of the warehousing period the prices are averaged and the securities allocated among clients. Warehousing has the advantage of providing for fewer settlements while the position builds up. Currently, the mathematical aspects of allocation are generally addressed using a hand-held calculator. The potential benefits of automation are clear.

PART IV

REPACKAGED PRODUCTS

11

DEPOSITARY RECEIPTS AND MANAGED FUNDS[1]

Earlier chapters of this book have considered how electronic settlement and cus- **11.01**
tody arrangements have the effect of altering the nature of the investor's asset, and
that of the collateral taker. Rather than securities held directly from the issuer,
their rights of property are indirect and unallocated, and these rights constitute
intangible assets. In this book, these assets have been called interests in securities.

This and the following chapter will consider another process whereby securities **11.02**
are replaced by interests in securities, namely repackaging. Electronic settlement
and custody were introduced for operational reasons, and their impact on the
legal nature of assets in the securities markets was an inadvertent consequence,
which has only recently been recognised. In contrast, the purpose of repackaging
is to alter the legal nature and status of the repackaged asset. However, this chapter will argue, the legal result in both cases is the same. Thus, a very wide variety
of techniques in the securities markets serve to replicate the same legal structure
whereby investors and collateral takers acquire interests in securities that are indirect, unallocated and intangible. Although, in economic and operational terms,
the rapidly evolving products of the financial markets are tremendously diverse,
the fundamental legal structure of many of them is remarkably constant. It is

---

[1] The author is grateful for Madeleine Yates, Senior Associate, Clifford Chance, for kindly
reviewing the section on depositary receipts, and Tim Herrington, Partner, Clifford Chance, for
kindly reviewing the section on managed funds. The opinions expressed in this chapter and any
errors are the author's own.

hoped that this analysis will serve to simplify the legal analysis of the securities markets.

A. Overview

11.03   The focus of this chapter will be the substantive law of repackaging, and in particular its property law aspects. The regulatory and tax aspects of repackaging are complex and fundamentally important to practitioners; however, there is not available space to consider them in any detail here.

11.04   This chapter will consider in turn two different markets in which securities are repackaged, namely the markets in depositary receipts and managed funds. Collateralised bond obligations will be considered in Chapter 12. The history and practice of each of these markets, and their purpose in repackaging (interests in) securities, is very different. However, when one focuses on the repackaged asset in the hands of the investor, and considers its proprietary link to the underlying (interests in) securities, strong similarities emerge between each structure, and also between them and computerised settlement and custody arrangements.

B. Depositary Receipts

11.05   Depositary receipts or DRs are a form of repackaged asset. DRs were originally developed by US banks in order to facilitate cross border investment, by repackaging foreign securities as US law interests in securities. DRs permit local investors to acquire an interest in foreign securities in circumstances where direct investment would not have been possible or attractive, for example because of investment restrictions,[2] the inconvenience of local settlement and/or receipt of dividends in local currency. Usually, the underlying assets in DR programmes comprise shares.[3]

(1) Fundamental Structure

11.06   In a DR programme, the underlying foreign shares are acquired by a financial institution (usually a bank) acting as depositary, and (usually)[4] registered in its name (or that of its nominee) in the register of the issuer of the shares. A share cer-

---

[2] The issuer of the foreign securities may not permit local investors to make a direct investment. Alternatively, the investment powers of institutional local investors may not permit foreign investment. It is important to establish in each case that DRs are not subject to the same investment restrictions that affect the underlying shares.

[3] In some cases they may comprise debt securities and cash.

[4] In some cases, the shares are registered in the name of a custodian acting for the depositary.

tificate[5] representing the depositary's holding is held for the depositary by a custodian, which is responsible for administering the shareholding locally.[6] As registered shareholder, the depositary holds legal title to the underlying shares.[7] The depositary issues new securities in the form of DRs. DRs are registered securities, and the depositary maintains a register of DR holders and issues DR certificates.[8] The depositary holds its title to the underlying shares on trust for DR holders.[9] The deposit agreement specifies the arrangements whereby the depositary passes on benefits associated with the shares such as dividends and (possibly) voting rights.[10] The beneficiaries of the trust are DR holders from time to time;[11] where a DR holder transfers its DRs, the depositary ceases to hold the relevant proportion of underlying shares for the transferor, and instead holds it for the transferee. Thus, a DR constitutes a beneficial interest in the underlying shares.[12] DRs are governed by the law of the jurisdiction in which the depositary operates (in many cases, New York law or English law) and are settled through the major electronic settlement systems.[13]

Chapter 1 discussed direct settlement systems, such as CREST, in which participants have a direct interest in securities settled through them. When DRs are settled through CREST, the CREST participant is the DR holder. Chapter 1 also discussed indirect settlement systems such as Euroclear, Clearstream[14] and the **11.07**

---

[5] Or certificates; see below. If the shares are dematerialised, the depositary or its nominee may be registered in the books of the national securities depositary which confers legal title under local law.

[6] In most cases, the role of the custodian is limited to physical possession of the certificate (together with handling voting arrangements and other matters requiring action in the local jurisdiction); however, as indicated above, in some cases the custodian acquires legal title to the shares as well as possession of the certificate.

As indicated below, more than one certificate may be issued for regulatory reasons.

[7] Of course, if the custodian or its nominee is a registered shareholder, it will acquire legal title, which it will hold for the depositary under the terms of a (custody) agreement.

[8] In practice, where (interests in) DRs are settled through Euroclear, Clearstream or the DTC, a 'global' certificate will be held by the depositary acting for the settlement system.

[9] In English law arrangements the depositary holds the underlying shares as trustee. In New York law arrangements, the depositary holds as bailee.

[10] The depositary may have limited duties in relation to voting, eg to forward any notices and proxy forms received by the company, and to forward to the company duly completed voting instructions. In many cases DR holders are not permitted to direct voting on the shares. Terms and conditions of the DRs will also make provision for non-cash distributions by the issuer, rights issues and other corporate actions. In some cases these arrangements are subject to delays and difficulties. For example, it is necessary to establish that the depositary is able to vote both for and against the same resolution if the different DR holders so instruct.

[11] This is a trust in favour of a class.

[12] One DR does not represent always one share; the ratio between DRs and shares is determined so that the DRs have an initial market price that is customary in the markets in which they are traded.

[13] Settlement of the underlying securities in the local market may be slow and inefficient. In contrast, DRs generally settle through major electronic settlement systems such as Euroclear, Clearstream, DTC or CREST.

[14] ie Clearstream Banking, Société Anonyme, often referred to as 'Clearstream, Luxembourg'; see Chapter 9.

DTC, where one or more depositary or other intermediary is used by the system to stand in the chain of ownership between participant and issuer, so that the interest of the participant in the underlying securities is indirect. When (interests in) DRs are settled through Euroclear, Clearstream and/or the DTC, participants in those systems do not hold DRs, but rather interests in DRs.[15] English law DR documentation refers to the persons whose names are entered in the register of DRs maintained by the depositary as 'DR holders', and to participants in Euroclear, Clearstream and/or the DTC to whose accounts interests in DRs are credited as 'owners'.[16]

11.08 In many DR programmes, the number of DRs in issue varies from time to time. Investors are permitted (subject to local law ownership restrictions affecting the issuer of the shares) to have shares transferred out of the name of the depositary into their name or as they direct. At the same time, the corresponding number of DRs are cancelled. Conversely, in some cases investors are permitted to arrange for new shares to be transferred into the name of the depositary, and for new DRs to be issued to them or as they direct.

11.09 DR programmes may be established with the co-operation of the issuer of the underlying shares (in a sponsored programme) or without it (in an unsponsored programme). In a sponsored programme the issuer issues the underlying shares to the depositary, and in an unsponsored programme the underlying shares are (generally) purchased by the depositary in the secondary market. An issuer may wish to sponsor a DR programme in order more readily to access foreign capital markets and to raise its profile abroad.

---

[15] Where DTC is used, the person holding the DRs (whose name is entered in the register of DRs maintained by the depositary) is Cede & Co, the depositary used by DTC, and the certificates are held by a custodian for DTC (who may be an associate of the depositary issuing the DRs). Where Euroclear and Clearstream are used, DRs are registered in the name of a common nominee for those systems (which again may be an associate of the depositary); a common depositary also holds the DR certificates on behalf of Euroclear and Clearstream.

On the basis that the interests in DRs remain within the settlement systems, the names entered on the register of DR holders would not change. If interests in DRs are transferred from participants in Euroclear to participants in Clearstream or vice versa across the bridge between those two systems, the register would be amended to reflect the new proportions in which the depositary holds the DRs for Euroclear and Clearstream respectively.

It is customary to refer to the certificates issued by the depositary as 'global certificates' because a single certificate represents the entire European and/or US holding. This language comes from the bond markets; where eurobonds are immobilised, global certificates (representing the entire issue) are issued in place of definitive bearer certificates, as discussed in Chapter 1. As discussed in Chapter 2, global and definitives are different types of assets; definitives are divided and globals are undivided. It is slightly misleading to refer to global certificates, because they are not different types of assets from certificates in favour of individual investors. A 'global certificate' is merely a regular certificate in respect of a large holding.

[16] US law documentation refers to persons on the DR register as 'owners' and persons with beneficial interests in the DRs as 'beneficial owners'.

(2) Markets

DRs were originally developed in the early part of the twentieth century by US **11.10**
banks as American Depositary Receipts or ADRs. ADRs are issued into the US
markets.[17] A later development was the Global Depositary Receipt or GDR.
GDRs are issued both into the US and European markets.[18] The term European
Depositary Receipts, or EDRs, is sometimes used for DRs issued into Europe
only.

GDRs and EDRs (which do not involve public offers of DRs in the USA or US **11.11**
listing or quotation) generally observe selling restrictions which enable them to
rely on two exemptions that are available from US registration requirements.[19]
Very broadly, rule 144A (of the General Rules and Regulations, Securities Act of
1933) permits private placements of securities to US qualified institutional buyers (QIBs). Regulation S of the same clarifies the circumstances in which sales of
securities outside the USA (with no directed selling efforts into the US), are free
from USA registration requirements.

In 1994, the requirements for listing DRs on the London Stock Exchange were **11.12**
significantly relaxed, providing further support for the market in GDRs.[20]

(3) Governing Law and Situs

An important legal advantage of repackaging securities in a DR programme is that **11.13**
it changes the governing law of the asset which investors hold. Where the investment powers of institutional investors restricts their ability to hold foreign assets,
the use of a local law DRs programme enables them to acquire or increase an exposure to foreign markets.[21] Other institutions have other reasons to wish to convert
foreign assets into local law assets in this way. As discussed in Chapter 8, the chief
technique whereby interests in foreign securities may be brought into CREST for
settlement is through CREST Depositary Interests or CDIs. These are a form of

---

[17] Customarily, ADRs are denominated in US dollars and investors receive dividends in US dollars. ADRs trade on US markets (the NYSE, NASDAQ or over the counter) and are settled through
DTC.

[18] GDRs are generally listed in London or Luxembourg, and settled through Euroclear,
Clearstream and the DTC.

[19] In particular, GDRs and EDRs seek exemption from the full registration requirements under
the US Securities Act 1933 and the financial reporting requirements under the Securities Exchange
Act 1934.

[20] See section 23.45 onwards in the FSA's Listing Rules. Equivalent provisions are contained in
Sch C to the Luxembourg Listing Rules. Other UK rules have been relaxed in favour of DRs. The
Financial Services Act 1986, s 75(6)(h), takes DRs outside the definition of a collective investment
scheme. (The promotion of such schemes is regulated under s 76.) Also, SFA Board Notice 444 provides a waiver from the normal client asset rules.

[21] Equally, DRs may enable investors to overcome local restrictions on foreign ownership of
shares in the underlying jurisdiction.

depositary receipt. CDIs are governed by English law, and therefore subject to the Uncertificated Securities Regulations 1995, SI 1995/3272. Although in theory foreign securities might be brought into CREST on the basis of foreign legislation providing for dematerialisation, in practice CRESTCo only permits this where the foreign legislation is very closely modelled on the Uncertificated Securities Regulations.[22] This is presumably because, under those regulations, CRESTCo as the operator of CREST has the benefit of very significant limitations of liability.

11.14 A second significant legal result of a DR programme is to change the situs of the asset. As discussed in Chapter 7, the situs of an asset is its legal location. DRs are a form of registered security. The situs of registered securities is (broadly) the place where the relevant register is maintained. As also discussed in Chapter 7, lex situs (or the law of the place where an asset is located) is important in establishing robust collateral arrangements. Under the rules of conflict of laws, it is relevant to the perfection of a security interest and (possibly) to the recharacterisation of an outright transfer arrangement. As indicated in Chapters 7 and 6, the approach of some jurisdictions to perfection and recharacterisation is robust, while in others it is unhelpful to collateral takers. One technique for avoiding the requirements of an unhelpful jurisdiction in relation to local shares which are used as collateral, is to establish a DR programme and place the DR register in a robust jurisdiction.[23]

(4) Property Rights

11.15 This section will consider the nature of the property interest of DR holders in respect of the underlying shares, and argue that it equates with the interests of participants in commingled electronic custody and settlement arrangements in the underlying securities.

11.16 The first point is of course that, as against the depositary, this interest is proprietary. DR holders acquire the beneficial interests in the underlying shares, which the depositary holds on trust for them, under the terms of the deposit agreement. Because the underlying shares are held by the depositary as trustee for DR holders, they are not available to the creditors of the depositary in its insolvency. In other words the effect of the trust is to ring-fence the shares in the hands of the depositary by conferring a property interest on DR holders as beneficiaries.

Indirect

11.17 The interest of DR holders in the underlying shares is beneficial and not legal, arising under a trust. As discussed in Chapter 2, the interest of a beneficiary in

---

[22] In the case of Ireland, the Isle of Man, and Jersey.

[23] See Chapter 7 for a discussion of the strengths and weaknesses of this approach. Of course, if interests in DRs are settled through a settlement system in a jurisdiction other than that where the register is maintained (such as Euroclear or Clearstream), the interests of the participants in such a settlement system are, it is argued, located in the jurisdiction of the settlement system.

trust assets is indirect, in the sense that in the normal course there is no direct recourse against the underlying assets. Where the trust assets consist of shares, the trustee (in this case the depositary) is the shareholder and, in the normal course, the beneficiary (in this case the DR holder) has no direct right of action against the issuer.[24]

In sponsored programmes it is often sought to give the DR holder (or, where interests in DRs are settled through Euroclear, Clearstream and/or the DTC, the participant in those system as owner) a direct right of recourse against the issuer, either contractually or under a deed poll.[25] However, this does not affect the proposition that the property rights of DR holders (ie their rights as beneficial owners of the shares) are indirect. Such direct personal rights do not arise under the trust which confers the DR holders' property rights, but instead arise under contract or deed poll. In other words, they are personal rights, which run concurrently with the property rights of DR holders.   **11.18**

---

[24] She cannot sue the issuer under company law as a shareholder (because she is not one) nor can she sue the issuer as beneficial owner of shares (because the company is not obliged to take notice of trusts under English law; see the Companies Act 1985, s 360). Chapter 13 will discuss the common paradigm, which (mistakenly) treats property rights as rights against assets, as opposed to rights against persons (in respect of assets). In the light of the common paradigm, it might be considered inconsistent to treat indirect rights (ie rights giving no direct recourse against assets, which can only be enforced through an intermediary) as proprietary. Any such apparent inconsistency is resolved when one understands that all legal rights are rights against persons. As discussed in Chapter 13, the test of a personal right is that it relates to the obligation of the defendant to the plaintiff. If it does not, it is a property right. Because obligations are affected by the insolvency of the obligor, the following test applies; a right is proprietary as against a particular person if it is not affected by the insolvency of that person. Intangible assets (such as shares) comprise the obligations of their issuers. Therefore, as against the issuers, they are always personal. They may only be the subject of property rights in the hands of intermediaries (from whose insolvency they are protected). Thus, the indirect nature of rights such as DRs is not incompatible with their proprietary nature; rather, it is its precondition.

[25] In a sponsored programme, the issuer of the underlying shares will enter into a deposit agreement with the depositary, under which it will assume various obligations including obligations to maintain the listing of the shares; appoint a successor depositary on the retirement or removal of the depositary; provide accounts and financial statements, notices and other shareholder information; and provision of information required by US regulatory requirements. The depositary assumes no liability in the event of the default of the issuer to perform these obligations. Because such default may affect the value of the DRs, it is necessary to consider the recourse of DR holders in the event of such default. DR holders are not parties to the deposit agreement. In the past, it was not possible under English law to confer an enforceable right under a contract on a person who was not a party to that contract, because of the requirement for privity of contract. (The position has now changed under the Contracts (Rights of Third Parties) Act 1999.) In contrast, New York law permitted third party contractual rights, and New York law deposit agreements were effective to confer enforceable contractual rights on DR holders. In order to replicate such rights under English law deposit agreements prior to the 1999 Act, it was necessary in the past to use deed polls. The issuer would execute a deed poll in which it would undertake inter alia to provide information on request to holders and beneficial owners, and otherwise comply with its obligations under the deposit agreement. (Certain standard deposit agreements provide for direct enforcement rights only for holders (ie persons named on the DR register), whereas under US regulatory requirements information is required to be provided to both holders and beneficial owners.)

11.19 As an indirect property interest, the interest of the DR holder equates with that of the client of a global custodian or a participant in an electronic settlement system.

Unallocated

11.20 A further point of similarity between the interests of clients of electronic custody and settlement arrangements and those of DR holders, is that both are unallocated. There is no allocation between any particular DR holder and any particular underlying share.

Unitary, dual and bifurcated structures

11.21 The interests of DR holders is unallocated notwithstanding the fact that DR programmes may be dual or bifurcated in structure.

11.22 As indicated above, issues of GDRs characteristically seek to rely on exemptions from US registration requirements. Such issues are made in two parts, with a rule 144A private placement to QIBs in the USA, and a regulation S public offer outside the USA.

11.23 If no distinction is made between shares held by the depositary which are subject to the US private placement and those which are subject to the non-US public offer, it is necessary to impose the US selling restrictions required by rule 144A on the entire holding, so that they can only be sold in the USA to QIBs.[26] For this reason, it is no longer customary to adopt a structure that makes no such distinction (a unitary structure).[27]

11.24 In a bifurcated structure, the depositary holds two separate shareholdings, so that there are two entries in the register of the issuer and two share certificates.[28] In turn, the depositary issues two classes of DR represented by two DR certificates. One class of DRs comprises DRs originally sold to European investors under regulation S, (the 'reg S DRs') and the other class of DRs comprises DRs originally sold to US QIBs under rule 144A (the 'rule 144A DRs').[29] The two classes of DRs

---

[26] These are continuing restrictions. Restrictive legends appear on the DR certificates, and managers involved in the issue of DRs are required to enter into appropriate undertakings in the subscription agreement. Also, when any investor deposits or withdraws shares from the DR programme, she is required to certify her non-US status. In contrast, where only reg S applies, European investors can generally resell into the US markets after 40 days.

[27] In a unitary structure, the depositary holds one holding of shares (for which a single certificate is issued). All the DRs are held through DTC and subject to rule 144A selling restrictions. European investors hold indirect interest in the DRs through Euroclear and Clearstream, who have accounts at DTC.

[28] Where legal title to the shares is held by the custodian, the custodian will create two separate accounts in favour of the depositary in its records.

[29] The reg S DRs (and certificate) are held by a common depositary for Euroclear and Clearstream, and the rule 144A DRs (and certificate) are held by Cede & Co for the DTC. (Alternatively, it is possible for both classes of DRs to be held through the DTC, with European participation through Euroclear and Clearstream as in a unitary structure.)

comprise different assets;[30] they are not fungible with each other and have different CUSIP or CINS numbers. The advantage of the bifurcated structure is that rule 144A selling restrictions need only apply to the US DRs.

A third alternative is a dual structure. This represents a compromise between unitary and bifurcated structures. In a dual structure as in a bifurcated structure, the depositary issues two classes of DRs, namely reg S DRs and rule 144A DRs. However, in a dual structure as in a unitary structure, there is no segregation of the underlying shares. This has the result that all the DRs must be subject to US selling restrictions, so that they can only be held in the USA by QIBs. For this reason this structure is not generally used.[31] **11.25**

Thus, in unitary and dual structures, there is one pool of underlying assets, and in a bifurcated structure there are two pools of underlying assets. In respect of each pool, however, there is no allocation of particular shares to particular DR holders. Therefore, under any structure, the interest of a DR holder is unallocated. **11.26**

Tenancy in common

Chapter 2 considered unallocated custody arrangements, in which an intermediary holds (interests in) securities for clients on a pooled basis. Where the assets held by the intermediary are intangible, it was noted that the only way of protecting the assets from the creditors of the intermediary is under a trust. Chapter 2 went on to consider the case law relevant to the question of how such a trust can take effect in the absence of allocation. It was suggested that the prudent interpretation of the relevant case law is that such a trust may take effect in favour of clients as equitable tenants in common. **11.27**

This interpretation of custody trusts coincides with the express provisions of DR arrangements. It is expressly provided that in the deposit agreement that DR holders will beneficially co-own the underlying shares as equitable tenants in common. In a bifurcated structure, one tenancy in common will arise in favour of reg S DR holders and one in favour of rule 144A holders respectively.[32] **11.28**

Intangible

As indicated above, DRs are characteristically issued in registered form. As discussed in Chapter 2, registered securities are a form of intangible asset. It was also **11.29**

---

[30] Although the depositary holds all the shares under a single trust, the rule 144A DRs are defined as DRs representing rule 144A shares, and reg S DRs as representing reg S shares. Thus, the different classes of DRs represent the beneficial interests in the different classes of shares respectively.

[31] Euroclear and Clearstream have objected to this structure as they do not want to take responsibility for monitoring compliance with US selling restrictions under rule 144A.

[32] Standard wording provides that 'Holders will accordingly be tenants in common of such Deposited Property to the extent of the Deposited Property represented by the GDRs in respect of which they are the Holders'.

indicated above that in most DR programmes the underlying securities comprise shares. Shares are generally issued in registered form, and are therefore intangible. On this basis, both the underlying securities and the interests in them are intangible. There may be exceptional cases where the underlying assets are physical bearer securities. However, even in these cases, because the DRs are unallocated, they do not attach to any physical asset. Thus the DRs remain intangible.

11.30 As indirect, unallocated and intangible assets, DRs equate to the interests of clients in electronic custody and settlement arrangements.

Shortfall risk

11.31 In DR programmes where the number of DRs in issue changes from time to time, the risk of shortfall may arise. By this it is meant that the number of shares held by the depositary at any time may fall short of the number of shares purportedly represented by the DRs in issue. Shortfall may arise due to administrative error[33] or bad deliveries affecting the transfer of the underlying shares to the depositary. As discussed in Chapter 9, a bad delivery occurs when a credit to a securities account (in this case, the registration of a transfer of shares to the depositary on the register of the issuer) is subsequently reversed. Bad deliveries may arise where a transfer proves to have been made in breach of nationality restrictions affecting the shares of the issuer, or pursuant to a court order where the transferor is affected by fraud or insolvency.[34]

11.32 Shortfall risk is significantly increased where depositaries engage in a practice known as 'pre-release'. This is a service offered by depositaries to brokers who deal in DRs. Where a broker's client wishes to buy DRs, the broker may acquire the DRs for its client by delivering the underlying shares to the depositary and having the depositary issue new DRs to the broker, for onward delivery to the broker's client. In order to save costs, the broker may wish to use the purchase price of the DRs paid to it by its client to fund its purchase of the underlying shares. This necessitates the synchronisation of the two transactions. As indicated above, DRs are usually settled through the major electronic settlement systems, and therefore their settlement cycle is short. In contrast, the settlement cycle of the underlying shares is likely to be slower.[35] The overall result is that the depositary is required to issue new DRs prior to its receipt of the corresponding underlying shares.

11.33 Therefore, during the excess of the settlement cycle of the underlying shares over the settlement cycle of the DRs, there is a temporary shortfall. If for any reason

---

[33] It is understood that, in any arrangement where two sets of active securities accounts are required to be reconciled, irreconciliations are commonplace.
[34] ie the transfer is reversed under a tracing action or insolvency displacement rules. See Chapters 4 and 9.
[35] The inefficiency of local settlement is one of the motives for the issue of DRs.

the delivery of the underlying shares fails, the shortfall may become less temporary.[36]

In the ordinary course of business, temporary shortfalls will arise and be elimi-   **11.34**
nated from time to time. Where less temporary shortfalls arise, the depositary may
eliminate them by buying in shares at its own expense, in order to protect its reputation. However, if a very large shortfall arises, the depositary may be unwilling
to meet the cost of eliminating it. In these circumstances, the question arises how
the cost of the shortfall is to be borne.

As discussed in Chapter 10, trustees are not strictly liable to make good shortfalls   **11.35**
to the trust assets. They are so liable only where the shortfall has been caused by
their breach of duty. Whether or not pre-release involves breach of duty by the
depositary may depend in part on whether it has been expressly disclosed to
investors in the listing particulars for the DRs. Where there has been a breach of
duty, investors will have a personal right of action against the depositary in respect
of their losses.[37] Of course, if the depositary is insolvent, such personal rights may
be worthless.

It is necessary therefore to identify the method by which the courts would allocate   **11.36**
the shortfall between DR holders. If on the facts it is possible to identify the DR
holder in respect of whom a shortfall arose (the shortfall DR holder),[38] then it
seems likely that the courts would seek to eliminate the shortfall by cancelling that
holder's DRs.[39] However, it may well be that, by the time the shortfall comes to
light, the shortfall DR holder may have redeemed her DRs or transferred them to
a bona fide purchaser without notice of the shortfall.

In these circumstances, one possibility is that the courts would seek to identify the   **11.37**
DRs that were originally held by the shortfall DR holder ('the bad DRs') in the

---

[36] Of course, in these circumstances, the depositary will require the broker to make good the
shortfall. However, if the broker has become insolvent, it is most unlikely to comply. Usually the
depositary collateralises the broker's delivery obligations to it by taking collateral in the form of cash
or high liquid debt securities. It is understood that these assets are not generally segregated from the
general assets of the depositary, so that in the depositary's insolvency, they may not be available to
DR holders to make good the shortfall.

[37] Where pre-release involves breach of trust and the depositary received identifiable assets from
brokers under the pre-release arrangements, DR holders may have a property claim against such
assets under a constructive trust.

[38] ie the DR holder to whom new DRs were issued against the transfer to the depositary of new
shares, in circumstances where that transfer either failed or was reversed.

[39] Or, possibly, requiring that DR holder to transfer new shares to the depositary. This approach
accords with common sense. There is authority for it in the rule of case law (supported by detailed
reference in Lionel Smith, *The Law of Tracing* (Oxford: Clarendon Press, 1997) 87 and n 78) that
where the assets of different persons are mixed, and a loss occurs to the mixture due to the fault of
one of the persons, the loss will come out of that person's contribution to the mixture. (Strictly, Dr
Smith discusses losses caused by the *intentional* wrong of one of the parties, which would not be the
case here.)

hands of a new DR holder (ie to follow them)[40] and to attribute the shortfall to their current holder. However, in many cases there will be no factual evidence to permit following, ie no record of where the bad DRs went.[41] If so, the courts might apply the rules of equitable tracing notionally to designate certain DRs as bad.[42]

11.38 Where the entitlements of different persons in a mixed fund are recorded by debits and credits (in a current bank account or, by analogy, a register of registered securities) the traditional rule of tracing is 'first in, first out').[43] In practice, this approach may lead to arbitrary results. Therefore the alternative (but complex) 'rolling charge' approach was developed.[44] However, in a programme where DRs are frequently issued and redeemed, the application of these traditional tracing rules would be unduly complex. It was held in *Barlow Clowes v Vaughan*[45] that, where a loss occurs to a global fund due to a common misfortune, the loss will in general be borne rateably by the beneficiaries. In that case, loss to a managed fund was suffered due to the fraud of a fiduciary. It was held that to have sought to allocate particular losses to particular investors would have been impracticable and arbitrary, and the losses were therefore borne rateably.[46]

11.39 Pro ration (under the rule in *Barlow Clowes*) is simpler to apply and less arbitrary in its result than the traditional rules of tracing, and it is therefore to be preferred.[47] Further support for the proposition that shortfalls would be pro rated between DR holders is provided by the common law rules for allocated losses among tenants in common. 'The cases also support the conclusion that any losses be borne ratably between contributors.'[48]

---

[40] Lionel Smith distinguishes between tracing and following as follows: 'The process of tracing can be used to identify a new asset which might be subject to the plaintiff's claim; this must first be distinguished from the process of following, which is concerned with the plaintiff's original asset': Smith (n 39 above) 4.

[41] If the shortfall DR holder cancelled the bad DRs, they no longer exist, and there is no factual method of linking them with new DRs subsequently issued.

[42] Here, tracing is used not to identify assets, but to identify shortfalls.

[43] *Devaynes v Noble, Clayton's Case* (1816) 1 Mer 572, per Sir Wm Grant MR at 798. ie 'the first drawings out are attributed to the first payments in': D J Hayton, *Underhill and Hayton, Law Relating to Trusts and Trustees* (15th edn, London: Butterworths, 1995) 860.

[44] 'This solution involves treating credits to a bank account made at different dates and from different sources as a blend or cocktail with the result that when a withdrawal is made from the account it is treated as a withdrawal in the same proportions as the different interests in the account bear to each other at the moment before the withdrawal is made': *Barlow Clowes International Ltd v Vaughan* [1992] 4 All ER 22, per Woolf LJ at 35.

[45] *Barlow Clowes International Ltd (in liquidation) and others v Vaughan and others* [1992] 4 All ER 22. See also *Re Eastern Capital Futures (in liquidation)* [1989] BCLC 371.

[46] See generally *Underhill and Hayton* (n 43 above) 860–863.

[47] In a bifurcated structure, shortfalls would possibly be pro rated among a single class of DR holders (ie reg S holders or rule 144A holders) in cases where the original shortfall was attributable to a particular class of holder.

[48] Lionel Smith (n 39 above) 76. Numerous authorities for pro ration are cited in n 45 above.

C. Managed Funds

Another market in which securities are repackaged, so that investors hold interests   **11.40**
in securities rather than securities, is the managed funds industry. A managed
fund is an arrangement whereby the assets of different investors are pooled and
invested on a collective basis by a professional manager.[49] As discussed below, a
variety of different legal structures are available for managed funds.

In this discussion, investors in managed funds will be called 'participants'. Invest-   **11.41**
ment in managed funds offers clear advantages to the participant as compared to
direct investment in the underlying assets. These advantages include professional
management,[50] diversification,[51] economies of scale[52] and market access.[53]

Managed funds constitute a major industry. Anecdotally, in the USA in 1994, for   **11.42**
the first time the value of units purchased in managed funds exceeded the value of
bank deposits, and the importance of the managed funds industry continues to
grow. Important factors in this growth are the rise of personal pension schemes,
and the development of wholesale funds (including hedge funds) both for investment purposes and for infrastructure purposes. (In the market turbulence in the
Far East in the late 1990s, infrastructure funds were used as a means of repackaging distressed assets.) Risks associated with hedge funds have generated an important debate in recent years, as discussed in Chapter 10.

In general terms, the universe of managed funds is divided into retail funds and   **11.43**
wholesale funds. Broadly speaking, retail funds may be promoted to the general
public in the United Kingdom and are subject to detailed regulation in all aspects
of their constitution, operation and management. In contrast, the promotion
of wholesale funds is narrowly restricted, but the constitution, operation and
management of wholesale funds is unregulated.[54] A regime permitting the cross

---

[49] While there is a debate about the correct definition of a managed fund, this definition seems
to be the most widely accepted in practice.

[50] A professional manager is likely to have greater specialised market expertise than the investor.

[51] A managed fund may have a very large asset value, and is therefore likely to be able to achieve
a higher degree of investment diversification than an individual investor. Diversification is a method
of managing the risks associated with securities investment.

[52] A fund manager dealing with brokers on a wholesale basis will be able to do business more
cheaply than an individual investor dealing on a retail basis.

[53] As an institutional investor, the fund manager may have access to investment opportunities,
including privately placed securities, that are unavailable to the private investor for regulatory and
other reasons.

[54] The marketing restrictions are contained in the Financial Services Act (FSA) 1986, s 76 and
the Financial Services (Promotion of Unregulated Schemes) Regulations 1991 made under that section ('the PUS Regulations'). Section 76(1) provides (broadly) that a person who is authorised to
carry on investment business in the United Kingdom under the FSA 1986 shall not promote a collective investment scheme in the United Kingdom unless that scheme is a regulated scheme. A regulated scheme for this purpose is an authorised unit trust scheme, an open-ended investment
company or foreign scheme which has been recognised by the Financial Services Authority (under

border marketing of retail securities funds within the EC and EEA is created under the UCITS Directive.[55]

11.44 It is important to participants (and fund managers seeking to attract participants) that a fund should be tax transparent. This means that the tax position of the participant is no less favourable than it would have been, had the participant directly acquired the underlying assets comprised in the fund's portfolio. In many jurisdictions, special favourable taxation regimes permit tax transparency for retail funds. In order to assist wholesale funds in achieving tax transparency, such funds are customarily generally in low tax jurisdictions.[56]

(1) Collective Investment Schemes

11.45 In the United Kingdom, managed funds are sometimes referred to by the technical term 'collective investment schemes'. A collective investment scheme (CIS) is defined in section 75 of the Financial Services Act 1986. Although the purpose of the definition in section 75 is regulatory,[57] its terms broadly correspond with the general commercial understanding of what constitutes a managed fund.

---

the Financial Services Act, ss 86, 87, 88). 'There are three types of recognised scheme which can be marketed to the public in the United Kingdom: (i) schemes, authorised in other Member States of the European Community, which comply with the requirements of the European Community Directive on Undertakings for Collective Investment in Transferable Securities (UCITS). Such schemes can obtain recognition under section 86 of the Act; (ii) schemes authorised in designated countries or territories which are of a class specified by the Treasury. Such schemes can obtain recognition under section 87 of the Act, and (iii) overseas schemes which do not qualify for recognition under either section 86 or 87 of the Act. Such schemes may seek recognition under section 88 of the Act': Financial Services (Regulated Schemes) Regulations 1999, explanation to Part 14.

FSA 1986, s 76(2) provides (broadly) that the above restriction does not apply to promotions to other authorised persons or professional investors. The PUS Regulations were made under s 76(3) and create a number of further exemptions, including (very broadly) ones in favour of promotions to existing and recent participants of substantially similar schemes to the one promoted; established customers of the promoter for whom the promoted scheme is suitable; and non-private customers.

[55] Council Directive on the Coordination of Laws, Regulations and Administrative Provisions relating to Undertakings for Collective Investment in Transferable Securities (UCITS) (85/611/EEC, as amended by 88/220/EEC). The objective of the Directive is to harmonise the laws relating to undertakings for collective investment in transferable securities (or UCITS) and to permit their free marketing within Europe. A UCITS which is authorised in its home Member State can be marketed throughout Europe without further authorisations. However, it must comply with host state marketing rules. Criteria for UCITS status include open-ended status; investment in transferable securities; and promotion to the public in the EU. At the time of writing, the European Commission has approved two amended proposals to the Directive. These involve first, wider investment powers so that UCITS can invest, not only in listed shares and bonds, but also in bank deposits, money market instruments, financial derivatives and units in other funds, and secondly conferring on management companies a European passport to operate throughout the EU.

[56] Such as Bermuda, the Cayman Islands, Luxembourg, Jersey and Ireland. The establishment of hedge funds in such common law jurisdictions lent urgency to the question of establishing the situs of interests in securities held through such jurisdictions; see Chapter 7.

[57] As indicated above a CIS is subject to the marketing restrictions in FSA 1986, s 76 and regulations made under it. In the United Kingdom, FSA 1986, s 76 and regulations made thereunder

Section 75 provides as follows: **11.46**

> In this Act 'a collective investment scheme' means, subject to the provisions of this section, arrangements with respect to property of any description, including money, the purpose or effect of which is to enable persons taking part in the arrangements . . . to participate in or receive profits or income from the acquisition, holding, management or disposal of the property or sums paid out of such profits or income.

The definition goes on to provide that participants must not be involved in managing the CIS,[58] which must either be professionally managed or pooled (so that no part of the underlying portfolio is allocated to any particular participants).[59] The general commercial understanding of the term 'managed fund' features both characteristics of professional management and pooling. **11.47**

(2) The Parties

Although a managed fund may adopt one of a range of different legal structures, the different parties involved in a managed fund, and their respective roles, are the same in most cases. **11.48**

A fund manager assumes a leading role in establishing and promoting a new fund.[60] Once the fund is established, the manager will manage the fund; this involves investing and reinvesting the fund's assets on a discretionary basis.[61] In the case of funds in which units are issued and redeemed from time to time, the fund manager arranges for such issues and redemptions. In retail funds the manager generally has an obligation as a principal to redeem units at the unit holder's request: see Article 1.2 of the UCITS Directive. Fund managers receive **11.49**

---

make a distinction between regulated CISs (which can be sold to the general public and which are subject to detailed regulation in their constitution, operation, investment powers and promotion), and unregulated CISs, which may not be sold to the general public, and which are not so regulated.

In the USA, an equivalent distinction is made under the Investment Companies Act 1940. The SEC regulates investment companies under this Act, subject to an exemption in s 3(c)(1), which provides that the definition of investment company does not include (broadly) funds which are not sold to the general public: '[not include] Any issuer whose outstanding securities (other than short term paper) are beneficially owned by not more than one hundred persons and which is not making and does not presently propose to make a public offering of its securities'. Very broadly, the marketing of unregulated schemes is narrowly restricted.

[58] 'The arrangements must be such that the persons who are to participate as mentioned in subsection (1) above (in this Act referred to as "participants") do not have day to day control over the management of the property in question, whether or not they have the right to be consulted or to give directions' (s 75(2)).

[59] 'and the arrangements must also have either or both of the characteristics mentioned in subsection (3) below . . . (3) Those characteristics are—(a) that the contributions of the participants and the profits or income out of which payments are to be made to them are pooled; (b) that the property in question is managed as a whole by or on behalf of the operator of the scheme' (s 75(2) and (3)).

[60] The industry is led by the different fund management houses, each of whom manages a 'stable' of different funds, either itself or through its associated companies.

[61] In accordance with the investment powers and objectives of the fund.

significant remuneration for their efforts, which is linked to the performance of the fund's portfolio.

11.50 A custodian is appointed to hold the assets of the fund, either directly or through sub-custodians.[62] In some cases the custodian will also assume a fiduciary responsibility for overseeing the manager. Trades in (interests in) securities, derivatives and foreign exchange for the account of the fund are entered into by brokers in the relevant markets. The triangular relationship between fund managers (who instigate trades), brokers (who execute them) and custodians (who settle them) is a fascinating and relatively unexamined area of commercial law.[63]

11.51 Because a fund may be subject to taxation in the jurisdiction from which it is managed, it is customary in the case of wholesale funds to use a manager established in the same low tax jurisdiction as the fund itself. In many cases it is desired to draw on the expertise of personnel based in the head office of the management group (for example in London or New York). In such cases, an associated London or New York entity may be appointed to act as investment adviser to the manager.[64]

11.52 An administrator[65] may also be engaged and where fund units are traded in the secondary market, a registrar.[66]

(3) Legal Structures

11.53 A number of different legal structures have been developed for managed funds, including (importantly) unit trusts, limited partnerships and open-ended investment companies. These will be considered in turn in the discussion below.

11.54 In each of these structures, the participant's interest in the fund's portfolio is intermediated, in that the underlying assets are held by an intermediary on their behalf. The simple explanation for the use of intermediaries in the managed funds industry is the need for continuity of title. Successful fund management may involve a medium or long term strategy, so that it is necessary to establish a continuing fund that will comprise the managed portfolio over a number of years. However, because participants' investment policies and/or circumstances may change unforeseeably, units in managed funds (particularly retail funds) will in general be more attractive to them if they may be readily disposed of for cash by the partici-

---

[62] See Chapter 10 for a discussion of global custody.

[63] L van Setten of State Street Bank has particular expertise in this area. The author very much looks forward to reading his proposed book on this subject.

[64] Care is taken in practice to ensure that the role of the London or New York adviser is not recharacterised as management, with adverse tax consequences.

[65] Sometimes administrative functions are undertaken by a secretary.

[66] Or transfer agent.

[67] It will be seen below that units may be rendered liquid either by being redeemable, or by being listed on a stock exchange. However, units in limited partnerships are generally not redeemable, and transfers are restricted, as discussed below.

pant, ie if they are liquid.[67] The legal challenge is to reconcile these two character-istics. English law has developed two techniques whereby a changing class of investors can hold continuous property rights in a changing fund, namely trust and corporation.[68] Thus, most managed funds are constituted either as trusts, or as corporations, or as limited partnerships which involve elements of both trust and corporation, as discussed below.

The choice of a particular structure as most suitable in particular circumstances **11.55** involves a number of factors, including importantly tax and regulatory consider-ations, which are beyond the scope of this chapter.

Unit trusts

A unit trust is a form of fund which has been developed in Anglo-Saxon jurisdic- **11.56** tions.[69]

Legal structure

A unit trust is constituted by a trust deed,[70] which is executed by a trustee and a **11.57** manager.[71] Although the trustee has primary responsibility for the custody of the trust assets, this function is usually delegated by the trustee to a custodian. The trustee also assumes fiduciary functions of oversight of the manager.[72] The origi-nal trust assets comprise the cash contributed by participants. This cash is invested from time to time by the manager to create a portfolio of investments.[73]

---

[68] For a superb discussion of the historic and jurisprudential relationship between trust and cor-poration, see F W Maitland, 'Trust and Corporation' in *Selected Essays* (Cambridge: Cambridge University Press, 1936). See also the discussion in R R Formoy, *The Historical Foundations of Modern Company Law* (London: Sweet & Maxwell, 1923) and Kam Fan Sin, *The Legal Nature of the Unit Trust* (Oxford: Clarendon Press, 1997).

[69] Dr Sin identifies the Foreign and Colonial Government Trust as the first unit trust in 1868. See Sin (n 68 above) 19.

[70] Dr Sin argues that the unit trust is the creature of both trust and contract. This is undoubtedly correct. Authorised unit trust schemes (see below) are creatures of trust, contract and statutory reg-ulation. See the Financial Services (Regulated Schemes) Regulations 1991, regs 7.12.1, 7.12.2.

[71] As an alternative, in the case of an unauthorised scheme (see below), the trust deed might be executed by the trustee alone, with the manager being appointed contractually by the trustee. 'In particular, the manager, as a party dominating the investment decision process, may be character-ized as a fiduciary of the unitholders in many facets of the trust operations and therefore may be sub-ject to fiduciary duties of loyalty and, as argued, of skill and care': Sin (n 68 above) 5.

[72] The trustee oversees the compliance of the fund manager with the terms of the trust and (with authorised unit trust schemes, discussed below) with applicable regulations. The unreported case of *Galmerrow Securities Ltd v National Westminster Bank plc* (1990) considered the position of the trustee of an unauthorised unit trust scheme. Harman J noted that the trust deed conferred exclusive power of and responsibility for management of the scheme on the managers. 'Plainly these terms are inconsistent with NatWest as Trustee exercising a general supervision over the choice of property': at 25. On this basis, the trustee was held not to be liable for losses attributable to bad management.

[73] 'Generally the manager has the executive responsibility for the scheme, in that he manages the investments, performs the valuations and determines the prices. The trustee has the duty of over-sight and supervision and safeguards the title to the investments and the interests of the unitholders in them': Financial Services (Regulated Schemes) Regulations 1991, explanation to Part 7.

The original cash and the portfolio in which it is invested is held on trust by the trustee for participants as beneficiaries. Participants are known as unit holders, and their investments are known as units.

11.58   The trust fund is regularly valued, and units are issued and redeemed at net asset value at the request of existing and new unit holders from time to time. Unit trusts may be sold to the general public in the United Kingdom if they are authorised.[74] Authorised status is conferred by the Financial Services Authority.[75] Authorised unit trust schemes are regulated in accordance with the Financial Services (Regulated Schemes) Regulations 1991 ('the Regulated Schemes Regulations'). The Regulated Schemes Regulations impose detailed requirements on trustees and managers relating to all aspects of the constitution, operation and management of the scheme.[76] The Regulated Schemes Regulations prescribe matters which must be contained in the trust deed,[77] as well as matters which may be so contained.[78] Disclosure documents (called scheme particulars) containing prescribed information concerning the scheme must be published.[79] A range of categories of unit trust may be authorised; the different categories have different investment powers.[80] Certain classes of authorised unit trust scheme are eligible for UCITS status.[81]

---

[74]   Authorised unit trust schemes are exempt from capital gains tax (CGT), but unauthorised unit trust schemes are not. Therefore unauthorised unit trust schemes are generally only attractive to unit holders which are exempt from CGT, such as pension funds.

[75]   Under the Financial Services Act 1986, s 78. The Act specifies a number of criteria for the trustees and managers of authorised unit trust schemes. These include the following. The trustee and manager must be independent of each other (s 78(2)); each must be a body corporate incorporated in the United Kingdom or another Member State (s 78(3)); each must be an authorised person under the Act (s 78(4)).

[76]   The provisions of the regulations relate (inter alia) to the constitution of the scheme; the preparation and publication of an information disclosure document called 'scheme particulars'; pricing of and dealing in units of the scheme; investment and borrowing powers; title to and transfer of units; powers and duties of the manager and trustee; payments and benefits to the manager and trustee; income; reports; meetings and modifications.

[77]   In reg 2.02 and in Sch 1, Part 1. Part 1 requires the declaration of trust to be made 'subject to the provisions of . . . all regulations made under section 81 of the [Financial Services Act 1986] and for the time being in force'. This serves to incorporate the provisions of the Regulated Schemes Regulations into the deed by reference, and has the result that the deeds of authorised unit trust schemes are much shorter than those for unauthorised schemes.

[78]   In reg 2.02 and Sch 1, Part 2.

[79]   See reg 3.02 and Sch 2.

[80]   The categories of authorised unit trust are as follows: securities funds; money market funds; futures and options funds; geared futures and options funds; property funds; warrant funds; feeder funds; funds of funds and umbrella funds. For the investment powers of the different categories of fund, see Part 5 of the Regulated Schemes Regulations.

[81]   These are securities funds, warrant funds and correspondingly invested umbrella funds. However, as indicated above, the European Commission has approved proposed amendments to the UCITS Directive to permit funds with wider investment powers to enjoy UCITS status.

Units may be issued in two classes, namely income units (on which the income is distributed to unit holders) and accumulation units (on which the income is automatically reinvested).[82] **11.59**

Units in authorised unit trust schemes are eligible for settlement in CREST. **11.60**

Nature of rights of participants in the portfolio

The express terms of the declaration of trust that are prescribed for authorised unit trust schemes confer undivided co-ownership rights on unit holders in the trust assets.[83] **11.61**

Comparison with DRs and custody and settlement arrangements

There are very strong similarities between the legal nature of a unit holder's interest in the unit trust portfolio, and that of a DR holder in respect of the shares held by the depositary. Both types of interest are indirect and unallocated, comprising an intangible asset, and both arise under an express equitable tenancy in common. Of course, the economic purposes of a DR programme and a unit trust are different. Unlike a DR programme, a unit trust has a manager with discretionary investment powers. The portfolio of a unit trust may comprise a wide and changing range of securities, derivatives and cash assets,[84] whereas the assets underlying a DR typically comprise only a single type of security and associated cash balances.[85] However, even though the composition of the underlying portfolio differs in the two structures, the investor's proprietary rights in respect of it are the same in each case. **11.62**

---

[82] Regulated Schemes Regulations, regs 2.06, 9.05 and 9.06.

[83] See reg 2.02 and Sch Part I, of which require the trust deed of an authorised unit trust scheme to contain: 'A declaration that . . . the property of the scheme . . . is held by the trustee on trust for the holders of the units pari passu according to the number of units held by each holder or, in the case where income units and accumulation units are both in issue, according to the number of undivided shares in the property of the scheme represented by the units held by each holder'. Regulation 2.05 provides that that each unit represents 'one undivided share in the property of the scheme'. This accords with the argument in Chapter 2 that the beneficiary of a trust has proprietary rights in the trust assets as against the trustee. The author therefore does not share Dr Sin's view that the unit holder 'does not have any proprietary interest in the underlying assets': Sin, (n 68 above) 73.

[84] Within the investment powers and policy of the unit trust.

[85] A regulatory restriction on the development of DR programmes with more than one type of underlying security is as follows. As indicated above, the Financial Services Act 1986, s 76, restricts the promotion of unregulated collective investment schemes. Section 76(6)(h) removes from the definition of collective investment schemes 'arrangements under which the rights or interests of the participants are investments falling within paragraph 5 of Schedule 1 to this Act'. Paragraph 5 relates to certificates representing securities. As registered securities, DRs are generally certificated. However, a note to para 5 states that 'This paragraph does not apply to any instrument which confers rights in respect of two or more investments issued by different persons or in respect of two or more different investments falling within paragraph 3 above [government and public securities] and issued by the same person'.

11.63 A considerable body of case law concerning unit trusts has been developed (largely by the Australian courts, and considered in a recent book by Dr Sin.[86] Because of the likeness of unit trusts to DRs (and, it will be argued below, other structures in the securities markets), it may be possible to apply much of this case law more widely.

11.64 Just as unit trusts are akin to DRs, DRs are akin to the custody and settlement trust arrangements, as was argued above. It is uncontroversial that a unit in a unit trust comprises (as a matter of law) a different asset from the components of underlying portfolio. This supports the argument, set out in Chapters 1 and 2, that interests in securities (arising in custody and settlement trusts) comprise assets which are different from the underlying securities.

Limited partnerships

11.65 Another legal structure used in managed funds, which has strong similarities to the unit trust, is the limited partnership.

Nature of limited partnership

11.66 A limited partnership is a form of partnership, in relation to which the general law of partnership has been modified.[87] Partners are divided into two classes, namely general partners (who are responsible for managing the business and assets of the partnership) and limited partners (who do not take part in management).[88] As long as they take no part in management,[89] the liability of limited partners in respect of the business of the partnership is limited to the capital they have contributed.[90] (This contrasts with the position under the general law of partnerships, in which all partners have unlimited joint and several liability.) Under a limited partnership, only the general partners have unlimited liability.[91]

11.67 Limited partnerships are required to be publicly registered,[92] and must file particulars of changes in the partnership.[93] Thus, limited partnerships constitute a form of hybrid between limited liability companies (in which the liability of sharehold-

---

[86] See Sin (n 68 above).

[87] 'Subject to the provisions of this Act, the Partnership Act 1890 and the rules of equity and of common law applicable to partnerships, except so far as they are inconsistent with the express provisions of the last-mentioned Act, shall apply to limited partnerships': Limited Partnerships Act 1907, s 7.

[88] ibid s 6(1).

[89] 'If a limited partner takes part in the management of the partnership business he shall be liable for all debts and obligations of the firm incurred while he so takes part in the management as though he were a general partner': ibid s 6(1).

[90] However, the status of limited partner, and the associated limitation of liability, is lost if they take any part in management.

[91] Limited Partnerships Act 1907, s 4(2).

[92] ibid ss 5, 8 and 15.

[93] ibid s 9.

ers is limited to their capital contribution, and which are required to file returns)[94] and general partnerships (in which all partners have unlimited liability, and which conduct their affairs in private).

In the United Kingdom, a regime for limited partnerships was created by the **11.68** Limited Partnerships Act 1907 (which requires limited partnerships to be registered with the Registrar of Companies).[95] The limited partnership must have a principal place of business in England and Wales.

Like most general partnerships,[96] limited partnerships may have no more than 20 **11.69** partners.[97]

Private equity funds

The limited partnership structure is suitable for use as a wholesale fund, with par- **11.70** ticipants assuming the role of limited partners,[98] and management being undertaken by one or more general partner.[99] Limited partnerships can be highly profitable for the general partner.[100] The fund is constituted by a partnership agreement made between the general partner and the limited partners whose interests in the fund is referred to as 'limited partnership interests'. The general partner may be assisted by an investment adviser. Although limited partners are not able to take any part in management, they are usually represented by an advisory committee, which provides advice (but not instructions) to the general partner.

Because of the '20 partner rule', where more than 20 investors are found, a num- **11.71** ber of limited partnerships are constituted. The same manager acts as general partner in each. The different partnerships are linked contractually so as to form a single fund, and the monies of this fund are invested together in the same assets (with each partnership taking a ratable proportion of each asset).

---

[94] Limited liability was considered desirable in order to encourage enterprise. As a quid pro quo, publicity of financial and other information was required so that creditors could make an informed decision as to the likelihood of the company being affected by insolvency.

[95] Limited Partnerships Act 1907, s 5. If unregistered, the partnership will be deemed to be a general partnership.

[96] Exceptions from the 20 partner rule are made for solicitors, accountants and brokers; see the Companies Act 1985, s 717.

[97] See the Limited Partnerships Act 1907, s 4(2).

[98] Some institutions are not permitted to invest in limited partnerships; such institutional investors may be able to make such investment indirectly, where another type of vehicle such as a unit trust is interposed between the investor and the limited partnership.

[99] In some cases, the general partner may delegate the management function to a separate entity.

[100] After limited partners have received the return of their original investment plus profits of perhaps 10 per cent, the general partners receive a share of excess profits (known as carried interest) of perhaps 20 per cent. This is in addition to regular management fees of up to 2 per cent of (broadly) total commitments to the fund. This is a very brief summary of typically complex on-going fee calculations.

11.72 This is not a suitable structure for retail funds for a number of reasons,[101] including the fact that limited partnership interests are illiquid.[102] Moreover, maintenance of capital rules restrict the return of limited partners' capital investment until the partnership is wound up.[103] However, in order to enable limited partners to realise the profits of the fund's investments from time to time, a large proportion of their contribution is made up of a loan to the fund, which the general partner is permitted to repay from time to time.[104]

11.73 Limited partnerships have long been used in the USA as a vehicle for wholesale funds. However, this structure was rarely used by the UK managed funds industry until its tax transparency was confirmed in 1987 by a statement issued by the British Venture Capital Association, with the agreement of the Inland Revenue. Following the BVCA statement, this structure is widely used for UK wholesale private equity funds.[105]

Nature of limited partner's interest in underlying property

11.74 A large part of the fund's investment will be in the form of equities. These are registered in the name of the general partner, with a note in the register that the general partner holds the shares for and on behalf of the partnership.[106] It is provided in the limited partnership deed that the general partner holds these assets on trust for the partners from time to time.[107] There is no allocation between particular partners and particular assets in the fund's portfolio. The assets of general partnerships are co-owned by the partners.

---

[101] As unregulated funds, the marketing of limited partnerships to retail investors is narrowly restricted (see above). Limited partnership agreements are complex documents, and are typically heavily negotiated between limited partners and the general partner. Return to investors is over the medium and not the short term.

[102] Limited partnership interests are not redeemable, and in typical fund structures may be transferred only with the consent of the general partner. (Provision in the Limited Partnership Act 1907, s 6(5)(b) for the assignment of limited partnership interests is subject to contrary agreement by the partners.)

[103] ibid s 4(3). Once realised, fund investments are not reinvested. Limited partnerships are generally wound up after some ten years.

[104] Perhaps 0.01 per cent of a limited partner's contribution is by way of capital. The remainder is by way of a loan commitment made when the fund is established. The loan is drawn down from time to time by the general partner over the course of perhaps five or six years in order to make investments on behalf of the fund, and returned thereafter as investments are realised. Realised investments are not reinvested. The fund may have a life of ten to 12 years.

[105] A private equity fund, also known as a venture capital fund, is a fund the investment policy of which is to invest in small companies at an early stage in their business development, with important prospects for growth. This is a high risk, high reward policy; profits associated with successful 'start up' companies are large, but a significant number may fail.

[106] Where the fund invests in bearer securities, these are usually held by a custodian on behalf of the general partner.

[107] As with custody and settlement trusts, DRs and unit trusts, this is a trust in favour of a class.

Corporate funds

A third important fund structure is the corporation. Unlike either a trust or a partnership,[108] a corporation is a separate legal personality. A legal person can hold property and contract in its own name. Whereas brokers and other third parties dealing with unit trusts have to contract with the trustee, and those dealing with limited partnerships have to contract with the general partner, third parties dealing with a corporate fund can contract with the fund itself.[109] **11.75**

Corporate funds take the form of limited liability companies. Participants are shareholders in such companies, and their liability is limited to the sum of their capital contribution. It was seen above that an equivalent limitation of liability is achieved in a limited partnership, but only on the basis that participants take no part in management. **11.76**

The corporate structure is available for managed funds in most jurisdictions, and this is probably the most internationally common fund structure. **11.77**

A corporate fund may be open-ended or closed-ended. Participants in an open-ended corporate fund may redeem their shares at net asset value. The issued share capital of open-ended companies fluctuates from time to time as shares are redeemed and new shares issued, and hence their name. Closed-ended companies are subject to the usual rules on maintenance of capital, and cannot readily redeem their own shares. Participants in closed-ended companies wishing to dispose of their investment must transfer them to a purchaser in the secondary market. **11.78**

In the United Kingdom, two forms of corporate fund are available, namely investment trusts (which are closed-ended) and open-ended investment companies, or OEICS. **11.79**

Investment trusts

In spite of their somewhat misleading name, investment trusts are not trusts but companies. They have a very long history.[110] **11.80**

---

[108] A limited partnership is not a legal person: *Re Barnard, Martin's Bank v Trustee* [1932] 1 Ch 269.

[109] This represents a real advantage for third party creditors, who are able to enforce judgment debts against the fund's assets, and therefore take the credit risk of the fund itself. In contrast, in the case of limited partnerships and unit trusts, third party creditors are in the first instance only able to enforce their claims against the trustee (or general partner as trustee of the fund's assets). The trustee has a right of indemnity against the fund's assets in respect of its debts and expenses, provided they were properly incurred in the course of the trustee's duties. Third parties have a right of subrogation to this right of indemnity. However, the indemnity is not available (so that the right of subrogation is valueless) in respect of debts and expenses incurred in breach of trust.

[110] The development of investment trusts in the nineteenth century, and their common ancestry with the unit trust is discussed by Sin (n 68 above) 22 and 23.

11.81 Investment trusts are public limited companies whose shares are listed in London and admitted to trading on the London Stock Exchange. Investment trusts are exempt from capital gains tax. The status of investment trust is conferred by the Inland Revenue, in accordance with criteria set down in the Income and Corporation Taxes Act 1988.[111] A custodian, manager and (in some cases) investment adviser are appointed by contract by the investment trust. The performance of the manager is supervised by the board of directors of the investment trust, and a company secretary carries out administrative functions.

11.82 Investment trusts are retail funds, and their shares may be marketed to the general public.[112] In this respect they represent a rival product to the authorised unit trust. Their shares customarily trade below net asset value, although where an investment trust is performing well and its shares are in demand they can trade at a premium.

OEICs

11.83 Under the general principles of UK company law, maintenance of capital rules restrict the redemption of issued shares.[113] Therefore, traditionally, it was necessary to structure open-ended funds as unit trusts. Corporate funds (in the form of investment trusts) were closed-ended, and stock exchange listing provided liquidity. However, in civil law jurisdictions (including continental Europe) open-ended investment companies have long been familiar to the investing public, and the unit trust structure is unknown. The UK managed fund industry found that the unfamiliarity of their retail product to Belgian dentists (and other continental retail investors) placed it at a competitive disadvantage. In an attempt to overcome this problem, the Open-Ended Investment Companies (Investment Companies with Variable Capital) Regulations 1996, SI 1996/2827 (the 'ECA Regulations') were made.[114]

11.84 OEICs are limited liability companies in respect of which the general provisions of English company law have been modified so as to permit their shares to be read-

---

[111] Criteria for investment trust status under ICTA 1988, s 842, include the following: the company must be UK resident; its income must consist mainly of eligible investment income (ie derive from securities and rental income); it must be listed on the London Stock Exchange; and it must not retain more than 15 per cent of its eligible investment income in any year.

[112] As closed-ended companies, they fall outside the definition of collective investment scheme in FSA 1986, s 75(7) and therefore are not subject to the marketing restrictions under ibid s 76. However, as listed corporate shares offered to the general public their promotion is subject to the requirements of Part IV of the FSA 1986 and the London Stock Exchange listing requirements.

[113] See Part V of the Companies Act 1985.

[114] These regulations are defined in the Financial Services (Open-Ended Investment Companies) Regulations 1997 (reg 3), and have become known in the market, as the ECA Regulations because they were enacted under the European Communities Act 1972.

ily redeemable at net asset value.[115] An OEIC is constituted by an instrument of incorporation.[116]

OEICs are authorisable by the Financial Services Authority,[117] and regulated **11.85** under the Financial Services (Open-Ended Investment Companies) Regulations 1997 (the 'OEIC Regulations'), which contain detailed provisions relating to all aspects of their constitution, operation and management.[118] An OEIC is eligible for UCITS status.[119]

The manager of an OEIC takes the role of authorised corporate director **11.86** (ACD).[120] It may be assisted by an investment adviser. A depositary acts as custodian of the OEIC's assets[121] (directly or through sub-custodians),[122] and has a supervisory role, overseeing compliance with the OEIC Regulations.[123] A prospectus containing prescribed information must be prepared.[124] OEICs may belong to one of three categories having different investment powers,[125] namely a securities company, a warrant company or an umbrella company.[126] Shares may be issued in a number of different classes.[127] An OEIC is permitted to issue shares in bearer form.[128] Like units in unit trusts, OEIC shares are redeemed at net asset

---

[115] An OEIC is not generally subject to the provisions of the Companies Act 1985. These apply to a 'company', which is defined in s 735 of the 1985 Act as 'a company formed and registered under this Act, or an existing company [ie one formed under former Companies Acts]'. In contrast, an OEIC is formed and registered under the ECA Regulations.

[116] This must comply with the ECA Regulations and the OEIC Regulations (see below). A model instrument of incorporation has been prepared by AUTIF. The ECA Regulations, regs 3 and 4, provide that the FSA (formerly SIB) shall make an authorisation order; immediately upon its coming into effect the OEIC will be incorporated; and as soon as reasonably practicable thereafter the authorisation order will be sent to the Registrar of Companies, which will register the instrument of incorporation and relevant details. After incorporation, the OEIC must register its prospectus and from time to time notify the registrar of companies of various matters: reg 65.

[117] Under the Financial Services (Open Ended Investment Companies) Regulations 1997, reg 9.

[118] The structure of the OEIC Regulations broadly follows that of the Financial Services (Regulated Schemes) Regulations 1991 discussed above, with Parts dealing with (inter alia): the constitution of the scheme; the preparation and publication of a prospectus; pricing of and dealing with shares; investment and borrowing powers; powers and duties of the director and depositary; income; reports and accounts; shareholders' meetings and amendments to the instrument of incorporation.

[119] ECA Regulations, reg 12.

[120] See the OEIC Regulations, regs 6.01, 6.02. This is a director of the company which is itself incorporated, and authorised to carry on investment business in the United Kingdom under the FSA 1986. The ACD is appointed to the OEIC pursuant to the authorisation order.

[121] ECA Regulations, reg 5.

[122] ibid reg 5(2) provides an express power of sub-delegation.

[123] See the OEIC Regulations, reg 6.05.

[124] See the OEIC Regulations, reg 3.01, Sch 1.

[125] See Part 5 of the OEIC Regulations.

[126] OEIC Regulations, reg 2.03.

[127] 'These include "income shares", "net accumulation shares", "gross accumulation shares", and currency class shares in the form of any such class': OEIC Regulations, explanation to Part 2. See ibid reg 2.04.

[128] ECA Regulations, reg 42.

value; unlike unit trusts, dual pricing is not permitted, and shares are issued and redeemed on the basis of single pricing.[129] Shares in OEICs are proposed to be eligible for settlement in CREST.

Offshore corporate funds

11.87 Many offshore wholesale funds are structured as open-ended investment companies. This may be particularly suitable where targeted investors are restricted in their ability to invest in limited partnerships. The management structure is similar to that of a limited partnership, but fund managers are appointed under a simple contract of services, and not as a general partner.

Nature of rights of shareholders in underlying assets

11.88 It was seen above that participants in unit trusts and limited partnerships co-own the fund's assets under equitable tenancies in common. Thus, their property rights equate to those of DR holders and clients of custody and settlement trusts.

11.89 In contrast, participants in both investment trusts and OEICs have the status of shareholders. Their proprietary rights are therefore somewhat different. 'Today a share in a registered company is unequivocally a species of transferable personal property, which does not include an interest, legal or equitable, in the assets of the company.'[130] This is because a company has legal personality, distinct from its shareholders. The company owns the company's assets legally and beneficially; in turn, the shareholders own the company.[131] However, the rights of shareholders in relation to the company's assets may be economically indistinguishable from ownership.[132]

11.90 *Historic origin of corporation in trust and partnerships*

The history of company law shows that there are strong links between the proprietary position of a shareholder and that of a unit holder and of a limited partner. The concept of separate corporate legal personality was clearly developed in the mid-nineteenth century. Prior to that, the old deed of settlement companies of the eighteenth and early nineteenth centuries (which were the ancestors of modern

---

[129] Only one price is given, rather than separate bid and offer prices, as for unit trusts. See Part 4 of the OEIC Regulations.

[130] Glen Barton, 'The Legal Nature of a Share', in Palmer and McKendrick (eds) *Interests in Goods* (2nd edn, London: LLP, 1998) 114.

[131] See Barton (n 130 above).

[132] 'Whilst a share will not entail any direct proprietary interest in the assets of the corporation, its substance may include rights of control. At the point where control is such that the controllers (or controller) can cause the company to transfer its assets or their proceeds to themselves or third parties, control and ownership become commercially, if not legally, indistinguishable': Barton (n 130 above) 114. See the ECA Regulations, reg 39(2), which provides that a shareholder in an OEIC does not have an interest in the scheme property.

[133] 'Legally speaking, these bodies were partnerships': P S Atiyah, *The Rise and Fall of Freedom of Contract* (Oxford: Clarendon Press, 1979) 562.

incorporated companies) were constituted as partnerships.[133] Their assets were held in trust for shareholders.[134] Thus company shares were originally a form of equitable interest, akin to both units in a unit trust scheme and to limited partnership interests.[135] Thus, it may be seen that the differences between the proprietary position of participants in corporate and non-corporate funds is merely a technical consequence of the development of legal personality.

(4) Comparison of Repackaging Structures

11.91

To recap, it has been argued that interests arising under DRs, unit trusts and limited partnerships are fundamentally akin to those arising under fungible custody and settlement arrangements. All arise under a form of repackaging arrangement, whereby a new asset is created which is legally distinct from the underlying asset, but economically the same as it. All are interests in securities. All are indirect, in that in the normal course they confer no direct rights of action against the issuer of the underlying securities. All are, as against the intermediary, proprietary (because the asset is not available to the creditors of the intermediary). All are unallocated, in that no client's interest in securities attaches to particular underlying securities. All arise under equitable tenancies in common. Because they do not attach, all constitute intangible assets (even where the underlying securities are themselves tangible). In the conflict of laws, it has been argued, all are legally located where they are recorded, in the books of the intermediary, against whom they are enforceable (even where the underlying securities are located elsewhere). Where there is a shortfall, it has been argued, all are pro rated.

11.92

Units in corporate funds are different, but only because a corporate intermediary has separate legal personality. The difference is technical and relatively recent. Moreover, strong points of similarity remain. The shareholder has an economic interest in the corporate assets, but no direct or allocated legal rights against them. Shares are intangible, even where corporate assets are tangible. In the conflict of laws, shares are legally located where they are recorded, with the register of the issuer. If there is a shortfall, the loss is borne rateably by shareholders.

11.93

It is interesting to compare the legal development of new forms of capital investment vehicle in the early modern period and that of new forms of investment

---

[134] See Formoy (n 68 above) 41, 42. Glen Barton (n 130 above) cites *Child v Hudson Bay Co* (1723) 2 PWMS 207, per Lord Maccelsfield: 'the legal interest of all the stock is in the company who are trustees for the several members'. See also Maitland, 'Trust and Corporation', in *Selected Essays* (Cambridge University Pess, 1936) 214: 'the connection between Trust and Corporation is very ancient'.

[135] Indeed, all three structures have a common ancestor in the deed of settlement companies. Shares were brought out of equity and into the common law by the Joint Stock Companies Act of 1856, which replaced the deed of settlement with a memorandum of association, and thereby ended the central role of the trust in the constitution of companies. However, it is still customary for issues of registered debentures to be made under a trust deed, so that registered corporate debt remains in most cases equitable and not legal, as discussed in Chapter 2.

intermediary in recent decades. Originally, the courts did not take the point that shares were a new form of asset, distinct from the underlying assets of the company. However, in 1837, *Bligh v Brent*[136] the shares in a company were held to comprise assets distinct from the underlying assets of a company. That moment in the history of company law might be compared to the present development of the law of the securities markets, where it is being established that interests in securities are distinct assets from the securities that underlie them.

D. Conclusions

11.94

This chapter has argued that the interests of investors in depositary receipts, managed funds and custody and settlement arrangements have in common the following characteristics. (1) The investor is separated from the underlying (interests in) securities by an intermediary. (2) The asset in the hands of the intermediary is intangible. (3) The intermediary holds the investor's asset commingled with the like assets of other investors. (4) The investor's asset is not available to the creditors of the intermediary. In each case, the structure relies on the following legal concepts: characteristics (1) and (4) involve the assertion of indirect property rights in favour of the client or collateral taker; this is reconciled with characteristic (2) by the concept of an equitable interest;[137] it is reconciled with characteristic (3) by the concept of co-ownership.

---

[136] (1837) 2 Y & C Ex 268.
[137] Arising under a trust in CBOs, the equivalent equitable interest is a charge. See Chapter 12.

12

COLLATERALISED BOND OBLIGATIONS AND RELATED STRUCTURES[1]

Plus ça change, plus c'est la même chose

This chapter will consider a relatively recent form of repackaging known as collateralised bond obligations ('CBOs').[2] CBOs were originally developed in the USA in the late 1980s. During the course of the 1990s the use of CBOs grew tremendously, with CBOs being established in Europe and (more recently) issued outside the USA. The last half of 1999 saw English law CBOs issued as a European product, and these are expected to grow significantly in the new millennium. CBO combines elements of a number of traditional structures. Indeed, they are of so hybrid a nature that their correct categorisation is controversial, and **12.01**

---

[1] The author is grateful to Andrew Coats of Clifford Chance for kindly reviewing this section and Rachel Kelly of Clifford Chance for her general comments. The opinions expressed in it and any errors are the author's own. CBOs are often discussed together with CDOs and CLOs: see below.

[2] The discussion of CBOs in this section represents a considerable simplification of a complex and evolving market. The author was assisted in preparing this section by her former student, Xin Zhang, who wrote a dissertation on securitisation (JIBFL, forthcoming).

perhaps premature; the better view may be that they are an original product.[3] Much published material presents CBOs as a new variety of securitisation, and their relationship with traditional securitisation structures is considered below. However, it may be helpful briefly to place CBOs in the context of the simpler structures of which they may be said to be a development. These simpler structures are asset swaps and repackagings.[4]

A. Asset Swaps

12.02 As discussed in Chapter 1, eurobonds generally pay fixed rates of interest. However, investors often wish to receive floating rates of interest.[5] Moreover, many potential investors in (interests in) eurobonds wish to receive income in US dollars, which may not be the currency in which income of eurobonds are paid. The asset swap market developed in the early 1980s to address these problems. An asset swap is a simple technique developed by investment banks for converting the currency and/or interest rate benchmark of the income payable on (interests in) eurobonds, thereby making investment in such eurobonds more attractive to investors.

12.03 In practice an asset swap might be structured as follows. An investment bank sells (interests in) eurobonds to an investor, and simultaneously enters into an interest rate and/or currency swap with the investor. The investor receives fixed rate (and/or non-dollar) income from the (interests in) eurobonds. Under the swap agreement, the investor pays sums equal to this eurobond income to the investment bank, and receives from it floating rate (and/or dollar) income payments.[6]

12.04 Although they have been an important source of liquidity in the eurobond markets, asset swaps remain a blunt instrument for a number of reasons. First, they are illiquid. If the investor wishes to dispose of the eurobonds, it must either terminate the swap[7] or assign it.[8] Moreover, if the issuer of the eurobonds defaults (so that the income stream ceases), the investor will remain bound by the swap agree-

---

[3] The repackaging, securitisation and managed funds markets all claim parentage of this successful product.

[4] See C Lewis, 'Asset Repackaging Wins Further Followers', IFLR (November 1996) 23 and R Mannix, 'Repackaging: the Key Structures in the Euromarket' IFLR (May 1999) 9.

[5] This is generally because investors have to borrow the funds with which to invest from commercial banks at a floating rate of interest. In these circumstances investors will wish to be able to pay this floating rate liability out of a (somewhat higher) floating rate income. Of course, floating rate notes pay floating rates of income: see Chapter 1.

[6] In practice these income payments between the parties to the swap are netted. Swaps are discussed in more detail in Chapter 6.

[7] If it wishes to be released from its obligations under the swap agreement, it will typically incur 'break costs'.

[8] This may not be a practical solution. Other disadvantages of asset swaps are possible tax and accounting inefficiencies, and (for the swap counterparty) the credit risk of the investor.

ment.[9] To address these shortcomings, a solution was developed in the form of repackaging. The original repackagings were simple, and complex repackagings were developed later.

B. Simple Repackaging

Repackaging develops the asset swap structure by the use of a special purpose vehi- **12.05** cle, or SPV. The SPV undertakes no business (and therefore has no assets or, it is hoped liabilities)[10] other than those associated with the transaction or transactions for which it was established. The SPV is established in a jurisdiction with favourable taxation, accounting and regulatory regimes, such as the Cayman Islands and Jersey,[11] but, depending on the assets being repackaged, may need to be established in a jurisdiction having the benefit of a double taxation treaty, such as Luxembourg. It usually takes the form of a corporation, but may also be a trust or a partnership. In order to ensure that the SPV is not affected by the insolvency of the investment bank, and that its accounts need not be consolidated with those of the investment bank, it is important that the investment bank does not control the management of the SPV nor hold its shares.[12]

A simple repackaging might be structured as follows. Rather than sell the (inter- **12.06** ests in) fixed rate eurobonds directly to investors, the investment bank sells them to the SPV. The SPV issues new securities in the form of floating rate dollar notes to investors. A trustee is appointed to the issue of new notes, which are constituted by a trust deed. Their issue price is used to fund the purchase price of the (interests in) eurobonds.

The investment bank enters into a swap with the SPV. Under the swap the SPV pays **12.07** the fixed income it receives from the (interests in) eurobonds to the investment bank; the floating rate dollar income which it receives from the investment bank under the swap is used to meet the SPV's payment obligations to noteholders.

In order to address credit risk, security interests are used in the structure as follows. **12.08** The SPV grants a first security interest over the (interests in) eurobonds to the trustee. Also, the benefit of contracts entered into by the SPV are assigned by way

---

[9] Conversely, if the investment bank defaults, the investor will continue to receive unswapped income.

[10] As discussed below, it is crucial to establish that the SPV is insolvency remote. This means both that it is most unlikely to become insolvent (either because it has excess liabilities, or because it has shareholders who might have an interest in its liquidation) and that it will not be affected by the insolvency of the originator (for example because it is substantively consolidated with the originator in the latter's insolvency).

[11] Where it is usually administered by a local bank.

[12] The SPV is established as an 'orphan company', with its shares being held by a local institution (usually) on trust for noteholders so long as notes are outstanding and, thereafter, for a charity.

of security to the trustee. The trustee holds the benefit of these security arrangements for noteholders and other secured parties, including the swap counterparty. Under the terms of the trust, it is provided that the trustee will apply the proceeds of sale, first to meet the obligations of the SPV to the swap counterparty under the swap, and secondly to make payment to noteholders under the notes.

12.09 Together, the charge and the trust serve to confer on noteholders a property interest in the (interests in) eurobonds and the rights under the swap. The obligation of the SPV to make payments to noteholders is limited to sums equal to the sums it receives under the bonds and the swap agreement. The effect of this 'limited recourse' provision, together with the interest of noteholders under the trust of the charges, are intended to place noteholders in the same economic position they would have been in had the SPV not been interposed between them, the (interests in) eurobonds and the investment bank.[13]

12.10 The notes are generally settled through Euroclear and Clearstream (in the case of European investors) or another convenient settlement system. Thus (in contrast to illiquid asset swaps) repackagings create assets which are readily transferable[14] and easily settled.[15]

12.11 These relatively simple structures, in which the underlying assets comprise an unchanging holding of one type of (interests in) security, became known as 'one bond, one swap repackagings'. In this respect, they are comparable to DRs.

C. Complex Repackaging

12.12 Over time, complex forms of repackaging evolved, which differed from the one bond, one swap structure in a number of respects.

(1) Structured Note Programmes

12.13 In order to save costs and delays, structured[16] note programmes were developed, under which a series of repackaging transactions are undertaken using the same SPV, and on the basis of the same set of master documentation. New documentation for each new issue of notes is kept to a minimum.[17]

---

[13] ie if they had invested in the bonds and entered into the swap directly with the investment bank. Of course, whereas an asset swap is entered into by an investment bank with one investor, repackaged notes are usually issued to a number of investors.

[14] Assuming of course that a buyer can be found.

[15] Moreover, their taxation and accounting treatment is simpler than that of asset swaps, and they do not expose the investment bank to the unsecured credit risk of the investor under the swap agreement.

[16] The term 'structured' in this context denotes the use of a segregated pool of assets which serve to collateralise the (interests in) securities. The phrase 'structured finance' is sometimes used interchangeably with the term 'securitisation'.

[17] These arrangements are modeled on MTN programmes, discussed briefly in Chapter 1.

It was seen above that a charge and trust are used to confer on noteholders a prop- **12.14**
erty interest in the underlying (interests in) bonds. In the case of structured note
programmes, it is important to ensure that the bonds underlying one issue of
notes are segregated in the hands of the SPV from those underlying each other
issue of notes under the programme. Such segregation is necessary to ensure that
a separate charge and trust takes effect in respect of each issue of notes. In turn,
this ensures that losses associated with the default under one class of underlying
bonds affect only holders of the notes issued in respect of those bonds, and not
holders of other notes issued under the programme.[18]

Notes issued to European investors under such programmes are normally listed in **12.15**
London or in Luxembourg; however, some issues are unlisted.

(2) Mixed Underlying Assets

A wide range of assets may be repackaged, including registered securities, loan **12.16**
participations and other forms of repackaged securities.[19] A further development
is the repackaging together of two or more types of asset in a single transaction
(multiple asset repackagings). Under a programme of single asset repackagings,
discussed above, the SPV will hold different classes of (interests in) bonds, but
holds each class subject to a separate charge. It must therefore hold each class of
asset separately. In contrast, under a multiple asset repackaging, the SPV may hold
different classes of assets subject to a single charge (in favour of noteholders under
a single transaction), and may therefore hold such assets fungibly. In this respect
complex structures are more akin to managed funds, in which investors participate in a portfolio of securities, as discussed in Chapter 11.

Of course, managed funds are managed in the sense that the fund manager buys **12.17**
and sells (interests in) securities in accordance with investment criteria and/or on
a discretionary basis. In a repackaging, it is more common for redemption monies
from the underlying assets to be used to redeem the notes. Under more recent
structures, however, redemption monies from the underlying assets may be reinvested, so that the composition of the underlying portfolio changes from time to
time. Such reinvestment is an important characteristic of CBOs.

---

[18] The credit rating agencies have been concerned to establish that such 'ring-fencing' (or 'fire-
walling') is effective. Doubt as to its effectiveness in certain jurisdictions has historically restricted
the development of the MTN programmes. Where the SPV appoints a custodian to hold the underlying assets in a settlement system, such segregation can be achieved by placing the different classes
of assets in different accounts in the settlement system.
[19] It is not uncommon for the same underlying assets to be repackaged several times, so that
repackaged assets are repackaged again and again.

D. Collateralised Bond Obligations

12.18   This discussion is concerned with collateralised bond obligations. CBOs have developed together with collateralised loan obligations or CLOs. In CLOs, the underlying portfolio consists not of (interests in) bonds but of loan obligations.[20] Structures in which the portfolio consists of both types of asset are called collateralised debt obligations, or CDOs.

12.19   Two distinct kinds of CBO have developed. In a 'traditional'[21] CBO, the issue of notes is supported by a portfolio of (interests in) bonds, in which noteholders acquire a property interest. In contrast, in synthetic CBOs, credit derivatives (usually credit default swaps) are used to replicate the economic effect of such property rights.[22] This discussion is concerned with traditional CBOs; a brief discussion of synthetic CBOs appears in the concluding chapter of this book.

12.20   CBOs may be balance sheet transactions (having the purpose of removing the underlying assets from the balance sheet of the originator)[23] or arbitrage transactions (in which a profit is made from the differences between the high rates of income on the relatively low grade underlying assets purchased in the market and the lower rates of income on high grade notes which are issued).[24] In CBOs, the composition of the underlying portfolio changes from time to time, for two reasons. First, at closing, the portfolio consists in large part (or even wholly) of the proceeds of the issue of notes, and this cash is invested in (interests in) bonds over a 'ramp up' period (of six months to one year). Secondly, during a reinvestment period (of a number of years), redemption monies will be reinvested in new (interests in) bonds.[25] Further, when existing (interests in) bonds fail to perform against defined criteria, there is provision for them to be disposed of, and others substi-

---

[20] In collateralised loan obligations or CLOs, the originator is usually a commercial bank securitising its corporate loan portfolio. In many cases, the purpose of a CLO is to increase the return of equity investment to shareholders, by removing corporate loans to high credit customers (which generate a low return for the bank), thus freeing up capital for higher risk and return loans to customers with lower credit.

[21] It may seem curious to describe anything as recent as CBOs as traditional.

[22] The author is grateful to Rachael Kelly of Clifford Chance for this point.

[23] 'Balance sheet deals are generally the securitisation of lower yielding, borderline investment grade loans, for the purpose of gaining capital relief, obtaining alternative funding or increasing the issuing entity's return on equity by removing lower yielding assets from its balance sheet': Morgan Stanley Dean Witter, *Collateralized Debt Obligation Handbook* (November 1998) 23.

[24] 'In an arbitrage transaction, the equity investor [ie junior noteholder] is capturing the spread difference between the relatively high yielding collateral and the yields at which the senior liabilities of the CDO are issued': *Collateralized Debt Obligation Handbook* (n 23 above) 1. A proposal for an arbitrage CBO may be initiated by a fund manager, which approaches an investment bank with a view to the bank acting as arranger.

[25] See 'Project Collateralized Loans and Bonds: Rating Considerations' *Standard & Poor's Structured Finance* (November 1999) 33, at 40.

tuted. Thus, the pool of assets underlying collateralised bond obligations are not only mixed, but also changing from time to time.

CBOs are divided into cash flow CBOs and market performance CBOs. Both require active management, but a higher degree of discretionary management is required for the latter.[26] The entity responsible for this management function may be referred to in the transaction documentation as the investment adviser.[27] However, this discussion will refer to this entity as the manager, in accordance with the practice of the managed funds industry (discussed in Chapter 11). The drafting of the agreement under which the manager of a CBO is appointed may be extensive and detailed. **12.21**

CBOs may be understood as a development of complex repackagings. Conversely, CBOs are often described as a simple form of securitisation. Undoubtedly CBOs rely on financial techniques that were traditionally developed in the securitisation markets, including the management of a changing portfolio and credit enhancement techniques. It will be argued below that CBOs are in functional terms a form of managed fund. **12.22**

A CBO involves the repackaging of a portfolio of underlying (interests in) bonds (which may be issued from more than one jurisdiction), in which direct investment would be relatively unattractive to investors, into new securities (usually notes) which represent more attractive investment opportunities. The underlying bonds may be unattractive because there is a significant risk that their issuers will default, for example because the issuer is a commercial company with a relatively low credit rating,[28] or an emerging markets issuer.[29] The new notes (or a preferred class of them) are more attractive for a number of reasons. Most importantly, they achieve a high credit rating.[30] Whereas the underlying (interests in) bonds are **12.23**

---

[26] 'A minority of CDOs have been cast as market-value transactions, in which the credit enhancement is reflected in a cushion between the current market value of the collateral and the face value of the structure's obligations. Within this framework, the collateral must normally be liquidated, either in whole or in part, if the ratio of the market value of the collateral to the obligations falls below some threshold. The liquidated collateral is used to pay down obligations, bringing the structure back into balance. In contrast, cash-flow transactions normally provide for the diversion of cash flows from junior to senior classes if certain tests that relate to the structure's soundness are not met': 'Moody's Approach to Rating Market-Value CDOs' *Structured Finance Special Report* (Moody's Investors Service, 3 April 1998).

[27] This may be because, in capital markets transactions, the term 'manager' traditionally denotes the party responsible for managing the issue of securities, rather than the underlying portfolio.

[28] A number of CBOs have been launched recently, using portfolios of Japanese corporate bonds, thus assisting their corporate issuers to raise capital at a time when banking finance was not readily available. See J Evans, 'Collateralised Bond Obligations in Japan' *The ISR Legal Guide to Securitisation* (July 1999) 31–36.

[29] Many CBOs are used to repackage emerging market debt.

[30] 'Ratings by one or more nationally recognized rating agencies . . . are invariably required in order to sell asset-backed securities in the public markets. Additionally, many financial institutions and investment funds that purchase asset-backed securities in the private markets require ratings in

below investment grade[31] or even ungraded, the new notes are usually graded triple A, through the use of credit enhancement techniques as discussed below.[32] In order to maintain this high credit rating and preserve the stream of payments to noteholders, the underlying portfolio of bonds is actively managed.

12.24 CBOs may serve a range of different purposes. They have recently been used to a significant extent by European banks as a method of enhancing their financial performance by reducing their regulatory capital burden. CBOs may also be used to assist corporate issuers who would not otherwise have access to the capital markets, by repackaging their new bonds as they are issued. Alternatively, CBOs may be used as a way of disposing of existing holdings of emerging market bonds or other underlying securities, for which there might be a less ready market.

(1) History of Securitisation

12.25 As indicated above, CBOs are often said to have evolved as a form of securitisation. Very broadly, securitisation has traditionally been a technique designed to assist institutions (known as originators) which hold or wish to acquire assets (the underlying assets) that would otherwise be burdensome to them. The underlying assets might be burdensome because they attract a heavy capital weighting, produce delayed income streams and/or generate a low level of return.[33]

12.26 As with repackaging, the central principle of securitisation is the ring-fencing of a pool of underlying assets (so that they are not at risk of the insolvency of the SPV that holds them,[34] nor in that of the originator).[35] New securities are issued and

---

order to satisfy either applicable regulatory requirements, investment guidelines, covenant restrictions or internal policies': 'Structured Financing Techniques' (n 35 below) 535.

[31] 'Investment grade: Being rated in one of the four highest rating categories (eg "AAA", "AA", "A", or "BBB" in the case of ratings assigned by S&P or "Aaa", "Aa", "A" or "Baa" in the case of ratings assigned by Moody's': 'Structured Financing Techniques' (n 35 below) 587.

[32] As further enhancements, income and principle on the notes will be paid in a currency different from that payable on the underlying bonds, and income will be paid at a different rate. Currency and interest rate swaps are used to convert the payment stream from the underlying bonds into that to noteholders.

[33] The originator does not simply sell the underlying assets to a commercial purchaser either because there is not a ready market for such sales, or such sale would be administratively impracticable due to the number and nature of the underlying assets, or alternatively because it wishes to maintain a commercial relationship with the persons whose obligations constitute the assets.

[34] Because the SPV is insolvency remote, and also because noteholders have the benefit of a charge in them.

[35] Because this transfer took effect as a true sale, and will not be recharacterised as a mere security interest—which might be void for want of registration or subject to an administration enforcement freeze—nor affected by insolvency displacement rules as a preference or otherwise. 'Structured financings are based on one central, core principle – a defined group of assets can be structurally isolated, and thus serve as the basis of a financing that is independent as a legal matter, from the bankruptcy risks of the former owner of the assets': the Committee on Bankruptcy and Corporate Reorganization of the Association of the Bar of the City of New York, 'Structured Financing Techniques' (1995) 50 The Business Lawyer 527, 529.

their holders enjoy the economic benefit of the underlying assets.[36] The originator is able to remove the underlying assets from its balance sheet.[37]

Securitisation was originally developed in the USA in the early 1970s in order to repackage residential mortgages, and was later applied to credit card receivables.[38] It was quickly established as an important factor in reducing the cost of raising consumer finance. Securitisation has been further developed as a technique for reducing regulatory capital requirements,[39] and thus for increasing income to capital ratios for regulated institutions including (importantly) banks and (more recently) insurance companies. Securitisation is also widely used by commercial companies as a technique for accelerating cash flows.[40] **12.27**

Originally the types of assets underlying securitisations were limited to those which were relatively homogenous and easily valued, with a steady income stream on which the rate of default was readily predictable.[41] More recently, however, a very wide range of assets have been securitised, including hospital and nursing home revenues, student loans and university accommodation rental streams, **12.28**

---

[36] Because together they hold the beneficial interest in them, under a charge and trust structure.

[37] The criteria for such off balance sheet treatment are set out (in the United Kingdom) in FRS 5 and (in the USA) in the Financial Accounting Standards Board's Statement No 125 (FASB 125), which brought in new accounting rules with effect from 1 January 1998 applicable to all transactions involving transfers of financial assets, including CBOs. (For the impact of these rules on repos, see the discussion in Chapter 6.) The central importance of off balance sheet treatment for regulated institutions is that regulators will generally relieve the originator from the position risk requirement in relation to off balance sheet assets, thus significantly relieving the burden of regulatory capital. In the United Kingdom, the regulatory criteria for such relief are set out in the FSA's section on 'Securitisation and Asset Transfers' in *Guide to Banking Supervisory Policy* (available at www.fsa.gov.uk/pubs/supervisor/). Off balance sheet financing permits the originator to use assets as collateral to raise finance in circumstances where, eg, the use of such assets under a registrable security interest would have been prohibited by negative pledges.

[38] 'While mortgage-backed securities held the limelight in the 1970s and even into the 1980s, during the late 1970s and the early 1980s securitisation of non-mortgage assets began': 'Structured Financing Techniques' (n 35 above) 538.

[39] In the Asian financial crisis of 1998, rapid falls in asset values caused many regulated institutions to be in breach of regulatory capital requirements, and securitisation was wisely used as a technique for restoring regulatory capital ratios.

[40] 'A bank may undertake a securitisation for a number of reasons. These include:
— portfolio management;
— reducing the need for capital to support assets on the balance sheet;
— risk management;
— enhancing equity return by allowing the redeployment of capital;
— restructuring the balance sheet for reasons connected with large exposures or sectoral concentrations;
— issuing securities as a means of funding with benefits for both cost and diversification of sources; and
— to provide funding of assets when the originator cannot obtain funding on its own part, for example to fund an acquisition': FSA, 'Securitisation and Asset Transfers' in *Guide to Banking Supervisory Policy*, section 2.1.2.

[41] As well as the more traditional residential mortgages and credit card receivables, securitised assets have included commercial mortgages, lease receivables, trade receivables, corporate loans, housing association loans, car loans and HP receivables.

aircraft, woodlands, entertainment ticket and hospitality revenues, revenues from sales of beer, electricity receivables and construction project receivables.[42]

12.29 Securitisation remains a very major international source of liquidity, permitting institutions whose poor or moderate credit rating would otherwise preclude them from accessing the capital markets, to raise long term, low cost funds by issuing securities on the back of relatively illiquid assets.

(2) Features of CBOs

12.30 A typical CBO might be structured as follows. An investment bank acting as originator identifies a portfolio of underlying (interests in) bonds (in its own balance sheet, or in the secondary market, or by arranging for them to be issued).[43] An SPV is established to which the originator (normally) makes a loan (although in some cases no such loan is made, and the underlying assets are purchased with the proceeds of the issue of notes). The SPV uses this loan to purchase the underlying (interests in) bonds. In many cases, the (interests in) bonds are eligible for settlement through one or more major settlement system. If so, delivery takes place by the crediting of interests in the bonds to the account of the SPV's custodian at Euroclear, Clearstream or DTC. Where the portfolio includes (interests in) bonds which are not so settled, delivery will be to one or more sub-custodians in the relevant local jurisdictions. Each sub-custodian will hold its interests in the bonds for the custodian of the SPV. The custodian will hold its interests in the bonds for the SPV under the terms of a custody agreement.

12.31 New notes are issued by the SPV, interests in which will be held through Euroclear and Clearstream.[44] The new notes are normally issued with senior and subordinated classes.[45]

12.32 The SPV enters into interest rate and currency swap agreements (and possibly other derivatives) with a bank (the swap counterparty) in order to enable it to

---

[42] See the discussion by Xing Zhang, JIBFL, forthcoming. 'Thus, securitisation techniques, which were once viewed primarily as a means of raising low-cost funds to finance mortgages and consumer receivables, are now used routinely to finance assets as diverse as tequila, motion picture revenues, stranded costs and intellectual copyrights': S Lumpkin, 'Trends and Developments in Securitisation' in OECD, *Financial Market Trends*, No 74 (October 1999).

[43] Where the underlying assets are newly issued into the repackaging structure, they may be issued either directly to the SPV, or alternatively to the originator, which transfers them to the SPV.

[44] Euroclear and Clearstream will be used in a euro issue of notes. Traditionally, CBOs have developed as a US product, and the earlier European CBOs were targeted at the US markets. More recently, however, truly European CBOs have been developed, which are sold only into the European markets. The notes will be immobilised in these systems in the normal way. Thus a global note or notes will be held by a common depositary for Euroclear and Clearstream, which will in turn credit the accounts of their participants. Payments under the notes will be made by the SPV to paying agents, which will in turn pass on these payments to the settlement systems.

[45] Senior notes have a priority claim on the cash flows from the underlying bonds. As a quid pro quo, subordinated debt pays a higher rate of interest.

adapt the cash flows it receives via the custodian from the underlying assets to meet its payment obligations to noteholders. In order to ensure it is able to pay noteholders in a timely manner, the SPV may obtain liquidity facilities.[46]

As with a repackaging, the SPV secures its payment obligations to noteholders by creating a security interest over its interest in the underlying assets; this security interest is given in favour of the trustee, which holds it beneficially for noteholders.[47]   **12.33**

The senior tranche of notes generally has a triple-A rating.[48] In order to achieve this rating, credit enhancement techniques are used. 'Credit enhancement can be "external" or "internal". Common forms of external credit enhancement include letters of credit issued by banks, surety bonds issued by insurance companies, and guarantees issued by financial assurance companies. Common forms of internal credit enhancement include capital contribution(s) to the equity of the special purpose vehicle and the use of a "senior-subordinated" structure whereby the senior asset-backed securities are protected by the quantum of the subordinated asset-backed securities'.[49] The subordination of junior notes to the senior notes serves as a form of credit enhancement as holders of the junior notes will bear losses associated with anticipated defaults on the underlying securities. Also, the originator may provide cash collateral to be held on deposit by the trustee,[50] or (commonly) the value of the underlying assets may exceed the value of the new securities ('over-collateralisation'). A variety of such techniques are often used in combination.   **12.34**

The new notes are issued to managed funds (including pension funds), insurance companies and other institutional investors. With the proceeds of issue of the notes, the SPV repays the loan from the originator.   **12.35**

In order to preserve the value of the notes (their credit rating), a manager[51] is appointed to manage the underlying assets in accordance with carefully defined criteria.   **12.36**

---

[46] 'Liquidity facilities enable SPVs to assure investors of timely payments. These include smoothing timing differences in the payment of interest and principal on pooled assets and ensuring payments to investors in the event of market disruptions': 'Securitisation and Asset Transfers' (n 37 above) section 10.1.1.

[47] Strictly, it holds it beneficially for a class of persons defined as 'secured parties'. Secured parties include all classes of noteholders, the trustee and the swap counterparty (as with a repackaging).

[48] Unfortunately, CBOs which were originally given a triple-A rating have been downgraded following the experience of default in emerging market debt in recent years.

[49] 'Structured Financing Techniques' (n 35 above) 534. In practice it is common to issue three classes of securities, namely senior debt (rated Aa), mezzanine debt (rated Baa) and junior debt (unrated). Junior debt is loosely referred to as 'the equity element' because, although a high rate of interest is potentially paid, income stream is uncertain, as with equity investment. Because both excess profits and losses associated with the whole portfolio are attributed to the junior debt, it is said to be highly leveraged.

[50] This is called a reserve account.

[51] In some cases the management function is undertaken by the custodian.

As with repackaged securities, a rolling programme of note issues is often established. Such programmes are generally called 'conduits'. Conduit structures may involve assets provided by more than one originator.

12.38 This discussion assumes that the custody agreement and the security interest are governed by English law; this will often be the case in practice. The taxation of CBOs is also a major factor, but this is beyond the scope of this discussion.[52]

E. Transfer to SPV

12.39 A considerable part of the legal complexity associated with traditional securitisations relates to the transfer of the underlying assets from the originator to the SPV. It is crucial to establish that this transfer is effective to confer property rights which are not at risk in the insolvency of the originator. If this is not established, credit rating agencies will not be willing to rate the new securities on the basis of the credit assessment of the underlying assets, rather than that of the originator. It is also necessary to establish that the transfer leaves the originator with no residual rights in the assets. If this is not established, the regulators of the originator will not relieve it of the regulatory capital burden of the underlying assets, and also recharacterisation risk may be present, as discussed below. It is necessary to establish that the transfer would not be subject to insolvency displacement under preference or similar rules in the insolvency of the originator, or subject to recharacterisation as a security interest, which might be void for want of registration.[53] In a traditional securitisation, where the documentation of the underlying assets is not uniform, establishing whether each asset is transferable[54] (and if so under which system of law)[55] may involve a major due diligence exercise. Where a range of legal systems are involved, foreign legal fees must be incurred in establishing their requirements. Complying with those requirements may not always be practicable.[56] Thus, in traditional securitisation, the transfer of the underlying assets is a major source of legal expense, and possibly of legal risk.

---

[52] Important taxation issues include the avoidance of withholding tax on payments by the issuers of the underlying securities, the custodian and the SPV, and the absence of corporation tax liability for the SPV.

[53] See Chapter 6 for a discussion of the disadvantages of recharacterisation risk. These include restrictions on enforcement under administration proceedings.

[54] Certain assets may have arisen under documentation that contains restrictions on assignment.

[55] In the case of debts, this will generally be the governing law of the assigned debt, in accordance with Article 12(2) of the Rome Convention, implemented in the United Kingdom by the Contracts (Applicable Law) Act 1990. See also the discussion in Chapter 7.

[56] Broadly speaking, civil law jurisdictions may not permit assignment to take place without notice to the debtor.

(1) Techniques of Transfer

Under English law, a number of techniques could in theory be used to transfer intangible assets (such as those which are traditionally securitised).[57] As discussed in Chapter 3, intangibles may be transferred by novation or by legal or equitable assignment. However, these techniques are not always feasible in practice. Novation involves the active participation of the debtor, which will clearly be impracticable where a very significant number of underlying assets are securitised. Legal assignment requires written notice of assignment to be given to the debtor, and in many cases this will also be impracticable (because of the large number of assets involved) or undesirable (where for example the originator wishes to preserve its commercial relationship with the debtor).[58]

The alternative of equitable assignment involves no formalities or publicity, but **12.41** has a number of disadvantages. Because the debtors will continue to treat the originator as their creditor, the SPV must rely on the originator (or a third party) to collect sums payable from debtors, and remit them to the SPV.[59] Moreover, in the absence of notice of assignment, set off may continue to apply between the debtor and the originator.[60] Under English law, a transfer of the underlying assets without

---

[57] In 'Securitisation and Asset Transfers' (n 37 above), the FSA indicates four methods that 'can be used to make an effective transfer of a loan off the supervisory balance sheet.' (section 5.1.2). These are novation, assignment, declaration of trust and sub-participation. 'Sub-participation does not transfer any of the seller's rights, remedies or obligations against the borrower to the buyer, but is an entirely separate, back-to-back, non-recourse funding arrangement, under which the buyer places funds with the seller in exchange for acquiring a covenant from the latter under which he passes on to the buyer payments under the underlying asset which the borrower makes to him, but the asset itself is not transferred . . . The sub-participant may, but is not required to, obtain a charge over the underlying assets. Such a charge would, among other things, allow the sub-participant to report on the basis of the capital charge on the underlying assets': 'Securitisation and Asset Transfers' (n 37 above) section 5.5. The FSA also indicates that it expects the bank 'to have evidence available in its records that its auditors are satisfied that the terms of [the] scheme comply with FRS 5' (section 6.3.6.a).

[58] Even where it is feasible, legal assignment has certain disadvantages, as discussed in Chapter 4. The benefit but not the burden of a contract can be assigned, so that any obligations associated with the underlying investment (such as the duty to make further advances under a loan, or to meet calls on partly paid investments) remain with the originator.

[59] If for any reason legal title to the underlying assets remains with the originator, then the income stream on the underlying assets will be paid by the obligors to the originator. In this case, it will be necessary to arrange for the originator to administer the underlying assets on the SPV's behalf, and to account to it for income which it receives. Ideally income should be segregated in the hands of the originator, so that it is not lost to the SPV if the originator becomes insolvent after receiving and before accounting for it. In some cases a third party (called a servicer) will be appointed to administer the assets in place of the originator, for a range of reasons including a desire to address recharacterisation risk and protect the assets from the insolvency of the originator.

[60] Other disadvantages of equitable as opposed to legal assignment are the risk of double dealing (if the originator subsequently transferred the asset to a third party under a legal assignment, the third party would take priority provided it had no notice of the prior equitable assignment) and enforcement formalities (the SPV as equitable assignee cannot sue the debtor in its own name, but must join the originator in any enforcement action).

notice to the debtors is generally effective to protect the SPV from the insolvency of the originator;[61] but involves administrative inconvenience, and may leave the SPV exposed to the fraud of the originator. Under other systems of law, it may not be straightforward to achieve insolvency protection in such circumstances.

12.42 In contrast, the transfer of the underlying assets in a CBO is tremendously simplified by the use of the major settlement systems.[62] In a CBO structure involving underlying Ruritanian bonds held through Euroclear, the assets are transferred by a simple credit to the Euroclear account of the custodian of the SPV. As discussed in Chapters 2 and 7, the transferred assets are not Ruritanian bonds, but rather Belgian law interests in Ruritanian bonds. Because the transferred assets are Belgian, the opinion of Belgian lawyers should be sufficient to establish their transferability.[63]

12.43 It was argued in Chapter 3 that the effect of debiting one securities account and crediting another is not assignment but novation. By debiting the account of the originator or other transferor, Euroclear reduces or extinguishes one asset. By crediting the account of the SPV's custodian, Euroclear creates a new asset. Thus, no notice to the underlying debtors or other formalities are required. The disadvantages of equitable assignments discussed above are avoided.

12.44 The use of the major settlement systems confers another potential advantage by simplifying the conflict of laws analysis, as discussed below.

(2) True Sale

12.45 In arbitrage CBOs, the underlying assets are generally purchased in the open market after the note issue, so that the concerns about recharacterisation discussed in this section do not arise.[64] However, in balance sheet CBOs, where the underlying assets are transferred from a single originator, it is important to establish that the transfer of assets by the originator to the SPV will not be recharacterised as a security interest. This might result in the interest of the SPV being void for want of registration as a security interest, or subject to an enforcement freeze in the administration of the originator.[65] Other disadvantages of recharacterisation were con-

---

[61] An equitable assignment is effective to confer a property right in the assigned asset. However, this is subject to the comments below on insolvency displacement and recharacterisation risk.

[62] It is hoped that the legal analysis that has been advanced in this book may simplify it further.

[63] They are transferable under the Belgian Royal Decree No 62 of 1967, which establishes the regime under which Euroclear operates.

[64] The investment bank acting as arranger does not lend the SPV the purchase price of the underlying assets, so the risk of the interest of the SPV being recharacterised as a security interest does not arise.

[65] Or equivalent foreign law proceedings.

[66] The FSA indicates the circumstances in which (broadly) it will let an originator which is a UK regulated bank remove the underlying assets from its balance sheet in the section on 'Securitisation and Asset Transfers' in its *Guide to Banking Supervisory Policy* (n 37 above). 'If the bank fails to

sidered in Chapter 6. Furthermore, with a CBO, it will not be possible to remove the underlying assets from the originator's balance sheet[66] or obtain the desired credit rating for the new securities unless recharacterisation risk is addressed.

In traditional securitisations, the continued involvement of the originator in administering the underlying assets may be a source of recharacterisation risk, and there is no such involvement in CBOs. However, a potential sensitivity is the treatment of cash surpluses. **12.46**

As indicated, CBOs are characteristically overcollateralised, to address the risk of default on the underlying (interests in) bonds. The likely effect of overcollateralisation is that monies received by the SPV in respect of the underlying (interests in) bonds is likely to exceed the fixed sums which the SPV is contractually obliged to pay to noteholders. It is important to consider who is entitled to receive this excess, which will be called surplus cash. It was seen in Chapter 4 that the defining characteristic of a security interest (as opposed to an outright transfer of collateral) is that the collateral giver retains the equity of redemption. The equity of redemption is a residual property right in the collateral assets which confers the right to the return of the collateral assets on the discharge of the secured obligation. As discussed in Chapter 4, the equity of redemption is economically equal to ownership of the surplus value of the collateral (ie the extent to which its value exceeds that of the secured obligation). Therefore, if the originator has the right to receive the surplus cash, it is possible that this would be construed as indicating that its interest is in the nature of a security interest. **12.47**

In practice, as indicated above, holders of subordinated notes are generally given the right to receive any surplus cash. It may be that, on the issue of CBOs, the subordinated notes cannot be successfully placed in the market, so that the originator is obliged to hold some or all of them.[67] In this case, it is important to consider the documentation of the transaction as a whole. If it could be argued that, when the transfer was made, the originator was obliged to acquire unplaced subordinated debt, it might be argued that the transfer was made on the basis that it would be entitled to cash surpluses. On this basis, recharacterisation risk may be present.[68] **12.48**

---

comply with the requirements of this policy, the FSA will regard the assets as being on the solo and consolidated balance sheet' (section 1.1.1). The policy requires inter alia that the bank 'has no residual economic interest in the principal amount of the asset (or that part which has been transferred) and the buyer has no formal recourse to the seller for losses' (section 6.4.4.b).

[67] This is not a desirable option for the originator, as the capital treatment of holding subordinated notes significantly compromises the capital efficiencies achieved by the CBO.

[68] This may be a particular sensitivity in a balance sheet transaction.

F. Security Interest[69]

12.49 This section will consider the security interest which is given by the SPV to the trustee. This security interest is given by the SPV in the trust deed constituting the notes.

12.50 As discussed in Chapter 1, the use of a security interest over identified assets to collateralise the obligations of the issuer of securities is not new. Indeed, the term 'securities' itself indicates that investments including bonds reflect the fact that originally such investments were invariably secured (so that the asset became linguistically conflated with the collateral arrangement that traditionally supported it).[70]

(1) Type of Security Interest

12.51 In a typical CBO, the security interest would be expressed to take effect as a fixed charge. As discussed in Chapter 5, a fixed charge has the same legal effect as an equitable mortgage. Recharacterisation as a floating charge would arguably be undesirable for a range of reasons, including that a floating charge may be registrable, depending on the jurisdiction of the issuer.[71] (However, in practice 'Slavenburg' registration is normal.)

12.52 As indicated above, the charged assets may change from time to time as the composition of the underlying portfolio changes. However, as discussed in Chapter 5, this is not incompatible with a fixed charge. The defining characteristic of a floating charge is that the collateral giver retains the freedom to deal in the charged assets in the ordinary course of its business. Thus, in practice, if the SPV as collateral giver has freedom to dispose of assets so as to remove them from the collateral pool, the danger of recharacterisation arises.

12.53 The SPV is not given any right to remove assets from the collateral pool. However, such a right is given to the manager in order to enable it to manage the portfolio.[72]

---

[69] The security language in the trust deed comprises a series of charges and assignments of a range of assets including the interest of the SPV in the (interests in) bonds, and also the balance of various cash accounts and its rights under certain contracts. This discussion focuses only on the charge over the (interests in) bonds.

[70] See the discussion in Chapter 1. On this basis, the common term 'asset backed securities' is tautologous. However, it is meaningful today as the term securities has been extended to include equities and other forms of unsecured asset.

[71] Floating charges created by a company incorporated in or having a branch in England are registrable under the Companies Act 1985, s 395. Of course, for taxation and other reasons the SPV will be incorporated in an offshore centre, with no place of business in England. It is therefore important to establish what registration requirements apply under the law of that offshore centre. Other disadvantages of floating charges as against fixed charges are discussed in Chapter 5.

[72] The manager of a fund (and particularly an unregulated fund) will generally have a much higher degree of discretion in managing the portfolio than the manger of a CBO. The former may have an unfettered discretion to invest in certain markets or to pursue certain strategies, whereas the

Under customary documentation, the appointment of the manager is so drafted that it may be construed as an appointment by the SPV of the manager to act as its agent. On the basis that the manager is the agent of the SPV, it may be said to be exercising the right of the SPV to dispose of collateral assets. Arguably, therefore, the risk arises that the security interest may be recharacterised as a floating charge.[73]

Of course, the fund manager does not have complete freedom to deal with the portfolio, and its rights of disposal may be carefully defined in accordance with strict criteria. CBOs are generally divided into cash flow funds and market value funds. The latter are more actively managed than the former. However, following *Re Cosslett*[74] it is clear that recharacterisation risk is not addressed by merely restricting (but not removing) such freedom. The risk of such recharacterisation may be referred to in the offering memorandum for the notes, and in a qualification to the English law legal opinions given in connection with the issue of notes.

12.54

This concern might be addressed by making the manager the agent of some other person.[75] Alternatively, a property interest in the bonds might be given under a trust rather than under a charge.[76] However, the tax implications of such structures would need to be carefully considered.

12.55

(2) Lex Situs

Economically, the interest in the underlying bonds which the SPV charges to the trustee, and the interest in the underlying bonds which is delivered to the custodian of the SPV, are the same. Legally, however, they are different, because the latter is intermediated by the custodian. If the custody agreement is governed by English law, the charged asset will be an English law trust interest (ie the interest of the SPV under the custody trust).[77]

12.56

---

powers of the latter may be limited by carefully defined formulae. However, there is wide variation, and these are differences of degree and not of kind.

[73] Of course, this depends on the precise terms of the documentation and the circumstances of the transaction as a whole.

[74] [1997] 4 All ER 115. See Chapter 5 for a further discussion.

[75] It is customary to provide that the manager acts as agent for the SPV, but that on the default of the SPV the trustee may require them henceforth to act as agent for the trustee. One possible option might be to have the manager act as agent for the trustee from the outset.

[76] In US structures, as an alternative to issuing bonds secured on the underlying assets, investors are in some cases issued with trust certificates, representing undivided co-ownership rights under a trust of the underlying assets. A further alternative is for the SPV to act as both the issuer of the notes and the trustee of the underlying assets in favour of noteholders. This obviates the need for a security interest, and is very akin to a DR structure. 'In structured financing jargon, where a special purpose vehicle (corporation or trust) issues debt securities it is called a "pay-through" financing. Where a special purpose trust issues certificates of beneficial interest, it is called a "pass-through" financing': 'Structured Financing Techniques' (n 35 above) 534, n 8.

[77] This assumes that the custody agreement is in industry standard terms, and that the custodian segregates the SPV's assets from its own assets (ie holds them in a client account at the relevant settlement system).

12.57 As discussed in Chapter 7, the rules of conflict of laws require security interests to be perfected under the lex situs. Chapter 7 argued that the situs of the unallo-cated[78] interest of a beneficiary under a trust is the location of the trustee. On the basis that the charged asset is an English law trust interest, therefore, its situs is England. No formalities are required by English law to perfect such a charge.

12.58 Notwithstanding this analysis, the author would consider it prudent also to ensure that the security interest is perfected in accordance with the law of the settlement system.[79] It is understood that in practice it is sometimes sought also to perfect the security interest in accordance with the law of the underlying assets, on the basis of local law opinions. Where these comprise bonds issued from a range of jurisdictions, this will be an onerous exercise. This would only be necessary in cases where these underlying jurisdictions do not accept this approach to conflict of laws, which was considered in Chapter 7.

(3) Multiple Security Interests

12.59 Chapter 4 discussed the problem of intermediation and multiple security inter-ests. When interests in securities (which are held through chains of intermedi-aries) are delivered as collateral, a potential problem for the collateral taker is that the collateral assets are subject to the competing security interests of the interme-diaries through whom they are held. This may significantly diminish the value of the collateral. In CBOs, therefore, it may be important to ensure that both the custodian and either the settlement system or the sub-custodians holding the underlying assets for the custodian waive the security interests which they would otherwise take in standard custody and settlement arrangements.[80]

G. Nature of the Interest of Noteholders in the Underlying Bonds

12.60 In the other types of repackaged asset discussed in Chapter 11 (DRs and managed funds) and also in custody and settlement arrangements, the proprietary link between investors and the underlying assets is a trust.[81] In contrast, in the case of a CBO, that link takes the form of a charge. It will be argued in this section that this difference may be more apparent than real.

---

[78] It is assumed that the custody arrangements, in common with standard industry practice, are fungible.

[79] ie Belgian law in the case of Euroclear. This will involve the use of a special collateral account.

[80] It is understood that both Euroclear and Clearstream are willing to release the participants' client accounts, at least where the regulators of the participants require this.

[81] In the case of participants in the major settlement systems, it is the statutory equivalent of a trust, as discussed in Chapter 2.

Both the charge and the trust are creatures of equity. Neither confers legal title,[82] **12.61** but both confer equitable property interests in the assets that are subject to them.[83] Both can relate to a changing pool of assets. The similarities between the two legal structures are so strong that in some circumstances the courts have difficulty in characterising a particular interest as either a trust interest or a charge.[84] In other circumstances, a trust interest can change into a charge, and then change back.[85]

There appear to be two essential differences between a trust interest and a charge. **12.62** The first relates to the requirement for allocation. Traditionally, it is not possible for a trust interest to take effect over an unallocated part of an asset or pool of assets, because of the requirement for certainty of subject matter. In contrast, it is normal for the value of charged assets to exceed the charged exposure.[86] This distinction will be called 'the allocation distinction'.

The second distinction (which is closely related to the first) concerns changes in **12.63** the value of the underlying assets. If the value of trust assets increases or diminishes, the value of the beneficial interest increases and diminishes accordingly. In contrast, the chargee does not benefit from increases in the value of the charged asset. When it enforces its charge by exercising its power of sale, the chargee is obliged to return any excess of the proceeds of sale over the charged exposure to the chargor or its liquidator. Conversely, the chargee does not suffer loss when the charged assets diminish in value, in the following sense. If the proceeds of sale of the charged asset fall short of the debt, the debt remains outstanding to the extent of that shortfall.[87] This will be called the 'excess and shortfall distinction'.

As indicated above, in a typical CBO any cash surpluses are payable to subordi- **12.64** nated noteholders. On this basis, the charged exposure (ie sums payable to noteholders) cannot fall short of the charged assets. Thus the allocation distinction cannot apply.[88] Because of the limited recourse nature of the rights of noteholders, the charged exposure cannot exceed the value of the charged assets. Because no excess or shortfall can arise, the excess and shortfall distinction does not apply. Thus in practice, the potential differences between a charge and a trust are never realised, and the fact that interest in noteholders arises under a charge, and that of holders of other types of interests in securities, makes no functional difference.

---

[82] As discussed in Chapter 5, a charge cannot arise at law (except by statute, over land).

[83] This means that the interest of the beneficiary survives the insolvency of the trustee, and that of the chargee the insolvency of the chargor.

[84] See the discussion in *Swiss Bank Corporation v Lloyds* [1979] Ch 548, [1982] AC 584.

[85] This can arise in the course of a tracing action supporting a tracing claim.

[86] ie there is no allocation by exhaustion or otherwise.

[87] Of course, this is still bad news for the chargee, because to the extent of the shortfall its exposure is unsecured.

[88] In any case it was argued in Chapter 4 that trusts over intangibles may not require allocation, following the judgment in *Hunter v Moss* and the arguments set out in that chapter.

H. Likeness to Traditional Managed Funds

12.65   The rise of CBOs has strong links with the managed funds industry. The appetite of institutional investors including fund managers for (interests in) securities which combine high returns with high credit ratings ensures the continued success of CBO issues.[89] A CBO is in many ways more akin to a managed fund than to a traditional securitisation. A CBO is largely free of the complex legal considerations associated with the transfer of the underlying assets from the originator, which is not involved in the continuing administration of the portfolio. Both CBOs and managed funds involve the establishment of a SPV in a low tax jurisdiction. In order to avoid the risk that the SPV may become subject to tax in the jurisdiction of the promoters of either type of transaction, it is important to ensure that they do not have day-to-day control of the management of the SPV. In both, the SPV may be structured as a corporation, a trust or a limited partnership. In both, the portfolios are managed, and professional fund management houses are routinely involved in CBOs. Moreover, the credit enhancement techniques of CBOs are widely used in the managed fund industry.[90] As CBOs develop with more sophisticated management strategies and even open-ended structures,[91] they become indistinguishable from managed funds.

12.66   Just as the banks responsible for the development of the CBO markets continue to borrow techniques from the managed funds industry, fund managers are beginning to structure their products as CBOs.[92] CBOs combine techniques developed in both the traditional securitisation and managed funds markets. They thus represent the product of a marriage between the most dynamic branches of the banking and securities industries respectively.[93] This process of convergent evolution might be compared to the experience of financial institutions taking securities collateral. Whereas in the 1980s the repo and securities lending markets were quite distinct, towards the end of the 1990s institutions began to use repo and securities lending documentation interchangeably, in order to achieve netting efficiencies. The breakdown of the traditional sectors of the financial markets is wholly welcome, as participants are increasingly free to select and combine the best features

---

[89] The demands of fund managers as investors in the shares of banks for high returns on their equity investments constitute part of the motivation towards CLOs. Thus, fund managers might be said to drive securitisation at both ends.

[90] In relation to guaranteed funds.

[91] ie with units which can be issued and redeemed from time to time.

[92] One possible reason for a fund manager to choose a CBO structure is the shorter timeframes typically involved in establishing CBOs than traditional fund structures.

[93] Growth has been phenomenal. 'The market for collateralized debt obligations (CDOs) is the fastest growing sector of the asset backed securities market': *Collateralized Debt Obligation Handbook* (n 23 above) 1. The deal volume for CDO funds was $3 billion in 1995, and $107 billion in 1998: quoted by the Panel on Collateralised Loan and Bond Obligations Funds at the IBA/ABA International Conference on Private Investment Funds, London, November 1999.

of the different traditional sectors. The other great advantage of this process of convergence is that it simplifies the legal analysis, as lessons learned in one sector can be applied in another.

This section has compared CBOs to traditional managed funds, but other com-   **12.67**
parisons may also be made. The proprietary nature of the noteholders' interest is also very akin to that of DR holders, participants in settlement systems and custody clients. As with other types of interests in securities, the rights of noteholders are indirect. As with other types, they are unallocated.[94] They are also intangible, for there is no tangible asset to which they can attach. CBOs therefore form part of the large family of indirect, unallocated and intangible interests in securities that has been considered in this book. The analysis of such interests in this book under domestic and private international law may therefore apply equally to CBOs as to DRs, interests in managed funds, and the assets of settlement system participants and custody clients.

---

[94] Although different classes of CBO may be issued, a single charge over the interests of the SPV in the underlying bonds secures the rights of all noteholders.

PART V

CONCLUSIONS

13

PROPERTY RIGHTS IN INTERESTS IN SECURITIES

Assuredly this is true of our real property law, it has been secreted in the interstices of the forms of action.[1]

This chapter will develop the proposition that, as against the intermediary, the **13.01** client enjoys property rights in interests in securities. This discussion involves a certain amount of legal history[2] and technical material which may not interest practitioners, and has therefore been delayed until the penultimate chapter of this book.

---

[1] F W Maitland, *The Forms of Action at Common Law* (A H Chaytor and W J Whittaker (eds), Cambridge University Press, 1997 (first published 1909)) 1, paraphrasing Maine.

[2] 'The obsolete doctrines of our laws are frequently the foundation, upon which what remains is erected; and that it is impracticable to comprehend many rules of the modern law, in a scholarlike scientifical manner, without having recourse to the antient': Blackstone, *Commentaries on the Laws of England* (facsimile of 1st edn, Chicago: University of Chicago Press, 1979) 2, 44.

A. Overview

13.02 Interests in securities have been defined as the asset of a client for whom an intermediary holds (interests in) securities on an unallocated basis, commingled with the interests in securities of other clients. As against the intermediary, it has been argued, the rights of the client are proprietary.

13.03 This argument is not uncontroversial, particularly for civil lawyers. Some commentators reject the possibility of property rights subsisting in relation to intangible assets, especially where such rights are asserted through intermediaries and in the absence of allocation. However, this chapter will seek to show that, although the assertion of property rights in such circumstances is relatively recent, it accords with the traditional principles of classical and English property law. This chapter will go on to consider why such property rights have been developed only relatively recently, and seek to explain why there is some conceptual resistance to their development, particularly among civil lawyers.

13.04 To support this discussion, this chapter will briefly consider the historical development of the law of property in the writings of a small number of key authors in the classical and common law traditions, particularly Justinian, Bracton, Blackstone, Maitland and Hohfeld.

B. Property Rights in Relation to Intangible Assets

13.05 This section will argue that the assertion of property rights in relation to intangible assets accords with the traditional principles of the law of property. In order to do this, it is necessary to return to the real actions from which property rights have historically been extrapolated in ancient[3] and common law.[4]

(1) Real and Personal Actions

13.06 Justinian distinguishes real actions from personal actions as follows:

> A plaintiff may sue a defendant who is under an obligation to him, from contract or from wrongdoing. The personal actions lie for these claims . . . Or else he may sue a defendant *who is not under any kind of obligation to him* but is someone with whom he is in dispute about a thing. Here the real actions lie. [emphasis added][5]

13.07 The term 'real actions' is a translation of '*actiones in rem*'. '*Rem*' is the accusative form of the word '*res*' or 'thing'.

---

[3] However, by the time Blackstone was writing, the original real actions had fallen into disuse. See *Commentaries* (n 2 above) vol 3, 266, 267.

[4] '[T]he forms of action are given, the causes of action must be deduced therefrom': Maitland (n 1 above) 5, commenting on Bracton.

[5] *Justinian's Institutes* (Birks and McLeod (trans.), London: Duckworth, 1987) 129, J.4.6.2.

(2) Things Include Intangibles

Crucially, in Justinian, things include *intangible* things such as obligations: 'Some **13.08** things are corporeal, some incorporeal . . . Incorporeal things cannot be touched. They consist of legal rights—inheritance, usufruct, obligations however contracted.'[6] This reification of obligations is continued in *Bracton on the Laws and Customs of England*[7] and in Blackstone's *Commentaries on the Laws of England*, in which discussion of things includes choses in action.[8] If an intangible is a thing or *res*, linguistically and therefore conceptually it is a candidate to be the subject of a *real* action.

(3) All Actions Concern Things

As obligations are things to Justinian and the Western legal tradition which fol- **13.09** lows him, a personal action (which relates to the obligation of the defendant to the plaintiff) involves a thing as much as a real action. The difference between the two types of action is not the presence or absence of a thing (for things are present in both). Rather it is the presence or absence of an obligation of the defendant to the plaintiff (which is present in a personal action and absent in a real action).[9]

C. Intermediated Property Rights in Intangible Assets

It follows that an intangible asset may be the subject of a real action, but only as **13.10** against a third party.[10] For example, as against the debtor, the creditor can only assert personal rights in relation to the debt.[11] However, if the debt is held through an intermediary, the creditor can assert real rights in relation to the debt, as against the intermediary.[12] On this basis, intermediation is not merely compatible with property rights in relation to intangibles; it is their precondition.

Chapter 2 considered the legal arrangements under which a client may enjoy **13.11** property rights in relation to assets held by an intermediary. In English law, as

---

[6] ibid J.2.2.pr-2. The reification of obligations by Gaius before Justinian is described by Birks and McLeod (n 5 above) as 'a brilliant leap' (at 15).

[7] 'Incorporeal things are such as are intangible, which exist in contemplation of law, as inheritance, usufruct, advowsons of churches, obligations, actions and the like': vol II, 48. Bracton is described as 'that great cathedral of the thirteenth century': 'Introduction' to *Justinian's Institutes* (n 5 above) 26.

[8] See ch XXV. Of course, the legal French term 'chose' means 'thing', and is a fair translation of the Latin '*res*'.

[9] This point has been somewhat obscured by the terms 'actions in *personam*' and 'actions in *rem*'. More helpful terminology might have been 'actions in *personam*' and 'other actions'.

[10] ie someone other than the obligor.

[11] See the discussion of charge backs in Chapter 5.

[12] Professor Schroeder has clearly shown that the proprietary nature of a chose in action arises only in the hands of third parties. See for example 'Chix Nix Bundle-O-Stix', (1994) 93 Mich L Rev 239.

discussed in that chapter, while property rights in *tangible* assets may be intermediated under a bailment, property rights in *intangible* assets may only be intermediated under a trust. Thus, the law of property rights in relation to intangibles is
the law of trusts.[13]

13.12   Incidentally, the author would suggest that the old vexed question of whether the
rights of the beneficiary under a trust are personal or proprietary,[14] may be readily
answered by applying Justinian's test of real and personal actions. *As against the
trustee*, the rights of the beneficiary are personal: the courts of equity are the courts
of conscience, and the law of trusts is built on the personal obligations of the
trustee to the beneficiary.[15] This accords with the Justinian definition of a personal
action as one where the defendant owes a personal obligation to the plaintiff.
However, if the trustee becomes insolvent, the beneficiary may be obliged to protect the trust assets from the trustee's general creditors. The general creditors owe
no personal obligation to the beneficiary, so that *as against them*, the rights of the
beneficiary are proprietary. Thus the trust assets are not available to creditors of
the insolvent trustee. The same reasoning protects the trust assets against judgment creditors of the trustee, and persons to whom the trustee transfers the trust
assets in breach of duty (other than the bona fide purchaser for value without
notice of the legal estate).[16]

---

   [13] Hence perhaps their strangeness to civil lawyers. Another historic reason for the greater readiness of common lawyers than civil lawyers to see the rights of clients in (heavily) intermediated interests in securities as proprietary, may be that common law (unlike civil law) has developed
uninterrupted from the Middle Ages. English property law originated with indirect rights of land
tenure. 'Almost all the real property of this kingdom is by the policy of our laws supposed to be
granted by, dependent upon, and *holden* of some superior or lord . . . The thing holden is therefore
stiled a *tenement*, the possessors thereof *tenants*, and the manner of their possession a *tenure*':
Blackstone (n 2 above) Book 2, 59. The author has been struck by the likeness of interests in securities, held through chains of financial intermediaries, with feudal land tenures, held through chains
of landlords. Both are intangible: see Jeremy Waldron, 'Property Law', in Dennis Patterson (ed), *A
Companion to Philosophy of Law and Legal Theory* (London: Blackwell, 1996) 4; see also Blackstone
(n 2 above) vol 1, 18 and vol 2, 59–60.
   [14] See eg the opening passages of Hohfeld, *Fundamental Legal Conceptions* (New Haven: Yale
University Press, 1919); Maitland, 'Trust and Corporation' in *Selected Essays* (Cambridge:
Cambridge University Press, 1936) 144–147; and, more recently, Kam Fan Sin, *The Legal Nature
of the Unit Trust* (Oxford: Clarendon Press, 1997) 265 and the materials referred to there.
   [15] Hence the maxim, 'Equity acts in personam'. 'The Courts of Equity in England are, and
always have been, Courts of conscience, operating in personam and not in rem': *Ewing v Orr Ewing*
(1883) 9 App Cas 34, per Lord Selborne at 40.
   [16] Admittedly, in theory, the historic development of the class of third parties against whom the
beneficiary could assert its rights has been based on the proposition that the conscience of those persons is affected: see Maitland (n 14 above) 165, 166, 169. See also Blackstone, (n 2 above) vol 2,
328. However, 'it is to be remembered that the making of great theories is not and never has been
our strong point. The theory that lies upon the surface is sometimes a borrowed theory which has
never penetrated far, while the really vital principles must be sought for in out-of-the-way places':
Maitland (n 14 above) 218, 219.

D. Property Rights in Unallocated Intangible Assets

This section will argue that interests in securities confer on clients property rights **13.13** in relation to the client assets held by intermediaries, even though there is no allocation of particular interests in securities to particular client assets.

Chapter 2 considered the question of how property rights can arise in relation to **13.14** an unallocated part of a pool of client assets (the allocation question), and indicated two possible answers. The first answer is that the interest of each client relates to the whole of the pool, which she co-owns with each other client. This approach serves to allocate the client's interest,[17] but at the cost of reducing it to a co-ownership interest.

Where the pool of assets held by the intermediary for clients comprises intangible **13.15** assets such as (interests in) shares, the second possible answer to the allocation question is as follows: the client owns part of the pool outright, without allocation. This is on the basis that there is no requirement for property interests in intangible assets to be allocated. As discussed in Chapter 2, this argument accords with the judgments in *Hunter v Moss* and *CA Pacific*. In the author's view, these were bold judgments, which went beyond the settled scope of English law. However, it will be argued below that they can be reconciled with the traditional principles of the law of property, and may therefore indicate the way in which English law should develop in the future.

To support this argument, the requirement for allocation will be considered in **13.16** relation to tangible assets and intangible assets in turn.

(1) Allocation Required for Property Rights in Tangible Assets

As discussed below, property rights originated in real actions, and the original real **13.17** action was vindication. Vindication enabled the plaintiff to recover a specific asset *in specie* from the defendant.[18] As a practical matter, a plaintiff cannot succeed in *recovering* a specific asset without first *identifying* that asset, and therefore allocation is a precondition of vindication.

The historic link between property and vindication may explain the conceptual **13.18** difficulty lawyers often experience in considering unallocated property rights.[19]

---

[17] The interest is allocated by exhaustion.

[18] And not merely an asset equivalent to it, or its monetary value. See eg *Bracton on the Laws and Customs of England* (Thorn (trans.), Cambridge, Mass: Harvard University Press, 1968) vol II, 292: 'Actions in rem are those given against a possessor . . . as where one claims a specific thing, an estate or a piece of land, from another and asserts that he is its owner, and seeks the thing itself, not its price or its value or an equivalent of the same kind'.

[19] A way around the difficulty, indicated by Hohfeld as discussed below, is to understand property rights, not as relationships between persons and things, but as relationships between persons in respect of things. This approach accords with the author's suggestion below that the contemporary

However, vindication is no longer relevant to property rights in the securities markets. As a technical matter, vindication cannot take place in relation to fungible assets such as interests in securities.[20]

13.19 However, even in the absence of vindication, it might be argued that there remains a conceptual requirement for allocation where property rights are asserted in *tangible* assets. This is because tangible assets exist physically, whereas legal rights are notional. In order to show that (notional) property rights relate to (physical) assets, some step is required to link the two. Such a link is required, because the notional and physical worlds are discontinuous.[21]

(2) Whether Allocation Required for Property Rights in Intangible Assets

13.20 By the same token, it might be argued, no link is required between property rights and intangible assets, because both are notional. Obligations are deemed by the law to be things, and therefore the establishment of an obligation automatically causes a notional thing to arise.[22] Because the law reifies obligations, an obligation automatically attaches to the thing which is its notional reification. No act of allocation is required, because both the right and the thing come into being together.

13.21 However, this reasoning, although compatible with old authority, is (as far as the author knows) novel. In contrast, a number of cases have held that, in order to assert property rights in a third party obligation, the plaintiff must link that obligation with a particular *asset* in the defendant's hands, which can serve as the thing to which her claims relates. Thus, in order for a trust of a debt to arise, the trust asset must be segregated in an empirically observable manner, for example by the opening of a separate bank account; a purported trust over part of a bank balance cannot take effect.[23] The same reasoning lies behind the rule that a proprietary

---

functional purpose of asserting property rights in interests in securities is not to recover particular assets, but rather to achieve 'super priority' in the insolvency of an intermediary.

[20] This is because the individual identity of the client's assets is lost on commingling within the pool held by the intermediary.

[21] 'for it is not enough to say "I claim a thing", unless it is said "I claim such a thing"': Bracton (n 18 above) 342, 343.

[22] See Blackstone's discussion of the original form of the action for debt (detinue), which involved the creditor claiming the debt *as a thing* in the hands of the debtor. 'The form of the writ of *debt* is sometimes in the *debet* and *detinet*, sometimes in the *detinet* only: that is, the writ states, either that the defendant *owes* and unjustly *detains* the debt or thing in question, or only that he unjustly *detains* it': *Commentaries* (n 2 above) Book III, ch 9, 155. This approach also accords with the language of a House of Lords judgment, which described a creditor as *owning* a debt which was owed to it: 'The relationship of the bank with the solicitors was essentially that of debtor and creditor, . . . It must follow . . . that the solicitors *as owners of the chose in action constituted by the indebtedness of the bank to them* in respect of the sums paid into the client account, could trace their property in that chose in action into its direct product, the money drawn from the account by Cass' [emphasis added]: *Lipkin Gorman v Karpnale Ltd* [1991] 2 AC 548, per Lord Goff at 573, 574.

[23] See the discussion of *Mac-Jordan Construction Ltd v Brookmount Erostin Ltd (in receivership)* [1992] BCLC 350 in Chapter 2.

claim can only be traced into a continuing trust fund,[24] so that in general it is not possible to trace through an overdrawn account.[25] While it was argued in *Space Investments*[26] that a beneficial interest could take effect without allocation, as a general charge over the assets of the defendant, this approach was rejected in *Bishopsgate Investment Management Ltd v Homan.*[27]

These cases have attracted criticism, and arguably wrought hardship on the **13.22** unsuccessful plaintiffs.[28] It might be argued that these decisions are not well founded, and conflate notional things (to which property rights automatically attach) with physical things (to which property rights require to be allocated). It is therefore hoped that the ideas which are implicit in *Hunter v Moss* will be judicially developed in the years ahead.[29] In the meantime, clients of unallocated custody and settlement arrangements may rely on the classical law of co-ownership when asserting property rights against intermediaries.[30]

E. Late Development of Property Rights in Obligations

This chapter has argued that it is possible to assert property rights in relation to **13.23** intangible assets such as interests in securities, and further that such proprietary rights accord with the traditional principles of the law of property. It might be objected that if such property rights did accord with such traditional principles, they would have a long history, and it must be conceded that they are relatively novel. To answer this possible objection, this section will seek to explain the late development of property rights in obligations.

English common law has always allowed real actions in relation to incorporeal **13.24** hereditaments (ie servitudes).[31] These are intangible rights associated with land, such as rights of way.[32]

---

[24] See *Re Diplock* [1948] Ch 465 per Lord Greene at 521.

[25] See eg *Westdeutsche Landesbank Girozentrale v Islington LBC* [1996] AC 669, per Lord Browne-Wilkinson at 706.

[26] *Space Investments Ltd v Canadian Imperial Bank of Commerce Trust Co (Bahamas) Ltd* [1986] 1 WLR 1072, per Lord Templeman at 1074.

[27] [1995] Ch 211 per Dillon LJ at 271 and Leggatt LJ at 221.

[28] It is hard to see how justice is served by penalising a plaintiff for the defendant's inadequate banking arrangements.

[29] This development may involve resurrecting the concept of a 'general charge' in the judgment in *Space Investments Limited* (n 26 above).

[30] See the discussion of co-ownership in *Justinian's Institutes* (n 5 above) 57–59, J2.125–129; Bracton (n 18 above) (discussion of acquiring dominion by confusion, vol 2, 47); and Blackstone (n 2 above) (vol 2, 180, 191, 192.

[31] 'Incorporeal herediaments are principally of ten sorts: advowsons, tithes, commons, ways, offices, dignities, franchises, corodies or pensions, annuities, and rents': Blackstone (n 2 above) vol 2, 21.

[32] 'It is called an action *in rem* because you are claiming your incorporeal *res*, that is, the right of going over his land': Bracton (n 18 above) Book 2, 294.

13.25 However, neither Roman nor English law developed real actions in relation to other types of intangibles such as obligations. Thus, although Justinian created, and the traditional common law authors sustained, the conceptual possibility of property rights in relation to third party obligations, they did not write of them. The reasons for this are both practical and procedural.

(1) Practical Reasons

13.26 In order to understand the practical reasons for the relatively late development of property rights in relation to obligations, it is helpful to consider the purposes that have been served by the assertion of property rights at different periods in legal history.

13.27 As indicated above, the original real action was vindication. Of course, an obligation cannot be vindicated, because the enforcement of an obligation discharges it.[33] This is an obvious practical reason why early lawyers did not assert property rights in relation to obligations.

13.28 During the late medieval and early modern periods, a benefit of property rights was transferability.[34] In order to render bearer debt securities transferable, they were recategorised as chattels.[35] It was not possible to assert property rights in debt securities as obligations, for policy reasons.[36]

13.29 The enduring usefulness of property rights in the securities markets lies in their ability to bind third parties. If a client places assets with an intermediary, she faces the risk that the intermediary will have a judgment debt enforced against it or become insolvent. She will only be able to protect her assets against these risks if she can assert property rights in the assets, which will bind third party creditors.[37]

---

[33] See *Justinian's Institutes* (n 5 above) 119, 3.29.pr.

[34] As discussed in Chapter 3, in the late medieval period to the early modern period, property rights were transferable, but a policy against maintenance, or the trafficking in claims, prohibited the transfer of obligations. Therefore an important consequence of establishing proprietary status for an asset was to render that asset transferable. With the rise of commerce, it became economically necessary to deliver debt obligations person to person. See the interesting discussion in J E Penner, *The Idea of Property in Law* (Oxford: Clarendon Press, 1997) 112, in which the test of 'contingency' is preferred to the test of 'transferability'.

[35] This was achieved by a legal fiction which conflated a debt obligation with the negotiable instrument issued in respect of it; a piece of paper was transferred, with the debt locked up inside it.

As more fully discussed in Chapter 3, other techniques were developed over time to by-pass the common law restrictions, including equitable assignment. With the Judicature Act 1873, the assignment of choses in action was generally permitted at common law, subject to certain formalities. With these developments, the old rule against the transfer of personal rights was overcome, and the second historical purpose of asserting property rights became otiose.

[36] It was necessary to resort to the fiction, which had the effect of notionally converting intangibles into tangible assets, because any attempt to assert proprietary (and therefore transferable) status on intangible debt obligations would have been defeated by the policy against maintenance.

[37] Where the intermediary is an individual, assets held for clients are excluded from the intermediary's bankruptcy by the Insolvency Act 1986, s 283(3)(a). Where the intermediary is a company, the same result is achieved by the general principle that only assets beneficially owned by the

Thus, property rights are needed in the contemporary securities markets in order to address intermediary credit risk, in effect by giving the client 'super priority' in the insolvency of the intermediary, so that the client ranks ahead of all creditors.

Since ancient times, domestic and international trade has been conducted **13.30** through agents, and commercial people have been obliged to entrust their goods, bearer instruments and other tangible assets to intermediaries. Traditionally, tangible assets have been protected in the hands of intermediaries by the law of bailment, under which the client retains title to the assets as bailor.

However, in relation to intangible assets, the concept of reserving property rights **13.31** so as to protect the assets in the hands of intermediaries is more recent. The two most commercially important categories of intangible asset are intellectual property rights and financial assets. Intellectual property rights are not regularly intermediated. Among financial assets, cash at bank is not protected from the bank's creditors,[38] and securities have only recently been dematerialised.

With the computerisation of the securities markets, the asset of the investor has **13.32** become both intangible (with the elimination of paper instruments) and intermediated (as the investor is unable to participate directly in computerised settlement systems).[39] With the advent of interests in securities, very significant values of intangible assets are entrusted to intermediaries, in circumstances where clients seek to avoid the intermediaries' credit risk.[40] Therefore the urgency of asserting property rights in intangible assets is associated with the rise of interests in securities, and thus with a period of time starting with the last quarter of the twentieth century. In terms of legal history, it is a recent problem.

(2) Procedural Reasons

There are also procedural reasons why real actions did not develop in relation to **13.33** obligations. The class of assets for which real actions were traditionally available comprised land, tenements and hereditaments. As indicated above, this class included certain intangibles (incorporeal hereditaments). It also excluded certain tangible assets.[41] The criterion for the inclusion of an asset in that class was not its tangibility, but rather its association with land.[42]

---

company are available to its creditors, as reflected in case law. See for example *Barclays Bank Ltd v Quistclose Investors Ltd* [1963] 3 All ER 651 and *Re Kayford Ltd* [1975] 1 All ER 604.

[38] *Foley v Hill* [1848] 2 HL Cas 28.

[39] See Chapter 1.

[40] The culture of the financial markets, including the policies of the credit rating agencies and regulatory, taxation and accounting authorities, requires that investors and collateral takers are protected from the intermediaries' credit risk.

[41] Real actions were not available for chattels until the nineteenth century (when the Common Law Procedure Act 1854, s 78, enabled the court to order restitution of a chattel to a plaintiff, and removed the defendant's traditional option of paying its value). See Maitland (n 1 above) 58.

[42] See eg Blackstone (n 2 above) Book 2, 384: 'Under the name of things *personal* are included all

13.34 The land-based values of feudal society receded in favour of commercialism in the early modern period. However, prior to the procedural reforms of the nineteenth century, the class of assets for which real actions were available was closed.

13.35 With the abolition of the fixed forms of action,[43] no obstacle remained to bringing real actions in relation to obligations, should the need arise. As indicated above, this need arose with the computerisation of the securities markets.

F. Physical Model

13.36 It was argued above that the development of property rights in intangible assets such as interests in securities was long delayed for practical and procedural reasons. In addition, there is a mistaken but widespread conception of property rights which must be overcome in order to assert property rights in relation to intangible assets, particularly where such rights arise indirectly and without allocation. This mistaken view will be called the 'Physical Model'.

13.37 The Physical Model (mistakenly) conceives of property rights as a legal relationship between a person and a physical asset, as distinct from personal rights (which are conceived of as legal relationships between persons).

(1) Possessory Basis

13.38 'It should be remembered that there has always been a very close association between ownership and possession in English law.'[44] It seems clear that the origin of the Physical Model is the historic legal association between property and possession.[45] This association continues to be very strong.[46] 'The law of *England* has

---

sorts of things *moveable*, which . . . are not esteemed of so high a nature, nor paid so much regard to by the law, as things that are in their nature more permanent and *immoveable*, as lands, and houses, and the profits issuing thereout. These being constantly within the reach, and under the protection of the law, were the principal favourites of our first legislators: who took all imaginable care in ascertaining the rights, and directing the disposition, of such property as they imagined to be lasting, and which would answer to posterity the troubles and pains that their ancestors employed about them; but at the same time entertained a very low and contemptuous opinion of all personal estate, which they regarded only as a transient commodity'.

[43] Common Law Procedure Act 1852 and the Judicature Acts 1873–75.

[44] N Palmer and A Hudson, 'Pledge', in Palmer and McKendrick (eds), *Interests in Goods* (2nd edn, London: LLP, 1998) 633.

[45] As discussed in Chapter 2, possession involves the physical control of a tangible asset. The association between property and possession is discussed in Pollock and Wright, *An Essay on Possession in the Common Law* (Oxford: Clarendon Press, 1888).

[46] 'The common law has recognised the taking of possession as essential to the transfer of title in various ways, in the delivery of chattels, for example, or in the ancient common law ritual of "livery of seisin", in which the transferor of land picked up a piece of the earth and placed it in the hand of the transferee before witnesses': Penner (n 34 above) 84, 85. See Blackstone (n 2 above) vol 2, 312, 313 and vol 3, 201.

always been, that personal property passes by delivery of possession; and it is possession which determines the apparent ownership.'[47] Property confers the right to possession; possession raises the presumption of ownership,[48] and long-standing possession confers it.[49]

Property rights were originally developed in English law in relation to the posses- **13.39** sion of land, and applied to other assets including intangibles by analogy.[50] The factual relationship of control between a person and the physical assets in her possession was used as a metaphor for the notional relationship between a person and the intangibles in which she has a property interest.[51]

It can take tremendous intellectual energy always to remember that a metaphori- **13.40** cal statement is not a literal statement, and hence the understandable tendency to conflate intangibles with the tangible assets to which they are metaphorically linked in legal writing.

Another aspect of the basis of the Physical Model in possession is vindication. As **13.41** indicated above, property rights originated historically and conceptually in legal remedies, and the original legal action was vindication. Because vindication was not available for chattels until the Common Law Procedure Act 1854, chattels were long considered not to be subject to *in rem* rights,[52] and are still excluded from the definition of real property. The connection between property and vindication is so ancient that for many it still remains counterintuitive to assert property rights in fungible assets such as interests in securities, where vindication is not sought and indeed not possible. Whereas vindication is the ancient purpose for asserting property rights, the current purpose in the securities markets (avoiding the credit risk of intermediaries) is fairly recent: corporate insolvency only dates from 1844.[53]

---

[47] *Dearle v Hall* (1823) ER 38, 475, per Sir Thomas Plumer MR at 483.

[48] In *Interests in Goods* (n 44 above) ch 3, N Palmer offers a fascinating discussion of possessory title. Following a careful analysis of case law, he concludes that 'in some respects at least, the immediate right to possession partakes of the nature of property' (at 89). See the discussion of the doctrine of false wealth in Philip Wood, *The Principles of International Insolvency* (London: Sweet & Maxwell, 1995) 36, 37.

[49] See the law of prescription. 'To prevent uncertainty over title, the old state law laid down that, where someone dealt with a non-owner in the belief that he was dealing with an owner, and obtained something in good faith by purchase or gift or on some other legally sufficient basis, he should become owner by usucaption, ie possession over time': *Justinian's Institutes* (n 5 above) 63, J.2.6.pr.

[50] See for example, Bracton (n 18 above) vol II, 121: 'incorporeal things cannot be possessed . . . They therefore are said to be quasi-possessed [and] can be transferred or quasi-transferred by acquiescence and use'.

[51] 'you must give notice to the legal holder of the fund; in the case of a debt, for instance, notice to the debtor is, for many purposes, tantamount to possession': *Dearle v Hall* (n 47 above), per Sir Thomas Plumer MR at 848.

[52] See Maitland, *The Forms of Action at Common Law* (Cambridge Univeristy Press, 1997 (first printed 1909)) 81.

[53] With the Joint Stock Companies Act 1844.

(2) Rationalist Basis

13.42 Another factor contributing to the persistence of the Physical Model is its conceptual attraction to rationalist thinkers. This factor also explains why English common lawyers, who belong to an empirical intellectual traditional, have been better able to resist the Physical Model than continental civil lawyers.[54]

13.43 In order to develop these comments, it is necessary to return to the real and personal actions from which property rights and obligations have historically been derived.

Actions

13.44 Early Roman law 'can be very fully expounded as nothing but a law of actions',[55] and the early textbooks of English law are collections of writs.[56] In both classical and common law, the forms of action precede substantive law, both historically and conceptually.[57]

Persons, things, actions[58]

13.45 The induction of substantive law from the forms of action begins with the classical trinity around which *Justinian's Institutes* is organised: 'All our law is about persons, things, or actions'.[59] In the thirteenth century this trinity is picked up in

---

[54] Broadly speaking, whereas the judges who wrote English commercial law in the eighteenth and nineteenth centuries read John Locke, and thought empirically, the civilians who wrote the continental Civil Codes read Descartes, and thought *a priori*.

Another factor in assisting English judges in resisting rationalist thought is the role of equity: 'equity thus depending, essentially, upon the particular circumstances of each individual case, there can be no established rules and fixed precepts of equity laid down, without destroying its very essence': Blackstone (n 2 above) vol 21, 61. (In contrast, it might have been thought that empirical thought, with its emphasis on the world available to the senses, would have been more drawn to the Physical Model, but English judges seem to have resisted this danger.)

[55] 'Introduction' to *Justinian's Institutes* (n 5 above) 17.

[56] *The Treatise on the Laws and Customs of the Realm of England Commonly called Glanvill* (Hall (ed), Oxford: Clarendon Press, 1965), ('Glanvill') probably written around 1198 'is the first textbook of the common law': (Introduction, xi); 'writs, and the procedure connected with them, bulk so large is this treatise that it is tempting . . . to regard the work as a commentary on writs': (ibid xxxvii). The reader will search in vain for substantive law. Moreover, 'Bracton, with the Institutes scheme before him, gives about 100 folios to Persons and Things and about 350 to the law of Actions' (ibid 8).

[57] With Bracton '[T]he forms of action are given, the causes of action must be deduced therefrom': Maitland (n 1 above) 5.

[58] In the Introduction to their translation of *Justinian's Institutes*, Peter Birks and Grant McLeod discuss two points concerning the Roman conceptual trichotomy of persons, things and actions. 'One is the strength of its grip of the law of modern Europe. The other is the proper credit for it. Unless he too had predecessors whom we do not know, it was Gaius, not Justinian, who invented it . . . the truth is that the inventor of the institutional scheme was a genius and deserves to be remembered as a Darwin among lawyers': (n 5 above) 13, 18.

[59] *Justinian's Institutes* (n 5 above) 39, J.1.2.12.

Bracton: 'the whole of the law with which we propose to deal relates either to persons or to things or to actions'.[60]

In the early modern era, the same conceptual framework is fundamental to the **13.46** structure of Blackstone's *Commentaries*.[61]

In Blackstone and Bracton, as in Justinian before them, the difference between **13.47** persons and things is not an *a priori* distinction, but a technique for categorising actions.[62]

Induction

Justinian did not induce property rights from real actions. In English law, the **13.48** induction of substantive law from legal procedure has been a very slow process. Indeed, it has never been completed.[63] From their emergence in the twelfth century until their abolition in the nineteenth, the forms of action provided the conceptual framework of English law, and 'they still rule us from their graves'.[64] Arguably, the process of abstraction only became plainly visible with Blackstone,[65] and did not develop very far. Common law has never been a rationalist science.[66]

> I think that the courts should be very slow to declare a practice of the commercial community to be conceptually impossible. Rules of law must obviously be consistent and not self-contradictory . . . But the law is fashioned to suit the practicalities of life and legal concepts like 'proprietary interest' and 'charge' are no more than labels

---

[60] Bracton (n 18 above) 29.

[61] 'The one great institutional writer of the common law still derived his structure ultimately from Justinian': 'Introduction' to *Justinian's Institutes* (n 5 above) 24. Volume 1 is entitled 'Of Rights of Persons', volume 2 'On Rights of Things', and volume 3 is devoted to legal procedure under the title 'Of Private Wrongs'. Volume 4 discusses criminal law, under the title 'Of Public Wrongs'. The four books reflect the division of *Justinian's Institutes* into four books, the first dealing with persons, the second and third dealing with things, and the fourth dealing with actions as well as criminal law.

[62] In the history of Roman law, the distinction between persons and things did not predate and inform the forms of action, but was induced from them. In their Introduction to *Justinian's Institutes*, Birks and McLeod discuss the fundamental importance of forms of action in Gaius. 'Gaius's book 4 is crucial . . . it gives a unique account of the classical and pre-classical forms of action. Gaius . . . was genuinely interested in legal history and rightly believed it essential to a proper understanding of law . . . the law can be very fully expounded as nothing but a law of actions' (at 17). See also Bracton: 'The first classification of actions . . . is this, that some are *in rem*, some *in personam* and some are mixed': (n 18 above) vol 2, 290.

[63] 'This dependence of right upon remedy . . . has given English law that close texture to which it owes its continuous existence despite the temptations of Romanism': Maitland (n 1 above) 63.

[64] Maitland (n 1 above) 1.

[65] However, Blackstone followed a scheme devised by Sir Matthew Hale in the seventeenth century.

[66] 'Also it is to be remembered that the making of grand theories is not and never has been our strong point': Maitland (n 14 above) 218, 219. See also Birks and McLeod 'Introduction' to *Justinian's Institutes* (n 5 above) 24: '*Halsbury*, the practitioner's work of reference in many volumes, sticks to the alphabet, much the commonest system of classification throughout the history of English law'.

given to clusters of related and self-consistent rules of law. Such concepts do not have a life of their own from which the rules of law are inexorably derived.[67]

13.49 The author would argue that the empirical, 'bottom up' approach of English law is its strength,[68] for it enabled English lawyers better to resist the Physical Model than their continental colleagues, for the reasons given below.

13.50 In contrast, continental civil lawyers extrapolated rights from Roman actions in the medieval period.[69] When continental civil law was codified in the early modern era, the forms of action were forgotten. In Grotius' *Introduction to the Jurisprudence of Holland*,[70] in the Napoleonic Code and in continental civil law generally, one reads only of persons and things, and not of actions. The distinction between persons and things ceases to be a technique for categorising actions, and becomes an *a priori* distinction.

Relative nature of property rights in relation to obligations

13.51 As discussed above, obligations can only be subject to property rights as against someone other than the obligor.[71] Personal or proprietary status is not unchangeably inherent in the asset, but depends upon whom one is suing. In other words, property is a function of particular actions, and not of particular assets.

13.52 Because the *in personam/in rem* distinction applies to actions (and the rights that are extrapolated from actions) and not to assets, it follows that both tangible and intangible assets may be subject to both personal and property rights. This might be represented diagrammatically as shown in Figure 13.1.

Figure 13.1: *In personam/in rem* distinction

	Personal rights	*Property rights*
Tangible assets	eg an unsettled bargain for the purchase of bearer bonds	eg a holding of bearer bonds
Intangible assets	eg registered securities (as against the issuer)	eg interests in registered securities (as against the intermediary)

---

[67] *In re BCCI (No 8)* [1889] AC 214, per Lord Hoffmann at 228.

[68] For a famous defence of this approach, see Karl N Llewellyn, *The Common Law Tradition* (Boston: Little, Brown and Company, 1960).

[69] 'The terms "*jus in rem*" and "*jus in personam*" were devised by the Civilians of the Middle Ages, or arose in times still more recent': Austin, *Lectures on Jurisprudence or The Philosophy of Positive Law* (5th edn, 1995) vol I, 369, quoted in Hohfeld, *Fundamental Legal Conceptions* (New Haven: Yale University Press, 1964 (first printed 1919)) 82.

[70] Published 1631.

[71] For example, if I invest in debt securities, as against the issuer my rights are personal, so that my investment is at risk in the insolvency of the issuer. However, if I hold my debt securities through a custodian, as against the custodian my rights are proprietary, so that my investment is not at risk in the insolvency of the custodian.

However in modern civil law, the relative, action-based nature of property is lost, **13.53** and the distinction between the personal and the proprietary becomes an *a priori* distinction. The cost of such abstract thought is clear. If one starts with the distinction between the personal and the proprietary, and then categorises assets in the light of it, personal status is taken to be an invariable quality of certain assets. If obligations are personal for some purposes, they are considered to be personal for all purposes. Thus civil lawyers may be drawn to the Physical Model, and consider the assertion of property rights in relation to intangible assets to be misconceived.

(3) Critique of the Physical Model

A distinguished line of Anglo-American legal writers including, notably, Hohfeld, **13.54** have developed a critique of the Physical Model.[72] There are two key themes in this critique.

First, it is shown that rights of property are not rights *against things*, but rather **13.55** rights against persons in respect of things.[73] As Hohfeld famously pointed out in *Fundamental Legal Conceptions*, legal rights are enforced by action,[74] and all legal actions, whether personal or real, are brought against the person of the defendant. By remembering the action-based nature of legal rights, their interpersonal nature becomes clear: 'All proceedings, *like all rights*, are *really against persons*'.[75] Thus: 'A right *in rem* is not a right "against a thing" . . . all rights *in rem* are against persons'.[76] Although a real action *relates to* a thing in the hands of a person, it necessarily *lies against* a person, for only a person can be a defendant in a legal action.[77]

The inter-personal nature of property rights is particularly clear in the English law **13.56** of property, because of its derivation from the rules of medieval land tenure.[78] Moreover, the continuing close association in English law between rights and

---

[72] See in particular Hohfeld, *Fundamental Legal Conceptions* (n 69 above) and Schroeder, 'The Myth that the UCC Killed "Property"' (1996) 69 Temple Law Review 1282–1341.

[73] See Pavlos Eleftheriadis, 'The Analysis of Property Rights' (1996) Oxford Journal of Legal Studies (Spring) 31–54. 'The law of property is about *things*, and our relations with one another in respect of the use and control of things': Jeremy Waldron, 'Property Law', in D Patterson (ed), *A Companion to Philosophy of Law and Legal Theory* (London: Blackwell, 1996) 4. See also Kevin Grey, 'Property in Thin Air' (1991) 51 Cambridge Law Journal 252.

[74] With the exception of limited 'self help' remedies; see Blackstone (n 2 above) vol 3, 22.

[75] Chief Justice Holmes in *Tyler v Court of Registration* (1900) 175 Mass, 71, 76, quoted by Hohfeld (n 69 above) 75.

[76] ibid 74, 76.

[77] Thus, the nature of personal and real rights can only be understood by reference to the potential actions whereby they might be enforced, and (Hohfeld argues) the difference between such rights is the identity of the potential defendants to such actions. (Intriguingly, Hohfeld refuses to understand rights in terms of actions; see 69, 102 et seq. The emphasis on actions is the author's.)

[78] Under the rules of feudal land tenure, a freeholder does not own land, but rather an interest in land. The nature of that interest is defined by the mutual rights and duties arising between the freeholder and his feudal lord. This is a reciprocal personal relationship, as symbolised by the ceremony of fealty. See Blackstone (n 2 above) vol 1, 57.

actions assists English lawyers in remembering that property rights lie against persons. However, civilian lawyers who approach law *a priori*, and seek to understand the law of property without reference to the practicalities of real actions, may face the danger of mistaking property rights for rights *against assets* and, on the basis of this false premise, as rights against *physical* assets only.[79]

13.57 The second element in the common law critique of the Physical Model is as follows. It is argued that, by equating property with physical things, the Physical Model conflates rights of property with the assets in relation to which they are asserted. This is a danger against which Justinian[80] warned us, and the warning has been repeated by common lawyers ever since.[81]

13.58 Hohfeld points out that property is intangible, because property comprises legal rights, which are notional and not physical things, even if they happen to relate to tangible assets.[82]

13.59 Historically, much of our commercial law was developed in the pre-electronic era, in relation to the sale and delivery of tangible assets. The conflation of intangible rights of property with tangible things presented no conceptual problem in the pre-electronic era.[83] However, in the electronic era, the Physical Model is burdensome, because it cuts across the assertion of property rights in intangible assets. In relation to interests in securities, therefore, it is important to reject the Physical Model.

13.60 This chapter has argued that the traditional principles of the law of property are quite equal to the challenge of computerisation. The impression that they are not,

---

[79] This error is forgivable because of the traditional terminology, which has been a false friend. If one uses Justinian's terminology for categorising actions (without carefully reading his definitions), one is tempted to take actions (and therefore rights) *in personam* as lying against persons, and actions (and therefore rights) *in rem* as lying against things. An opposition between rights against persons and rights against things suggests (falsely) that a personal obligation (which clearly confers a right against the obligor) cannot be a thing. If an obligation were not a thing or *res*, it could not be the subject of an *in rem* right. The attraction of this false conclusion is linguistic as much as logical.

[80] See eg Justinian: 'It is irrelevant that an inheritance may include corporeal things. What a usufructuary takes from the land will also be corporeal. And what is owed to us by virtue of an obligation is usually corporeal, such as land, a slave, or money. The point is that the actual right of inheritance is an incorporeal, as is the actual right to the use and fruits of a thing, and the right inherent in an obligation': J.2.2.2, p. 61.

[81] See eg Bracton: 'Incorporeal things are such as are intangible, which exist in contemplation of law, as inheritance, usufruct, advowsons of churches, obligation, actions and the like. It is no objection to this that corporeal things are comprised in inheritance, usufruct and such, for what is due us under an obligation is in most cases corporeal, as land, a slave, money and the like, but the right of succession itself, that is the right of inheritance, is incorporeal': (n 18 above) vol II, 48. See also Blackstone (n 2 above) Book II, 20, 21.

[82] Even a microscopic physical examination of a shipment of grain will not reveal its ownership.

[83] Although incorrect, the Physical Model is not burdensome in a physical commercial environment. This is because, in relation to tangible assets, the legal results of the Physical Model coincide with the legal results of the correct model of property rights as intangible and inter-personal legal rights.

and that the law of property is the law of tangible things, involves conflating legal rights of property with the things to which they relate, and further conflating things with tangible things.

(4) Cultural Context of the Physical Model

The Physical Model conflates the intangible with the physical. The same materi- **13.61** alism is a characteristic of modern Western culture, with the decline of popular religion and the rise of empirical science. It may therefore be unsurprising that the Physical Model belongs to the modern period, and coincides historically with these cultural developments.

This links financial law to the wider culture in which it has been developed. The **13.62** role of the Physical Model, and the history of Western lawyers in alternately resisting and succumbing to it, have direct parallels, for example, in the history of Western theology. The historic debate among financial lawyers on the status of the bearer bond (whether it constitutes, or merely represents, the debt) recalls the debate between transubstantiation and consubstantiation, and may express the same underlying concerns. This may explain the beautiful and haunting quality of problems that recur in this area of law, and the great cultural status of the leading judgments.

It is all too human to mistake the physical for the intangible. But just as Moses **13.63** taught us not to worship the golden calf, and just as Lacan advised us that tangible possessions will never make us happy,[84] so the computerisation of the international financial markets reminds us to return to Justinian, and the knowledge that the law has never belonged to the physical world.

---

[84] See also *Pirke Avot*, ch 2, verse 8.

14

CONCLUSIONS

By way of conclusion, this chapter will summarise the arguments that have been **14.01** advanced in this book concerning the legal nature of interests in securities. It will go on to raise four issues relating to the proprietary rights conferred by interests in securities. These issues are: the role of the law of trusts in permitting such rights to arise; whether this area of law requires codification; the development of 'synthetic' techniques in the financial markets that serve contractually to replicate such property rights; and the technical basis for unallocated and intermediated property rights in relation to intangible assets.

A. Interests in Securities

This book has defined interests in securities as the assets of a client for whom an **14.02** intermediary holds (interests in) securities on a commingled basis, together with the interests in securities of other clients. The author has used the term 'interests' because it has traditionally denoted (equitable) property rights. Interests in securities are akin to US law securities entitlements (arising under article 8 of the Uniform Commercial Code). They are also akin to the rights of participants in Euroclear (arising under the Belgian Royal Decree No 62 of 1967).

Intermediaries hold securities[1] for clients on a pooled basis in a very wide range of **14.03** products and services. These include custody,[2] settlement,[3] clearing,[4] collateral,[5]

---

[1] And interests in securities.
[2] See Chapter 10.
[3] See Chapter 9.
[4] See Chapter 8.
[5] See Chapters 4, 5 and 6.

depositary receipt,[6] fund management[7] and collateralised bond obligation[8] arrangements. As all these arrangements are in widespread use, and all create interests in securities, it is hoped that the legal analysis developed in this book will be of practical use to financial lawyers. This book has argued that the same fundamental legal structure lies at the heart of each of these arrangements, and it is hoped that this argument will simplify the legal aspects of the contemporary financial markets. These markets might be compared to a coral reef, because of the bewildering diversity of forms that have evolved, their strangeness to the unfamiliar eye and indeed their beauty. However, the student or young practitioner venturing into these warm waters may take comfort from the fact that the same underlying structure recurs.

14.04　There has been very significant growth in the use of interests in securities, and this trend is expected to continue. In the past the student of finance studied banking, and possibly regarded the securities markets as an esoteric area. However, today interests in securities are fundamental to the structure of international finance through their wide and innovative use, particularly in collateral and repackaging arrangements (see Chapters 1, 4 and 11 and 12). They therefore merit more analytic attention than they have traditionally received, and this book is intended in some measure to correct that relative neglect.

14.05　This book has offered the following conclusions about interests in securities.[9]

14.06　(1) The economic value of interests in securities derives from the underlying assets held by the intermediary, so that for balance sheet, regulatory and taxation purposes, the two are indistinguishable.[10]

14.07　(2) However, interests in securities comprise assets which are legally distinct from the underlying (interests in) securities.[11] The relevance of this distinction arises primarily in the context of collateral arrangements.

---

[6] See Chapter 11.　　　　　　　　　　[7] See Chapter 11.

[8] See Chapter 12.

[9] As with all the comments in this book, these are offered as general conclusions, and not as legal advice. Legal advice should always be sought as to the application of these conclusions to any particular arrangements.

[10] This assumes the assets are properly segregated in the hands of the intermediary, so that they would be available to its creditors in the event of its insolvency or otherwise, and also that the intermediary is a regulated entity with high standards of internal controls, so that the risk of fraud and error are not significant. Clearly, special contractual arrangements may serve economically to distinguish interests in securities from the underlying assets. For example, in repackaging arrangements, credit enhancement techniques may serve to improve the credit rating of the interests in securities relative to the underlying assets: see Chapter 12. Conversely, in depositary receipt structures, depositary receipt holders may be deprived of the benefit of certain corporate actions in relation to the underlying assets: see Chapter 11.

[11] For the same conclusion in relation to units in unit trusts, see Kam Fan Sin, *The Legal Nature of the Unit Trust* (Oxford: Clarendon Press, Oxford, 1997) 328: 'Units are items of property in their own right'. See also T Austen-Peters, *Custody of Investments* (Oxford University Press, 2000) paragraphs 4.11–4.23 and s. 19.

(3) Interests in securities are intangible assets (or choses in action), evidenced **14.08** only by electronic records. This is true even if the intermediary holds physical bearer securities, because (in the absence of allocation) no interest in securities attaches to any such physical asset (see Chapter 2).

(4) Therefore interests in securities cannot be the subject of legal arrangements **14.09** based on common law possession. A purported bailment may take effect as a trust (with higher implied levels of fiduciary duty: see Chapter 2); a purported negotiation may take effect as novation (with lower levels of security of transfer: see Chapter 3); and a purported pledge may take effect as a charge (which in some circumstances may be registrable as a floating charge: see Chapter 5).

(5) As against the intermediary, clients have property rights in the interests in **14.10** securities credited to their accounts. This means that their interests in securities are not available to the creditors of the intermediary in its insolvency or otherwise (see Chapters 2 and 13).

(6) In turn, interests in securities confer on clients property interests in the **14.11** underlying assets held by the intermediary for clients (see Chapters 2 and 13).

(7) These interests are indirect, in the sense that the client has in the normal **14.12** course no direct right of action against the issuer of the underlying securities or any sub-custodian, depositary or other intermediary through whom her intermediary holds the assets (see Chapters 1 and 2).

(8) As a matter of English law, the relationship between the client and the inter- **14.13** mediary is a trust,[12] and the interest of the client is equitable and not legal (see Chapter 2).

(9) This may place the client or its counterparties at a disadvantage for the pur- **14.14** poses of priority in the event of a tracing action (see Chapter 3) or in the event of competing security interests (see Chapters 4 and 5).

(10) The equitable status of the client's interest may also mean that it is not recog- **14.15** nised in certain civil law jurisdictions, raising possible insolvency risk (see Chapters 2 and 13).

(11) The interest of the client in the underlying assets is unallocated. Under the **14.16** existing principles of English law, it takes effect as a co-ownership interest, under an equitable tenancy in common (see Chapters 2 and 13).

(12) On this basis, shortfalls in the pool of assets held by the intermediary should, **14.17** in the intermediary's insolvency, be borne rateably by all clients (see Chapter 11).

---

[12] Or, in the case of a repackaging, a charge, the proprietary effect of which is the same as a trust because of the contractual arrangements in place: see Chapter 12.

14.18 (13) English law may (and arguably should) develop so that the interest of the client is an outright interest and not a co-ownership interest, even in the absence of allocation (see Chapters 2 and 13). It is not considered that such a development would change any of the conclusions above, other than conclusion No 11 and, possibly, No 12.

14.19 (14) Interests in securities are akin to registered securities and not to bearer securities (see Chapter 2).

14.20 (15) Therefore their transfer takes effect by novation (and not by assignment nor by negotiation) (see Chapter 3).

14.21 (16) Because their transfer does not involve assignment, they are not subject to the traditional formalities and restrictions on the assignment of choses in actions (see Chapter 3).

14.22 (17) Because their transfer does not involve negotiation, they may enjoy lower security of transfer than negotiable instruments (see Chapter 3).

14.23 (18) Interests in securities may be subject to competing security interests from multiple intermediaries (see Chapter 4).

14.24 (19) Where one client uses its interests in securities as collateral, the interests in securities of other clients credited to the same commingled client account may in some circumstances be claimed by the collateral taker (see Chapter 4).

14.25 (20) For conflict of laws purposes, interests in securities are located in the place where the intermediary maintains the account to which they are credited (see Chapter 7). This is relevant for the perfection of security interests (see Chapters 5 and 7) and, possibly, the recharacterisation of outright collateral transfers (see Chapters 6 and 7).

14.26 Until fairly recently, the proposition that a custody client did not own bonds, but rather owned interests in bonds, was controversial. However, this book has argued that the term 'my bonds at the custodian' is almost as inaccurate as the term 'my money at the bank'.[13] It is not suggested that the terminology should change, because (in economic terms) interests in securities are equivalent to securities. The difference between them is a technical legal one, which is relevant only in limited contexts. The most important of such contexts is cross border collateral arrangements. Here, conflating interests in securities with securities is a source of legal risk.

14.27 At a technical level, interests in securities may *confer* property rights in securities, but they *are not* securities. Western lawyers during the modern era have regularly

---

[13] Of course, there is an important difference. Whereas the rights of the depositor against her bank are merely personal, the rights of the custody client against the custodian are proprietary, although they are unallocated and indirect.

confused property rights with the assets to which they relate (see Chapter 13), and this may in part explain why the distinction between interests in securities and securities has not been made more readily.

B. Trusts

The law of equity in general, and trusts in particular, has sometimes been considered unwelcome in commercial arrangements. This has been largely because of concern that equitable concepts such as fiduciary duty and constructive notice may disturb commercial expectations and undermine commercial contracts.[14] These concepts impose non-contractual duties based on conscience. **14.28**

However, the view that conscience has no place in commerce is somewhat out of date, and the author does not share it. In any case, the author wishes to emphasise the enormous *technical* contribution that trusts have made to financial law, by permitting a range of innovative proprietary structures that could not otherwise have arisen. Whereas some have argued that the dominance of common law (as opposed to civil law) in international finance is due to the supremacy of the bargain and the suppression of implied duties, the author would suggest that it is largely due to the creative development of property rights in equity. **14.29**

As discussed in Chapter 13, the enduring value of property rights in the financial markets is that they permit assets to be protected from the insolvency of intermediaries and counterparties. The fundamental achievement of equity is to permit property rights to extend to the intangible and unallocated assets on which the international financial markets are based. The intangible and unallocated nature of these assets will be considered in turn. **14.30**

First, equity permits the ownership of *intangible* assets, through an intermediary as trustee. (Indeed, some have argued that equitable interests always relate to intangible assets, even where the trustee holds physical things.)[15] While some commentators have argued that this uniquely Anglo-Saxon possibility compromises the classical distinction between property and obligation, the author has argued (in Chapter 13) that, on the contrary, it follows from a correct understanding of that distinction. Today, its importance cannot be underestimated. Because we can assert property rights in intangibles, we can have secure custodial **14.31**

---

[14] For a recent judicial example, see *Westdeutsche Landesbank Gironzentrale v Islington LCH* [1996] AC 669, per Lord Browne-Wilkinson at 704, 705.

[15] The judgment in *Re Diplock* [1948] Ch 465 refers to the 'metaphysical approach' of equity at 520. See also Maitland, 'Trust and Corporation', in *Selected Essays* (Cambridge: Cambridge University Press, 1936) 164, 165 : 'We might say that "the use" is turned into an incorporeal thing, an incorporeal piece of land; and in this incorporeal thing you may have all those rights, those "estates", which you could have in a real, tangible piece of land'.

and collateral arrangements, and thereby manage credit risk. This is why the *conceptual* transition to computerisation has been relatively effortless in London, and also why statutory adaptations that have been necessary in civil law jurisdictions introduce concepts that common lawyers readily recognise as trusts, charges and other creatures of equity. This is an important respect in which English law can contribute to the development of commercial law in Europe.

14.32 Secondly, equity permits property rights to be asserted in circumstances where allocation is not possible. Hence the equitable charge, and hence the ability to trace in equity (but not at common law) through a pool of assets. Moreover, equity permits property rights to subsist in a *changing* pool of assets, through the concepts of the trust fund,[16] and the floating charge. This flexibility is fundamental to the development of custody,[17] collateral[18] and repackaging[19] structures that relate to interests in securities which are credited to a particular account from time to time.

14.33 It is therefore unsurprising that the use of trusts[20] in the securities and financial markets is increasing.[21] Readers will be familiar with the traditional uses of trusts in these markets. For example, in issues of debt securities, a trustee may be expressly appointed in order to protect the interests of holders and to simplify the enforcement of their rights, as discussed in Chapter 1. A further traditional use of the trust is in collateral arrangements, where the benefit of a security interest over (interests in) securities is held by a trustee for a changing group of secured creditors.[22]

14.34 In addition, this book has shown that trusts are widely used in custody[23] and repackaging[24] structures. In the settlement industry, trusts (and trust-like civil law statutory arrangements) are used to protect participants from the credit risk of depositaries, and also to protect purchasers from the credit risk of vendors.[25] As a matter of legal history, security interests were importantly developed in the law of

---

[16] 'The Court of Chancery . . . converted the "trust fund" into an incorporeal thing, capable of being "invested" in different ways.' Observe that metaphor of "investment". We conceive that the "trust fund" can change its dress, but maintain its identity.' Maitland (n 15 above) 171, 172. See the interesting discussion of funds in J E Penner, *The Idea of Property in Law* (Oxford: Clarendon Press, 1997) 110.

[17] See Chapter 10.

[18] See Chapters 5, 6, 8 and 9.

[19] See Chapters 11 and 12.

[20] And charges.

[21] Also, many of the important investors and counterparties in the wholesale securities and financial markets are trustees of pension funds and unit trusts.

[22] Of course, trusts are widely used in tax planning structures but that is beyond the scope of this book.

[23] See Chapter 10.

[24] See Chapters 11 and 12.

[25] See Chapter 9.

equity,[26] and today the interest of many collateral takers is equitable.[27] 'We have here a very elastic form of thought into which all manner of materials can be brought.'[28]

C. Codification

Professor Sir Roy Goode has proposed[29] the development of an English and, possibly, UK commercial code, and this proposal has found widespread support among academics and practitioners,[30] as well as the public sector. Of course it is not suggested that England should cease to be a common law jurisdiction, and this author has argued that, in the financial markets, common law has a unique conceptual advantage over civil law.[31] Sir Roy has cited the US Uniform Commercial Code as an interesting example of successful codification in a common law context.[32]   **14.35**

Such an initiative would be highly beneficial to the financial markets in general and the securities markets in particular, and would assist the internationally competitive position of London. Major law reform would not be necessary. This book has argued that existing principles of English law are well adapted to the computerisation of the financial markets, through the concept of interests in securities.   **14.36**

However, the concept of interests in securities recommended in this book has, at the time of writing, not yet been widely taken up. Largely because of the long-standing 'Physical Model' of property rights, discussed in Chapter 13, many commentators continue to conflate interests in securities with the underlying physical securities, and this is a source of legal risk. The strength of English law is in some important respects more latent than obvious. Therefore it would be helpful to have legislative clarification that where an intermediary holds (interests in) securities for clients on a commingled basis, the asset of each client differs from the underlying assets held by the intermediary. In the USA, this has been achieved with the concept of the 'securities entitlement' developed in article 8 of the   **14.37**

---

[26] 'The true construction of *securities* for money lent is another fountain of jurisdiction in the courts of equity': Blackstone, *Commentaries on the Laws of England* (facsimile of 1st edn, Chicago: University of Chicago Press, 1979) vol 3, 439. Clearly, the *equity* of redemption is a creature of equity.

[27] See Chapters 4, 5 and 6.

[28] Maitland (n 15 above) 220.

[29] See Roy Goode, 'The Codification of Commercial Law' (1988) 14 Monash University Law Review (September) 135.

[30] This support was expressed at a DTI seminar on a Commercial Code for England/United Kingdom, 11 May 2000.

[31] See Chapter 13, and the concluding section of this chapter.

[32] Of course, Louisiana operates under civil law, but the other states, notably the leading commercial states of New York and California, operate under common law.

Uniform Commercial Code. The clarity of article 8 and the intellectual strength that lies behind it, are tremendous. Of course, an English commercial code would be based on English law and practice, and US drafting cannot provide an exact model. However, as a successful result of creative collaboration between the public and private sectors, article 8 is a good model for our jurisdiction.

14.38 While the traditional principles of English law operate well in the electronic environment, there are (unsurprisingly) some points of detail which are less satisfactory, and some limited, technical law reform would be appropriate. There are two areas in particular where the case for law reform is clear.

14.39 The first involves security of transfer. As discussed in Chapter 3 (and conclusions 4 and 17 above), the loss of negotiable status which follows computerisation may reduce security of transfer. Although the statutory regimes which have been developed to protect key settlement systems from systemic risk[33] address the impact of insolvency on security of transfer, they neglect the risk of fraud. There may therefore be a case for replicating the benefits of negotiability within major settlement systems.[34]

14.40 On a related point, as discussed in Chapters 2 and 3 (and conclusion 9) the equitable status of interests in securities may also reduce security of transfer in the event of fraud, by removing the defence of bona fide purchaser of the *legal* estate for value without notice. The rule that a subsequent legal interest has priority over a prior equitable interest[35] may be in part based on the following view. Traditionally a client who chooses to entrust her assets to an intermediary to hold as trustee must bear the risk that the intermediary will fraudulently dispose of her assets.[36] Today, however there is no element of choice. Because of patterns of cross border investment and restrictions on participation in the wholesale financial settlement systems, it is not possible for most investors to participate in the international financial markets without relying on institutional intermediaries to hold their assets. Therefore the policy reasons that may lie behind the traditional rule are no longer safe, and should be re-examined.[37]

14.41 The second area where law reform would be appropriate relates to security interests. The computerisation of the securities markets may serve to convert a purported pledge into a charge (see Chapter 5 and conclusion 4 above), which is weaker in priority and which in turn may be registrable as a floating charge. The

---

[33] The Settlement Finality Directive (98/26/EC), and Part VII of the Companies Act 1989.

[34] Chapter 9 discusses the statutory protections available for CREST. Whether or not CREST has special protections, there may be a case for making security of transfer available in a wider range of systems.

[35] Provided it is acquired bona fide without notice of the prior interest.

[36] See eg the discussion in J A Ewart, *Negotiability and Estoppel* (1900) 14 LQR 135.

[37] See Birks, 'The Necessity of a Unitary Law of Tracing' in R Cranston (ed), *Making Commercial Law: Essays in Honour of Roy Goode* (Oxford: Oxford University Press, 1997).

existence of a large number of different types of security interest, enjoying different relative priorities and only some of which are registrable, is a source of legal risk. A number of distinguished writers have stressed the urgency of reform in the area of security interests over personal property. Many would share the author's regret that the recommendation of the *Diamond Report*[38] for major reform is unlikely to be implemented.[39] The UK financial markets are arguably at a competitive disadvantage to the US markets, which benefit from the elegant simplicity of a unified regime under article 9 of the Uniform Commercial Code.

The reforms suggested above in relation to adverse claims in transferred assets and security interests, would address the differences in priority between legal and equitable interests. This a nettle which was not grasped in the great reforms of the Judicature Acts of 1873–1875. Today, however, when the computerisation and intermediation of the financial markets has diverted so much of our economic wealth out of the law and into equity, the time may be ripe.   **14.42**

The nineteenth century also saw many other pieces of important legislation which codified parts of our commercial law, and which served to clarify traditional principle, simplify its operation and remove anomalous detail. This provides a good model for what is needed today. While contemporary English commercial lawyers may have rejected many of the values of our Victorian ancestors, we share their tremendous pride in our commercial law, as well as their faith in and commitment to the future of London as a commercial centre.   **14.43**

D. Synthetic Arrangements

This book has analysed property rights. As explained in Chapters 2, 4 and 13, the presence or absence of property rights are crucial in assessing counterparty credit risk. However, the proprietary analysis is not always informative as to the economic position.   **14.44**

As indicated above, one case in which the legal proprietary analysis differs from the economic analysis relates to interests in securities. The difference between interests in securities and securities is legally significant and economically insignificant.[40] 'Repos' or repurchase agreements provide another case; these transactions transfer title to assets, but are balance sheet neutral.[41]   **14.45**

---

[38] Prof A Diamond, *Security Interests in Property* (Department of Trade and Industry, 1989).

[39] For example, in N Palmer and E McKendrick (eds), *Interests in Goods* (2nd edn, London, 1998), ch 39, John Phillips considers the case law relating to equitable liens, and comments, 'within this "rag bag", it is not easy to discern any coherent statements of principle'. Certainly, few would disagree with Gerard McCormack (ibid ch 28) that the rules for the registration of corporate charges are in a muddle, and require urgent reform.

[40] See above, and Chapters 1 and 2.

[41] See Chapter 6.

14.46   A third and important case where the legal proprietary analysis differs from the economic analysis is the development of synthetic arrangements in the contemporary financial markets. These enable market participants contractually to acquire and dispose of economic positions in securities and other assets, without affecting the proprietary position. Derivatives such as financial futures and options have long been used to acquire exposures to the securities markets, and to hedge such exposures, and the size of the markets in financial derivatives greatly exceeds that of the underlying cash (ie non-derivative) markets. More recently, the financial markets have seen the development of credit derivatives to manage the credit exposures otherwise associated with holding financial assets including securities. Credit derivatives, including credit default swaps and credit linked notes, are now widely used in securitisations and other repackaging structures, known as 'synthetic repackagings', so as economically to transfer assets from a market counterparty or an originator to a special purpose vehicle, without any change in the property rights enjoyed in the assets.

14.47   In broad terms, the regulatory capital[42] and balance sheet[43] treatment of transactions follows the economic and not the legal proprietary position. The legal proprietary analysis developed in this book is of most relevance in relation to cross border collateral arrangements.

E. Property Rights

14.48   Some commentators have argued that the traditional law of property is unequal to the challenge of the computerisation of the financial markets.[44] Chapter 13 has argued that it is. This is a pleasing result, both in the interests of credit risk management in the highly intermediated securities markets, and also in the interests of legal continuity, for today '[t]he distinction between property and obligations lies at the heart of our jurisprudence'.[45] Indeed, it always has: as Professor Birks has argued, 'when the truth is that those same categories of legal thought have been surviving critical onslaughts in different jurisdictions and under different political systems since the time of Justinian in the sixth century and Gaius in the sec-

---

[42] See 'Securitisation and Asset Transfers' in *Guide to Banking Supervisory Policy* (FSA), available at www.fsa.gov.uk/pubs/supervisor
[43] See (in the United Kingdom) Financial Reporting Standard 5 (FRS 5) 'Reporting the Substance of Transactions' and (in the USA) Statement of Financial Accounting Standard 125 (FAS 125) 'Accounting for Transfers and Servicing of Financial Assets and Extinguishment of Liabilities'.
[44] 'the fact remains that modern securities markets have moved so far beyond the movement of pieces of negotiable paper that the property law construct is inadequate and unworkable': C W Mooney, 'Beyond Negotiability' (1990) 12 Cardozo Law Review 305.
[45] *Re BCCI (No 8)* [1996] 2 All ER 121, per Rose LJ at 131.

ond, we are bound to approach the issue of radical reform at least with some self-doubt'.[46]

Chapter 13 argued that the proprietary/personal distinction applies to actions **14.49** (and the legal rights that are asserted in actions). Because the same asset can be subject to different kinds of legal action, proprietary status does not inhere in assets, and the same asset may be subject to both personal and proprietary claims.

It is important to concede that the analysis of property rights in financial law is dif-**14.50** ferent from the analysis of property rights in general, because financial assets are predominantly intangible. Whereas tangible assets are physical things having actual locations, the reification and location of intangible assets is notional. Whereas the ownership of tangible things is bound up with their possession,[47] intangibles are incapable of possession at common law. Whereas physical assets may be transferred by physical delivery, intangible interests in securities are transferred by novation.[48]

Moreover, and crucially, the traditional function of asserting property rights in **14.51** tangible assets is to determine rights of use and enjoyment of the physical resources of this world.[49] In contrast, intangible assets such as interests in securities exist not in the physical world but rather in the notional legal world. In the financial markets, the significant purpose of asserting property rights in them also relates to a notional legal phenomenon, namely insolvency.

Chapter 13 discussed the Physical Model, which erroneously conflates rights of **14.52** property with the tangible assets to which they may relate. Following the Physical Model, tangible assets are (wrongly) equated with property and intangible assets considered to be (invariably) personal assets. This leads to the consequential error of considering intangible assets to be incapable of property rights.

The Physical Model has served commercial law well from ancient times until the **14.53** middle of the twentieth century, during which time most commercial assets have been physical. However, it is unhelpful today, when property rights are required in the financial markets to address intermediary credit risk, by ring-fencing intangible client assets such as interests in securities.

Chapter 13 argued that the Physical Model is associated with rationalist thought, **14.54** because such thought is based on deduction from general principles, whereas

---

[46] Birks and McLeod, 'Introduction' to *Justinian's Institutes* (London: Duckworth, 1987) 26.
[47] See Chapter 13.
[48] See Chapter 3.
[49] This is (quite properly) the focus of the traditional jurisprudence of the law of property, from the discussions of property in Locke's *Two Treatises of Government* (1690), Hume's *A Treatise of Human Nature*, to the more recent discussions in Jeremy Waldron's 'Property Law' in *A Companion to Philosophy of Law and Legal Theory* (London: Blackwell, 1996) and Penner, *The Idea of Property in Law* (Oxford: Clarendon Press, 1997).

empirical thought is based on the induction of the general from the particular. Accordingly the Physical Model has been more dominant in continental law than in common law. The ring-fencing of unallocated intangible client assets in the hands of intermediaries is difficult to achieve under the general principles of continental civil law. This is why continental settlement systems require statutory support in order to address depositary credit risk. This reliance on (public sector) statute represents a drag on (private sector) financial initiatives involving the intermediation of intangible assets.[50] This places civil law jurisdictions at a competitive disadvantage in the international financial markets.

14.55 Chapter 13 argued further that, because of its long association with the forms of action, common law has been better able to resist the Physical Model, and is therefore able effortlessly to recognise property rights in the electronic environment. As indicated above, this is a respect in which English law may be able to make an important contribution to financial law in Europe.

14.56 The distinction between assets and property rights may be unwelcome to some. This is because it involves rejecting the equation of property with physical things, and the notion that property is an invariable feature of certain assets. In contrast, it involves accepting that an asset is subject to property rights for some purposes only. As discussed in Chapter 13, property is contingent upon who is suing whom in actual or hypothetical litigation, and depends on the relationship between plaintiff and defendant.[51]

14.57 This 'action based' view of property as intangible, contingent and relative may be unattractive to those in the Enlightenment tradition, who have sought certainty through the intellectual mastery of the physical world. However, it may be that the 'action based' view of property better enables financial lawyers in the twenty-first century to remain useful to their clients, as those clients leave the physical world and enter the virtual.

---

[50] Including custody, settlement and repackaging.
[51] ie the absence of an obligation of the defendant to the plaintiff.

INDEX